James Joyce, Rural Ireland and Modernity

James Joyce, Rural Ireland and Modernity

Beyond the Pale

Niall Ó Cuileagáin

EDINBURGH
University Press

Edinburgh University Press is one of the leading university presses in the UK. We publish academic books and journals in our selected subject areas across the humanities and social sciences, combining cutting-edge scholarship with high editorial and production values to produce academic works of lasting importance. For more information visit our website: edinburghuniversitypress.com

Grateful acknowledgement is made to the sources listed in the List of Illustrations for permission to reproduce material previously published elsewhere. Every effort has been made to trace the copyright holders, but if any have been inadvertently overlooked, the publisher will be pleased to make the necessary arrangements at the first opportunity.

Edinburgh University Press Ltd
13 Infirmary Street
Edinburgh EH1 1LT

Typeset in 11/13 Adobe Sabon by
IDSUK (DataConnection) Ltd, and
printed and bound in the UK using 100% Renewable Electricity by
CPI Group (UK) Ltd

A CIP record for this book is available from the British Library

ISBN 978 1 3995 3280 8 (hardback)
ISBN 978 1 3995 3282 2 (webready PDF)
ISBN 978 1 3995 3283 9 (epub)

This book is printed using paper from well-managed forests, recycling and other controlled sources

Contents

Figures

Acknowledgements

Beginning a list of acknowledgements is a daunting endeavour, given that there are so many people I must thank for helping to bring this book to fruition, not all of whom I know by name. It is easy to know where to begin, however, and that is with Scarlett Baron, who has been a wonderful mentor and friend over the past number of years and whose enthusiasm for this project was a major encouragement from the very start. Her profound expertise on all things Joycean (and beyond) has been both an inspiration and an invaluable resource. I would also like to thank Anne Fogarty and Frank Shovlin for their deep engagement with the research upon which this work is based and for helping me to hone my argument. The majority of the research for this book was carried out within the halls of University College London, and therefore I would like to thank the university for its institutional support over many years. I owe thanks to many members of the English Department at UCL for their academic support, as well as their regular words of advice and encouragement. In particular, my thanks go to Matthew Sperling, Matthew Beaumont and Julia Jordan, who all read earlier versions of these chapters and helped to direct my research over the years. I would also like to thank the entire staff at the British Library as well as the numerous librarians at UCL who helped to source, scan and send material to me over the course of the various lockdowns during the pandemic – without them, this work would simply not exist.

I would like to express my sincere gratitude to the Wolfson Foundation, whose generous funding made the research upon which this work is based possible, as well as the International James Joyce Foundation and the Trieste Joyce School for providing scholarships to attend conferences during the past few years. My thanks also go to all those who engaged with and provided feedback on papers I delivered at the UCL English Department's conference and research seminar, the Italian James Joyce Foundation's 2019 conference, the

International James Joyce Symposia of 2021 and 2022, and the Dublin James Joyce Summer School of 2023.

My sincere thanks to all those at Edinburgh University Press who have helped to bring this work into being, most especially Jackie Jones and Elizabeth Fraser. I would also like to thank the various editors and peer reviewers of other articles for their insightful readings and advice. In particular, I would like to thank Luca Crispi and Anne Fogarty at the *Dublin James Joyce Journal* for their editorial help and for granting me permission to adapt material that first appeared in the article '"Rus in Urbe": The Semi-Rural Liminal Zones of *Ulysses*', *Dublin James Joyce Journal* 14–15 (2021–22), 18–35. I would also like to thank Yen-Chi Wu and Phyllis Boumans who helped to sharpen up some of my arguments for the article '"A Joycean Smutmonger": Echoes of Joyce in Máirtín Ó Cadhain's Rural Modernism', *Review of Irish Studies in Europe* 7 (2024), 58–76, and who granted permission for their reuse here. I am also very grateful to Rosemarie Langtry for allowing me to use her painting 'Uisneach' as the cover image of this book.

I am very fortunate to be surrounded by a close-knit and supportive group of friends who have all helped to elucidate matters relating to research – and matters mercifully unrelated. In particular, I would like to thank Sam Caleb, Sarah Chambré, Harry Chancellor, John Daly, Jake Elliott, Will Fleming, Jess Hannah, Naomi Hinds, Gearóid Looney, James Reath, Zara Regan, Seán Reynolds, Alberto Tondello and Tymek Woodham, as well as the late and dearly missed Hannah Tran.

Finally, I want to express my eternal love and gratitude to my family for their constant support, and most of all to Rebecca, for all her advice, patience and affection. *Mo ghrá go daingean tú.*

Abbreviations

Works by James Joyce

D   *Dubliners* (1914; Oxford: Oxford University Press, 2008)

FW   *Finnegans Wake* (1939; London: Penguin, 2000). References are given in the following form: *FW* page number: line number. Chapters are referred to in the following form: part number in Roman numerals, chapter number in Arabic numerals.

JJA   *The James Joyce Archive*, ed. Michael Groden et al. (New York: Garland, 1977–79). References are given in the following form: *JJA* volume number: page number.

L1   *Letters of James Joyce*, ed. Stuart Gilbert (London: Faber and Faber, 1957)

L2   *Letters of James Joyce*, vol. 2, ed. Richard Ellmann (London: Faber and Faber, 1966)

L3   *Letters of James Joyce*, vol. 3, ed. Richard Ellmann (London: Faber and Faber, 1966)

OCPW   *Occasional, Critical, and Political Writing*, ed. Kevin Barry (London: Oxford University Press, 2000)

P   *A Portrait of the Artist as a Young Man* (1916; London: Penguin, 1966)

PSW   *Poems and Shorter Writings*, ed. Richard Ellmann, A. Walton Litz and John Whittier-Ferguson (London: Faber and Faber, 1991)

SH   *Stephen Hero* (1944; London: Granada, 1981)

SL   *Selected Letters of James Joyce*, ed. Richard Ellmann (London: Faber and Faber, 1975)

U   *Ulysses*, ed. Hans Walter Gabler (1922; New York: Vintage, 1986). References are given in the following form: *U* episode number: line number.

Other Works

FGB   Niall Ó Dónaill, *Foclóir Gaeilge-Béarla* [*Irish-English Dictionary*] (Dublin: An Gúm, 1977)

JJII   Richard Ellmann, *James Joyce*, rev. edn (Oxford: Oxford University Press, 1982)

MBK   Stanislaus Joyce, *My Brother's Keeper*, ed. Richard Ellmann (London: Faber and Faber, 1958)

OED   *Oxford English Dictionary Online* (Oxford University Press, https://www.oed.com/)

Introduction: Within, Upon and Beyond the Pale

Poplinstown, [. . .] goodwalldabout, with talus and counterscarp and pale of palisades (*FW* 539.24–6)

There is nothing particularly new about partition on the island of Ireland. Indeed, one of the country's most famous borders was first constructed around Dublin and its environs during the late Middle Ages. Known as 'the English Pale' due to its being constructed out of stakes (*palus* in Latin), it served the purpose of protecting English colonial settlers on the east coast from the so-called 'wild Irish' who lay beyond its frontiers. In an Irish context, to go 'beyond the Pale' has therefore a very literal signification. Over time, the Pale has come to stand for the notion of Ireland being divided between east and west: roughly speaking, Dublin and the rest of the country. Such a division inevitably splits Ireland along simplified and not always accurate lines: rural versus urban, provincial versus cosmopolitan, traditional versus modern, Irish-speaking versus English-speaking – sometimes also Catholic versus Protestant and nationalist versus unionist. In short, then, Gael versus Pale. In Part III, Chapter 3 of *Finnegans Wake* (1939), the work's main character HCE boasts of the cities he has founded, including the Irish capital, Dublin, which in the above epigraph is rendered 'Poplinstown' in reference to its tradition of poplin weaving.[1] HCE describes in particular the fortified nature of the city, being protected from troublesome outsiders by a wall, a sloping earthwork (*OED*, 'talus, n.1', 1a), another fortifying wall or ditch (*OED*, 'counterscarp, n.', 1), and finally by a 'pale of palisades'. This last protection of palisades – 'a fence made of wooden pales or stakes fixed in the ground, forming an enclosure or defence' (*OED*, 'palisade, n.', 1) – is evidently a reference to the Pale.

James Joyce has traditionally been read solely as a writer of the Pale – even the earliest Irish commentators emphasised his connection to urban Dublin above all else, with Mary Colum stating that '[n]obody has ever written of the life of a city, so identified himself with that city and its history, as Joyce has with Dublin'.[2] For generations of critics since then, Joyce has become 'the archetypal urban writer'.[3] These readings are of course not without some justification: Joyce was primarily an urban man and an urban writer, with Dublin the main subject of his life's work. This book, however, sets itself out as a measured corrective, to show that by limiting our view of Joyce to Dublin alone, we ignore the many pages devoted to Ireland beyond the Pale in his work, and risk telling only half the story.

Joyce himself had a personal connection to the Pale from a young age. Upon being sent to board at Clongowes Wood College in 1888, Joyce would in fact have lived on the remains of the Pale boundary itself (*JJII* 27). The Pale boundary can be seen marked on the Ordnance Survey map from 1908, running down from the college towards Clane (fig. I.1). The building at Clongowes, established in 1450, took on the function of a 'Pale castle' in order 'to protect the English land from incursions by the Irish clans in search of cattle and plunder'.[4] Sinéad Quirke writes that today the rampart runs for about 170 metres and is around four metres wide, with a 'deep fosse to its eastern side'.[5] Indeed, the very first issue of the college's journal *The Clongownian* – published in 1895, just four years after Joyce had left – features a detailed history of the Pale and its rampart near the college, showing a deep awareness in the institution of its connection to this structure (*JJII* 34).[6] The article, written by a certain 'Logographos', describes the historical significance of the fence as follows:

> It seems strange – almost incredible – that in the fifteenth century this, not very formidable, fence was raised to mark and to defend the western limit of the British Empire. West of it the king's writ did not run nor English law bind, while on the east lay the English Pale, organised completely on the mode of feudal England, and designated by the writers of the time the 'English land.' Hence it is that the structure is nowadays spoken of as the 'rampart of the Pale.'[7]

The rampart itself is described by the writer as 'nothing more than an ordinary "double ditch" with a bridle path on its summit'.[8] This path along the top was in itself significant, as it provided a shortcut between Clane and the college.[9] This shortcut was not a one-way route either, as '[a]t the same time as the locals were accessing the college via the rampart the students were visiting the village to shop for tuck, also via the rampart'.[10] We can therefore very plausibly imagine a young James Joyce literally atop the Pale rampart – or what remained of it – during a walk into Clane or some other similar excursion. And it is this hypothetical image that I would like to home in on: the young Joyce, atop the boundary between rural Ireland and the Pale, with an ideal vantage point from which to examine and dissect both cultures.

Figure I.1   Clongowes Wood College, with the Pale running southwards from the college. Ordnance Survey, *Kildare, Ikeathy and Oughterany, North Salt, Clane, North Naas*, sheet XIV.2, 25 inches to 1 mile, Dublin, 1911.

This image is useful, for it strikes at a basic truth about Joyce's life and also, I argue, his work: his was never a solely urban, Dublin experience. His father, a fiercely proud Corkonian – he is reported to have said that '[t]here is not a field in County Cork that I don't know' (*JJII* 14) – impressed upon his eldest son his links to the southern county. When an early biographer confused Joyce's family origins as being from the west of Ireland, Joyce wrote a letter to correct him on this point, emphasising the connection to Cork (*L1* 115). Nevertheless, Joyce was aware that his surname linked him with the west, especially the area known as 'Joyce Country' in Galway and Mayo. His eventual marriage to Nora Barnacle of Galway furthered this connection with the west; indeed, Frank Shovlin remarks that Joyce 'was very pleased that Nora was a native' of Galway.[11] Joyce's letters to her, especially during his trip there in 1909, delight in stressing the fact of Nora being a Galwegian, calling her his 'little Galway bride' and luxuriating in 'those strange places whose names thrill on your lips, Oughterard, Clare-Galway, Coleraine, Oranmore' (*L2* 242, 273). He was also aware that the Joyce family was one of the traditional tribes of Galway city. After *Pomes Penyeach* (1927) was published, Joyce had a copy presented to only three libraries in Europe: the Bibliothèque Nationale in Paris, the British Museum in London, and the university library in Galway (*L3* 371). Joyce explained his reasons for doing so to his daughter Lucia: 'I presented it in our name (that is, yours and mine) to the library of the University of Galway, as you are a grandchild of that ancient city and I a descendant of one of its tribes' (*L3* 375).

What these few selected examples from Joyce's own life demonstrate is that Ireland beyond the Pale needs to be considered as far more than just a contextual background or atmospheric shading in his works. Joyce's relationship with Ireland outside Dublin went deep to the core of his own familial identity. The notion, which has for so long been taken as a truism, that Joyce was a uniquely urban man who created uniquely urban works must be called into question once we factor in the reality of his own life. Joyce came to maturity in an Ireland whose cultural titans – the Revivalists – had their gaze fixed firmly on the west of Ireland as the source of inspiration for a country on the road to self-actualisation. That Joyce did not align himself with them does not mean that he did not also look westwards. Borrowing Bonnie Kime Scott's assertion that her pioneering work *Joyce and Feminism* (1984) 'does not invent or substitute a subject, but reclaims one that was there, too little recognized and worked, from the start', this book does not propose to 'take' Joyce out of the city and beyond the Pale, but rather to show that Joyce had already gone on that journey himself.[12] It seems time for us, as readers, to follow him.

* * *

The Pale in Ireland was not the only Pale to have existed, with an area going under the title of the 'English Pale' in Calais, France, before the Irish one had been established. Michael Potterton notes that Edward Poynings, who set about constructing the boundary in Ireland in 1494, had been the deputy lieutenant in Calais before then.[13] The term 'Pale of Settlement' is also used in English to refer to the area in Tsarist Russia, established in 1791, within which Jews were obliged to live.[14] In fact, John Everett-Heath posits that it is from the Russian Pale of Settlement that we get the phrase 'beyond the pale', meaning 'outside the limits of acceptable behaviour; unacceptable or improper' (*OED*, 'pale, n.1', 5c).[15] Going 'beyond the pale' has slightly different connotations depending on whether one sees the phrase originating from the English Pale in Ireland or the Pale of Settlement in Russia. For a Jewish person to go beyond the Pale of Settlement is unacceptable because it is illegal: this Pale is intended to keep its repressed subjects trapped within it. For someone in medieval Ireland who was loyal to England, going beyond the Pale was to risk confrontation with behaviour that was unacceptable – the customs of the Gaelic people, or 'wild Irish'. The Pale in an Irish context serves the primary function of keeping people out rather than trapping them within. Therefore, when someone in Ireland goes 'beyond the pale', the connotation is not just that the very act of doing so is unacceptable, but rather that the behaviour that will be encountered outside will be unacceptable. The difference may seem slight, but it is important: going 'beyond the pale' in an Irish context, while potentially frowned upon and advised against for the English colonist, is a phrase connoting exoticism in addition to fear, the chance to observe an alien people. Certainly, for many of his more conservative contemporaries, Joyce went 'beyond the pale' in his description of sexuality, religion, and even his use of language itself. However, for Joyce as an Irishman, going 'beyond the pale' would have also suggested a sense of exploration, the mapping of *terra incognita* and the observation of the primitive.

While the boundary itself was not constructed until 1494, the concept of the Pale goes back further into Irish history. Potterton writes that boundaries had existed before this, though they were 'in some places quite different and in many instances quite fluid [. . .]

The greater part of the Pale's edge was defined by natural features – rivers, lakes, mountains, bogland and the coast.'[16] It appears that the first reference to the Pale in Ireland comes from the Irish leader Aodh Ruadh Mac Mathghamhna in 1446–47 who promised 'to carrie nothing owte of the inglishe pale contrarie to the statutes'.[17] Even this first reference indicates that the area denoted by the Pale was potentially vulnerable and liable to raids by the Gaelic Irish and rebellious Anglo-Irish beyond its boundaries. At its height following the twelfth-century Anglo-Norman invasion, the area along the east coast under English control stretched from Dundalk down to Waterford and extended up to sixty miles inland.[18] However, following repeated attacks and shrinkage of this area of control, the colonists sought to construct a literal barrier to the area. Art Cosgrove writes that '[i]n 1454 commissioners were appointed to recruit "labourers and workmen . . . to make trenches and fortresses upon the borders and marches" of the four Pale counties of Meath, Louth, Kildare, and Dublin'.[19] The eventual result was the construction of linear earthworks serving as a barrier, as well as numerous towerhouses.[20]

While the area within the Pale officially used English and followed English law, beyond this Gaelic culture and language predominated and, as Cosgrove writes, '[s]ome parts of the country, like the O'Donnells' territory in the north-west, had never experienced Anglo-Norman or English settlement'.[21] By the latter half of the fifteenth century, Brehon law (the Gaelic system of law) was once again so dominant over the majority of the country that it 'threatened to engulf even the Pale itself'.[22] Indeed, the prior unfixed nature of the Pale border meant that a clean division between the Pale and Gaelic Ireland was always going to be somewhat false. R. F. Foster notes that 'Gaelic patterns survived within the Pale, in peasant society', while Pale agricultural practices persisted in areas beyond the frontier, such as in County Cavan.[23] Likewise, certain areas that remained predominantly loyal to the English crown, such as Kilkenny, were outside the Pale, while the Irish language was in fact spoken within the Pale.[24] The Pale, therefore, is not as neat a division between two civilisations as might previously have been thought, and its construction was quite evidently an act born out of fear and desperation over loss of control rather than a triumphant claiming of territory for England.

Whatever the mutability of the Pale area itself, Ireland became, for English writers, very much an island divided into two culturally incompatible areas, one inhabited by the English and the other by the 'wild Irish'. This is apparent as early as Gerald of Wales's (alias Giraldus Cambrensis) account of Ireland in *Topographia Hibernica*

(*The History and Topography of Ireland* [c. 1188]), written following the Anglo-Norman invasion. Joep Leerssen writes that for Gerald, the Gaelic Irish were wild because they lived in the countryside, rather than in towns; they were a *gens silvestris*, 'a people of forest-dwellers, and inhospitable; a people living off beasts and like beasts; a people that still adheres to the most primitive way of pastoral living'.[25] Clearly, even as far back as the twelfth century, Ireland's wildness was inherently bound up with its rurality. Gerald was writing before the construction of the Pale, but his idea of a *gens silvestris*, already founded on distinctions relating to place of habitat, would be applied to those living beyond the Pale from the sixteenth century onwards.

In *The Fyrst Boke of the Introduction of Knowledge* (1547) – considered 'the first English guidebook to Europe'[26] – the sixteenth-century English physician and author Andrew Boorde wrote that Ireland was 'devyded in ii. partes .i. is the English pale. & the other, the wyld Iryshe'.[27] Boorde's account is particularly dualistic, describing the Pale as being 'a good countrey' where 'the english fashion is' and where the people 'be metely well mannered'.[28] By contrast, beyond the Pale, the people 'lak maners & honesti, & be untaught & rude'.[29] Like Gerald of Wales, Boorde links the Pale and 'english fashion' with 'good townes & cities', while the Gaelic Irish inhabit a countryside that is 'wylde, wast & vast, full of marryces & mountains'.[30] Indeed, it is of note that Boorde includes Waterford, not technically part of the Pale at this point, as culturally English by virtue of its urbanity. Interestingly, though Boorde acknowledges the 'testy' nature of some within the Pale, this is primarily blamed on their being 'vexed', presumedly by frequent attacks from the wild Irish; in contrast, the Irish beyond the Pale are 'testy without a cause'.[31] The concept of the wild, barbarous Irish living beyond the Pale takes on a life of its own from the sixteenth century, as the country came under wave after wave of plantations, with William Camden's *Britannia* (1586) describing them as 'they who reject all Laws, and live after a barbarous manner'.[32] Camden provides an even more Manichean account of the country than Boorde, contrasting the wild Irish with those 'who inhabit the Engliſh Pale' and 'are defective in no point of civility, or breeding; which they owe to the Engliſh Conqueſt'.[33] In these accounts, race and place are inherently bound up with civility; to be beyond the Pale is to be beyond redemption.

The division between the urban(e), eastern Pale and the wilderness of the west can also be seen in maps produced around this time. Abraham Ortelius's *Theatrum Orbis Terrarum* (1570) features a map of Ireland, viewed from the vantage point of Britain. Even a quick glance reveals the disparity in detail between the eastern coast (i.e. the Pale) and the western and northern regions of Ireland (fig. I.2). While the Pale has references to numerous towns, the west and most especially the north is *terra incognita*, featuring vast swathes of empty space, to the point that a large section of Ulster is filled up with an account of Lough Erne by Gerald of Wales. It is not, however, *terra nullius*, or unclaimed land, for what is certainly known is that this land is under ownership. The western and northern areas of the map are dotted with Gaelic surnames, reflecting the fact that these regions are under the control of Gaelic chieftains. Potterton describes numerous Renaissance maps that similarly distort the topography of Ireland, overemphasising the extent of the Pale, while William Smith draws attention to one map from the 1520s that 'greatly exaggerates the area of the Dublin/English Pale with the islands off Skerries shown around Co. Down and the island of Dalkey drifting southwards towards Wicklow and Arklow', while it is suggested that Dublin city extended as far as 'the lands of the Kildare Fitzgeralds'.[34] Meanwhile, John Speed's early seventeenth-century

Figure I.2   Reproduction of Abraham Ortelius's 1570 map of Ireland in *Theatrum Orbis Terrarum. Hiberniae Britannicae Insvlæ, Nova Descriptio*, The Topographical Collection of King George III, The British Library, 1573.

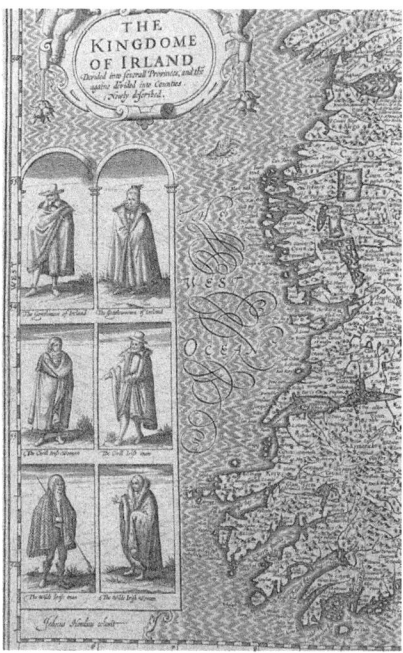

Figure I.3   Detail of the types of people to be found in Ireland, from John Speed's *The Theatre of the Empire of Great Britaine* (1611–12), in *A Prospect of the Most Famous Parts of the World . . . Together with All the Provinces, Counties and Shires, Contained in . . . Great Brittaines Empire. (A Description of the Civill Warres . . . in England, Etc.)*, 1631, n.p.

maps of Ireland include a guide to the inhabitants of the island, showing the 'Gentleman' and 'Gentlewoman of Ireland', the 'Civill Irifh' man and woman, and the 'Wilde Irifh' man and woman (fig. I.3). The semantics are worth commenting upon here: while the latter two groups, evidently of Gaelic origin or custom, are described as 'Irifh', the first group, originally of Anglo stock, is instead described as being 'of Ireland', an important distinction. Speed compiled his map in the wake of the Irish plantations, and hence many of these gentlemen and women would have belonged to families who had arrived in Ireland only a few decades previously. Even if they have been born in Ireland, Speed is careful not to suggest that this makes them 'Irifh'; it is safer, instead, to have them simply be 'of Ireland'. What is clear from these maps is that even for the cartographer, if the island of Ireland itself is one land and one country, it is most evidently not one culture.

Ireland beyond the Pale gradually became less threatening – if no less bewildering and even reprehensible, depending on who was viewing it – as the country increasingly came under the control of the growing British Empire. By the eighteenth century, going beyond the Pale had become an opportunity for touristic exploration and ethnographic observation. Glenn Hooper writes that the 'relatively pacific nature' of eighteenth-century Ireland resulted in it becoming 'a viable alternative to traditional Grand Tour destinations' for British tourists.[35] Ireland had the advantage of being 'both a spectacle and a domestic arena; a place apparently not that different from Britain, yet utterly so'.[36] In the nineteenth century, however, the increasing scale of Irish poverty meant that even the most blinkered of tourists could no longer ignore the dramatic discrepancy between the quality of life within and beyond the Pale. Hooper quotes from Thomas Kitson Cromwell's 1820 account of a tour of Ireland in which he compares the 'ruddy open countenances of English rustics' to their violent Irish equivalents, who resemble 'banditti [. . .] beings detached from civilized society, and ready for the perpetration of any attack upon its legal institutions'.[37] In 1887 the *Fortnightly Review* featured an article entitled 'Ireland Beyond the Pale' by Arthur D. Hayter that recounts a journey from Dublin to Connacht, and describes with some sympathy the plight of the local peasantry, 'whose life is one long struggle for existence'.[38] This article, written at the height of the Land War, searches for a solution to the peasantry's interminable impoverishment and battle with starvation. It depicts another revealing flashpoint in England's relationship with Ireland beyond the Pale: the 'wild Irish' have progressed from an existential threat just outside the barricades, to ethnographic fascination, and finally to a political problem and moral responsibility.

Yet throughout all of this, they remained totally other, wild, existing 'beyond the pale' first literally and then figuratively. Ireland was defined, even tainted, by the otherness that existed on its western edge; and for those middle-class Catholic Irish who resided in the Pale, the wretches beyond its former frontier weighed heavily on their sense of self-esteem. Edward Hirsch writes that middle-class Catholics associated the western peasantry 'with a strong and debilitating sense of cultural inferiority, and they were at least partially ashamed of their own rural background'.[39] As a result, Hirsch notes that

Many Catholic Dubliners affected English manners, styles, and habits, stigmatizing the Gaelic language and peasant customs as a badge of social inferiority and backwardness. Their insecurity suggests that as colonials they had internalized English attitudes and stereotypes. But because they were also nationalists, they liked to idealize and sentimentalize their roots, and they were especially vulnerable when attacked for their 'West Britonism.'[40]

These conflicted attitudes betray an awareness on the part of the middle-class Dubliners that, to those in Britain, the Catholic Irish, no matter where they lived, would always to some extent be seen as beyond the Pale. Such attitudes are frequently dramatised by Joyce, through the middle-class pretensions of Gabriel Conroy in 'The Dead' and the youthful shame and fear felt by Stephen D(a)edalus when travelling through the countryside in *Stephen Hero* (posthumously published in 1944) and *A Portrait of the Artist as a Young Man* (1916). Meanwhile, in *Ulysses* (1922), Stephen clearly believes that English attitudes to the Catholic Irish have not changed much over the centuries when he describes the Englishman Haines as 'smiling at wild Irish' (*U* 1.731).

Things changed quite dramatically towards the latter half of the nineteenth century, however. Rural Ireland, so long a source of trouble to the English and shame to the socially mobile Irish, now became a model for a new vision of Ireland and, most particularly, of Irish literature. Ireland beyond the Pale became *the* Ireland, as a complex history featuring waves of invasions and intermarriage was reduced to a simple formula: to be 'Gaelic' is to be Irish in its purest form. This reached its apogee during the Irish Literary Revival, as Revivalists took inspiration from the folklore, language and noble poverty of the western peasantry. Early Revivalists, especially those from the Anglo-Irish Protestant ascendancy, attempted to form an alliance between 'the noble and the beggar-man', thus making a claim for their continued role as aristocratic overseers in a new Ireland.[41] But this '[d]ream', as Yeats rightly labels it, for it never progressed beyond such a state, was instead overshadowed by the narrow identity confines espoused by the conservative revolutionaries who would go on to lead the Irish Free State following independence.[42]

Perhaps the best exponent of this conservatism in twentieth-century Irish nationalism is the journalist and author D. P. Moran (1869–1936), whose writings at the turn of the century led to the birth of the 'Irish Ireland' movement. His 1905 book *The Philosophy of Irish Ireland* argues for a Catholic, Gaelic, Irish-speaking island independent of Britain. Moran saw this battle as one between two civilisations, and this resulted, as P. J. Mathews argues, in him taking 'a steadfastly essentialist view of Irish identity' in which 'Irish

culture and Gaelic Catholic experience were simply coterminous'.[43]
One chapter of *The Philosophy of Irish Ireland*, entitled 'The Pale
and the Gael', makes clear where Moran drew the line between these
two civilisations. Moran placed the blame squarely on the concept
of the Pale and its supposed adherents, writing that '[t]he next few
years will decide for all time whether the Gael is to lift up the Irish
race once more, or whether the Pale is to complete its effacement'.[44]
For Moran, the epithet 'Paleman' ranked among the worst of insults
to inflict upon the Irish.[45] For those of an Anglo-Irish background,
the situation was quite hopeless: they would be forever 'Palemen'.
Mathews underscores this and notes how Moran 'did not see any
distinction between the younger generation of Anglo-Irish revivalists
and die-hard ascendancy colonials'.[46] Even when Moran acknowledges the patriotism of some Anglo-Irish Protestant politicians, he
nevertheless writes that 'they had no conception of an Irish nation',
emphasising instead that the 'foundation of Ireland is the Gael'.[47]

Strangely enough, the Gaels, for Moran, existed as a more mutable
species. They, by embracing what Moran sees as English habits of
materialism, can lose their status as 'Gaels' and become 'Palemen'.
For example, Moran admonishes those Gaels who 'stay[ed] at home,
learned a bit of English, and became Palemen'.[48] According to Moran,
then, being a Gael is a state of mind and behaviour as much as it
is an ethnic fact – but only if you come from a Gaelic background
in the first place. The status of a Gael is therefore something one
can lose but not gain. Those from beyond the Pale, though finding
themselves perhaps for the first time being lauded in the English language, were now caught in a bind: remain proud, poor and Gaelic –
or become a Paleman. Moran's vitriolic philosophy resulted in what
Joseph Valente calls a group of 'em-paled or impaled Gaels', whose
allegiances were divided between Gael and Pale, and among whose
tormented membership Valente counts Joyce.[49]

D. P. Moran's binary division of Ireland into Pale and Gael was evidently reductive, though it struck a nerve with many of Joyce's peers.
Timothy G. McMahon writes that Moran's newspaper *The Leader*
'became extremely popular with the students at University College
during Joyce's student days', and argues for Moran being a major
influence on the writing of 'Cyclops' and 'Circe'.[50] Vincent Deane
similarly writes of the influence that Moran's rhetoric had on Joyce's
writing, noting that 'Joyce belonged to the demographic championed
by the *Leader* and a number of his writings show him to be equally
engaged in a battle of two civilizations'.[51] We know, for instance, that
Joyce had a copy of Moran's 1905 novel *Tom O'Kelly* in Trieste.[52]

He also clearly followed Moran's arguments in *The Leader*, though it seems likely that he did not agree with most of them, responding with irony in 1904 to a remark in one of his brother Stanislaus's letters: 'As for the comments of "Irish Ireland" – she [Nora] seems to have as high an opinion of them as I have' (*L2* 71).

Nevertheless, if Moran's idealisation of the 'Gael' did not exactly persuade Joyce, his demonisation of the 'Paleman' can be seen creeping into Joyce's work. It is noteworthy in *Ulysses*, for example, that English characters are at several points referred to as 'Palefaces'. Even within the first few pages, Stephen imagines, with some disdain, the English scholars whom Buck Mulligan befriended at Oxford – 'the moneyed voices' – as 'Palefaces' (*U* 1.165–6). Later, in 'Wandering Rocks', we are presented with two cars of English tourists passing in front of Trinity College: 'Two carfuls of tourists passed slowly, their women sitting fore, gripping the handrests. Palefaces' (*U* 10.340–1). Later again, in 'Circe', the writer of *Matcham's Masterstroke*, Philip Beaufoy of the 'Playgoers' Club, London', is described as being '*palefaced*' (*U* 4.502–3, 15.814). The term 'paleface' was a moniker used by Native Americans for their white conquerors, appropriated in turn by Irish nationalists for their English conquerors, probably being attractive given its emphasis on the Pale, thereby recalling a time when the English had to fence themselves off from the rest of the country for fear of being overrun by Gaelic attackers.[53] It also seems quite possible that Joyce might have been offering his own variation on the frequently used term for Protestants in the pages of Moran's paper: 'sourfaces'.[54] It is also significant that 'pale face' appears as a negative description more than once in Moran's writing; for example, in an article for *The Leader* in 1907, Moran refers to 'the procession of pale-faces that passes you in every street' in London,[55] while in his novel *Tom O'Kelly*, he includes a caustic authorial aside directed at Yeats-esque Celtic Twilight poets:

> My parting word is reserved to the young gentlemen in the cloaks, with long hair and solemn, pale faces, who hear 'lake water lapping' even when they are stirring their punch. Lifting up their voices they will mournfully chant, 'Where, oh where, is the Celtic Note?'[56]

Moran and Joyce shared a disdain for the pretensions of the Revivalists, and this mocking depiction of the Irish poet searching after the 'Celtic Note' is echoed in Joyce's portrayal of Little Chandler in 'A Little Cloud', who imagines how he might compose poems that would be accepted by English critics as containing the all-important '*Celtic note*' (*D* 56).

While the Pale, and pale faces, are both primarily associated with Englishness and English characters in Moran and Joyce, the latter was also willing to direct such descriptions towards Irish-born characters. In *Finnegans Wake*, on at least two occasions the police are associated with the Pale: in Phoenix Park, we meet 'a brace of palesmen' on the beat, and later again there is a reference to 'that bunch of palers on their round' as Joyce plays on the term 'peeler' for a policeman (*FW* 42.34, 323.30). In pre-independence Ireland, the police of the Royal Irish Constabulary, though often from so-called Gaelic backgrounds, were, for nationalists, easily associated with colonialism – and later considered a legitimate target for Republicans. Here, as in Moran, we see Irish men making the transition from Gael to Pale.

When Ireland was finally partitioned, the line of division that for so long separated Dublin from the rest moved northwards as the capital city increasingly Gaelicised itself and the new state of Northern Ireland was crafted as a Protestant, unionist state. The north-eastern portion of Ulster now became what for so long the eastern strip of the Pale had been for southern nationalists. This, too, is represented in Joyce through the old dichotomy of Pale/Gael: 'men on the two sides in New South Ireland and Vetera Uladh, bluemin and pillfaces' (*FW* 78.26–7). The Ulster unionists (*Uladh* being the Irish for Ulster) now take on the mantle of 'pillfaces', while the nationalists in the south are 'bluemin', perhaps a reference to the Blueshirts, Ireland's flirtation with fascism in the 1930s.

Another example comes from the start of the *Wake*, when Joyce retells the story of the sixteenth-century Gaelic pirate queen Gráinne Ní Mháille, or 'the prankquean' (*FW* 21.15), who is said to have kidnapped a child of the Anglo-Irish St Lawrence family of Howth Castle upon being refused hospitality there.[57] In Joyce's retelling, 'her grace o'malice kidsnapped up the jiminy Tristopher and into the shandy westerness she rain, rain, rain' (*FW* 21.20–2). The prankquean twice more kidnaps 'a paly one' before the tale comes to a sudden end (*FW* 22.3). Amid this farcical train of events, this episode sets up a clear east/west dichotomy, represented respectively by the Anglo-Irish St Lawrence family and Gráinne Ní Mháille as Gaelic Taoiseach. As the above quotation demonstrates, the prankquean flees with Tristopher to 'the shandy westerness', 'shandy' meaning 'wild' or 'boisterous' (*OED*, 'shandy, adj.'), but also possibly a play on *seanda*, Irish for 'ancient', placing emphasis on the idea of western Ireland being rooted in the past (*FGB*, 'seanda'). Meanwhile, 'westerness' also appropriately aligns the west with 'wilderness'. Tristopher's description as 'a paly one' evidently links him to the Pale, while his father Jarl van Hoother's foreignness is emphasised as he speaks to the prankquean 'with dovesgall', a reference to *dubh gall*, an Irish term meaning 'black foreigner' and employed to describe the Norse invaders. Van Hoother is also sartorially English, as he wears 'soxan-gloves': Anglo-Saxon socks and gloves (*FW* 21.23, 22.35). Meteo-rological variances between east and west are also to the fore here, as on two occasions the prankquean's escape with the young Baron is described thus: 'she rain, rain, rain' (*FW* 21.22, 22.8–9). Later again she flees 'raining, raining' (*FW* 22.18). F. H. A. Aalen notes the importance of this meteorological difference between east and west in understanding the political power-balance of the country, writing that '[t]he eastern coastlands between Dublin and Drogheda are the driest parts of the country, which has helped their evolution as a geopolitical focus'.[58]

The prankquean's 'invasion' of Howth Castle recalls the raids carried out by Gaelic leaders on the Pale and upends the apparent hegemonic structures on the island. What might appear an outland-ishly comic passage in fact contains within it many references to the geopolitical divisions on the island throughout history. Evidently, the Pale/Gael dichotomy had a lasting imaginative appeal, even for a writer such as Joyce who rejected the binaries fostered by 'Irish Irelanders'.

*   *   *

Susan Stanford Friedman borrows Dipesh Chakrabarty's phrase 'provincializing Europe' to note that the idea of a unified 'West' has led to the repression of 'the heterogeneities and peripheries *within* Europe'.[59] 'Provincializing' a writer such as Joyce might seem an excessively revisionist undertaking – though he did at one point intend to write a sequel to *Dubliners* entitled *Provincials* (*L2* 63) – while the turn towards an Irish Studies approach to Joyce since the 1990s might sometimes appear to overly ground and localise a famously peripatetic writer. Barry McCrea addresses this concern when he writes that

> [m]uch scholarship indeed now reads *Ulysses* as though Irishness were not the frame for its expression, but instead the essence residing at its interpretative core, an irreducible, indispensable, secret code for

understanding the book. As though, in short, *Ulysses* were important because it belongs to Ireland, and not the other way around.[60]

McCrea's intervention is a reminder, particularly to Irish critics, that there is always more to Joyce than just Ireland. For all the useful corrections that the 'Irish turn' in Joycean studies has provided, it is important to remember that he was, in McCrea's words, 'never a working writer in Ireland'.[61]

Where does this leave a work that insists not just on an Irish reading of Joyce, but on a rural and provincial one? Is this not the 'Irish turn' in Joyce taken to its final, absurd, myopic conclusion? This reading might be especially problematic in a country where ruralism has for so long been associated with the most conservative elements of Irish culture. If, as McCrea argues, *Ulysses* and Joyce have become so accepted in modern Ireland because they have been seen to represent an Ireland that is urban, cosmopolitan and inter-nationalist in outlook – qualities with which Ireland is now happy to be associated – what happens to this sense of national and cultural selfhood if both the man and the works can be shown to be equally as influenced by the rural, 'traditional' Ireland long banished to the remote realms of the national psyche?

It has become common in much Irish criticism to lambast an anti-urban bias in the Irish cultural imagination, particularly of the early twentieth century.[62] Indeed, Alison Lacivita has argued that it has often been 'scholars working to (re-)place Joyce into an Irish con-text that are most emphatic about his urban quality, a trend that is also indicative of the urban-focused trend of Irish studies in recent decades'.[63] Such tendencies need to be tempered with a consider-ation of what basis, if any, the clichés about rural Ireland have in fact. Luke Gibbons usefully points out that the problem with the idea that rural Ireland and rural values are at fault for the failings of modern Ireland 'is that it assumes that the rural ideology which pre-sided over the national revival was a genuine expression of country life'.[64] Instead, Gibbons writes, the 'idealizations of rural existence [. . .] are the product of an *urban* sensibility, and are cultural fic-tions imposed on the lives of those they purport to represent'.[65] By 'provincializing' Joyce, this study is not attempting to turn him into a signed-up Revivalist – rather, it will show the extent to which he was attuned to the fantasy version of rural Ireland that was gaining dominance in certain Revivalist circles, and outline how he offered his own interpretation. Rather than merely pointing out Joyce's scepticism towards the Revivalist utopia of rural Ireland, this book argues instead for the full incorporation of a modern, unidealised rural Ireland into the Joycean landscape.

Joycean critics have in the past sporadically ventured away from the city and into rural Ireland. An important, early contribution to this area of Joycean criticism came in a 1992 article by Cóilín Owens that added some much-needed nuance to understandings of Joyce's relationship with the Revivalists. Owens argues that, though a critic of the movement, Joyce was nevertheless a product of the same cultural and political forces that were at play during this time, and therefore 'was not entirely impervious to the mystique of the Gaelic West'.[66] Marjorie Howes similarly deals with Joyce's relationship to the west in a primarily geographical reading of 'The Dead', where she also investigates Stephen's interactions with the peasantry in *A Portrait* and argues for what she calls 'rural Ireland's perverse partial modernity' as a vital element in Joyce's work.[67] Another examination of a 'rural Joyce' can be found in Oona Frawley's compelling work *Irish Pastoral* (2005), in which she rightly notes that 'as critics we have not often looked beyond the template of the "urban Joyce"', but nevertheless remains of the view that Joyce 'refus[es] rural Ireland a significant existence in his work'.[68] Instead, focusing on *Dubliners* and *Ulysses*, Frawley claims that 'the vast majority of non-Dublin space [. . .] is foreign: not only not rural, but not Irish', and she is more interested in Joyce's depiction of pastoral spaces beyond Ireland, such as Gibraltar and Palestine, for example.[69] However, the most important and extended treatment of Joyce beyond Dublin is Frank Shovlin's *Journey Westward: Joyce, 'Dubliners' and the Literary Revival* (2012). While Shovlin examines Joyce's relationship to the west of Ireland more broadly, the primary focus of this work is, as the title suggests, *Dubliners* (1914). Shovlin convincingly argues that 'Joyce, too, was interested in what lay beyond the Shannon' and had an attitude towards the west that was 'considerably more ambiguous than many critics have allowed'.[70] Shovlin contends that Joyce's interest in the west was 'more historically grounded, and sometimes more personal' than the typical Revivalist romanticism, an argument that this book also sets out.[71] More recently still, Heather Laird's 2022 article on the 'agrarian code' in *Ulysses* concludes that while *Ulysses* 'is undoubtedly an urban text', it is 'one with an important rural context', and that viewing the work 'through a rural lens reveals further nuances in its treatment of Irish nationalism and the colonial relationship between Ireland and England'.[72]

It will probably come as little surprise that, given its concluding promise to 'journey westward', many of the important early studies of Joyce beyond the Pale focus on 'The Dead'. However, the more recent ecocritical turn in Joycean studies has opened up new avenues for exploring Joyce's engagement with the rural landscape across his oeuvre, particularly in *Finnegans Wake*. The 2014 collection *Eco-Joyce: The Environmental Imagination of James Joyce* includes many important ecocritical contributions to the Joycean critical canon, including one by Brandon Kershner entitled 'Joyce Beyond the Pale'. While this piece does not deal with much of Joyce's writing set beyond the Pale itself, Kershner does elucidate how nature encroaches upon urban spaces in Joyce, 'as a kind of horizon to their action or vision'.[73] This is indeed a revealing aspect of Joyce's depiction of the city space, and one that is explored in the fourth chapter of this book. Alison Lacivita's *The Ecology of 'Finnegans Wake'* (2015) deals at length with how Joyce's final work delves into both urban and rural environments, showing how the *Wake*'s effort to give a totalising account of human history and experience is mirrored in its depiction of environmental diversity: '*Finnegans Wake* deals with all kinds of Irish environments, from inner-city slums to the coasts of Cork and the mountains of Kerry, to the suburban village of Chapelizod and the purgatorial identity of the Phoenix Park.'[74] Lacivita places ecological concerns at the centre of the *Wake*, noting how Joyce's final work 'is exemplary as a subject for ecocritical inquiry because of the way in which it addresses the interaction and interdependence between city and country', connections that this book also seeks to draw out across Joyce's works.[75] Perhaps of most relevance to the current study is Lacivita's insistence on how Joyce's engagement with ecological concerns is fundamentally linked to the experience of modernity, writing that '[m]odernity is the condition wherein humans begin to separate from the earth that once defined their lives'.[76] In a country where colonial modernity so often goes hand-in-hand with ecological disaster – be it through the deliberate felling of forests or *laissez-faire* attitudes to potato blight – Lacivita's point is a salient one, and one that insists upon the political and the ecological as central to any exploration of rural modernity in Joyce.

While there are many other individual articles of particular relevance to Joyce and ecology, it is important to mention the recent work of Katherine O'Callaghan and her centring of the 'west' in Joycean ecocriticism, once again in relation to the *Wake*.[77] Like Lacivita, O'Callaghan argues that the *Wake* is 'remarkable, not just for its evocations of the Irish landscape (and the West) but for the extraordinary manner in which it resonates with understandings of environmental connectivity, ecological systems, and communication (and a thorough dismantling of an urban-rural dichotomy)'.[78] Finally, O'Callaghan cautions against the 'rush to deem Joyce "urban"', which she argues only serves to deny 'the subtleties of Joyce's representation of both the land and culture of the country'.[79]

Ecocritical approaches to Joyce's work have provided insightful commentaries on his portrayal of both urban and rural space. While parts of this book are greatly influenced by such approaches – particularly in Chapter 5 – it is nevertheless not solely a work of eco-criticism. Instead, the interdisciplinary nature of this study bespeaks a desire not to limit Joyce's writing on rural life to just its ecological aspects. My contention is that Joyce's interaction with rural Ireland is as influenced by its politics and people as it is by its landscape or ecology. Of course, the environmental humanities have now gone well beyond merely having 'nature' as their main focus. Nevertheless, by maintaining a focus solely on the ecological, there remains a risk that one might imply that to speak of the rural is to necessarily only speak of the ecological. Such a focus can potentially end up stripping rural communities of their legacies of political engagement, reducing them to nothing beyond the landscape that envelops them.

This book is therefore instead primarily grounded in the concept of rural modernity, which is based on the relatively straightforward notion that 'rural regions, communities, classes and figures can orig-inate and sustain histories of and criticism on modernity and the modern'.[80] This concept need not, however, be limited only to writers from rural regions, as Kristin Bluemel and Michael McCluskey argue in *Rural Modernity in Britain* (2018), but relates to all '[w]riters, artists and designers who granted rural people subjectivity and repre-sented rural places and activities as central to the nation's experience of modernity'.[81] I contend that Joyce is one such writer. While the concept of rural modernity is discussed primarily in the first chap-ter, it remains the guiding principle that runs throughout the book. At this point it is also important to note that 'rural' is a somewhat catch-all term: while acres of agricultural landscape might comfort-ably fit under the rubric of 'rural', where, for example, does one draw the line between 'rural' and 'provincial'? Often, these terms are used somewhat interchangeably to describe the opposite of a metro-politan centre, though there is of course a clear difference between a purely 'rural' area, far from any significant urban zone, and a small provincial town or city. There is also, however, an argument to be made for there being a shared identity between those living in rural areas and those living in provincial cities, such as Limerick or Cork,

formed out of a sense of commonality in opposition to the metropolitan centre. While the primary focus of this book is rural Ireland,
there are sections that deal with the provincial more broadly, including Joyce's account of towns and cities beyond the Pale.

This study takes a thematic rather than a chronological approach
in an effort to show how ideas regarding rural Ireland warp and
weave their way through Joyce's entire oeuvre. While certain chapters focus on particular works more than others, the aim is to show
that these concerns were career-long ones that did not stop at the
final page of any one of Joyce's novels. The book is divided into two
parts, the first of which, 'Politics and People', attempts to establish
the political and cultural context by investigating how Joyce was
both influenced by and reacted against Revivalist narratives of rural
Ireland. Chapter 1 explores rural modernity, looking at it through
the lens of the co-operative movement and *The Irish Homestead*,
where Joyce had his first stories published, and finally the legacy of
the Land War, framing them within critical debates regarding tradition and modernity. Chapter 2 looks into Revivalist debates regarding the merits of crafting an urban and cosmopolitan nation versus a
'provincial' or rural one – whether the country should, in the words
of the *Wake*, be 'ruric or cospolite' (*FW* 309.10). Rather, however,
than accepting these facile binaries, the chapter shows how Joyce
was aware of the complexities of such issues in a decolonising country. The third chapter turns its focus on to one of the core obsessions
of Revivalism: the rural peasantry. It insists on the importance of
drawing out the nuances of Joyce's portrayal of peasant characters,
particularly in comparing how the peasantry are recast from *Stephen
Hero* through to *A Portrait of the Artist as a Young Man*. Joyce's
aestheticisation of the peasantry is one that views them as a complex
and modern group, rejecting both negative colonial stereotypes and
Revivalist notions of a pure peasantry.

The second part, 'Place and Peregrinations', turns its focus on to
Joyce's literal and literary journeys through rural Ireland, as well as
his geographical depictions of it. Chapter 4 looks at how elements
of rural life enter and transform the city streets, such as the quite
literal examples of rural migrants to the city and cattle on their way
to the docks. It also explores the liminal areas between the rural and
the urban on the city's periphery, showing the border around Joyce's
cityscapes to be a porous one. Chapter 5 follows Joyce on his journeys out of Dublin, looking especially at spatial and geographical rep-
resentations of rural and provincial Ireland, particularly the trip to
Cork in *A Portrait* and the imaginative 'tours' of Ireland throughout

Ulysses. The final chapter is concerned with provincial acrimony in *Finnegans Wake*, where the Four Old Men represent the provinces of Ireland. This comes to the fore in Chapter III.3 of the *Wake* where Shaun forms a 'landshape', sprawled across the Hill of Uisneach in the centre of Ireland (*FW* 474.2–3).

In short, *James Joyce, Rural Ireland and Modernity* argues that, for all Joyce's obsession with the city of his youth, he shows a consistent interest in rural and provincial Ireland throughout his writing, testament to the powerful grip that life beyond the Pale had on the early twentieth-century Irish cultural imagination. Standing at the Pale's edge, Joyce did not follow some Revivalist contemporaries by relocating to the west, but neither did he avert his gaze. If the Pale might at times have seemed to act as a boundary to Irish readings of Joyce, this work instead argues for surmounting its ramparts and straying beyond.

Notes

1. Roland McHugh, *Annotations to 'Finnegans Wake'*, 4th edn (Baltimore, MD: John Hopkins University Press, 2016), 539.
2. Mary Colum, *Life and the Dream* (New York: Doubleday, 1947), 379.
3. Peter Costello, *The Heart Grown Brutal: Irish Revolution in Literature from Parnell to the Death of Yeats, 1891–1939* (Dublin: Gill and Macmillan, 1977), 53, cited in Katherine O'Callaghan, 'Solastalgic Modernism and the West in Irish Literature, 1900–1950', in Malcolm Sen (ed.), *A History of Irish Literature and the Environment* (Cambridge: Cambridge University Press, 2022), 162 n.64.
4. Brendan Cullen, 'The Pale Rampart at Clongowes Wood College', *Local History Journal* 21 (2016), 32, https://localhistory.ie/?mdocs-file=455 (accessed 22 February 2021).
5. Sinéad Quirke, 'A Gatehouse to Beyond the Boundaries of the Pale: Reflection on Rathcoffey, Co. Kildare', in Michael Potterton and Thomas Herron (eds), *Dublin and the Pale in the Renaissance, c.1540–1660* (Dublin: Four Courts Press, 2011), 118.
6. I would like to express my gratitude to Margaret Doyle, archivist at Clongowes, for directing my attention to this article.
7. Logographos, 'The Rampart of the Pale', *The Clongownian* 1 (1895), 10.
8. Ibid., 10.
9. Cullen, 'The Pale Rampart at Clongowes Wood College', 32.
10. Ibid., 33.
11. Frank Shovlin, *Journey Westward: Joyce, Dubliners and the Literary Revival* (Liverpool: Liverpool University Press, 2012), 3.

12. Bonnie Kime Scott, *Joyce and Feminism* (Bloomington, IN: Indiana University Press, 1984), 201–2.
13. Michael Potterton, 'Introduction: the FitzGeralds, Florence, St Fiachra and a Few Fragments', in Michael Potterton and Thomas Herron (eds), *Dublin and the Pale in the Renaissance, c.1540–1660* (Dublin: Four Courts Press, 2011), 41.
14. John Everett-Heath, 'Pale of Settlement', in *The Concise Oxford Dictionary of World Place Names*, 5th edn (Oxford: Oxford University Press, 2019), https://www.oxfordreference.com/view/10.1093/acref/9780191882913.001.0001/acref-9780191882913-e-10232 (accessed 19 January 2022).
15. Ibid. The *OED* casts doubt on the idea that this phrase relates to any of the specific regions mentioned here, and instead argues that it 'is likely to be a later rationalization' (*OED*, 'pale, n.1', 5c).
16. Potterton, 'Introduction', 41.
17. *Calendar of the Carew manuscripts preserved in the archiepiscopal library at Lambeth*, I (London: 1867–73), 290, cited in Art Cosgrove, 'The Emergence of the Pale', in Art Cosgrove (ed.), *A New History of Ireland: Volume II, Medieval Ireland 1169–1534* (Oxford: Oxford University Press, 2008), 533.
18. Charles Knight, *The Popular History of England: An Illustrated History of Society and Government from the Earliest Period to Our Own Times*, II (Boston, MA: Estes and Lauriat, 1874), 386.
19. Art Cosgrove, 'Anglo-Ireland and the Yorkist Cause', in Art Cosgrove (ed.), *A New History of Ireland: Volume II, Medieval Ireland 1169–1534* (Oxford: Oxford University Press, 2008), 563.
20. Geraldine Stout and Matthew Stout, 'Early Landscapes: From Prehistory to Plantation', in F. H. A. Aalen, Kevin Whelan and Matthew Stout (eds), *Atlas of the Irish Rural Landscape* (Toronto: University of Toronto Press, 1997), 57–8.
21. Art Cosgrove, 'Ireland beyond the Pale, 1399–1460', in Art Cosgrove (ed.), *A New History of Ireland: Volume II, Medieval Ireland 1169–1534* (Oxford: Oxford University Press, 2008), 569.
22. Ibid., 590.
23. R. F. Foster, *Modern Ireland, 1600–1972* (London: Penguin, 1989), 9.
24. See John Bradley, 'The Purpose of the Pale: A View from Kilkenny', in Michael Potterton and Thomas Herron (eds), *Dublin and the Pale in the Renaissance, c.1540–1660* (Dublin: Four Courts Press, 2011), 51–67; and Brendan Kane, 'Languages of Legitimacy? *An Ghaeilge*, the Earl of Thomond and British Politics in the Renaissance Pale, 1600–24', in Michael Potterton and Thomas Herron (eds), *Dublin and the Pale in the Renaissance, c.1540–1660* (Dublin: Four Courts Press, 2011), 267–79.
25. Giraldus Cambrensis, *Topographia Hibernica*, cited in Joseph Theodoor Leerssen, 'Wildness, Wilderness, and Ireland: Medieval and

Early-Modern Patterns in the Demarcation of Civility', *Journal of the History of Ideas* 56/1 (1995), 30.

26. 'Andrew Boorde', in *Britannica Academic*, Encyclopædia Britannica, 20 July 1998, https://www.britannica.com/biography/Andrew-Boorde (accessed 14 September 2024).

27. Andrew Boorde, *The first boke of the introduction of knowledge* (1552; repr. London, 1814), n.p., cited in Joseph Theodoor Leerssen, *Mere Irish & Fíor-ghael: Studies in the Idea of Irish Nationality, Its Development and Literary Expression Prior to the Nineteenth Century* (Amsterdam: John Benjamins, 1986), 42.

28. Ibid., 42.

29. Ibid., 42.

30. Ibid., 42.

31. Ibid., 42.

32. William Camden, *Camden's Britannia* (Oxford: Edmund Gibson, 1695), 973.

33. Ibid., 1048.

34. William Smyth, *Map-making, Landscapes and Memory: A Geography of Colonial and Early Modern Ireland, c.1530–1750* (Cork: Cork University Press, 2006), 21–2, cited in Potterton, 'Introduction', 23.

35. Glenn Hooper, 'The Isles/Ireland: The Wilder Shore', in Peter Hulme and Tim Young (eds), *The Cambridge Companion to Travel Writing* (Cambridge: Cambridge University Press, 2002), 178.

36. Ibid., 179.

37. Thomas Kitson Cromwell, *Historical and Descriptive Sketch of the Past and Present State of Ireland*, II (London: Longman, 1820), 145, cited in Hooper, 'The Isles/Ireland', 180–1.

38. Arthur D. Hayter, 'Ireland Beyond the Pale', *Fortnightly Review* 41/241 (1887), 72.

39. Edward Hirsch, 'The Imaginary Irish Peasant', *PMLA* 106/5 (1991), 1123.

40. Ibid., 1123–4.

41. William Butler Yeats, 'The Municipal Gallery Revisited', in *Yeats's Poems*, ed. A. Norman Jeffares (London: Palgrave Macmillan, 1989), 439.

42. Ibid., 439.

43. P. J. Mathews, *Revival: the Abbey Theatre, Sinn Féin, the Gaelic League and the Co-operative Movement* (Cork: Cork University Press in association with Field Day, 2003), 97.

44. D. P. Moran, *The Philosophy of Irish Ireland* (Dublin: James Duffy, 1905), 51.

45. Ibid., 35.

46. Mathews, *Revival*, 98.

47. Moran, *The Philosophy of Irish Ireland*, 37.

48. Ibid., 36.

49. Joseph Valente, 'James Joyce and the Cosmopolitan Sublime', in Mark A. Wollaeger, Victor Luftig and Robert Spoo (eds), *Joyce and the Subject of History* (Ann Arbor, MI: University of Michigan Press, 1996), 62.

50. Timothy G. McMahon, 'Cultural Nativism and Irish-Ireland: *The Leader* as a Source for Joyce's *Ulysses*', *Joyce Studies Annual* 7 (1996), 74, 68.

51. Vincent Deane, 'Joyce, Moranism, and the Opal Hush Poets', *Dublin James Joyce Journal* 5 (2012), 76.

52. Richard Ellmann, *The Consciousness of Joyce* (Oxford: Oxford University Press, 1977), 120.

53. Sam Slote, Marc A. Mamigonian and John Turner, *Annotations to James Joyce's 'Ulysses'* (Oxford: Oxford University Press, 2022), 13.

54. Deane, 'Joyce, Moranism', 70.

55. D. P. Moran, 'The Capital of West-Britain', *The Leader*, 5 January 1907, 325, cited in Liam Lanigan, *James Joyce, Urban Planning, and Irish Modernism: Dublins of the Future* (London: Palgrave Macmillan, 2014), 134.

56. D. P. Moran, *Tom O'Kelly* (Dublin: Cahill, James Duffy, 1905), 232.

57. Brendan O Hehir, *A Gaelic Lexicon for 'Finnegans Wake' and Glossary for Joyce's Other Works* (Berkeley, CA: University of California Press, 1967), 403.

58. F. H. A. Aalen, 'The Irish Rural Landscape: Synthesis of Habitat and History', in F. H. A. Aalen, Kevin Whelan and Matthew Stout (eds), *Atlas of the Irish Rural Landscape* (Toronto: University of Toronto Press, 1997), 16.

59. Susan Stanford Friedman, *Planetary Modernisms: Provocations on Modernity Across Time* (New York: Columbia University Press, 2015), 54. See also Dipesh Chakrabarty, *Provincializing Europe: Postcolonial Thought and Historical Difference*, 2nd edn (2000; Princeton, NJ: Princeton University Press, 2008).

60. Barry McCrea, 'Privatising *Ulysses*: Joyce before, during and after the "Celtic Tiger"', *European Joyce Studies* 22 (2013), 82.

61. Ibid., 92.

62. For an epitomisation of this view, see Fintan O'Toole, 'Going West: The Country versus the City in Irish Writing', *The Crane Bag* 9/2 (1985), 111–16. O'Toole writes that 'Irish culture and in particular Irish writing has been marked by this dominance of the rural over the urban, a dominance based on a false opposition of the country to the city which has been vital to the maintenence [*sic*] of a conservative political culture in the country' (111). For an overarching account of the perceived anti-urban bias in early twentieth-century Ireland, see Mervyn Horgan, 'Anti-Urbanism as a Way of Life: Disdain for Dublin in the Nationalist Imaginary', *The Canadian Journal of Irish Studies* 30/2 (2004), 38–47. Horgan argues that '[i]f the very substance of the nation is premised on a particular ideology that views rural life as the truth and ideal of Irish

life, then general disdain for Dublin, as the place where what is not Irish occurs, was inevitable' (40).

63. Alison Lacivita, *The Ecology of 'Finnegans Wake'* (Gainesville, FL: University Press of Florida, 2015), 19.

64. Luke Gibbons, *Transformations in Irish Culture* (Cork: Cork University Press in Association with Field Day, 1996), 85.

65. Ibid., 85.

66. Cóilín Owens, 'The Mystique of the West in Joyce's "The Dead"', *Irish University Review* 22/1 (1992), 91.

67. Marjorie Howes, '"Goodbye Ireland I'm going to Gort": Geography, Scale, and Narrating the Nation', in Marjorie Howes and Derek Attridge (eds), *Semicolonial Joyce* (Cambridge: Cambridge University Press, 2000), 65.

68. Oona Frawley, *Irish Pastoral: Nostalgia and Twentieth-Century Irish Literature* (Dublin: Irish Academic Press, 2005), 106, 109.

69. Ibid., 108.

70. Shovlin, *Journey Westward*, 3, 131.

71. Ibid., 3.

72. Heather Laird, '"[H]e daren't show his nose with the Molly Maguires looking for him to let daylight through him for grabbing the holding of an evicted tenant": *Ulysses*, the Cattle Economy, and the Unwritten Agrarian Code', *James Joyce Quarterly* 59/2 (2022), 223.

73. Brandon Kershner, 'Joyce Beyond the Pale', in Robert Brazeau and Derek Gladwin (eds), *Eco-Joyce: The Environmental Imagination of James Joyce* (Cork: Cork University Press, 2014), 126–7.

74. Lacivita, *The Ecology of 'Finnegans Wake'*, 7.

75. Ibid., 84.

76. Ibid., 228.

77. See, for example, Katherine O'Callaghan, 'The Riddle of the Brocken Spectre: Reading *Finnegans Wake* on the Top of Croagh Patrick', *James Joyce Quarterly* 56/1–2 (2018–19), 133–53, as well as the aforementioned essay on 'Solastalgic Modernism'.

78. O'Callaghan, 'Solastalgic Modernism', 162.

79. Ibid., 162.

80. Kristin Bluemel and Michael McCluskey, 'Introduction: Rural Modernity in Britain', in Kristin Bluemel and Michael McCluskey (eds), *Rural Modernity in Britain: A Critical Intervention* (Edinburgh: Edinburgh University Press, 2018), 2.

81. Ibid., 15.

Part I

Politics and People

Chapter 1

'The west shall shake the east awake': James Joyce and Rural Modernity

In the summer of 1904, the poet George Russell (known as 'Æ') sent a letter to a young aspiring writer in Dublin, suggesting that he submit a short story to *The Irish Homestead*, a newspaper focusing on rural affairs, particularly the co-operative movement, with which Russell was affiliated. Russell made the case for appearing in this less than prestigious publication in the following terms:

> Could you write anything simple, rural?, livemaking?, pathos?, which could be inserted so as not to shock the readers. If you could furnish a short story about 1800 words suitable for insertion the editor will pay £1. It is easily earned money if you can write fluently and don't mind playing to the common understanding and liking for once in a way. You can sign it any name you like as a pseudonym. (*L2* 43)

Perhaps reassured by the permission to publish under a pseudonym, on 13 August 1904 a short story entitled 'The Sisters' appeared in *The Irish Homestead*, written by a certain 'Stephen Dædalus' (fig. 1.1). A little later, the young James Joyce was paid his pound, and thus the major figure of Irish modernism received his literary debut – in a paper bought mostly for its advice on farming methods.

Joyce would go on to publish two more stories in the *Homestead*, early versions of what became 'Eveline' and 'After the Race' in *Dubliners*, before failing to get any others accepted due to supposed 'letters of complaint from readers in both the country and the city' (*JJII* 165).[1] Many years later, Joyce had Stephen Dedalus refer to the *Homestead* as the 'pigs' paper' in *Ulysses*, perhaps indicative of a long-held grudge against it for refusing to publish any more of

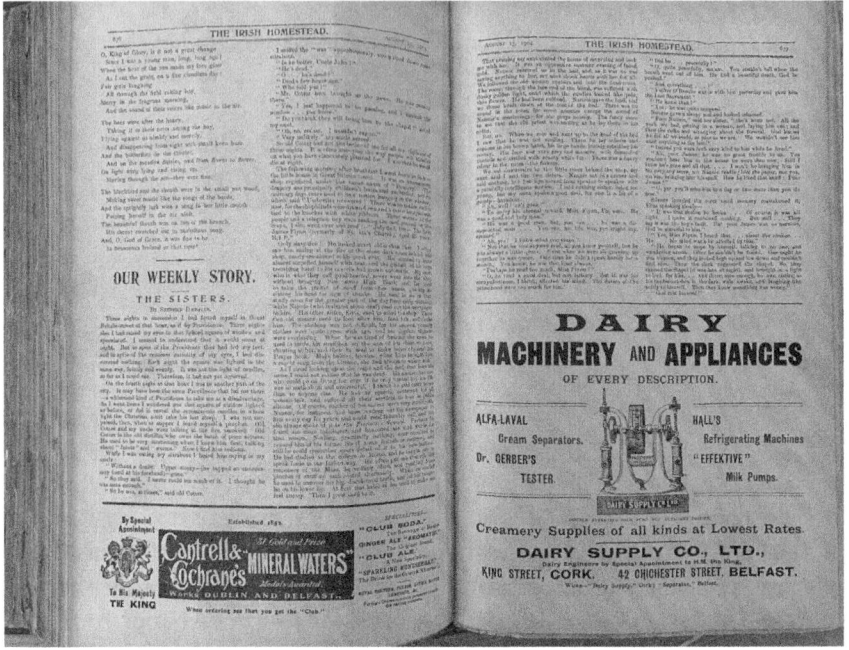

Figure 1.1   'The Sisters', as published in *The Irish Homestead*.
Stephen Dædalus [James Joyce], 'The Sisters', *The Irish Homestead*,
13 August 1904, 676–7.

his stories, or else a knowing and ironic suggestion from Joyce that
his fictional alter ego might find himself depending on it for publication just as he had in reality, though of course one should be wary
of aligning Joyce's post-1904 life with Stephen's hypothetical one
(*U* 9.321). Nevertheless, Stephen's seemingly trivial linguistic play on
Russell's Æ pseudonym – 'A.E.I.O.U.' (*U* 9.213) – takes on a greater
significance when we consider that Joyce, as a young, somewhat aim-
less writer, had been given his first major break by Russell and did
indeed 'owe' him a great deal. A few months prior to being published
in the *Homestead*, Joyce had submitted an essay entitled 'A Portrait
of the Artist' to the literary journal *Dana*, under the editorship of
John Eglinton, who refused it by saying 'I can't print what I can't
understand' (*JJII* 147). Ironically, Joyce's urban and cosmopolitan
peers were not willing to take a chance on his writing while ruralists
such as Russell and the *Homestead* were.

The fact of Joyce's initial publication in *The Irish Homestead*
should encourage us to reconsider how his relationship to questions

of rurality and tradition have thus far been framed. The critical consensus has generally tended to view Joyce's writing as existing in opposition to both, with rurality and tradition bordering on being synonymous, and therefore of little interest to a writer so immersed in the depiction of modernity. This chapter, however, will instead delve into Joyce's representation of *rural modernity*, a phenomenon that exists in a symbiotic relationship with tradition. It will argue for the centrality of the rural in any discussion of modernity, most particularly in an Irish context, and give an overview of the theoretical concerns relating to this relatively new area of study. It will then discuss in detail how Joyce's writing engaged with one of the most emphatic examples of rural modernity from his early childhood: the Land War.

To begin with, however, it is worth returning to the original publication of 'The Sisters' in *The Irish Homestead*. Though later heavily revised and expanded for inclusion in *Dubliners*, the original 'The Sisters' hardly conformed to Russell's idea of something simple and rural, though it did stand in marked contrast to the density of his refused essay 'A Portrait of the Artist'. Indeed, critics have argued for viewing Joyce's later style as having been influenced by the type of story usually published in the *Homestead*. For example, Dathalinn O'Dea makes the case for *The Irish Homestead*'s influence on Joyce's early stories, arguing that his 'stories borrow the regionalism of the editorials and cooperative fiction featured in the paper, emphasizing local settings and characters, but are set apart chiefly by Joyce's use of modernist narrative techniques'.[2] She goes on to argue that the oft-noted village-like quality of Joyce's Dublin 'bears a clear resemblance to the rural villages and country towns featured in the *Homestead*'s other fiction and articles'.[3] Rather than retracing this territory, however, I suggest instead examining the other major feature of this double spread: the advertisement for 'DAIRY MACHINERY AND APPLIANCES OF EVERY DESCRIPTION'. While it might seem incongruous for Ireland's great literary modernist to appear above an advertisement for cream separators, sediment testers, refrigerating machines and 'Effektive' milk pumps, in fact this dairy machinery was a symbol of a bold leap into modernity, not just for agricultural Ireland, but for the nation as a whole.

Co-comeraid Joyce

In 1889 the first co-operative creamery was established in rural Ireland. A few years later, in 1894, the Irish Agricultural Organisation

Society (IAOS) was founded by the Anglo-Irish politician Sir Horace Plunkett. The aim of the IAOS was to support the establishment of a 'network of creameries, credit societies and agricultural stores' across rural Ireland.[4] The following year, 1895, the IAOS created *The Irish Homestead* newspaper 'to propagandise the objectives and ideas of the co-operative movement'.[5] Key to the movement was the establishment of co-operative creameries, set up on a 'one farmer, one vote' principle, which allowed farmers to collectively own the latest technology.[6] This allowed societies to buy the kinds of appliances listed in the advertisement that appeared below 'The Sisters'. Indeed, in an account by the *British Medical Journal* of a visit to a typical Irish creamery in 1903, the author lists a number of these appliances, including cream separators, milk pumps and Gerber's sediment tester.[7] The success of the co-operative movement was dramatic: by 1900 there were already 236 dairy societies in the country with over 26,000 members,[8] with numbers peaking in 1920 at 1,000 societies and 150,000 members.[9] Bell and Watson note that farmers stood to increase their profits from dairying by 30–35% by supplying milk to these societies.[10] Indeed, such was the vital importance of the creameries to rural Ireland that during the War of Independence British forces specifically targeted them during reprisals for IRA attacks.[11]

Plunkett's hope for the movement was, in his own words, that the Irish farmer should 'be satisfied that remaining on the land does not imply being in the backwater of modern progress'.[12] The movement dreamed of creating a modern 'civilisation among the fields', according to the *Homestead* itself.[13] However, it is arguable that the movement's success was due, in large part, to its harnessing of older traditions of a communal vision of farming and ownership, as epitomised by the *clachan* and the 'rundale' system of land division. Kevin Whelan describes the *clachan* as 'a nucleated group of farmhouses, where land-holding was organised communally, frequently on a townland basis, and often with considerable ties of kinship between the families involved'.[14] The best available patch of land encompassed a large field 'with a multiplicity of "strips"', which were 'periodically redistributed' between families to ensure an equal division of land quality over time.[15] This redistributive system was called 'rundale' and amounted, in Whelan's words, to a form of 'environmental egalitarianism'.[16] David Lloyd writes extensively about this system, which 'refuse[d] and resist[ed] permanent and rationalized boundaries, knowing neither walls nor established hedges', and thereby allowed tenants to 'have access to a variety of available land types, from the higher reaches of the mountain where a few sheep might be grazed to the more fertile patches where potatoes or, on occasion, oats could be cultivated'.[17] Lloyd notes 'the horror of modernizing foreign observers' when confronted with Irish 'patchwork patterns of landholding', which they desired to see swiftly obliterated.[18] Indeed, the revolutionary socialist James Connolly noted the similarities between these older rural traditions and the new co-operatives when discussing the possibilities of the movement, writing that other leaders had never 'been able to take from the peasantry the possession of traditions which kept alive in their midst the memory of the common ownership and common control of land by their ancestors'.[19] As such, the Irish peasantry did not need to be taught the collectivist principles of the co-operative movement, but rather needed to be afforded the space and opportunity to put them into practice. As Lloyd argues, 'far from being a backward element in the need of radical conscientization, the peasantry can be seen as already possessing, if in inarticulate ways, the counter-cultural consciousness that would be the basis for the syndicalist co-operative commonwealth'.[20] While the movement was rooted in making the most out of the capitalist market, it was still seen as radical enough by the *Skibbereen Eagle* for it to be described as a 'scheme for the introduction of continental socialism'.[21]

Russell was a firm supporter of the movement and became editor of the *Homestead* in 1905, the year after he had advised Joyce to submit fiction to the paper.[22] Throughout his writing career, Russell wrote essays outlining a broader national philosophy stemming from the co-operative movement. In 'Ideals of the New Rural Society', published in the 1915 collection of essays *Imaginations and Reveries*, Russell argued that a 'rural commune or co-operative community ought to have, to a large extent, the character of a nation'.[23] Russell saw rural Ireland as existing independently of urban rule, managing its affairs in small parish-led assemblies, taking many of the ideas regarding the right of small nations to self-determination and applying them to rural communities. Russell's philosophy rejected the macro-level nationalist politics that campaigned for independence or Home Rule, instead focusing on the local, arguing that '[a]s great work can be done in a parish as in the legislative assemblies with a nation at gaze'.[24] Despite the somewhat socialist influence behind the co-operative movement's policies, Russell rejected any such conflation of the two, admonishing the 'officious interferer [. . .] who would offer on behalf of the State to do for us what we should, and could, do far better ourselves'.[25]

As a member of the Anglo-Irish aristocracy, Plunkett's involvement with the co-operative movement can be interpreted as an effort to ensure that his class maintained a paternalistic role over the Irish peasantry.[26] Indeed, Plunkett was, in Doyle's words, 'an unapologetic defender of the role played by members of the landlord class in the regeneration of Irish soil and society', who had a steadfast 'faith in the innate moral and intellectual superiority of his class'.[27] It is of little surprise, therefore, that Joyce was less than enthusiastic about Russell's dream of an agricultural nation, formed upon a vague rural ideal, with dutiful peasants toiling in the fields while the paternal aristocrat watched over and advised.[28] In 1904's 'A Portrait of the Artist' essay and again in a letter to Oliver St John Gogarty a few months later, Joyce refers to what he calls 'Their Intensities and Their Bullockships' who form a 'joint government' (*PSW* 218) and 'continue to flourish' (*L1* 54). While Stuart Gilbert is confident that 'Their Intensities' is a nod to Irish nationalists, he speculates that 'Their Bullockships' might be a general reference to 'countrified louts' or indeed 'priests' (*L1* 54n4). It would seem just as possible, however, that 'Their Bullockships' are the likes of Russell and Plunkett, members of the Anglo-Irish class attempting to hold on to their status by exploiting Ireland's agricultural economy. Joyce was certainly more than happy to take every opportunity to mock Russell, ridiculing him for his theosophical and agricultural concerns in *Ulysses*. Throughout the novel Joyce has Russell wear a watch that is described on more than one occasion as being 'cooperative' (*U* 9.270, 15.2273), while the *Homestead* is referred to as 'his farmer's gazette' (*U* 14.525). Later, in 'Circe', Russell transforms into Mananaun MacLir, sea-god of Irish mythology, declaring 'I am the light of the homestead! I am the dreamery creamery butter' (*U* 15.2275–6). The hostility would appear to have been mutual by the time of *Ulysses*' publication, with Joyce hearing that Russell deemed that the novel 'did not contain a single sentence worth reading' (*L1* 176).

The disparaging references to the 'farmer's gazette' and 'pigs' paper' do not, however, do justice to the singular nature of the publication. As Doyle notes, the *Homestead* 'maintained an eclectic focus that encompassed national and international news, instruction on innovative farming methods, information about agricultural markets and news about individual societies, as well as literary pages that placed the journal within the contemporary cultural revival'.[29] The young Joyce no doubt saw the *Homestead* as simply another wing of Revivalism – which to a large extent it was – but it set itself apart in its balancing of nostalgia for a bucolic past with an embrace of rural modernisation. The best example of this rapid modernisation was the cream separator mentioned in the advert below 'The Sisters', and which, as O'Dea notes, featured prominently on the front page of the *Homestead*'s first issue in 1895.[30] This invention greatly accelerated the separation of cream from milk and, in Doyle's words, 'revolutionised the butter industry'.[31] Its quick adoption by Danish dairy farmers gave them 'a distinct competitive advantage over their Irish counterparts' in the late nineteenth century.[32] This was a lesson for Irish farmers in the eyes of co-operative leaders: in order to survive they would have to modernise. In fact, the very issue of the *Homestead* in which 'The Sisters' was published contains a leader entitled 'The Danish Parallel' that reviews the success of Ireland's farmers having followed their Danish counterparts into modern agricultural methods.[33] Joyce was evidently aware of Irish dairy farmers' rivalry with Denmark – in a 1906 letter to Stanislaus he notes an article that he had recently read by Arthur Griffith in which the nationalist leader claimed 'that it cost a Danish merchant less to send butter to Christiania and then by sea to London than it costs an Irish merchant to send his from Mullingar to Dublin' (*L2* 167). Many years later, in *Finnegans Wake*, Joyce once again refers to this rivalry when he describes a 'gathering, convened by the Irish Angricultural and Prepostoral Ouraganisations, to help the Irish muck to look his brother dane in the face' (*FW* 86.20–2). With its rendering of the IAOS as angry, preposterous and hurricane-like (French: *ouragan*), and the description of the peasantry as 'muck', this is hardly the most flattering depiction of the movement. It does show, however, just how aware Joyce was of the debates within agricultural circles regarding how desperately rural Ireland needed to modernise in order to be able to compete with its Danish rivals. Indeed, the detail of Joyce's knowledge of dairy technology is highlighted by Philip Keel Geheber, who notes a sentence from the Burrus and Caseous tale in the *Wake* (a tale ostensibly about butter and cheese production) in which Joyce describes 'the Silkebjorg tyrondynamon machine for the more economical helixtrolysis of these amboadipates' (*FW* 163.30–1). Keel Geheber glosses this by noting that Silkeborg is the town in Denmark from which Ireland began to import centrifugal separators in the early 1880s, while '"[e]lectrolysis" ("helixtrolysis") is chemical decomposition by electricity, so the Danish butter churns use electricity to separate the fats, *adipes* (Latin), from the milk'.[34]

These are not, however, the only fleeting references to the co-operative movement in the *Wake*. In Part I, Chapter 2, HCE meets the Cad in Phoenix Park near the Wellington monument and is addressed by the Cad in Irish. This incites a panicked, stuttering and guilt-laden response from HCE, as he offers a defence of himself that is filled with references to the co-operative movement. It is possible that, having been addressed in Irish, HCE assumes that by referencing the movement he will curry favour with the presumedly nationalist Cad. His outburst begins:

> Shsh shake, co-comeraid! Me only, them five ones, he is equal combat. I have won straight. Hence my nonation wide hotel and creamery establishments which for the honours of our mewmew daughters, credit me, I am woowoo willing to take my stand, sir, upon the monument, that sign of our ruru redemption, any hygienic day to this hour and to make my hoath to my sinnfinners, even if I get life for it, upon the Open Bible and before the Great Taskmaster's (I lift my hat!) and in the presence of the Deity Itself andwell of Bishop and Mrs. Michan of High Church of England as of all such of said my immediate withdwellers and of every living sohole in every corner wheresoever of this globe in general which useth of my British to my backbone tongue and commutative justice that there is not one tittle of truth, allow me to tell you, in that purest of fibfib fabrications. (*FW* 36.20–34)

HCE addresses the Cad as a 'co-comeraid', the 'co-' prefix calling to mind the co-operative movement, while its radical collectivism is hinted at in 'comeraid'. However, unlike the *Skibbereen Eagle*, Joyce is alive to the contradiction of thinking of the movement in purely socialist terms – as it was above all else focused on the capitalist market – and therefore 'comrade' is disfigured into 'comeraid', the movement being at its core an *aid* to *commerce*. HCE himself is subsumed into the co-operative creameries, becoming the 'hotel and creamery establishments' located across the remote stretches of rural Ireland – the adjective 'nonation' is listed by the *OED* as a regional term for '[r]emote; uncouth; wild; undesirable' (*OED*, 'no-nation, adj.'). HCE's declaration that he will take the stand 'for the honours of our mewmew mutual daughters' references the 'mutualist' organisation of the co-operative movement, while his stutter – 'mewmew' – is a not-so-subtle reminder of the sounds these farming daughters are likely to hear as they milk the cows. Meanwhile, his exhortation to 'credit me' is probably a reference to the numerous credit societies that operated under the umbrella of the co-operative movement. His stutter is again revealing when he talks of the Wellington monument as 'that sign of our ruru redemption', 'ruru' suggesting the rural as the locus of national redemption. It is also significant that when the Cad later spreads the story of HCE's outburst, it eventually makes its way to a certain 'Philly Thurnston, a layteacher of rural science' (*FW* 38.35). HCE's oath is sworn to his 'sinnfinners', which would appear to be another attempt to appeal to what he presumes are the Cad's nationalist leanings, but there seems to be another layer to the political backdrop to this passage. William York Tindall sees HCE as '[l]ooking to the Wellington Monument and the Church of England for assurance', and indeed towards the end of the passage HCE declares his tongue to be 'British to my backbone'.[35] Such declarations of fealty to the symbols of British rule in Ireland would seem to work in contradiction to the references to the co-operative movement, but, as noted, the movement was one moulded in the image of Anglo-Irish notions of aristocratic paternalism. Viewed in such a context, the co-operative movement manages to be symbolic of both the last vestiges of Anglo-Irish power in Ireland and the beginnings of rural modernisation and efforts at self-definition among the sons and daughters of previously tenant farmers. It is little wonder, then, that HCE finds himself getting confused between symbols of nationalism and unionism, tradition and modernity.

Bar the notable examples already highlighted, Joyce's first publication in the *Homestead* has generally been treated as an amusing idiosyncrasy in the trajectory of his literary career and of little other significance. However, as mentioned, the village-like nature of Joyce's Dublin might owe much to the kind of provincial fiction generally published in the *Homestead*, and indeed it might not be an accident that the start of 'Eveline' laments the disappearance of fields in favour of brick houses (*JJA* 4: 3b). The version of 'After the Race' that appears in *Dubliners*, bar some changes to punctuation and the odd word here and there, is indistinguishable from the story that was published in the *Homestead*. While the narrative deals primarily with the return of the motorists to Dublin, it is worth remembering that shortly before the story begins the cars had been 'careering along the country roads' (*JJA* 4: 3d). The race is based on the 1903 Gordon Bennett Cup race, which took place on roads in the counties of Carlow, Kildare and Laois, then known as Queen's County.[36] As such, the appearance of 'After the Race' in the pages of the *Homestead* makes thematic sense, as it deals with a phenomenon that is the very definition of rural modernity: the rural countryside being the laboratory site for the pinnacle of motoring technology, even if it is only briefly mentioned in the story itself.

Joyce's publications in the *Homestead* should therefore not really surprise us too much: the newspaper and its agricultural concerns were emblematic of the modernising tendencies of early twentieth-century

Ireland, and most especially of the rural parts of the country. Even more so, the fact that Joyce's uncompromising stories were accepted by the *Homestead* – while he had been rejected by the self-professed literary urbanites of 1900s Dublin – is indicative of the influence that rural modernity had not just on Ireland's economic, but also its cultural pursuits. In writing about *The Irish Homestead*, Mathews notes that 'it was not uncommon to see a poem by Yeats or a short story by James Joyce published side-by-side with an article on fertilizers or foot-and-mouth disease'.[37] The cultural eclecticism of early twentieth-century Ireland and its experience of modernisation needs to be justly acknowledged, particularly with regard to its rural modernisers. Given that it was responsible for first publishing Ireland's most celebrated modernist, it is essential that rural modernity is factored into discussions of his work.

The Lantern of Tradition and Rural Modernity

In *Stephen Hero*, Stephen affirms that '[n]o esthetic [*sic*] theory [. . .] is of any value which investigates with the aid of the lantern of tradition' (*SH* 189). It has been commonplace to view tradition as being at loggerheads with modernity, and indeed Joyce, in his early writings, has Stephen place himself firmly in the camp of modernity as opposed to that of tradition, putatively represented by the Revivalists. Just as tradition has been viewed as being at odds with modernity, so too has the rural generally come to be associated with traditional values. In *The Country and the City* (1973), Raymond Williams writes that in modernist work, particularly that of T. S. Eliot, we find a 'regular association of rural living with the past and with tradition'.[38] As such, the notion of a 'rural modernity' might seem oxymoronic. In *Stephen Hero*'s rejection of the 'lantern of tradition', we find a clear link with the Italian Futurists, champions of modernity and technological progress, who viewed the world as divided 'between those docile slaves of tradition and us free moderns who are confident in the radiant splendour of our future'.[39] It is noteworthy how light imagery is invoked by both Joyce and the Futurists, though with an emphatic contrast between the faint light emanating from an old-worldly lantern and the 'radiant splendour' of the future. Writing of the above quote from the Futurists, Marshall Berman notes: '[t]here are no ambiguities here: "tradition" – all the world's traditions thrown together – simply equals docile slavery, and modernity equals freedom; there are no loose ends'.[40] Berman famously described modernity as encompassing a 'terror of disorientation and disintegration, of life falling apart'; to be modern is to experience 'the thrill and the dread of a world in which "all that is solid melts into air"'.[41]

Berman is correct in noting the complexity of feelings elicited by modernity's maelstrom: while for some it was a 'thrill', for others it could only ever amount to 'dread'. Often, where one landed on this spectrum had as much to do with one's experience of tradition as it had with modernity. As Joe Cleary writes, 'the Futurists might feel that Italy was smothering under the excessive encumbrance of its once glorious past and heritage, but the real dilemma for the Irish was that so much of the native heritage had already been obliterated'.[42] The Irish modern, then, might find themselves less inclined to kill off tradition in the way that the Italian Futurist might; after all, slaying a tradition that is barely alive is not quite the same daring act of rebellion. In a conversation with Joyce during the writing of *Ulysses*, the English painter Frank Budgen quoted a line he had heard the Futurists proclaim: 'Noi futuristi italiani siamo senza passato', to which Joyce wryly responded, 'E senza avvenire.'[43] Clearly, by the time Joyce was writing *Ulysses* he had come to view the lantern of tradition as providing more light than the young Stephen allowed. Joyce's answer to Budgen is important in forming a sense of his relationship with tradition, a relationship that is never far removed from his relationship with rural Ireland.

The standard approach throughout the twentieth century to issues of modernity and tradition – in which they existed as binary opposites – has increasingly come under question from critics of a postcolonial or 'alternative modernities' orientation. Susan Stanford Friedman, for example, when discussing modernism as a movement, makes reference to Ezra Pound's famous exhortation to 'make it new', but instead argues for a relational approach that places tradition at its heart: 'Modernism requires tradition to "make it new." Tradition comes into being only as it is rebelled against.'[44] Modernist art can be considered a dialectic between the forces of tradition and modernity, which might go a long way to explaining why it often flourished in the postcolonial and/or 'peripheral' zones, rather than in the perceived centres. Berman's approach to modernity and the act of being modern is still relevant here in its insistence upon the dread and anxiety that are inherent in it:

> We might even say that to be fully modern is to be anti-modern: from Marx's and Dostoevsky's time to our own, it has been impossible to grasp and embrace the modern world's potentialities without loathing and fighting against some of its most palpable realities.[45]

As such we see that the act of being modern is one of continuous conflict with modernity itself. Friedman insists on this contradiction when she describes 'the struggle between modernizing and traditionalizing forces within a given society' as a 'defining characteristic of modernity', concluding that a 'past-oriented traditionalism is as much a feature of modernity as modernization'.[46]

The dismissal of tradition when discussing modernity and indeed modernism has often had colonial undertones. One such example is Eric Hobsbawm's notion of the 'invention of tradition'. Hobsbawm's argument is that '"traditions" that appear or claim to be old are often quite recent in origin and sometimes invented'.[47] Regarding movements that describe themselves as 'traditionalist' or 'revivalist', Hobsbawm dismisses the very appearance of such movements as proof of a 'break' in tradition, while traditions that are 'genuine' need no assistance to survive:

> Such movements [. . .] can never develop or even preserve a living past (except conceivably by setting up human natural sanctuaries for isolated corners of archaic life), but must become 'invented tradition'. On the other hand the strength and adaptability of genuine traditions is not to be confused with the 'invention of tradition'. Where the old ways are alive, traditions need be neither revived nor invented.[48]

As Cleary intimates, the death of Irish traditions was inherently bound up with colonial policies in the country. Hobsbawm here espouses a Darwinian view of tradition whereby the strongest and most authentic traditions survive, ignoring the fact that some traditions are deliberately destroyed. Mark Salber Phillips takes Hobsbawm to task for this view of tradition, writing that an emphasis on 'invented' traditions is particularly dangerous as it 'inevitably become[s] defining for the category of tradition as a whole'.[49] This results, Phillips argues, in the 'blurring together of tradition as such with a (putatively) bogus traditionalism', which then 'lends itself to a notion that tradition is necessarily static or reactionary, never adaptive, constructive, or creative'.[50] Ironically, even when subaltern groups act in ways that are stereotypically 'modern' – engaging in political revolution, for example – Hobsbawm continues to relegate these peasant movements to the category of 'pre-political' and 'archaic'.[51] Dipesh Chakrabarty highlights the problems of such historicist designations in *Provincializing Europe*, arguing instead that this kind of thinking falls into line with a version of colonialism that perennially argued that 'some people were less modern than others, and that the former needed a period of preparation and waiting before they could be recognized as full participants in political modernity'.[52]

It is perhaps the ultimate insult of colonialism that after doing its utmost to obliterate native traditions and cast subjugated people into the maelstrom of modernity, it then denies those same people the category of modern. Subaltern groups must be satisfied to suffer the consequences of modernity without reaping any of its potential – political, material and social – benefits. As is clear from Chakrabarty's critique of Hobsbawm, often the victims of such binary accounts of tradition/modernity were rural people, whose actions were condemned to being omitted from any discussion of 'true' modernity. This has significant implications in an Irish context, where rural Ireland came to stand as emblematic of Irish tradition and was, for a long period, banished from any discussion of modernity.

In an Irish context, the most prominent writers on questions of tradition and modernity in recent times have come from the left, including critics such as Joe Cleary, David Lloyd, Conor McCarthy and Luke Gibbons. All have written on the experience of colonial modernity in Ireland and problematise the binary opposition between tradition and modernity. Lloyd in particular is highly critical of historicism and modernisation theory, which, in his words, 'understand[] modernity as the progress from the backward to the advanced, from the pre-modern to the modern' and regard 'elements that resist modernization as residues of ideas and practices that belong to the past and remain to be overcome'.[53] Lloyd is suspicious of criticism that divides Ireland between traditional and modern elements, seeing post-Famine Ireland as 'inhabiting a temporal dimension composed simultaneously of multiple and often incommensurable temporalities for which the terms "tradition" and "modernity" are only partial and certainly inadequate designations'.[54] McCarthy similarly tackles the core tenets of modernisation theory, particularly as it pertains to tradition and nationalism. He notes how nationalism comes to be associated with tradition in this formulation and is therefore seen as 'atavistic, authoritarian, provincial, chauvinist'.[55] Instead, McCarthy argues for modernisation and nationalism as being 'related, intertwined but contradictory phenomena'.[56] To insist on viewing nationalism in a purely negative light is to 'fatally misunderstand the situation of countries like Ireland that still sit on the boundaries of tradition and modernity'.[57] Cleary, in particular, builds on this point, showing how in a colonial setting such as Ireland, 'the term "modernity" is stripped of its semblance of obviousness'.[58] In contrast to western

Europe, in Ireland 'modernity meant dispossession, subordination and the loss of sovereignty, the collapse of its indigenous social order, the gradual disintegration of its Gaelic cultural system, and successive waves of politically or economically enforced emigration'.[59] Ireland's experience of colonialism leads Gibbons to argue that 'Irish society did not have to await the twentieth century to undergo the shock of modernity: disintegration and fragmentation were already part of its history', with the result that 'Irish culture experienced modernity before its time'.[60] A destabilising modernity is, therefore, as Gibbons writes, 'the common inheritance of cultures subjected to the depredations of colonialism'.[61] Such an understanding of modernity should encourage us to rethink diffusionist models that conceive of modernity as something that begins in the metropolis and is then bestowed, gift-like, upon the natives in the colonial outposts. This is even more pertinent when one considers how peripheries were often the sites of modernising experimentation before the metropolitan centres.[62]

The reluctance to conceive of rural settings as sites of modernity and therefore potential objects of a modernist literary expression can be attributed to some scholars' preoccupation with urban life. Berman, for example, proclaims that 'the streets, our streets, are where modernism belongs', implicitly suggesting that modernism cannot exist outside the urban space.[63] Hugh Kenner goes further; for him '[m]odernism is distinctly urban',[64] writing elsewhere that, within modernism, 'the only story that [. . .] has adequate explanatory power' is 'a story of capitals'.[65] Likewise, Malcolm Bradbury defines modernism as 'an art of cities', writing that it was only in cities that 'the new aesthetics were distilled; generations argued, and movements contested; the new causes and forms became matters of struggle and campaign'.[66] However, new understandings of modernity encourage new conceptions of modernism, particularly in relation to its geographies. One of the most frequently cited analyses of this geographical rethinking of modernism is Douglas Mao and Rebecca Walkowitz's article, 'The New Modernist Studies' (2008), which documents the contributions of scholars who work 'under the umbrella of transnational modernism'.[67] Instead of adhering to older models that view modernism as being created by denationalised exiles located in intellectual centres such as Paris, London and Berlin, Mao and Walkowitz emphasise scholarly works that 'globalize modernism both by identifying new local strains in parts of the world not always associated with modernist production and by situating well-known modernist artifacts in a broader transnational past'.[68] Such work not only helps to recover modernisms in parts of the world far from Europe and North America, but can also help to identify variant modernisms in these countries as well. An example of this approach, focusing specifically on Ireland and Britain, can be found in *Regional Modernisms* (2013), where the authors argue that 'ideas of region and regional culture had considerable appeal for writers and intellectuals during the twentieth century'.[69]

Developments in new geographies of modernism are mirrored in similar new approaches to modernity and, in particular, to the notion of rural modernity. The first example of this can be found in Rosemary Shirley's *Rural Modernity, Everyday Life and Visual Culture* (2015), which sets out to specifically 'reactivat[e] the rural as a site of modernity'.[70] Shirley identifies 'four persistent narratives' that are promulgated about rural life, which she lists as insularity, artifice, stability and order, and which, she argues, 'contribute to the idea that the countryside, or its place in the national imaginary stands in opposition to some of the major characteristics associated with modernity'.[71] A sustained exploration of rural modernity in literature is found in the collection of essays *Rural Modernity in Britain*, which, as the editors Bluemel and McCluskey note, takes the novel approach of 'assuming that rural regions, communities, classes and figures can originate and sustain histories of and criticism on modernity and the modern'.[72] Rural modernity affirms that rural areas 'cannot be viewed only as retreats from modernity', but instead 'must also be seen as modern spaces inviting us to consider the diverse effects of new ways of moving, communicating, producing and perceiving'.[73]

Emerging rural literary studies have – understandably – focused mostly on highlighting contributions by rural writers tackling rural subjects. While often this has the felicitous consequence of prioritising previously understudied voices, it can also encourage critics to re-examine established authors under a different lens. For example, in *William Faulkner and the Faces of Modernity* (2019), Jay Watson studies Faulkner within the frame of rural modernity, arguing that modernisation is 'a process that ping-pongs back and forth between country and city, transforming both in the bargain – a process, in fact, in which the rural may in some instances take developmental precedence over the urban as the matrix and laboratory of modernity'.[74] Watson views modernisation in Faulkner's works as 'not just something that happens to them [i.e. rural people]. It is also something they *do*.'[75] Joyce is another such canonical writer whose work is refreshed by turning towards the rural aspects in his writing. What we find when we do so are characters who, even when they seem to resist modernity, are nevertheless still deeply engaged in the formation of modern Ireland.

This study is greatly informed by Marxist approaches to modernity, and while Irish critics on the left have done much work to complicate the binaries surrounding modernity and tradition, Marxist criticism in general has sometimes been guilty of sidelining the rural experience of modernity. Marxism's blind spot in relation to rural life appears to have been influenced in part by the mistranslation of the word '*Idiotismus*' in *The Communist Manifesto* (1848). This has traditionally been rendered as 'the idiocy of rural life',[76] but, as Hal Draper notes, in fact it means something closer to the 'isolation' of rural life.[77] Nevertheless, the original translation has had a lasting impact on Marxist criticism, from Hobsbawm's dismissal of peasant social movements as being 'pre-political' to Tom Nairn's claim that most ethnonationalist conflict stems from 'the curse of rurality', even when it occurs in urban areas. Indeed, Nairn argues that nationalist violence during the Troubles was an example of this, claiming that the urban violence associated with this period 'appears invariably to have its origin in the peasant or small town world' left behind by recent arrivals to the cities.[78] It is clear to see how easy it is to slip into well-worn biases regarding the rural, Catholic, 'wild' Irish.

Raymond Williams stands as one of the few Marxist critics to call out what he terms the 'long contempt' for rural life within intellectualism in general and Marxism in particular.[79] Williams argues that the fact that writers and intellectuals of the twentieth century have so often been located in cities has resulted in the feeling that there was 'little reality in any other mode of life; all sources of perception seemed to begin and end in the city, and if there was anything beyond it, it was also beyond life'.[80] For Williams, it is impossible to remove the growth of the city from the growth of capitalism, paraphrasing Trotsky, who, he writes, viewed 'the history of capitalism [as] the history of the victory of town over country'.[81]

Ironically, one of the few Marxists to investigate rural life is now known mostly for his writing on urbanity: Henri Lefebvre. Lefebvre began as a rural sociologist before turning his focus to urban life, and the transition from rural to urban is documented in the appropriately titled collection of essays, *Du rural à l'urbain* (1970).[82] His early work is a determined attempt to provide an outline of the complex structures of rural societies. The very first sentence of his 1949 essay 'Problems of Rural Sociology' ('Problèmes de sociologie rurale') admonishes those intellectuals who fail to see – or even look for – this complexity:

Among those – citizens, intellectuals, even historians and sociologists – who cross one of our villages, discovering its original or uncertain appearance, amazed at its torpor or admiring its 'picturesque' quality, how many know that this village cannot be reduced to an accidental mishmash of men, beasts and things, that an examination of it reveals a complex organisation, a 'structure'?[83]

Later in this essay, Lefebvre argues against a view of rural life that sees it as fixed and unchanging, especially in the wake of industrial agriculture: 'the peasant community has nothing immutable or eternal about it [. . .] Like every historical reality, the peasant community has developed, strengthened, dissolved.'[84] Lefebvre, then, depicts rural communities as being equally dynamic and reflective of modernity as their urban variants. In conclusion, Lefebvre offers a historical-sociological study of rural communities as providing 'one of the central threads to pursue in the entanglement of human facts'.[85] To make sense of the mess that is modernity, it is as essential to understand the processes at work in rural societies as it is those in urban communities.

In *Finnegans Wake* the conservative, nationalist figure of Shaun at one point declares that '[t]he west shall shake the east awake', a reference to the Thomas Davis ballad, 'The West's Asleep', a song documenting the 'slumber' in which the west of Ireland lies, and predicting a day when the west will awaken and '[l]et England quake' (*FW* 473.22–3).[86] However, this should not be dismissed as nothing more than the Revivalist/nationalist view that the west of Ireland is the real Ireland and therefore will awaken the east's sense of patriotism. Instead, we must remember that the rural west's defining features – bilingualism, mass emigration and violent rebellions – are all hallmarks of the destabilisation of modernity. If the capital city of Dublin is to enter into the modern world, it will at least in part be woken into it as a result of the upheaval and loss of tradition experienced in the west of the country.

The following section focuses on one of the most extreme examples of this upheaval in rural Ireland: the Land War of the late nineteenth and early twentieth centuries. Although a generally understudied event in Joycean studies, it features as an important contextual framework throughout his work. Not only is the Land War important to consider when gaining a sense of Joyce's political influences, it is also intrinsic to any discussion of his interaction with rural modernity.

'All his blather about home rule and the land league': Joyce and the Land War

Berman describes modern environments as encompassing a 'maelstrom of perpetual disintegration and renewal, of struggle and contradiction'.[87] In the context of late nineteenth-century Ireland, few environments seem to better meet this definition than those along the western fringes that became consumed by the Land War. Writing of the 1880s, Declan Kiberd concludes that '[t]he great issue of the decade was land'.[88] This was the decade into which James Joyce was born and whose political debates and controversies would come to define much of his outlook on the country of his birth. The issue of land, however, is key to understanding much of Irish history. As P. J. Drudy notes, 'land has been at the heart of the struggle for political, as well as social and economic, power' in Ireland since the time of the plantations in the sixteenth and seventeenth centuries.[89] Nevertheless, 'the land question', as it was known, ultimately came to a head during the so-called Land War of the late nineteenth and early twentieth centuries. Along with the debate over Home Rule, 'the land question' dominated the political careers of figures such as Charles Stewart Parnell and Michael Davitt during this time. While much has been written about the impact of the Home Rule debate and the Parnell affair upon Joyce's political outlook, comparatively little has been said regarding the Land War. One of the only exceptions is a 1992 article by Charles Ford, though even here Ford writes that Joyce 'obscures the role of the land question in the Irish revolution' and betrays 'an indifference to the historically crucial struggle over the ownership of the soil'.[90]

Spanning a period from the late 1870s to the early 1900s, the Land War's 'battles' came in sporadic waves. The eighteenth and nineteenth centuries had seen numerous, relatively small-scale attempts to challenge the structure of landlordism in rural Ireland, with agrarian rebel groups such as the Whiteboys and the Molly Maguires agitating for land reform, often violently and ultimately with limited success or impact. The first attempt by Westminster to address the land question came through William Gladstone's first Land Act of 1870, though the Act itself was limited in scope and did little to redress the problems facing most tenant farmers. The land question flared up again in the late 1870s when poor harvests drove many to desperation. Many tenant farmers were unable to pay their rents, resulting in mass evictions from 1879 onwards. In reaction to such evictions, the Irish National Land

League was formed, and thus the Land War began in earnest. Michael Davitt was a key figure in the establishment of the Land League and was instrumental in convincing Parnell, then a Home Rule MP, to become president of the League. Over the next two years the Land League became a mass movement, famous for its public demonstrations against evictions as well as its ability to whip up public disdain for what were known as 'landgrabbers': anyone who dared to take over the land of a farmer who had been evicted. Heather Laird frames this as part of a larger 'agrarian code', which she defines as 'a set of undocumented rules of behavior that was generally known and understood, particularly by poorer members of Irish rural communities'.[91] While the tactics employed by the Land League made a huge impact, in the short term evictions dramatically increased, which in turn led to increased agrarian violence, known as 'outrages'. In the early months of 1881, Gladstone unveiled a second Land Act, which, according to the historian F. S. L. Lyons, established 'the principle of co-partnership in the soil between landlord and tenant'.[92] Parnell's involvement in the land question lessened following this, though agitation continued, and two more Land Acts followed in 1887 and 1888. Subsequently, the battle for Home Rule fell apart with the revelation of Parnell's affair in 1890, the fallout from which is famously well documented throughout Joyce's work.

Following this, the land question was redefined somewhat: while the Land War has often been perceived as a battle between poor (usually Catholic) tenant farmers and wealthy (usually Protestant) landlords, the reality was in fact more nuanced. The Irish farming class comprised a hierarchy of farmers, from small breeders to larger and relatively wealthy farmers known as 'graziers', who purchased cattle from the breeders and fattened them before selling them on. The graziers were also often local shopkeepers whom the poorer farmers relied on for their essential goods and who heaped interest on the products that the tenant farmers bought on credit. As a result, the shopkeeper-grazier became 'a particular figure of hate' for the poorer tenant farmers.[93] A new organisation, the United Irish League, was founded in 1898 to wage the battle for land redistribution on behalf of the mostly western peasantry. By this point, the movement's focus was entirely on land rather than nationalism, with Fergus Campbell noting that while 'the demand for Home Rule was also expressed' at the first meeting of the United Irish League, 'most of the speakers called for the redistribution of grazing land'.[94] This phase of the Land War saw old tactics of social ostracism returned to, as 'shopkeepers who refused to display a United Irish League membership card in their window suffered serious loss in trade', while farmers who continued to work for graziers were ostracised.[95] Finally, after years of agitation as well as a decisive victory in the 1902 local government elections, the 'Wyndham' Land Act was passed in 1903. This was the most significant of the Land Acts and resulted in 'a revolutionary transformation of the Irish land question', whereby 200,000 Irish tenant farmers became owner-occupiers of their land.[96] The 'land question' was not entirely settled as a result of the 1903 Land Act, as another period of land agitation would follow between 1906 and 1909, known as the Ranch War, which campaigned against the powerful grazier farmers. However, by now the main period of the Land War itself was drawing to a close. Over thirty years, Irish rural society had undergone a dramatic change. During this time the peasantry had experienced the full brunt of the 'maelstrom' of modernity through waves of evictions and corresponding agrarian violence, before finally becoming owner-occupiers of their land.

The issue of land would have been impossible for Joyce to ignore, even in his youngest years. In *My Brother's Keeper*, Joyce's brother Stanislaus gives us an illuminating description of the characters who dominated the family home, particularly during their time living in Bray, County Wicklow. Stanislaus begins by mentioning Mrs Conway – who provides the model for 'Dante' Riordan in *A Portrait of the Artist as a Young Man* and *Ulysses* – as having a negative influence on the young James, writing that 'she inculcated a good deal of very bigoted Catholicism and bitterly anti-English patriotism' into the young boy (*MBK* 31). Beyond Mrs Conway, Stanislaus also mentions 'John Kelly of Tralee', the inspiration for Mr Casey in *A Portrait*, whom Stanislaus designates as '[t]he sincerest of the little group of my brother's well-wishers' (*MBK* 34). Stanislaus's depiction of Kelly is sympathetic, describing him as being 'of peasant stock', steadfastly loyal to Parnell, and devoid of Conway's 'narrow, restless, partisan bigotry' (*MBK* 36). While we are told that Casey in *A Portrait* had been sent to prison for 'making speeches from a wagonette', the subject of the speeches is not specified (*P* 37). However, in *My Brother's Keeper*, Stanislaus tells us that Kelly 'had been in and out of prison several times for making speeches in support of the Land League agitation', showing us that the Joyce family was clearly very close to a Land Leaguer (*MBK* 34–5). Stanislaus also recalls Kelly having to evade arrest one night by escaping to Dublin – this, too, is recounted in *A Portrait* when Stephen remembers Sergeant O'Neill calling at the house and a car arriving to take Mr Casey to Dublin (*P* 37).

Even if Kelly was less inclined than Conway towards indoctrination, it seems hardly likely that his links to the Land War would have gone unnoticed by the young Joyce. Indeed, a tendency towards agrarian agitation was something of an ancestral trait in the Joyce family. Richard Ellmann describes how Joyce's great-grandfather, also called James, had as a young man in County Cork joined the 'Whiteboys', a secret organisation in rural Munster which, as mentioned, provided something of a precursor to the Land Leaguers, albeit one that was more overtly violent in its defence of tenant farmers (*JJII* 12). The elder James Joyce was even sentenced to death for his involvement with the Whiteboys, though the sentence was never carried out (*JJII* 12). From Simon Dedalus's words in *A Portrait*, we know that Joyce was well aware of this familial legacy: 'Do you see that old chap up there, John? he said. He was a good Irishman when there was no money in the job. He was condemned to death as a whiteboy' (*P* 38). The Whiteboys are again referenced by Joyce in the first paragraphs of *Finnegans Wake* as the 'Whoyteboyce', during a passage filled with violent clashes (*FW* 4.5).

Indeed, violence was at the heart of the Land War, both in the actions taken in evicting tenants and in the reactions to such evictions. Lyons outlines the high number of murders, manslaughters and shootings at the person recorded between January 1881 and April 1882,[97] while Campbell notes how when the Land War reignited at the turn of the century, violence once again increased, causing an alarmed Neville Chamberlain to describe the state of Ireland as 'unparalleled in any civilized country at the present time'.[98] Joyce's first explicit mention of the Land War does not shy away from the violence intrinsic to it. This first reference comes in his article 'Ireland at the Bar' (1907) for *Il Piccolo della Sera*, which deals with the injustice surrounding the Maamtrasna murders. Towards the end of this article, Joyce writes sympathetically of the tendency of the Irish to 'employ extremely violent methods' when desperate (*OCPW* 147). Joyce gives the example of the Land Leaguers in particular, and links this to the contemporary agrarian violence associated with the later waves of the Land War:

For example, twenty years ago, seeing themselves reduced to poverty by the oppression of the large land owners, they refused to pay their rents and gained provisions and reforms from Gladstone. Today, seeing the pastures full of well-fed cattle while an eighth of the population is registered as being without the means of subsistence, they drive the cattle from the holdings. (*OCPW* 147)

Kevin Barry notes that this article was written by Joyce in the aftermath of rioting in Belfast throughout August and September of 1907, and refers also 'to various incidents in an anti-cattle-grazing agitation during July, August, and September 1907', part of the Ranch War (*OCPW* 326n4). Joyce's annoyance is primarily in relation to the sensationalist reporting of these stories in the English press, as he writes of how 'the London press dedicates weeks and innumerable articles to the agrarian crisis which, it says, is very serious, and publishes alarming items on the agrarian revolt that are then reprinted by foreign newspapers' (*OCPW* 147). Joyce's ironic tone here underlines the inability of the English press to fully understand the complexities of the Irish agrarian situation. While Joyce refrains from offering an 'exegesis of the Irish agrarian question', he nevertheless refuses to condemn the actions of the peasantry, dismissing as a 'complete misjudgement' the idea that 'Ireland is going through a stage of exceptional criminality' (*OCPW* 147). Joyce instead goes on the defence, going so far as to claim that '[c]riminality in Ireland is lower than in any other country in Europe; organized crime does not exist in Ireland' (*OCPW* 147). Whatever the accuracy of such statements, what appears clear here is that Joyce is drawing a distinction between political violence (such as cattle driving) and straightforward violence, a distinction that the press seems unable or unwilling to see.

The tense and often violent atmosphere of the time works its way into the pages of *A Portrait*, most particularly in its depiction of the schism that struck at the heart of the land movement, represented by Davitt and Parnell. While land reform was a personal mission for Davitt, for Parnell it provided a useful means to garner support for his overall goal of achieving Home Rule. Their alliance can be seen as symbolising a union of the interests of rural Ireland (land reform) with that of urban Ireland (Home Rule nationalism). However, this alliance was a loose one, as Parnell never came to share Davitt's obsession with peasant ownership of the land. This much was obvious from Parnell's reluctance to support the Plan of Campaign, a strategy devised by other land activists to assist tenants in their efforts to engage in collective bargaining on estates, for fear that it would lose him the support of the Liberal Party in Westminster. Following the revelation of Parnell's affair, Davitt became one of Parnell's earliest and most high-profile critics, and thus the short-lived alliance between rural and urban Ireland was ended, at least for the time being.

While it has often been noted that Parnell is mentioned on the opening page of *A Portrait*, acting as proof of the huge shadow he cast over Joyce's life and political thinking, it is worth remembering that his name appears alongside that of Davitt. The names are mentioned as Stephen recalls Dante's two brushes: 'The brush with the maroon velvet back was for Michael Davitt and the brush with the green velvet back was for Parnell' (*P* 7). Dante's two brushes can be seen as signifying this temporary unity of purpose between the two strands of Irish politics at this time, one focused on agrarian matters, the other on national. Parnell's green seems quite clearly representative of Irish nationalism, though it is less obvious why exactly maroon was chosen for Davitt. The schism that followed Parnell's affair is also dramatically symbolised when Dante rips off the green velvet from her brush, as the nationalist cause falls foul of the moral strictures of the Church as well as some within the agrarian movement. Interestingly, Mr Casey is described as taking the opposite side to Dante, suggesting that not all Land Leaguers blindly condemned Parnell. Following Parnell's death, Dante is seen wearing 'a maroon velvet dress and with a green velvet mantle hanging from her shoulders' (*P* 27). While the maroon of Davitt and the land movement now dominates, the incorporation of the green velvet mantle shows that Dante continues to cling on to the belief that the national movement can survive the death of Parnell, though, like the mantle on the dress, it rests on the strength of the agrarian movement. The entire episode has a deep impact on Stephen, causing him to question, 'which was right, to be for the green or for the maroon' (*P* 16).

Not only does this moment represent the end of a political alliance, it can also be seen as representing a profound division between rural and urban Ireland. Following Parnell's fall, only Dublin, Roscommon and a few other urban strongholds remained Parnellite.[99] Indeed, some rural agitators were quite explicit about the divisions now present in the two political movements, with one telling the author George Birmingham that 'it was the land they were after and to hell with Home Rule'.[100] Davitt also appears during the 'Circe' episode of *Ulysses*, where he is seen battling with Isaac Butt, the founder of the Irish Parliamentary Party and early campaigner for Home Rule (*U* 15.4684). Ford draws attention to this short scene, arguing that it shows Joyce's 'comprehension that the Home Rule League, which Butt founded, was essentially antagonistic to the agrarian revolutionaries, in spite of the historical fact of their coalition under Parnell'.[101] The land movement is, therefore, in Joyce's works, intrinsically associated with its schism from the nationalist campaign, as well as the part it played in Parnell's downfall.

The abovementioned hallucinatory appearance of Davitt is not the only mention of the land activist in *Ulysses*. In fact, we learn that

Davitt's politics had a strong impact on Leopold Bloom's political outlook during his younger years. During 'Ithaca', we are informed that Bloom was a dedicated adherent to the cause of land reform around 1885, when the land question was still raging. Bloom had, we are told,

> publicly expressed his adherence to the collective and national economic programme advocated by James Fintan Lalor, John Fisher Murray, John Mitchel, J. F. X. O'Brien and others, the agrarian policy of Michael Davitt, the constitutional agitation of Charles Stewart Parnell (M.P. for Cork City), the programme of peace, retrenchment and reform of William Ewart Gladstone [. . .] (*U* 17.1646–51)

As well as the quite explicit reference to Bloom's belief in the 'agrarian policy of Michael Davitt', the reference to James Fintan Lalor is also of importance here. Lalor was another influential advocate for land reform during the nineteenth century, propagating revolutionary ideas which argued that, by 'natural right, on the grant of God, the soil of Ireland belongs to the people of Ireland', who therefore 'have a clear vested right of property in the soil'.[102] Foster summarises Lalor's political philosophy as being founded on the belief that '[i]ndependence for the farming class must be the basis for national independence'.[103] In *The Fall of Feudalism in Ireland* (1904), Davitt claims that Lalor was instrumental in converting many others, such as the influential writer and activist John Mitchel – mentioned in the above extract from 'Ithaca' – to the cause of land reform.[104]

From the allusions to such figures, it is clear that Bloom's youthful enthusiasm for land reform bordered on the extreme. Indeed, in 'Eumaeus' we learn that he would even have gone 'a step farther than Michael Davitt', though it is not exactly clear what Bloom intends to mean by this (*U* 16.1592). Meanwhile in 'Ithaca', when we are taken through Bloom's library, we discover that one of the books on his shelf is *Laurence Bloomfield in Ireland* (1864) by William Allingham (*U* 17.1388). This verse-novel takes the land question as its primary theme and is sympathetic towards land reform, in spite of Allingham's own opposition to many of the core tenets of Irish nationalism, such as Home Rule and the revival of the Irish language.[105] In *Laurence Bloomfield in Ireland*, Allingham gives us a portrait of a sympathetic young landlord who disagrees with the approach taken by other landlords and his own land agent. Instead, he enacts land reforms that give the peasantry lower rents and fair leases, resulting in a state of harmony between Catholics and Protestants, tenants and landlords. While Joyce was almost certainly attracted to this book due to its main character's name echoing his own, it is also likely that Bloom's view of the land question has been formed from fictional accounts such as this, which, though radical for their time, still see the solution to the land question in a more sympathetic version of landlordism rather than full-scale land redistribution.

Whatever Bloom's belief in land reform, in 'Eumaeus' we learn that he sympathised with the evicted tenants without 'contributing a copper or pinning his faith absolutely to its dictums' (U 16.1587–8). Indeed, Bloom's view of the 'evicted tenants question' is based on theoretical 'sympathy with peasant possession as voicing the trend of modern opinion' (U 16.1589–90). Even if Bloom claims to have wished at one point to go 'a step farther than Michael Davitt', it appears now that his support for land reform came not from some deeply held belief, but rather because it was an intrinsic element of the political zeitgeist of 1880s Ireland. We might conclude from this that Bloom's allegiance in truth lay with the nationalist side of matters, represented by Parnell. For so long as the land question helped to further the national one, Bloom seems to have been happy enough to support it. Reflecting in 'Eumaeus', he now sees his former views towards land redistribution as a mistake that 'he was subsequently partially cured of' (U 16.1591), though of course the inclusion of 'partially' here suggests that some faint sympathy might still remain.

These thoughts occur to Bloom while he is sitting with Stephen in the cabman's shelter in 'Eumaeus', and the tone used throughout is that of the knowing, older man reflecting with wisdom on the passionate but misguided political idealism of his youth. Indeed, during 'Penelope' we get a sense from Molly of Bloom's prior – and perhaps irritating – passion for these movements when she says 'O wasnt I the born fool to believe all his blather about home rule and the land league' (U 18.1187–8). As much as this gives evidence of Bloom's previous inclination for what he calls those 'ultra ideas' (U 16.1585), Molly's dismissal of the rhetoric of these movements as 'blather' demonstrates not only Bloom's subsequent rejection of them, but also to what degree they had fallen out of fashion more generally by 1904 in urban circles at least.

Nevertheless, the reflections in 'Eumaeus' and 'Ithaca' show just how indelibly Bloom's political outlook was shaped by the events of the Land War. Indeed, throughout *Ulysses* we see that Bloom continues to harbour grudges towards the hate figures of the Land War. While Bloom's views of the Land War might have been influenced by the fictionalised versions found in *Laurence Bloomfield in Ireland* and the movement's general usefulness to the broader national debate, Bloom's own working life has been closely linked to the agricultural economy. Between 1893 and 1894 Bloom had worked under Joseph Cuffe at the cattle market in Stoneybatter, and would therefore have been intimately familiar with the debates and controversies raging in rural Ireland through his interaction with the farmers bringing cattle to market (*U* 17.483–6). However, it is unlikely that Bloom would have met many of the poorer tenant farmers, but rather the larger, wealthier graziers who sold cattle at the market for transport to England. As we have already discussed, the graziers were by this time particular figures of scorn for those agitating for land reform. Campbell writes that 'graziers were perceived to be the allies of the landlord class',[106] while Foster argues that 'many of them were, effectively, landlords, if not landowners'.[107] Paul Bew goes even further, writing that '[g]raziers were said not to be farmers in the proper sense of the word', given that '[t]hey had benefited by the destruction of the Irish peasant community and the depopulation of the island'.[108] Indeed, these views seem to have influenced Bloom, and it is this radicalisation that appears to have lost him his job, as we learn in 'Cyclops' that 'Joe Cuffe gave him the order of the boot for giving lip to a grazier' (*U* 12.837–8). It does not take a great leap of the imagination to guess why this erstwhile Davitt supporter found himself mouthing off at a grazier. It is worth pointing out, however, that this heightened disdain for the grazier figure was most especially a feature of the later Ranch War of 1906–09. As such, Bloom's hatred of the grazier might in fact be somewhat ahead of its time, or be another example of the sometimes ahistorical nature of *Ulysses*, with Joyce being more influenced by contemporary agrarian agitations than historical ones. In any case, while Bloom's enthusiasm for land reform might wane over the next few years, his disdain for the grazier figure does not. One of Bloom's plans for the cattle market, which is mentioned repeatedly throughout the novel, is for a tramline to bring the cattle directly to the quays. In Bloom's plan, the significant costs associated with this would 'be covered by graziers' fees' (*U* 17.1742–3). Later, in 'Circe', when Bloom imagines himself as leader of Bloomusalem, he strikes down with his sceptre and causes the '*instantaneous deaths of many powerful enemies*' (*U* 15.1566–7). These '*enemies*' are listed, and while it seems logical that a Parnellite such as Bloom would include '*members of parliament*' and '*members of standing committees*' – given that these were the figures who sealed the Irish leader's fate – it is telling that among them he also includes '*graziers*' (*U* 15.1567–8). The inclusion of graziers betrays just how much Bloom continues to harbour resentment towards these *bêtes noires* from the Land War, no doubt made all the more acute following the most recent agitation.

It should be noted that it is not only through Bloom that we feel the continuing influence of the Land War in *Ulysses*. The grazier farmers who also acted as rural shopkeepers found themselves acquiring another nickname around this time, and one that has stuck in Irish politics to the present day: 'gombeen'. As mentioned, the tenant farmer relied on buying goods from these shopkeepers, who then heaped huge levels of interest on their debts. The act of demanding such unfair levels of interest resulted in the shopkeeper being referred to as a 'gombeen' man, with *gaimbín* being the Irish word for exorbitant interest. In a particularly succinct summary of the situation, Father Joseph Alfred Pelly described the shopkeeper-grazier as someone who 'made their money out of the poor, and with the money they made out of the poor they barred the access of the poor to the land'.[109] The 'gombeen' man also often got involved in politics, with Campbell noting that '[t]he shopkeepers' economic power was enhanced by their involvement in local politics'.[110] Indeed, the hypocrisy of the 'gombeen' man was no more evident than during the later waves of the Land War, when they professed support for the cause of the United Irish League. One especially succinct example is that of a shopkeeper in Westport, who in 1898 began advertising his business with the slogan: 'Who fears to speak of '98, the United Irish League: Tea 2/6.'[111] Here the co-option of Irish nationalistic slogans and the professed support for political movements agitating for land reform – movements specifically targeting shopkeeper-grazier figures such as this – is all merely in the service of petty capitalism.

This appropriation of Land War rhetoric by local politicians is referenced in *Ulysses* during the 'Cyclops' episode, when we witness a parody of proceedings from the House of Commons. In this scene, a nationalist politician named Mr Cowe Conacre for Multifarnham in County Westmeath (one of the counties where larger graziers were most prevalent) is introduced to speak on the slaughter of animals with foot-and-mouth disease. While the politician's first name does not require great elaboration, his surname is more interesting, referencing what was known as the 'conacre system', a system of exploitation that became prevalent during the nineteenth century and one that the Land War specifically worked to defeat. Under this system, a wealthier tenant farmer would rent small tracts of land to a poorer, neighbouring farmer, usually at an exorbitant price. The poorer farmer would then use this patch of land to grow crops such as corn, from which the name conacre comes: *corn-acre*. In Cynthia E. Smith's words, this practice 'proved to be disastrous for Irish tenants'.[112] This particular nationalist politician appearing in 'Cyclops' might therefore express sympathy for the challenges facing Irish farmers, but the authenticity of this sympathy is called into question, given that the system that ensured that poorer Irish farmers remained in the grip of exploitation is inscribed into his very name. There is further irony in the 'Cyclops' episode when we learn that the Citizen, that self-proclaimed champion of the Irish peasant, cannot go to speak in Shanagolden as 'the Molly Maguires [are] looking for him to let daylight through him for grabbing the holding of an evicted tenant' (*U* 12.1314–16). Laird argues that this demonstrates the 'emerging chasm between mainstream Irish nationalists and agrarian agitators'.[113] In addition to the subtle references to gombeens and graziers, it certainly shows Joyce's intimate awareness of the multiple layers of exploitation at the heart of rural Irish society.

As in current Irish usage, the term 'gombeen' in *Ulysses* has been somewhat removed from its original rural context and come to be used for anyone seen as unfairly profiting from others. For example, it is levelled at historical figures, such as Queen Elizabeth I, whom Stephen describes as '[t]he gombeenwoman Eliza Tudor' (*U* 9.630). While this might at first seem an unusual descriptor for Elizabeth, it is appropriate given that '[u]nder her reign, land was forcibly seized from Irish Catholics and given over to English and Scottish Protestant settlers', thus setting in motion the system of land exploitation in Ireland.[114] As such, Elizabeth becomes the first gombeen figure in Irish nationalist history. However, the term gombeen also takes on more racially charged significations in *Ulysses*, most particularly in relation to Jewish people, as certain characters espouse the antisemitic trope of Jews being usurious. The most explicit example of this is directed at Reuben J. Dodd, a character based on a real Dublin solicitor and insurance agent of the same name who was also at one time a moneylender to John Stanislaus Joyce. Dodd was not actually Jewish but was easily suspected of being so due to his first name recalling the Israelite Reuben, son of Jacob and Leah, though Reuben was also a popular name among Christians at this time.[115] The Dodd of *Ulysses* is disdained by many characters, notably Simon Dedalus and Father Cowley, who are in his debt. Speaking to Dedalus, Cowley refers to Dodd as '[a] certain gombeen man of our acquaintance', using the specifically Irish term to reference Dodd's apparent greed (*U* 10.890). While Cowley and Dedalus are content to explain Dodd's usury by his supposed Jewishness, they are also implicitly admitting to the unracialised nature of exploitation through the use of an Irish expression that was usually only attached to fellow Irish Catholics and coming from a specifically Irish context, made even more ironic here by the real Dodd's being a Catholic. Cowley's antisemitic narrative is therefore undermined by the language through which it is expressed, though his choice of expression also reveals how urban spendthrifts such as Dedalus and himself look to align themselves with the plight of the genuinely exploited peasants. While the extent of Dodd's profiteering is unknown, Dedalus and Cowley's appropriation of Land War terminology provides them with an easy way to explain away their money problems and don the air of victimhood.

While terms such as 'gombeen' gained currency during the Land War, undoubtedly the most famous and influential piece of terminology to make its way into the English language during this time was the word 'boycott'. In the early days of the Land War, in September 1880, Parnell gave a speech in Ennis, County Clare, in which he encouraged farmers to ostracise a neighbour who attempted to 'grab' the land of evicted farmers by 'putting him in a moral Coventry, by isolating him from the rest of his country as if he were the leper of old'.[116] Shortly afterwards, the fruits of this policy were seen in County Mayo on Lord Erne's estate when locals stood up against the land agent that Erne had appointed, an English-born former soldier called Captain Boycott. In 1880 Boycott attempted to evict tenants from Erne's estate, with the Land League deciding to target him, in the historian Liam Ó Raghallaigh's words, as a 'test case'.[117] In fact, Ó Raghallaigh suggests that the local curate, Father O'Malley, had fallen out with Boycott and was keen to encourage his parishioners to ostracise the Captain. Indeed, O'Malley is credited with coining the term 'boycott', as he believed people would not be able to remember the word 'ostracise'.[118] In any case, the local farmers understood what was expected of them and duly ostracised Boycott, leaving him in a difficult situation whereby he had no one willing to take in the harvest and instead had to hire Ulster Orangemen to carry out the work.[119] The events were covered extensively in the press, making Boycott a household name; in the end, lacking protection, the Captain and his family were forced to leave their home and take the boat to Holyhead. Ó Raghallaigh writes that '[b]y the end of 1880 "boycotting" was widespread in Ireland and further afield, and within twenty years the word would appear in dictionaries all over the world'.[120]

This most famous legacy of the Land War plays a surprisingly significant role in *Ulysses*, standing as a useful subtext to consider in a number of key scenes. Captain Boycott is specifically mentioned in 'Cyclops' when he is ironically designated as a hero of Ireland in an absurd list that leaves major political figures such as Parnell and Daniel O'Connell conspicuously absent (*U* 12.182). However, there is a sort of strange logic to listing Boycott as one of the heroes of Ireland. By provoking the Land Leaguers in County Mayo, Boycott provided Irish nationalism with a blueprint for how to effect change in the country. The realisation that social ostracism could be even more effective than armed struggle was an important one for the agrarian and nationalist movements. Joyce himself highlights this in his 1907 article 'Home Rule Comes of Age', warning that the House of Lords, in vetoing Home Rule, would risk provoking 'a reaction from a people which, poor in everything else, is rich solely in political ideas, has perfected the tactics of obstructionism and has made the word "Boycott" an international battle-cry' (*OCPW* 143). Here, Joyce shows how a tactic once used by farmers in the west of Ireland had since very effectively transitioned into the realm of international politics. However, the willingness of the Irish to ostracise would end up being a double-edged sword for the nationalist movement, as Parnell was to discover following the revelation of his affair with Katharine O'Shea. While much has been made – most especially by Joyce himself – of the Church's role in condemning Parnell, as outlined earlier many of Parnell's political allies from the Land War became high-profile critics of his, losing him the support of almost all rural areas.

In *Ulysses*, Bloom is often the victim of the same kind of unrelenting ostracism as Parnell, perhaps most notably when he is put on trial in 'Circe'. Ford sees Bloom's mock trial as 'bear[ing] a resemblance to the O'Sheas' adultery trial', but the swiftness with which the Irish public turn on Bloom is also reminiscent of the boycotting of the Land War and the eventual use of this ostracism against Parnell.[121] Most strikingly, during the trial in 'Circe', 'The Irish Evicted Tenants' make an appearance, dressed in '*bodycoats, kneebreeches, with Donnybrook fair shillelaghs*' and, directing their ire at Bloom, cry 'Sjambok him!' (15.1883–4). The sjambok is a traditional Afrikaans leather whip used for driving cattle (*OED*, 'sjambok, n.'), as here the rural agitator's propensity for driving cattle off a wealthy grazier's land – which Joyce attempted to sympathetically explain in 'Ireland at the Bar' – appears to be the tactic that the evicted tenants turn to in meting out punishment to Bloom.

The sense that the much-sympathised-with tenant farmers might in fact have used the newfound power that boycotting provided for ill is suggested by Bloom in 'Eumaeus'. Here, Bloom reflects on what he deems to be the ingratitude of the tenant farmers towards Parnell, noting that

> his beloved evicted tenants for whom he had done yeoman service in the rural parts of the country by taking up the cudgels on their behalf in a way that exceeded their most sanguine expectations, very effectually cooked his matrimonial goose, thereby heaping coals of fire on his head, much in the same way as the fabled ass's kick. (*U* 16.1396–400)

As throughout this section, Bloom here depicts Parnell, 'the fallen leader', in grossly romanticised terms, as a chivalric hero who gave his all to better the lives of his inferiors and dependants, who then turn on him once they have got what they want. Later in the same episode, Bloom blames Parnell's subsequent electoral hammering on 'chiefly the belauded peasant class, probably the selfsame evicted tenants he had put in their holdings' (*U* 16.1731–2). Bloom's reading of the internecine wars in the Irish nationalist movement has Parnell as the innocent victim of those same peasants he sacrificed everything for (this view of the period, of course, conveniently ignores Parnell's ambiguous relationship with the agrarian movement). The once ingenious tactic of boycotting now appears as a dangerous weapon in the peasants' armoury. Without the guidance of their better-educated superiors, the rural peasantry are liable to use the strategies of the Land War in a way that sabotages the national movement.

How much all of this accorded with Joyce's own views is unclear, though in the aforementioned 'Home Rule Comes of Age' article, Joyce lambasts the current members of the Irish Parliamentary Party:

> From being peasants' sons, street traders and clientless lawyers, they have become salaried administrators, factory and company bosses, newspaper owners and large land holders. Only in 1891 did they give proof of their altruism when they sold Parnell, their master, to the pharisaical conscience of the English non-conformists, without exacting the thirty pieces of silver. (*OCPW* 144)

Joyce conspicuously puts 'peasants' sons' as the first of the ignoble origins of these petty politicians who have Parnell, 'their master', to thank for their current positions. Clearly 'the belauded peasant class' still incurred a significant degree of his wrath for the downfall of Parnell. The weariness felt towards the agrarian tactics of yesteryear by an entire generation is displayed by Molly when she mentions that 'there was a boycott', and immediately follows this with the exasperated 'I hate the mention of their politics' (*U* 18.387–8). Politics has become synonymous with agrarian boycotts for Molly and Leopold's generation, and also with the downfall of Ireland's lost leader. No wonder, therefore, that they should hate the mention of it.

Dominic Manganiello in *Joyce's Politics* (1980) sees the fall of Parnell as '*the* political event of [Joyce's] youth'.[122] While undoubtedly true, there is a major argument for asserting that the Land Wars and subsequent Acts had a more profound and lasting effect on Irish society, in ways both positive and negative. Indeed, without the Land War, it is not at all certain that Parnell would have become leader of the Irish Parliamentary Party – as Drudy puts it, the Land League 'made Parnell the leader of Irish politics'.[123] Certainly the Acts themselves did not achieve all the goals that land reformers had originally hoped for. Despite the gradual eroding of landlordism, inequality remained, except this time between fellow Irish Catholics. Kiberd summarises this period of Irish history by noting that while the rural middle class were the victors of the Land Acts, the losers were ultimately not only the upper-class gentry, but also the poor rural labourers.[124] Indeed, he paraphrases Shaw by claiming that the Land Acts led to a new form of 'landlordism of a more petty variety'.[125]

The Land Acts were no doubt intended to mollify the Irish appetite for independence, as part of the Westminster tactic of 'killing home rule by kindness'. They have also often been blamed by commentators for the conservative nature of Irish politics post-independence, overly obsessed with the ownership of property. Leon Trotsky made this very argument in 1916 when he wrote that, once Irish farmers had secured their land, they 'became transformed into conservative small proprietors, whose eyes could henceforth no longer be distracted from their little plots of land by the green flag of national freedom'.[126] Terry Eagleton has similarly argued that Ireland's modernisation was stunted because it was dependent on 'the rural middle class' who, inheriting 'a woefully inert brand of rural capitalism', ended up establishing a 'reactionary ruralism' in the country.[127] Such a view, however, arguably fails to acknowledge the radical origins of the land movement itself, instead focusing on the subsequent nationalist (and largely urban-based) politics that would go on to form the basis of the Free State. The Land War, in its most radical stirrings, represented a profound reaction against feudalist structures and a determination by the peasantry to take modernity into their own hands – to form it rather than merely be formed by it. Indeed, viewed from this perspective, the Land War represents not a 'reactionary ruralism' but rather rural radicalism – it should not be forgotten that the Land League chose as its enemies those who represented exploitative petty capitalism, the gombeen men who locked their neighbours in cycles of debt. Cleary argues for this rural form of radicalism, noting that, unlike in other more urbanised countries, 'in nineteenth-century Ireland [. . .] it was the rural lower and middle classes that remained the motor of radical social change'.[128] Indeed, in *Finnegans Wake*, when Shaun is lamenting his brother Shem's supposed radical ways, he compares him to one 'S. H. Devitt' of 'Sydney and Alibany', a seeming reference to Davitt and his time spent touring Australia (*FW* 489.30–2).

While Joyce's treatment of the Land War and its legacies is complicated by its association with Parnell's downfall, he nevertheless appears intimately aware of the profound changes that it wrought on Irish society at large and the model it provided to subsequent movements for change. There is a strong argument to be made for Irish independence beginning in these years of boycotting, cattle driving and eventual land redistribution, and so it seems appropriate when in the *Wake*, as Joyce reflects on his home country's newfound independence and membership of the League of Nations, he should refer to it as 'this landleague of many nations' (*FW* 540.2).

Conclusion: Joyce's Rural Modernity

On a return trip to Ireland in 1912, Joyce spent some time in Galway with Nora, during which he wrote two articles inspired by the west of Ireland for *Il Piccolo della Sera*, one on Galway city and the other on the Aran Islands. He planned, however, to write a third article, this time on the new Marconi wireless station situated in Clifden, Connemara. Joyce in fact travelled to the station, but was ultimately unable to complete the article. This brief period in the west is, however, revealing in terms of the topics that Joyce sought to uncover while there, perhaps none more so than the uncompleted Marconi article, as succinct an example of rural modernisation as one could find. Unlike many of his Irish peers at the time, Joyce was consistently interested in documenting rural Ireland's engagement with modernity. While this often manifests itself as a fascination with efforts to further rural industry or agriculture, it can also be seen in his portrayal of rural Ireland's more complicated relationship with modernity, particularly in terms of radical movements, agrarian violence and societal disharmony, at no time more evident than during the Land War. Joyce's works persistently emphasise that, when it comes to the 'maelstrom' of modernity, urban settings did not have a monopoly on the dizzying experience of rapid change and disintegration. To go west is not to go back in time, as some might have imagined it, but rather, to borrow Shaun's phrasing, to be shaken awake to the times one lives in.

Notes

1. Even by early 1905, after he had left for exile, Joyce still had hopes that the *Homestead* would publish 'Hallow Eve' (later 'Clay' in *Dubliners*). On 19 January 1905 he sent his brother Stanislaus a copy of the story, which he told him to 'offer at once to the Editor of the Irish Homestead', though he acknowledged that '[p]erhaps they are annoyed with me and won't honour me by printing any more' (*L2* 77). A month later he asked his brother '[w]here is "Hallow Eve" at present? Take it to the I.H. again and kiss Russell from me' (*L2* 83).
2. Dathalinn O'Dea, 'James Joyce the Regionalist: The *Irish Homestead*, *Dubliners*, and Modernism's Regional Affect', *Modern Fiction Studies* 63/3 (2017), 477.
3. O'Dea, 'James Joyce the Regionalist', 489. For more on the influence of the *Homestead* on Joyce, see P.J. Mathew, '"A.E.I.O.U": Joyce and the *Irish Homestead*', in Anne Fogarty and Timothy Martin (eds), *Joyce on the Threshold* (Gainesville, FL: University Press of Florida, 2005).
4. Patrick Doyle, *Civilising Rural Ireland: The Co-operative Movement, Development and the Nation-state, 1889–1939* (Manchester: Manchester University Press, 2019), 2.
5. Ibid., 48.
6. Ibid., 3.
7. 'A Report on The Milk Supply of Large Towns: Its Defects and Their Remedy. II Source and Distribution of the Milk to Towns', *British Medical Journal*, 28 March 1903, 741, https://doi.org/10.1136/bmj.1.2204.739 (accessed 10 June 2021).
8. Jonathan Bell and Mervyn Watson, *A History of Irish Farming, 1750–1950* (Dublin: Four Courts Press, 2008), 246.
9. Doyle, *Civilising Rural Ireland*, 3.
10. Bell and Watson, *A History of Irish Farming*, 246.
11. Ibid., 247.
12. Horace Plunkett, 'Rural Regeneration', *North American Review* 214/791 (1921), 474, cited in Doyle, *Civilising Rural Ireland*, 43.
13. 'The Struggle between Country and Town', *Irish Homestead*, 15 August 1908, 645–66, cited in Doyle, *Civilising Rural Ireland*, 41.

14. Kevin Whelan, 'The Modern Landscape: From Plantation to Present', in F. H. A. Aalen, Kevin Whelan and Matthew Stout (eds), *Atlas of the Irish Rural Landscape* (Toronto: University of Toronto Press, 1997), 80.
15. Ibid., 80.
16. Ibid., 80.
17. David Lloyd, *Irish Times: Temporalities of Modernity* (Dublin: Keough-Naughton Institute for Irish Studies, University of Notre Dame/Field Day, 2008), 19, 41. Lloyd also describes the radical communalism of the *clachan* and rundale in *Irish Culture and Colonial Modernity 1800–2000: The Transformation of Oral Space* (Cambridge: Cambridge University Press, 2011), 64–76.
18. Ibid., 41.
19. James Connolly, *Collected Works*, I (Dublin: New Books Publications, 1987), 258, cited in Lloyd, *Irish Times*, 110.
20. Lloyd, *Irish Times*, 110.
21. 'Mr Horace Plunkett's Disorganization Society Limited', *Skibbereen Eagle*, 12 October 1895, 2, cited in Doyle, *Civilising Rural Ireland*, 48.
22. Doyle, *Civilising Rural Ireland*, 49.
23. Æ [George Russell], *Imaginations and Reveries* (Dublin: Maunsel, 1915), 104.
24. Ibid., 100.
25. Ibid., 99.
26. For more on this argument, see Leeann Lane, '"It Is in the Cottages and Farmers' Houses That the Nation Is Born": AE's "Irish Homestead" and the Cultural Revival', *Irish University Review* 33/1 (2003), 165–81. Lane describes the co-operative movement as providing 'an alternative leadership role for the Anglo-Irish as a newly reconstituted cultural aristocracy' (165).
27. Doyle, *Civilising Rural Ireland*, 43.
28. This conflating of agricultural concerns with matters of the nation is nodded to in the *Wake* when Joyce refers to 'milk from a national cowse' (*FW* 615.27).
29. Doyle, *Civilising Rural Ireland*, 48.
30. O'Dea, 'James Joyce the Regionalist', 484.
31. Doyle, *Civilising Rural Ireland*, 15.
32. Ibid., 15.
33. 'The Danish Parallel', *Irish Homestead*, 13 August 1904, 662–3.
34. Philip Keel Geheber, 'Assimilating Shem into the Plural Polity: Burrus, Caseous, and Irish Free State Dairy Production', in Onno Kosters, Tim Conley and Peter de Voogd (eds), *A Long the Krommerun: Selected Papers from the Utrecht James Joyce Symposium* (Amsterdam: Brill/Rodopi, 2016), 133.
35. William York Tindall, *A Reader's Guide to 'Finnegans Wake'* (London: Thames and Hudson, 1969), 59.

36. Cóilín Owens, *Before Daybreak: 'After the Race' and the Origins of Joyce's Art* (Gainesville, FL: University of Florida Press, 2013), 25.
37. Mathews, '"A.E.I.O.U."', 155.
38. Raymond Williams, *The Country and the City* (London: Chatto and Windus, 1973), 240.
39. Umberto Boccioni et al., 'Manifesto of the Futurist Painters, 1910', in Umbro Apollonio (ed.), *Futurist Manifestos*, trans. Robert Brain (New York: Viking, 1973), 25, cited in Marshall Berman, *All That is Solid Melts into Air: The Experience of Modernity* (1982; London: Penguin, 1988), 25.
40. Berman, *All That is Solid Melts into Air*, 25.
41. Ibid., 13.
42. Joe Cleary, *Outrageous Fortune: Capital and Culture in Modern Ireland* (Dublin: Field Day, 2007), 89.
43. Frank Budgen, *James Joyce and the Making of 'Ulysses', and Other Writings* (Oxford: Oxford University Press, 1972), 198. 'We Italian Futurists are without a past.' 'And without a future.' (My translation.)
44. Friedman, *Planetary Modernisms*, 45.
45. Berman, *All That is Solid Melts into Air*, 13–14.
46. Friedman, *Planetary Modernisms*, 157.
47. Eric Hobsbawm, 'Introduction: Inventing Traditions', in Eric Hobsbawm and Terence Ranger (eds), *The Invention of Tradition* (Cambridge: Cambridge University Press, 1983), 1.
48. Ibid., 8.
49. Mark Salber Phillips, 'Introduction: What is Tradition When it is Not "Invented"? A Historiographical Introduction', in Mark Salber Phillips and Gordon Schochet (eds), *Questions of Tradition* (Toronto: University of Toronto Press, 2004), 6.
50. Ibid., 6.
51. Hobsbawm, *Primitive Rebels*, 3, cited in Chakrabarty, *Provincializing Europe*, 11–12.
52. Chakrabarty, *Provincializing Europe*, 9.
53. Lloyd, *Irish Times*, 3.
54. Ibid., 6.
55. Conor McCarthy, *Modernisation: Crisis and Culture in Ireland 1969–1992* (Dublin: Four Courts Press, 2000), 16.
56. Ibid., 16.
57. Ibid., 17.
58. Joe Cleary, 'Introduction: Ireland and modernity', in Joe Cleary and Claire Connolly (eds), *The Cambridge Companion to Modern Irish Culture* (Cambridge: Cambridge University Press, 2005), 2.
59. Cleary, *Outrageous Fortune*, 78.
60. Gibbons, *Transformations*, 6.
61. Ibid., 6.

62. This is especially true of technological experimentation in colonial outposts – see David Arnold, 'Europe, Technology, and Colonialism in the 20th Century', *History and Technology* 21/1 (2006), 85–106. Arnold writes how, even up until relatively recent times, 'colonies and ex-colonies provided overseas laboratories and testing-grounds, places where dangerous experiments could be conducted or ambitious schemes alike of social and physical engineering enacted, without the public scrutiny and political constraints that might inhibit – even prohibit – such ventures in Europe itself' (89).

63. Berman, *All That is Solid Melts into Air*, 12.

64. Hugh Kenner, *The Mechanic Muse* (Oxford: Oxford University Press, 1987), 14.

65. Hugh Kenner, 'The Making of the Modernist Canon', *Chicago Review* 34/2 (1984), 59.

66. Malcolm Bradbury, 'The Cities of Modernism', in Malcolm Bradbury and James McFarlane (eds), *Modernism: A Guide to European Literature 1890–1930* (1976; London: Penguin, 1991), 96.

67. Douglas Mao and Rebecca L. Walkowitz, 'The New Modernist Studies', *PMLA* 123/3 (2008), 739. See also the updated collection of essays charting these new developments in modernist criticism in more detail: Douglas Mao (ed.), *The New Modernist Studies* (Cambridge: Cambridge University Press, 2021). Other important works which take a broader, more globalised view of modernism include Laura Doyle and Laura Winkiel (eds), *Geomodernisms: Race, Modernism, Modernity* (Bloomington, IN: Indiana University Press, 2005), and Friedman's *Planetary Modernisms*.

68. Mao and Walkowitz, 'The New Modernist Studies', 739.

69. See Neal Alexander and James Moran, 'Introduction: Regional Modernisms', in Neal Alexander and James Moran (eds), *Regional Modernisms* (Edinburgh: Edinburgh University Press, 2013), 1. Dathalinn O'Dea in 'James Joyce the Regionalist' takes a regional modernist approach to Joyce, but treats Dublin as the region in question rather than looking at his portrayal of rural life.

70. Rosemary Shirley, *Rural Modernity, Everyday Life and Visual Culture* (Farnham: Ashgate, 2015), 3.

71. Ibid., 7.

72. Bluemel and McCluskey, 'Introduction', 2.

73. Ibid., 14–15.

74. Jay Watson, *William Faulkner and the Faces of Modernity* (Oxford: Oxford University Press, 2019), 42.

75. Ibid., 70.

76. Karl Marx and Friedrich Engels, *The Communist Manifesto*, trans. Samuel Moore (1848; London: Pluto Press, 2008), 40.

77. Hal Draper, *The Adventures of the Communist Manifesto* (Alameda, CA: Center for Socialist History, 2004), 220.

78. Tom Nairn, 'The Curse of Rurality: Limits of Modernisation Theory', in John A. Hall (ed.), *The State of the Nation: Ernest Gellner and the Theory of Nationalism* (Cambridge: Cambridge University Press, 1998), 108.

79. Williams, *The Country and the City*, 36.

80. Ibid., 235.

81. Ibid., 302.

82. Henri Lefebvre, *Du rural à l'urbain* (1970; Paris: Anthropos, 2001). Most of Lefebvre's writings on rural life went untranslated until the recent publication of *On the Rural: Economy, Sociology, Geography*, ed. Stuart Elden and Adam David Morton, trans. Robert Bononno (Minneapolis, MN: University of Minnesota Press, 2022). However, the quotations that follow are taken from *Du rural à l'urbain* and the translations are my own.

83. 'Parmi ceux qui – citadins, intellectuels, voire historiens ou sociologues – traversent un de nos villages, découvrent son visage original ou incertain, s'étonnent de sa torpeur ou admirent son « pittoresque », combien savent que ce village ne se réduit pas à un pêle-mêle accidentel d'hommes, de bêtes, et de choses, que son examen révèle une organisation complexe, une « structure » ?' (ibid., 21).

84. 'la communauté paysanne n'a rien d'immuable, d'éternel [. . .] Comme toute réalité historique, la communauté paysanne s'est développée, raffermie, dissoute' (ibid., 37–8).

85. 'un des fils conducteurs à suivre dans l'enchevêtrement des faits humains' (ibid., 39).

86. Thomas Osborne Davis, *The Poems of Thomas Davis* (Dublin: James Duffy, 1846), 10.

87. Berman, *All That is Solid Melts into Air*, 15.

88. Declan Kiberd, *Inventing Ireland: The Literature of the Modern Nation* (London: Vintage, 1996), 23.

89. P. J. Drudy, 'Introduction', in P. J. Drudy (ed.), *Ireland: Land, Politics and People* (Cambridge: Cambridge University Press, 1982), 1.

90. Charles Ford, 'Dante's Other Brush: *Ulysses* and the Irish Revolution', *James Joyce Quarterly* 29/4 (1992), 758, 755.

91. Laird, '"[H]e daren't show his nose"', 213.

92. F. S. L. Lyons, *Ireland Since the Famine* (London: Weidenfeld and Nicolson, 1971), 164.

93. Michael D. Higgins and John P. Gibbons, 'Shopkeeper-graziers and Land Agitation in Ireland, 1895–1900', in P. J. Drudy (ed.), *Ireland: Land, Politics and People* (Cambridge: Cambridge University Press, 1982), 95.

94. Fergus Campbell, *Land and Revolution: Nationalist Politics in the West of Ireland 1891–1921* (Oxford: Oxford University Press, 2005), 31.

95. Ibid., 33.

96. Ibid., 80.

97. Lyons, *Ireland Since the Famine*, 166.

98. Campbell, *Land and Revolution*, 72.

99. Foster, *Modern Ireland*, 424.

100. G. A. Birmingham, *An Irishman Looks at his World* (London, 1919), 208, cited in Higgins and Gibbons, 'Shopkeeper-graziers and Land Agitation', 113.

101. Ford, 'Dante's Other Brush', 758.

102. James Fintan Lalor, 'Tenant Right Meeting in Tipperary', in L. Fogarty, *James Fintan Lalor: Patriot & Political Essayist, 1807–1849* (Dublin: The Talbot Press 1918), 47–8.

103. Foster, *Modern Ireland*, 381.

104. Michael Davitt, *The Fall of Feudalism in Ireland or The Story of the Land League Revolution* (London and New York: Harper & Brothers, 1904), 55–6. Joyce's library in Trieste included a copy of Davitt's history of the Land War, with it therefore likely to have had a substantial influence on Joyce's account of it throughout his work (Ellmann, *Consciousness of Joyce*, 106).

105. Robert Lee Woolf, 'Introduction', in William Allingham, *Laurence Bloomfield in Ireland* (1864; New York: Garland, 1979), vi.

106. Campbell, *Land and Revolution*, 19.

107. Foster, *Modern Ireland*, 379.

108. Paul Bew, 'The Land League Ideal: Achievements and Contradictions', in P. J. Drudy (ed.), *Ireland: Land, Politics and People* (Cambridge: Cambridge University Press, 1982), 85.

109. *Royal Commission on Congestion in Ireland: appendix to the tenth report*, HC (1908) [Cd. 4007], xlii, 268, cited in Campbell, *Land and Revolution*, 24.

110. Campbell, *Land and Revolution*, 22.

111. Ibid., 22.

112. Cynthia E. Smith, 'The Land-Tenure System in Ireland: A Fatal Regime', *Marquette Law Review* 76/2 (1993), 473.

113. Laird, '"[H]e daren't show his nose"', 214.

114. Slote et al., *Annotations*, 395.

115. Ibid., 183.

116. 'The Land Question', *Freeman's Journal*, 20 September 1880, p. 7, col. 4, The British Newspaper Archive, https://www.britishnewspaper-archive.co.uk/viewer/BL/0000056/18800920/033/0007?browse=true (accessed 3 January 2024).

117. Liam Ó Raghallaigh, 'Captain Boycott: Man and Myth', *History Ireland* 19/1 (2011), 29.

118. Ibid., 29.

119. Ibid., 30.

120. Ibid., 31.

121. Ford, 'Dante's Other Brush', 755.

122. Dominic Manganiello, *Joyce's Politics* (London: Routledge and Kegan Paul, 1980), 8.
123. Drudy, 'Introduction', 4.
124. Kiberd, *Inventing Ireland*, 491.
125. Ibid., 490.
126. Leon Trotsky, 'Lessons of the Dublin Events', in *The Lace Curtain* 1, trans. Brian Pearce (Dublin: New Writers' Press, 1970), 59. My thanks to Will Fleming for alerting me to this article.
127. Terry Eagleton, *Heathcliff and the Great Hunger: Studies in Irish Culture* (London: Verso, 1995), 277.
128. Cleary, *Outrageous Fortune*, 42.

Chapter 2

'Ruric or cospolite': Cosmopolitans and Provincials in Joyce

Part II, Chapter 3 of *Finnegans Wake*, which unfolds in a Chapel-izod pub, opens with HCE and a group of 'Finnfannfawners, ruric or cospolite, for much or moment indispute' (*FW* 309.9–10). Roland McHugh suggests that 'Finnfannfawners' is a reference to Sinn Féiners who appear to be fawning over something or some-one, though it might also be a faint echo of the new Irish national anthem, which begins with the line 'Sinne Fianna Fáil'.[1] What is clear is that these barsponger nationalists do not compose a mono-lithic group. Within the group there are those who are 'ruric' (rural and rustic) as well as those who are 'cospolite' (cosmopolitan and polite). In addition, their conflicting ideas were ones that were very much 'indispute' as Joyce was coming of age in Ireland.

In their divisions, these men echo a debate that preoccupied the Irish Literary Revival at the turn of the twentieth century regarding the direction a future, free Ireland should take, both politically and culturally. Should it be centred on an ideal of a rural, Gaelic Ireland, or should it aim to mould itself into a cosmopolitan, outward-looking country? Vincent Cheng draws attention to this line and highlights how relevant these debates were to the construction of Irish identity at this time, especially in terms of a rural/urban divide:

> This binary of the rural/local versus the cosmopolitan/global plays itself out in a number of parallel variants (each side of which can be conveniently glorified or vilified): country versus city; peasant versus urban-dweller; primitive folk culture versus modernity and metropol-itan culture; rude primitives versus suave and urbane city-dwellers.[2]

While Revivalist Ireland, and Irish cultural nationalism in general, is usually thought to favour the peasant/rural/folk side of this binary, it would be a mistake to think of these movements as uniform in their composition and outlooks, as suggested by Joyce's 'Finnfannfawners' being 'ruric or cospolite'. In his influential study of the Revival, P. J. Mathews argues against this received 'notion of a solidly homogenous entity', one which 'invariably occludes the complex range of political positions that were developing and competing within nationalism at this time'.[3] Instead, Mathews argues that during 'this great moment of national "imagining", various different notions of Irish cultural identity began to crystallize and compete to become *the* emblem of Irish national identity'.[4] Similarly, Wim Van Mierlo has more recently written of the Revival as encompassing a 'broad group of artists and intellectuals whose ideas, ambitions and motivations diverge as much as they converge'.[5] Van Mierlo highlights how the Revival was implicated in forms of ethnic nationalism that were popular at the time, though he is quick to insist that 'among its many voices was also a modern cosmopolitan outlook that did not eschew European culture'.[6]

It is this chapter's contention that the contemporary debates surrounding the Revival's provincial/cosmopolitan divides influenced the young Joyce in subtle and not always acknowledged ways. Indeed, much of Joyce's work seeks to restage the postcolonial complexity of such debates, rather than taking one particular side. This chapter will look at examples of this, re-examining Joyce's works and interrogating the standard image of Joyce as an icon of urban, cosmopolitan modernism.

The framing of Joyce as a writer who embodies urban cosmopolitanism can be traced to some of the first commentators on his work. Some early Joycean criticism in particular sought to distance him from Ireland, and most especially from the rural Ireland so beloved of Yeats, Synge and other Revivalists. Ezra Pound's claiming of Joyce for urban, cosmopolitan modernism, in contrast to the literary landscape of Ireland, is among the earliest and most explicit examples of this tendency:

> It is surprising that Mr. Joyce is Irish. One is so tired of the Irish or 'Celtic' imagination (or 'phantasy' as I think they now call it) flopping about. Mr. Joyce does not flop about. He defines. He is not an institution for the promotion of Irish peasant industries. He accepts an international standard of prose writing and lives up to it.[7]

Similarly, Joyce's biographer, Richard Ellmann, saw the 18-year-old Joyce's brief correspondence with Henrik Ibsen as representing a pivotal break with his home country: 'Before Ibsen's letter Joyce was an Irishman; after it he was a European' (*JJII* 75). Van Mierlo writes that 'the brand of criticism that resulted from [Ellmann]' sought to celebrate Joyce as 'an urban – and urbane – author who looked towards the Continental literary traditions', thereby 'free[ing] himself from parochialism and resist[ing] the cultural binaries in which Yeats and the Revival were trapped'.[8] Van Mierlo writes that while this reading might appear attractive, it is simply 'not fully supported by events, nor by Joyce's early Irish reception'.[9] Postcolonial criticism from the 1990s onwards, particularly from critics such as Emer Nolan, Seamus Deane and Declan Kiberd, sought to correct this effacing of Joyce's nationality from his work; however, the image of an urban Joyce remains dominant even within this strand of Joycean criticism. While Joyce's Irish identity has been successfully reclaimed, one can argue that this has in truth been mostly a reclaiming of Joyce's Dublin identity at the expense of other aspects of his engagement with Ireland, particularly rural Ireland.[10] Seamus Deane, for example, still argues that Joyce's 'cosmopolitanism helped to avoid provincialism'.[11]

Cosmopolitanism, even when it does not necessarily efface nationality, does pose problems when dealing with rural specificity. Formed from the Greek words for world (*kosmos*) and citizen (*polites*), a cosmopolitan is a self-declared citizen of the world, espousing 'a universal humanism that transcends regional particularism'.[12] However, *polites* specifically denotes someone of the *polis*, or city, and as a result urbanity is embedded within cosmopolitanism's etymology. It is indeed also possible that by labelling the barspongers as 'cospolite', Joyce is making a veiled reference to that other pub-frequenting nationalist – and, as we shall see, perhaps conflicted cosmopolitan – of his oeuvre, the Citizen. In any case, by its very definition, cosmopolitanism assumes the urban location of any who would claim such an identity, and can even be read as denying this worldly identity to anyone of a rural background. Indeed, English is replete with insults that have their origins in descriptions of country people, such as 'villain' (from Old French and with the original sense of 'rustic' [*OED*, 'villain, n.']), 'boor' (from the Dutch for farmer [*OED*, 'boor, n.']) and 'churl' (from the West Germanic term for a peasant [*OED*, 'churl, n.']). Meanwhile, as the above quotation from Deane shows, the most frequent antonym to 'cosmopolitan' is 'provincial'.

The strength of Joyce's connection to Dublin for Irish-centred critics – as well as the cosmopolitanism of his writing for others – seems destined to preclude any potential association between Joyce and rural or provincial Ireland. This chapter seeks to problematise this assumption by first returning Joyce to the scene of Revivalist debates around such matters, when the binaries of cosmopolitan/provincial did not yet appear quite so set in stone. It will conduct a postcolonial reappraisal of Joyce's cosmopolitanism and examine to what extent his writing problematises such binaries. The chapter will begin by investigating a debate that took place in the *Daily Express* during Joyce's early days at university regarding how Irish literature should approach issues surrounding cosmopolitanism and nationalism, and how this likely influenced Joyce. From this will follow an analysis of the complexities of cosmopolitanism in colonial, and rural, settings. I will then carry out a series of readings from across Joyce's oeuvre which dramatise the aforementioned debates. Ultimately, this chapter argues that Joyce's work demonstrates that the binary opposition of 'ruric or cospolite' is a false one, unworkable and illogical in a colonial context. As Kevin Whelan writes, Ireland's 'provincialism and alienation were central to the condition of modernity, not its benighted opposite'.[13] In short, a cosmopolitanism that ignores the provincial is never fully 'of the world' – this chapter will attempt to show Joyce's intimate awareness of such a predicament.

The *Daily Express* Debates

Between October and December 1898, when the Revival was still in its infancy, a debate unfolded in the pages of the *Daily Express* between John Eglinton (the pseudonym of William Kirkpatrick Magee) and W. B. Yeats, with contributions from William Larminie and Æ (the pseudonym of George Russell). Their articles were collected in 1899 and published under the title *Literary Ideals in Ireland*. While the debate was largely well mannered, the ideas and ideals expressed in these articles represent a significant schism at the heart of the Revival movement as to the direction in which Irish literature should look. The impact this debate had on literary Ireland is made clear in the 'Editor's Note' to the collection:

> The following articles constitute a controversy which was not intended when the first article was written, but which spontane- ously grew from week to week in the Saturday issues of the DAILY EXPRESS, and developed, as will be seen, a certain organic unity. Written by men who are amongst the foremost of the modern school of Irish writers, they reveal aims and views so original and

so illustrative of the new movement of ideas which is observable in contemporary Ireland, that it was felt it would be interesting to bring them together in volume form, if only as furnishing a possible chapter of Irish literary history.[14]

The labelling of these debates as a 'controversy' shows the significant effect they had on the Revivalist literary landscape. Taking place as they did during Joyce's first weeks as an undergraduate in Dublin, it would have been impossible for him to have been unaware of these debates, and indeed his early enthusiasm for cosmopolitanism shows that, at least to some extent, he took up a personal position in relation to them. Even more importantly, the fact that the ideas debated in the *Daily Express* recur in every Joycean work shows just how influential the literary atmosphere of turn-of-the-century Dublin remained for the writer. This section will describe the tenor of the debates, as well as the primary individuals involved, arguing that Joyce's early writing should be read in the context in which they occurred.[15]

The 'controversy' itself began on 8 October 1898 with an article by John Eglinton entitled 'What Should be the Subjects of a National Drama?' In this article Eglinton imagined a scenario in which 'a writer of dramatic genius were to appear in Ireland' and questioned what dramatic subjects such a writer would choose: 'Would he look [. . .] in the Irish legends, or in the life of the peasantry and folklore, or in Irish history and patriotism, or in life at large as reflected in his own consciousness?'[16] For Eglinton, the latter option was the most appropriate for this future writer of genius, emphasising individuality over nationality. Eglinton was a librarian at the National Library of Ireland, and, like many in the first wave of Revivalism, he was of a Protestant Anglo-Irish background. It was an identity that he wore with pride, entitling his 1917 essay collection *Anglo-Irish Essays*, in which he referred to the Anglo-Irishman as the 'Modern Irishman', in contrast to the native Catholic individual whom he labelled a 'Mere Irishman'.[17] Eglinton attributed his own cosmopolitanism directly to the fact that he was a Protestant Anglo-Irishman and therefore possessed an 'open-mindedness [that] makes us ideal cosmopolitans'.[18] The preface to *Anglo-Irish Essays*, written in 1917 and so after the Revival's heyday, reflects the anxieties of the Protestant ascendancy following the Easter Rising. In it, Eglinton argues that 'destiny entrusted the task of unifying and governing Ireland' to the Anglo-Irish, 'the country's natural rulers'.[19] Eglinton's cosmopolitanism, therefore, often expressed itself in terms that seemed more anti-nationalism than pro-internationalism. This was not lost on contemporary nationalists, such as Arthur Griffith, the founder of Sinn Féin, who lambasted Eglinton's 'barbarous fetish of cosmopolitanism' in a 1901 article for the *United Irishman*.[20] Joyce, however, does not appear to have been upset by Eglinton's rhetoric, and kept his mockery to fairly gentle jibes. It is also clear that he had some respect for Eglinton's essays, with his Trieste library containing Eglinton's *Bards and Saints* (1906) and *Anglo-Irish Essays*.[21] Indeed, Scott notes that Joyce attempted to have another collection of Eglinton's essays, *Pebbles from a Brook* (1901), translated into Italian, suggesting a substantial degree of respect for his work.[22] Such consistent engagement with Eglinton's writings throughout his lifetime makes it more likely than not that Joyce followed Eglinton's arguments in the *Daily Express* in 1898.

W. B. Yeats responded to Eglinton's initial article in the *Express* by defending the recourse to ancient imagery in crafting a national literary ideal, citing the likes of Dante, Homer and Shakespeare. Eglinton responded to this argument in turn by claiming that the poet who

> looks too much away from himself and from his age, does not feel the facts of life enough, but seeks in art an escape from them. Consequently, the art he achieves cannot be the expression of the age and of himself – cannot be representative or national.[23]

For Eglinton, then, to be national, the artist had to be contemporary in their thematic expression and individualist. Eglinton, however, did not completely reject the notion of using material from the past or from mythology as part of a national literature, but he did note in a further article that such material 'can only be made to live again by something new added to them out of the author's age and personality'.[24]

While the debate initially involved only Eglinton and Yeats, after a number of weeks other Anglo-Irish Revivalist figures became involved, including William Larminie and George Russell. The latter is most interesting for this discussion, as it was he who summarised the crux of the debate in the final contribution to the controversy, entitled 'Nationality and Cosmopolitanism in Literature'. As was discussed in the previous chapter, Russell was an ardent supporter of rural and agricultural Ireland. He entered the debate firmly on the side of communal tradition, as opposed to Eglinton's individualist cosmopolitanism. Russell summarised the *Express* debate as being 'on the one side [. . .] a plea for nationality in our literature, and on the other a protest on behalf of individualism'.[25] His concern was that Irish literature, in becoming cosmopolitan and modern, would go the way of the rest of European writing, as he perceived it, losing all sense of national singularity. 'The cosmopolitan spirit,' he wrote, 'whether for good or for evil, is hastily obliterating distinctions.'[26] Ireland's uniqueness lay for Russell, as it did for Yeats, in its mythology. The ideal national literature is imagined 'as an offset to the cosmopolitan ideal', and involves 'the creation of heroic figures, types, whether legendary or taken from history, and enlarged to epic proportions by our writers'.[27] The emphasis on this 'national ideal' is founded to a large extent on the notion of Irish exceptionalism, as Russell makes clear:

> If nationality is to justify itself in the face of all this, it must be because the country which preserves its individuality does so with the profound conviction that its peculiar ideal is nobler than that which the cosmopolitan spirit suggests – that this ideal is so precious to it that its loss would be as the loss of the soul, and that it could not be realised without an aloofness from, if not an actual indifference to, the ideals which are spreading so rapidly over Europe.[28]

Cosmopolitanism is here portrayed as a significant threat to the establishment of the nation – spiritually more so than politically – to the extent that the securing of Irish nationhood can only be guaranteed by deliberate 'aloofness' or 'indifference' to European matters. This is the retreating of Irish thought into the cavern of national isolation so feared by Eglinton.

The sense that Eglinton and Russell represented opposite ends of the Revival's spectrum for Joyce is suggested by their appearance many years later in the 'Scylla and Charybdis' episode of *Ulysses*, in which the two characters continue to adhere to the positions they took in the *Express* debates. On hearing that the Englishman Haines is enthusiastic about Douglas Hyde's *Love Songs of Connacht* (1893), Eglinton dismisses this facet of the Revival by commenting that '[t]he peatsmoke is going to his head' (*U* 9.100). By contrast, Russell warns that such love songs can be 'dangerous', even radical, opining that '[t]he movements which work revolutions in the world are born out of the dreams and visions in a peasant's heart on the hillside' (*U* 9.103–6). Where Russell sees in rural Ireland the potential for radical change, Eglinton prioritises the urban centre, noting at one point that '[t]he highroads are dreary but they lead to the town' (*U* 9.408–9). Evidently, in the 1904 Dublin of *Ulysses*, theories regarding the direction that

Irish literature should take are still very much up for debate, the divisions represented as ever by Eglinton and Russell.

In *Imaginations and Reveries*, Russell included a slightly edited version of his *Express* article, this time under the title of 'Nationality or Cosmopolitanism'. This version is somewhat less strident in its attack on cosmopolitanism and refers to John Eglinton as 'one of our most thoughtful writers' and 'our first cosmopolitan'.[29] Here, Russell makes the claim for nationality and tradition in literature on the basis not just of Irish exceptionalism, but also on the capacity for ancient tales to hold 'a core of eternal truth'.[30] However, perhaps the most interesting indication of Russell's more nuanced take on this debate is contained in the preface, where he argues retrospectively that '[i]f I advocated a national ideal I felt immediately I could make an equal plea for more cosmopolitan and universal ideas'.[31] Here, we see that for Russell a 'national ideal' is not an end in itself, but instead is necessary in order to properly embrace cosmopolitanism or universality in literature. However, without that national ideal in place, cosmopolitanism appears to Russell as a threat to the independence of Irish nationhood and character. In expressing this view, Russell mirrored the thoughts of nationalists in many other emerging nations who were reluctant to espouse unbridled cosmopolitanism in their earliest stages. These nationalist figures were adamant, however, that this was not because they wished to close themselves off from the rest of the modern world. As Giuseppe Mazzini, the Italian revolutionary, warned: '[b]efore *associating* ourselves with the Nations which compose Humanity we must exist as a Nation'.[32] Sun Yat-sen, often considered modern China's 'father of the nation', similarly argued that 'cosmopolitanism grows out of nationalism; if we want to extend cosmopolitanism we must first establish strongly our own nationalism'.[33] Cosmopolitanism, therefore, can often be the ultimate goal of nationalism, but it is an aspiration that many nationalists feel is dangerous to indulge in before one's own sovereignty is secured. The arguments put forward by Russell fall into this mode of nationalist thinking.

In January 1900, a few months after the *Daily Express* controversy was published as *Literary Ideals in Ireland*, the 17-year-old Joyce presented a paper entitled 'Drama and Life' to the Literary and Historical Society at University College Dublin. The paper, extolling the merits of European, cosmopolitan writers, particularly Ibsen, appears to have been influenced by the debates raging at the time and echoes some of the arguments made by John Eglinton in the *Express*. Where Eglinton, in the first article that sparked the controversy, had written that 'Ireland must exchange the patriotism which looks back for the patriotism which looks forward',[34] Joyce, in his paper, writes that '[i]t is a sinful foolishness to sigh back for the good old times, to feed the hunger of us with the cold stones they afford' (*OCPW* 28).[35] Joyce took his listeners on a tour through European art, from ancient Greek drama to Wagnerian opera, all the while without mentioning a single Irish author. Ellmann notes that Joyce's paper provides his 'strongest early statement of method and intention' (*JJII* 73). In particular, Ellmann remarks that

> His defense of contemporary materials, his interest in Wagnerian myth, his aversion to conventions, and his insistence that the laws of life are the same always and everywhere, show him to be ready to fuse real people with mythical ones, and so find all ages to be one as in *A Portrait*, *Ulysses*, and *Finnegans Wake*. (*JJII* 73)

This allowance for ancient myth's potential as a raw material for elevating the present is also in line with Eglinton's acceptance that mythological materials 'can only be made to live again by something new added to them out of the author's age and personality'.[36] This is, in many ways, a succinct description of what T. S. Eliot called the 'mythical method' employed by Joyce throughout *Ulysses*, and indeed even more so in *Finnegans Wake*.[37]

Joyce's paper received a frosty reaction – in Ellmann's (figurative) words, 'his audience sprang to attack him' (*JJII* 73) – which Joyce went on to fictionalise in the pages of *Stephen Hero*. Joyce does not provide the reader with the text of the paper itself, but he does give us a depiction of the audience's reaction. One speaker, named Magee – despite sharing Eglinton's real surname they do not appear to have much else in common – lambasts the paper on account of its supposed atheism, describing it as 'a reproduction of the decadent literary opinions of exhausted European capitals' (*SH* 95). Another speaker, Hughes, a nationalist of the most close-minded kind, declares that

> They wanted no foreign filth. Mr Daedalus might read what authors he liked, of course, but the Irish people had their own glorious literature where they could always find fresh ideals to spur them on to new patriotic endeavours. (*SH* 95)

Hughes's lexical choice when he says that ancient Irish literature will provide 'fresh ideals' seems deliberate in the context of the recent debates in *Literary Ideals in Ireland*. Worst of all, Hughes proclaims that 'Mr Daedalus was himself a renegade from the Nationalist ranks: he professed cosmopolitanism. But a man that was of all countries was of no country – you must first have a nation before you have art' (*SH 95*). Stephen's cosmopolitanism – interestingly, apart from the Wakean 'cospolite', this is the only appearance of the word in Joyce's oeuvre – marks him as a traitor among Irish nationalists. Hughes's belief that one must first have a nation before one can create art aligns with the views expressed by Russell. While Stephen does not reply to his critics, it is quite clear that the young Joyce has set Stephen up as the heroic bringer of cosmopolitan ideals to these backward nationalists, his message doomed to be rejected. Where they worship the 'cold stones' of Irish tradition, Stephen preaches a gospel of modern European literature. Stephen, like Eglinton, far from serving his nation, does not even bother to wait for its formation – he jumps straight to the international sphere. Such, it is clear, was the young Joyce's literary ideal, one crafted in the context of intense debates that also appeared in the pages of Irish newspapers.

A few years later, in his 1904 essay 'A Portrait of the Artist', Joyce obliquely mentions that 'traditional and individual revelations were at that time pressing their claims', in what appears to be a reference to this period in recent Irish literary history (*PSW 215*). Even at this early point, however, there is a sense that Joyce now feels somewhat removed from the debate, or at least incapable of giving himself wholeheartedly to one or other camp, almost suffocating between these two factions 'pressing their claims'. By the time Joyce was living in 1920s Paris and basking in the celebrity of *Ulysses*, we get an even more surprising perspective on these issues from this supposedly arch-cosmopolitan. Arthur Power, at the time a young Irish artist, upon meeting Joyce told him that he would like to write in the style of French satirists, and reported the following response: 'You will never do it [. . .] you are an Irishman and you must write in your own tradition. Borrowed styles are no good. You must write what is in your blood and not what is in your brain.' When Power objected to this on the grounds that he wanted to be a great international writer rather than merely a national one, Joyce is said to have replied: 'They were national first [. . .] and it was the intensity of their own nationalism which made them international in the end [. . .]' (*JJII 505*). Here is a Joyce seemingly more in line with Russell, even perhaps with his own creation Hughes. While these words have been put into Joyce's mouth by Power in his recollections, nevertheless Joyce's later work does seem to testify to a change in attitude. Indeed, Margot Norris writes that Joyce's 'cosmopolitanism was balanced by a growing interest, in later life, for reappropriating Irish culture, tales, legends, and his own family lore, at a time when he was estranged from his native land'.[38]

What happened between the Joyce of 1900 and that of the 1920s and 1930s? What change in attitude has him reject a hasty cosmopolitanism in favour of a degree of nationality and even provincialism? Or has Joyce's urbane cosmopolitanism been overstated at the expense of his interest in these other areas? Reappraisals of cosmopolitanism over the past twenty years can help us to understand Joyce's developing relationship to it as a guiding principle as he matured.

Critical Cosmopolitanism

Apart from some retrospective nuance from Russell, the debate that occurred among Anglo-Irish Revivalists around the turn of the twentieth century can be summarised as a choice between the two binary options of nationalism and cosmopolitanism, with matters relating to provincialism and urbanity existing in the background throughout. The notion that nationalism and cosmopolitanism stand at opposite ends of the spectrum of ideas held sway for most of the twentieth century. However, towards the end of the century this neat binary began to come under investigation. In *Cosmopolitics: Thinking and Feeling Beyond the Nation* (1998), a number of writers question this binarism. Pheng Cheah looks into the historical disjunction in conceiving of nationalism and cosmopolitanism as opposites by noting how cosmopolitanism long precedes nationalism in the history of ideas. Cosmopolitanism is associated with the humanism of the Renaissance, long before 'the doctrine of nationalism [had] been fully articulated'.[39] In fact, even when nationalism first emerged, it did so as 'a *popular* movement distinct from the state it seeks to transform in its own image'.[40] Thus, Cheah argues, nationalism in its first guise – and before it was subsumed into the official nation-state – was a utopian movement *against* the status quo. As such, for Cheah, 'the ideals of cosmopolitanism and European nationalism in its early stirrings are almost indistinguishable'.[41] Bruce Robbins, in the same collection, makes the case for conceiving of numerous kinds of cosmopolitanism, arguing that 'there is a growing consensus that cosmopolitanism sometimes works together with nationalism rather than in opposition to it'.[42]

Just as we might say that there are different kinds of cosmopolitanism, so too, it is important to stress, are there many kinds of nationalism. As Cheah makes clear, the rebellious nationalism that exists *against* the state, and the 'official nationalism' *of* the nation-state, are two very different beasts. It is only the latter form of nationalism that makes sense as an antithesis to cosmopolitanism, according to Cheah.[43] This is an extremely important point with regard to nationalism in colonised countries. By definition, this form of nationalism exists *against* the colonial state. While it might look to the pre-colonial past for inspiration, it is always with the aim of creating a new future. In this way we have what might be termed the Janus-faced nature of decolonising nationalism: the need to look both to the past and to the future; to look both inside and outside the boundaries of one's country.[44] It is only after independence, when a particular brand of nationalism has become officially sanctioned by the new nation-state, that nationalism can become a purely conservative force and settle itself into a new role of maintaining the status quo – and, of course, this is not necessarily a given for all variations of nationalism post-independence.

The Janus-faced nature of Irish nationalism at this time is apparent even among its most ardent exponents, such as the writer and revolutionary Patrick Pearse. Pearse is most famous for his leading role in the 1916 Easter Rising, during which he read the Proclamation of the Irish Republic from the steps of the General Post Office and was declared the President of the Republic. He would eventually surrender to the British forces and be executed by firing squad. He was also a poet, teacher, barrister and prominent activist in the Gaelic League. Pearse taught the Irish language lessons that Joyce attended and, according to Ellmann, had a significant impact in turning Joyce against the language: 'Joyce gave them up because Patrick Pearse, the instructor, found it necessary to exalt Irish by denigrating English' (*JJII* 61). However, Pearse's attitude to the language and to Irish nationalism was more complicated than this simplified depiction. Louis de Paor describes Pearse's writing in the Irish language as offering 'a sophisticated model for a new literature in Irish that would re-establish a living connection with the pre-colonial Gaelic past while resuming its relationship with contemporary Europe, bypassing the monolithic influence of English'.[45]

De Paor also highlights that the interest shown by many nationalist writers in Irish was matched by a simultaneous interest in the languages of Europe: Pearse, '[l]ike many of his revivalist colleagues [. . .] was a Francophone for whom French provided access to contemporary European thought and culture and an enabling alternative to English'.[46] Indeed, from Wolfe Tone's republicanism and the 1798 United Irishmen rebellion onwards, Irish nationalism has a history of taking its inspiration from France. Scarlett Baron describes this Francophilia as being born out of 'Ireland's continuing sense of a prospective alliance with France' and a 'legacy of expectation'.[47] This 'alliance' can be seen in 'After the Race', particularly the 'sympathy' that the crowds have for 'the blue cars – the cars of their friends, the French', as well as in 'The Dead' through Gabriel Conroy's interest in French language and culture (D 30). It is also clear in *A Portrait*, when 'four French delegates' attend the setting of a slab in tribute to Wolfe Tone (P 183), and in *Ulysses* when Stephen recalls meeting the Fenian Kevin Egan who fled to Paris to escape the British forces (U 3.249–50). Indeed, it is also often forgotten that George Clancy, the inspiration for *A Portrait*'s arch-nationalist Davin, attended the same French classes as Joyce at university, while Davin's character speaks of one day serving 'the foreign legion of France' (*JJII* 60; P 181). France, therefore, provides Irish nationalists with an opportunity to escape the suffocating influence of British rule in Ireland, something that Joyce highlights in the Mookse and Gripes section of *Finnegans Wake* when the Mookse proclaims: 'Unionjok and be joined to yok! Parysis, *tu sais*, crucycrooks, belongs to him who parises himself' (*FW* 155.16–17). To be under the Union Jack is therefore to be under the yoke of Britain, whereas Paris offers an escape to those who are willing to embrace it.

Such was the thinking of figures such as Pearse who encouraged Irish nationalists to get in touch with European – and particularly French – culture. Indeed, Pearse even admonished those nationalists who might have had a tendency towards national navel-gazing in an editorial for the bilingual newspaper *An Claidheamh Soluis*:

> Do you seriously contend that we should be wise to cut ourselves adrift from the great world of European thought? . . . Were we then completely aloof from European thought when we were Irish, and are we more in touch with it now that we are more than half English?[48]

While many nationalists professed hostility towards cosmopolitanism as a guiding principle, often this was more a hostility towards Anglophone culture than outright xenophobia. In the same editorial, Pearse makes this clear by writing that '[w]e fear that in Ireland, "cosmopolitanism" . . . is only another word for Anglicisation, and that the "world" of which "we" are citizens is that portion of the British Empire which – we speak metaphorically – lies between Westminster and Fleet Street'.[49] The thinking of such nationalists was that

embracing a cosmopolitanism that was in reality a veiled Anglicisation would sound the death knell of Irish culture. Such a form of
cosmopolitanism, it was feared, might just be colonialism enforced
by the savant rather than the soldier.

Walter Mignolo tackles such issues by charting a history of 'cosmopolitan projects' from the spread of Christianity to the civilising mission
of the Enlightenment.[50] Both, Mignolo argues, are 'linked to coloniality
and to the emergence of the modern/colonial world'.[51] This leads him
to conclude that 'coloniality [. . .] is the hidden face of modernity' –
and, by extension, of cosmopolitanism as well.[52] Mignolo argues that
the reason this has tended to go unacknowledged is that 'most stories of modernity have been told from the perspective of modernity
itself'.[53] He differentiates between two '[n]arratives of cosmopolitan
orientation', one that has a 'managerial' purpose (such as Christianity, nineteenth-century imperialism or neoliberal globalisation) and
another that has an 'emancipatory' goal (such as Marxism), the latter
sometimes being 'oblivious to the saying of the people that are supposed to be emancipated'.[54] Mignolo calls instead for what he terms
a 'critical cosmopolitanism' that would 'reconceive cosmopolitanism
from the perspective of coloniality'.[55] He sees the world as composed
of multifarious 'local histories'; however, those local histories enacted
from a hegemonic position take on cosmopolitan, universalising roles –
what Mignolo terms 'global designs' – while the 'other local histories in
the planet' are relegated to the status of the provincial.[56]

The tendency for cosmopolitanism to act as a justification for
what were in reality colonial endeavours is clear from the words
of representatives of Empire themselves. For example, Edward
Dowden, a unionist Irish scholar, stated that '[t]he direction of such
work as I have done in literature has been (to give it a grand name)
imperial or cosmopolitan'.[57] Mathews draws particular attention to
Yeats's opposition to Dowden's supposed cosmopolitanism, which
'Yeats recognized [. . .] as quintessentially provincial in its deference
to London taste and values'.[58] The enthusiasm shown by imperialists
for cosmopolitanism, particularly when faced with subaltern nationalism, suggests that it was a convenient guise for furthering colonial
ends. In *Finnegans Wake* Joyce has the nationalist Shaun draw a link
between colonialism and his brother Shem's exile to Europe: 'How he
went to his switlersland after his lungs, my sad little brother, before
his coglionial expancian' (*FW* 488.30–2). Here, Shem's recuperative,
and apparently innocuous, trip to Switzerland is interpreted by his
jealous brother as preceding an act of colonial expansion, involving
his testicles (Italian: *coglioni*) and his stomach (Italian: *pancia*), as

McHugh notes.[59] *Coglione* also carries the signification of 'moronic' in Italian, meaning that Shem's exile can be viewed alternatively as imperialist, ballsy, consuming or moronic – or indeed all at the same time. While it is easy to dismiss this as no more than the usual Shaunian jealousy, it is also a good summation of the complexities of espousing cosmopolitanism in a colonised society.

Nels Pearson addresses how Joyce and other Irish writers were forced to tackle the binary choice provided by cosmopolitanism and nationalism. Pearson argues that progressive nationalists in decolonising states – who would naturally be sympathetic to the humanist ideals of cosmopolitanism – were faced with '[t]he paradox [. . .] that one must be "international" before ever fairly knowing what it is to be national'.[60] Pearson views Joyce as being particularly aware of this paradox and subsequently forced to find innovative ways to balance these two impulses: one that is sympathetic to Irish nationalism's desire to break free of limiting outside influences; the other that views global culture as the rightful domain of the artist above solely national culture. Pearson argues that this paradox led Joyce to develop '[a] modernism that derives not from choosing between national and cosmopolitan sympathies, but from the need to somehow make these concurrent principles'.[61] Similarly, Kevin Whelan warns against 'reduc[ing] Joyce's cultural politics to a crude and morally-charged choice between "national" and "cosmopolitan"'.[62] In contrast to his Revivalist peers, Whelan views Joyce's complexity as lying in his 'refusal to inhabit the binaries of Celtic or Saxon, Catholic or Protestant, modern or traditional, national or cosmopolitan, English or Irish'.[63] While the binaries of Celtic/Saxon, Catholic/Protestant and English/Irish were never really up for debate – Joyce would hardly ever have been considered Saxon, Protestant or English no matter how hard he might hypothetically have tried – Whelan is essentially correct in emphasising Joyce's rejection of the dominant binaries of the time. Indeed, once we begin to investigate the perceived binary division between cosmopolitanism and provincialism in Joyce's work, we come upon some of his most complex cultural critiques.

Ruric *and* Cospolite?

After getting his literary break from the farming newspaper, *The Irish Homestead*, in late 1904, Joyce left the country firmly set against the core tenets of Revivalism. His hostility towards the country and its institutions is made clear in his letters to Nora Barnacle as they prepared for their departure. He declares himself to be 'fighting a battle with every religious and social force in Ireland', concluding that '[t]here is no life here – no naturalness or honesty' (*L2* 53). It is with this attitude that *Stephen Hero* and most of the stories comprising *Dubliners* appear to have been written, until Joyce's ill-fated move to Rome in 1906 caused the writer to begin a reappraisal of his depiction of Ireland. In September 1906 he reflected in a letter to Stanislaus:

> Sometimes thinking of Ireland it seems to me that I have been unnecessarily harsh. I have reproduced (in *Dubliners* at least) none of the attraction of the city for I have never felt at my ease in any city since I left it except in Paris. I have not reproduced its ingenuous insularity and its hospitality. The latter 'virtue' so far as I can see does not exist elsewhere in Europe. I have not been just to its beauty: for it is more beautiful naturally in my opinion than what I have seen of England, Switzerland, France, Austria or Italy. (*L2* 166)

Joyce performs an interesting slippage here from 'Ireland' to 'the city' (i.e. Dublin), to the point that it is unclear whether he is talking about the virtues of Ireland or Dublin by the end of the paragraph. This kind of slippage of Dublin into Ireland is one that has been repeated in much criticism, and indeed it might be tempting to argue that for all Joyce's efforts to speak for his country, he invariably falls back into talking solely about his city. However, there is no doubt that Joyce's attitude to Ireland more broadly did shift after this point, and, as Ellmann notes, it was with this 'indulgent view of Ireland' that he began to write 'The Dead' (*JJII* 230). Such is the argument made by Cóilín Owens when he writes that '[a] few years of exile and the companionship of Nora Barnacle had led him to a new appreciation of some of the good humour and hospitality of his native land'.[64] Owens is right to note the influence of Nora, who became symbolic of the west of Ireland for Joyce, leading to a sudden growth of interest regarding rural Ireland and the western town of Galway. This change in view incited a desire to no longer place himself quite so emphatically on one side of the debate taking place in Ireland, but instead to document its complexities throughout the course of his work. 'The Dead' is the first example in Joyce's writing where the conflict between cosmopolitanism and provincialism is set up without a clear sense of where the author stands – a major development from similar sections in *Stephen Hero*.

'The Dead' establishes sets of binaries that correspond to contemporary debates in Ireland, pitting Gabriel Conroy, a self-professed urban cosmopolitan and sometime man of letters, first against Molly Ivors, a Gaelic League nationalist, and finally against Michael Furey, his wife's former sweetheart and a representative of rural Ireland. Gabriel's wife, Gretta, is also originally from Galway, an aspect of her identity that Gabriel attempts to erase, instead judging her 'people' to be from Connacht, not Gretta herself (*D* 148). Gabriel's very marriage is, therefore, a union of rural and urban, Gael and Pale, an argument in miniature against notions of ideological purity, but he does not at first seem willing or able to acknowledge this.

Gabriel's worldview first comes under scrutiny when Ivors invites him to join her and her fellow nationalists on an excursion to the Aran Islands off the west coast of Galway. In this instance, Irish nationalism is intrinsically linked to rural Ireland through the identification of the Aran Islands as a repository of an ancient Gaelic way of life. During their dance together Ivors reveals that she has seen through the pseudonym ('G.C.') that Gabriel uses for his literary reviews in the *Daily Express*.[65] This leads Ivors to mockingly label him a 'West Briton' (*D* 148). There is a bite to the jibe, and the comment clearly hurts Gabriel, despite his view that 'literature was above politics' (*D* 148). When Gabriel refuses her invitation to the Aran Islands in favour of going on a cycling trip 'to France or Belgium or perhaps Germany', the conversation takes on a more caustic edge (*D* 149). Ivors lists the usual nationalist reasons for going on an excursion to the west, including the opportunity to practise one's Irish – to which Gabriel replies, 'Irish is not my language' (*D* 149) – as well as the more general notion of getting to know 'your own land [. . .], your own people, and your own country' (*D* 149). It is at this point, in the course of the dance, that Gabriel loses his cool, declaring 'I'm sick of my own country', though when Ivors presses him for a reason why, he fails to give one (*D* 149). Gabriel's inability to provide an answer is telling here and is the beginning of a realisation that the form of cosmopolitanism that he has embraced has resulted in a poverty of knowledge regarding his own country. He can provide no clear reason why the lands and languages of Europe should take primacy over those of Ireland. Gabriel's cosmopolitanism might be termed, after Mignolo, an *uncritical* one, favouring the globalising narratives of the powerful, hegemonic cultures of Europe over the local histories in Ireland. When Ivors calls him a 'West Briton' again, Gabriel is stung by the public nature of her castigation of him, thinking that 'she had no right to call him a West Briton *before people*, even in joke' (*D* 150, my emphasis). Just as Gabriel uses a pseudonym to hide the fact that he writes in a unionist paper, so he seems happy to enjoy the trappings of his ability to partake in the British establishment in Ireland, until this is revealed to his fellow countrymen. Clearly, for Ivors, Gabriel's choice of holiday exposes a cosmopolitanism that imposes a global and imperial cultural system that refuses to accommodate local, subaltern cultures, knowing only how to erase them. Gabriel's inability to provide a response to Ivors is proof of his realisation that nothing – not literature nor holiday destinations – is now 'above politics'.

Molly Ivors, despite being the symbol of nationalism in 'The Dead', at no point can be easily dismissed as having a backward or so-called 'provincial' outlook – indeed, the nationalist movement that she is a part of is as much a modern, urban phenomenon as Gabriel's cosmopolitanism.[66] Ivors certainly looks towards the rural west for inspiration, but there is nothing in 'The Dead' that suggests that she is of rural or provincial origins herself – in any case, she is very much an urban figure now, residing not far from the site of the party at Usher's Island. Despite her loyalty to rural, Gaelic Ireland, Gabriel cannot claim that she is overly wedded to the past, as one might with other nationalist figures in Joyce's oeuvre, such as the Citizen and Shaun. There are hints that Ivors might be somewhat conservative – we are specifically informed that '[s]he did not wear a low-cut bodice', suggesting a Catholic brand of nationalism (*D* 147) – but mostly she shows herself to be a politically active and independent woman, not afraid to speak her mind. Indeed, her fervent opinions, allied with her youth, clearly perturb Gabriel: 'Of course the girl or woman, or whatever she was, was an enthusiast but there was a time for all things' (*D* 150). Her independent nature is most obvious when Gabriel offers to see her home, an offer she refuses, instead stating 'I'm quite well able to take care of myself' (*D* 154). Molly Ivors is proof, then, of the folly of dismissing nationalism as solely backward-looking.

Joyce returned to Trieste in 1907 and began contributing pieces of journalism to *Il Piccolo della Sera*, as well as giving lectures on Ireland at the city's university. His lectures and articles from this time provide the most explicit demonstration of a change in attitude towards Ireland. As Kevin Barry states in his introduction to Joyce's non-fictional writing, his purpose in the series of Triestine articles and lectures between 1907 and 1912 was 'to state the case of Ireland to an international audience which, he claimed, had been systemically misinformed through the agencies of the British press' (*OCPW* x). In the same 1906 letter to Stanislaus in which Joyce spoke of having been 'unnecessarily harsh' towards Ireland, he also admitted that 'once or twice in Trieste I felt myself humiliated when I heard the little Galatti girl sneering at my impoverished country' (*L2* 166–7). There is a definite sense that Joyce in his writing at the lectern and in *Il Piccolo* is trying to convey to his Triestine audience Ireland's justified place in the modern world.

Joyce's 1907 lecture, 'Ireland: Island of Saints and Sages', is his most extensive account of Ireland's history and of the malignant influence of colonialism on the country. Joyce even appears to betray some similarities to those contemporaries of his back in Dublin who looked into the past for inspiration, telling his listeners that 'the Irish nation's desire to create its own civilization is not so much the desire of a young nation wishing to link itself to Europe's concert, but the desire by an ancient nation to renew in a modern form the glories of a past civilization' (*OCPW* 111). This idea of renewing past glories in a modern form cuts to the heart of the Janus-faced nature of Irish cultural nationalism – looking into the past to create its present. Throughout this piece, Joyce places emphasis on ancient Ireland's cosmopolitanism, particularly its links to continental Europe, be it through Irish saints spreading the message of Christianity or the 'Wild Geese', the Gaelic leaders who fled to Europe to garner support for Ireland's cause in the late seventeenth century (*OCPW* 123). This allows Joyce to perform a kind of balancing act, by looking for cosmopolitanism in predominantly nationalist narratives. He does not, however, accept any notions of racial purity in doing so, instead noting that

> it is pointless searching for a thread that has remained pure, virgin and uninfluenced by other threads nearby. What race or language [. . .] can nowadays claim to be pure? No race has less right to make such a boast than the one presently inhabiting Ireland. (*OCPW* 118)

This lecture sees Joyce laying claim to many of the core elements of Irish nationalism but purging them of their notions of purity; for example, the Irish language, which in Joyce's hands becomes an emblem of cosmopolitanism: 'This language is eastern in origin and has been identified by many philologists with the ancient language of the Phoenicians, the discoverers, according to historians, of commerce and navigation' (*OCPW* 110).[67] Joyce seems particularly attracted to this Phoenician story of Ireland's origins because it would make the ancient proto-Irish a seafaring, trading and cosmopolitan people. When he imagines what an independent

Ireland might look like, he sees it as 'a rival, bilingual, republican, self-centred and enterprising island next to England, with its own commercial fleet and its ambassadors in every port throughout the world' (*OCPW* 125). Joyce's vision of Ireland's fleet is based on commerce rather than war, on trading with the rest of the world as opposed to fighting with it, while the idea of Ireland's ambassadors in every port emphasises a country enthusiastically engaged in international diplomacy. This is a nation at the crossroads of world trade, resuming, in Joyce's words, 'its ancient position as the Hellas of the north' (*OCPW* 124).

In 1909 Joyce made a journey to Galway to visit Nora's family. His time in the country seems to have been positive – bar a brief period when he suspected Nora of having had an affair in 1904 – and in his letters to Nora he refers to her as his 'little Galway bride' (*L2* 242), while during a trip to Cork in December 1909 he admitted that he would 'prefer to be going westward [. . .] towards those wild fields of Connacht in which God made to grow "my beautiful wild flower of the hedges, my dark-blue rain-drenched flower"' (*L2* 273).[68] Galway during this time appears to take on a romantic aura – in marked contrast to Dublin, which he describes at the same time as being 'a detestable city' where 'the people are most repulsive' (*L2* 243). Joyce returned to Galway in 1912, this time with Nora, and wrote two articles for *Il Piccolo della Sera*, one on Galway's history and the other on the Aran Islands. The first article is perhaps most fascinating for the strange temporal zone that Galway city seems to inhabit as described by Joyce. The opening paragraph of 'The City of the Tribes: Italian Memories in an Irish Port' makes clear the strange mix of provincialism and cosmopolitanism that he found in the town:

> The lazy Dubliner who does not travel much and knows his country only by hearsay thinks that the inhabitants of Galway are of Spanish stock, and that it is impossible to walk through the gloomy laneways of the city of the tribes without coming across a true Spanish type with olive features and crow-black hair. The Dubliner is both wrong and right. Nowadays, at least, dark hair and eyes are rare in Galway where, for the most part, a Titian hue of red dominates. The old Spanish houses are in ruins and tufts of weeds are growing in the splays of the bay windows. Outside the town walls rise the suburbs, new, gay and thoughtless of the past. However, it is enough to close one's eyes against this unsettling modernity just for a moment, and the 'Spanish City' can be seen in the shadows of history. (*OCPW* 197)

The first point to note here is Joyce's admonishment of the 'lazy Dubliner' who is ignorant of the west of the country – the kind of person Gabriel Conroy might be said to represent in 'The Dead'. Joyce, at this point, was clearly keen to distance himself from such a stereotype; perhaps because of his surname's strong association with Connacht and his wife's Galway origins, Joyce was now happy to disassociate himself from Dublin when the opportunity presented itself.

The object of this article, as shown by its title, was to convey Galway's historical links with Italy to Joyce's Triestine readers. However, this is more than a simple history lesson, and instead Joyce depicts Galway as a place at the crossroads between an old-world traditionalism and an 'unsettling' suburban modernity, 'thoughtless of the past'. Galway's modernity is unsettling precisely because it seems out of place in a western setting that has been lauded by Revivalists for its rural timelessness. Instead, Galway represents what Howes terms the 'perverse partial modernity' of rural Ireland.[69] Perhaps counterintuitively, Joyce has the Gaelic nature of Galway represent modernity – such as the red-hued hair taking over from the Spanish dark hair and eyes – while the cosmopolitanism of Galway's Mediterranean connections takes the place of tradition. Galway becomes a multicultural melting pot, with Joyce laying emphasis on its once thriving port, where peoples from different parts of Europe mingled:

> in the Middle Ages, these waters were ploughed by thousands of foreign ships. The signs on the street corners recall the connections of the city with Latin Europe: Madeira Street, Merchant Street, Spaniards Walk, Madeira island, Lombard Street, Velasquez Palmyra Avenue. Oliver Cromwell's letters testify that Galway was the second port of the United Kingdom, and the first in the whole kingdom for Spanish and Italian trade. (OCPW 197)

The street names represent the older cosmopolitan traditions that lurk stubbornly beneath the surface of this western town, persisting in spite of the suburban modernisation. As Joyce writes, 'it is enough to close one's eyes against this unsettling modernity just for a moment' in order to see these traditions. However, the act of 'clos[ing] one's eyes' does insinuate that any attempt to deny the historical cosmopolitanism of rural and provincial Ireland necessitates a certain self-deception. Joyce's Ireland beyond the Pale carries its traditions still, but they are inseparable from the cosmopolitan forces that have shaped them.

Ireland's harbours as being representative of cosmopolitanism also features in the 'Cyclops' episode of *Ulysses*, where the nationalist Citizen and his cronies seem to epitomise a regressive brand of Irish nationalism that only looks inward and to the past for inspiration, and that sees little contradiction in combating colonial injustice with equally racist rhetoric. This remains the dominant reading of the episode – and for good reason – though compelling revisions from critics such as Emer Nolan place emphasis on the overlap between some of the Citizen's opinions and Joyce's journalism.[70] One example is the Citizen's dream of an independent Ireland with bustling harbours, trading with the wider world:

> Our harbours that are empty will be full again, Queenstown, Kinsale, Galway, Blacksod Bay, Ventry in the kingdom of Kerry, Killybegs, the third largest harbour in the wide world with a fleet of masts of the Galway Lynches and the Cavan O'Reillys and the O'Kennedys of Dublin when the earl of Desmond could make a treaty with the emperor Charles the Fifth himself. And will again, says he, when the first Irish battleship is seen breasting the waves with our own flag to the fore, none of your Henry Tudor's harps, no, the oldest flag afloat, the flag of the province of Desmond and Thomond, three crowns on a blue field, the three sons of Milesius. (*U* 12.1301–10)

The Citizen's vision is one of a rejuvenated rural Ireland – each harbour he mentions is located along the western coast, facing towards the 'New World'. The new flag he imagines flying at the foremast of Irish battleships is that of Munster ('the province of Desmond and Thomond') rather than the harp of Leinster, an emphasis on the supposed heart of Gaelic Ireland as opposed to the English-influenced Pale.

While the emphasis on a future Ireland crafted in the image of the rural west is not surprising, the fact that this west would be defined by its engagement with the rest of the world is significant. The Citizen sees this not as a wholly new endeavour but as a return to a previous way of life in Ireland, one that existed in constant dialogue with Europe: 'And our eyes are on Europe, says the citizen. We had our trade with Spain and the French and with the Flemings before those mongrels were pupped, Spanish ale in Galway, the winebark on the winedark waterway' (*U* 12.1296–8). Despite the Citizen's evident xenophobia – '[w]e want no more strangers in our house' (*U* 12.1150–1) – his idealised rural Ireland is a modern, cosmopolitan one, reviving old connections with Europe, connections that have been cut off since British colonisation. As Pearson argues, the nation-alists in this episode are 'trying in their own way to imagine Ireland *internationally*'.[71] In contrast to Ireland – which J. J. O'Molloy, one of the Citizen's fellow barspongers, sees as being part of '[t]he Euro-pean family' (*U* 12.1202) – Britain is viewed as being removed from continental culture. The British, the Citizen argues, are 'not Euro-pean [. . .] You wouldn't see a trace of them or their language any-where in Europe except in a *cabinet d'aisance*' (*U* 12.1203–5). The Citizen's nationalism – while certainly xenophobic, racist and overly insistent on the past – remains, almost in spite of itself, cosmopoli-tan. He parrots, perhaps unwittingly and without full comprehen-sion, the kind of attitudes that more sophisticated nationalists such as Pearse espoused when they encouraged Irish nationalists to look towards Europe for inspiration. It is quite clear, however, whatever the overlaps, that Joyce's image of an independent Ireland differs significantly from the Citizen's, rejecting a myopic notion of a pure Gaelic past and future. Their differences might best be summed up by comparing the new ships that each imagines filling Irish waters and harbours: where for the Citizen these are battleships, for Joyce they are trading vessels.

In Joyce's final work, *Finnegans Wake*, he stages a prolonged clash between cosmopolitanism and provincialism/nationalism through the bitter brotherly battles of Shem and Shaun. The brothers echo the rela-tionship between Joyce and Stanislaus,[72] though primarily they stand for varying ideologies of nationhood, with Shem an exilic cosmopoli-tan living in Europe and Shaun a regressive nationalist who has more in common with post-independence nationalism in Ireland, a 'devil era' presided over by the Catholic conservatism of Éamon de Valera (*FW* 473.8). Shaun is emblematic of a generation of Catholic revolu-tionaries, greatly influenced by the cultural nationalism of the Revival, who would go on to shape the twenty-six counties of the Irish Free State. Like de Valera, Shaun exalts rural Ireland over the urban centre of Dublin, and at one point he is renamed 'rural Haun' (*FW* 471.35).

Shaun has much in common with the more egregious characteris-tics of the Citizen; he is even dressed in a similar attire to the national-ist. Joyce, as part of the gigantism of 'Cyclops', at one point has the Citizen wear what is apparently traditional clothing, placing emphasis on the animals that have provided its source material:

a long unsleeved garment of recently flayed oxhide reaching to the knees in a loose kilt and this was bound about his middle by a girdle of plaited straw and rushes. Beneath this he wore trews of deerskin, roughly stitched with gut. His nether extremities were encased in high Balbriggan buskins dyed in lichen purple, the feet being shod with brogues of salted cowhide laced with the windpipe of the same beast. (*U* 12.168–73)

Meanwhile, in *Finnegans Wake*, Shaun is

dressed like an earl in just the correct wear, in a classy mac Frieze o'coat of far suparior ruggedness, indigo braw, tracked and tramped, and an Irish ferrier collar, freeswinging with mereswin lacers from his shoulthern and thick welted brogues on him hammered to suit the scotsmost public and climate [. . .] (*FW* 404.16–21)

Like that of the Citizen, Shaun's clothing does not disguise the animals from which it derives: where the Citizen is covered in the hides of oxen, deer and cows, the collar of Shaun's coat would appear to be composed of the skin of an Irish terrier ('Irish ferrier collar')[73] while the laces swinging from his shoulders seem to come from mereswine, an archaic term for dolphins or porpoises. Both also wear traditional brogues, footwear associated with the Irish peasantry, while Shaun's 'mac Frieze o'coat' is a reference to the traditional Irish 'frieze-coat', made of coarse woollen cloth, which, as the *OED* notes, became a byword for an Irish peasant (*OED*, 'frieze, n.1', 1).

Shaun and the Citizen attempt to portray themselves as rugged noblemen ('suparior ruggedness') akin to ancient chieftains. Ironically, however, both seem to have melded what they believe are the traditions of Irish clothing with those of its perhaps more famous Celtic equivalent in Scotland. The Citizen wears a kilt, while Shaun's shoes have been 'hammered to suit the *scotsmost* public and climate' (*FW* 404.20–1, my emphasis). Hugh Trevor-Roper puts forward the kilt and the Highland garb of Scotland in general as an example of a Hobsbawmian 'invented tradition' by showing that it has little to do with ancient ways of Celtic dress and is instead 'a purely modern costume' popularised by the upper and middle classes, who began to wear it as part of the nineteenth-century tendency to romanticise the supposed primitiveness of Highland life.[74] It is perhaps of little surprise then that immediately following this paragraph, Shaun is described as 'a picture primitive' (*FW* 405.3). The adoption of the kilt as a symbol of Irish nationalism first occurred as part of Revivalism, and seemingly has little basis in ancient Irish sartorial culture before this point.[75] The confusion and melding together of Irish and Scottish culture by nationalists such as the Citizen and Shaun undercuts the supposed authenticity of these traditions (or at least the nationalists' conception of them). Towards the end of this description of Shaun, 'the blessings of God and Mary and Haggispatrick' are invoked, another blending of Scottish and Irish stereotypes (FW 404.34–5). Shaun, despite his nationalism, seems little better than any ignorant observer who is happy to collapse all Celtic cultures into one indifferentiable whole. And yet, despite this ironic ignorance, Shaun and the Citizen, by their attire, also bear witness to the cosmopolitan nature of Irish nationalism and its tendency to look beyond the boundaries of its own nation for influence and inspiration. The adoption of the kilt, though hypocritical in terms of its fake authenticity, is at the same time proof of an ability to imagine or invent new traditions, a desire to see opportunities for the reinvention and transformation of national identity. It embodies, in many ways, the complexities and ironies of the Janus-faced nature of decolonising communities, by harking back to a past that doesn't exist in order to create a future that might.

However, Shaun's harking back to the past takes on a more pernicious edge in III.2 during his sermon to the girls of St Bride's, as he embodies the nastier, more racially focused elements of Irish nationalism. Len Platt draws particular attention to this chapter and Shaun's performance in it, noting how 'he attempts to stamp his puritanist authority over the twenty-nine girls, warning them about the dangers of modernity, demanding their modesty and insisting on the importance of tradition and the national culture'.[76] Shaun's brand of nationalism resembles that espoused by D. P. Moran, the vituperative journalist and leader of the movement known as 'Irish Irelandism'. A favourite proposition of Moran, parroted by the Citizen in *Ulysses*, was to build an Irish nation that would be 'racy of the soil', a phrase taken from the motto of Thomas Davis's nationalist newspaper *The Nation*.[77] Variants of this phrase occur throughout *Finnegans Wake*, such as when a 'right-down regular racer from the soil' is opposed to 'a too pained whittlewit laden with the loot of learning' (FW 108.5–7). Here, the earthy, honest nationalist lies on the opposite end of the spectrum to the bespectacled ('too pained': two-paned) scholar, worn down with the stolen load of learning, where learning itself is associated with cultural theft.[78] Once again, there is suspicion regarding what might be termed 'intellectual cosmopolitanism', which here seems to resemble coloniality in its proclivity for cultural appropriation. However, in III.2, the phrase is linked entirely to a narrow, racialised form of conservative nationalism:

> The racist to the racy, rossy. The soil is for the self alone. Be own-kind. Be kithkinish. Be bloodysibby. Be irish. Be inish. Be offalia. Be hamlet. Be the property plot. Be Yorick and Lankystare. Be cool. Be mackinamucks of yourselves. Be finish. (*FW* 465.30–4)

The sense of this expression is here reduced to an insular nationalism based on narrow definitions of Irishness. The political philosophy of Sinn Féin has taken on its most literal and limited meaning, the motto 'we ourselves' resulting in a view of the world epitomised by '[t]he soil is for the self alone. Be ownkind. Be kithkinish', leaving no room for outside influence. The tragedy of such an isolationist view of the world, exemplified by de Valera's protectionist economic policies whereby excessive tariffs were imposed on imported goods, is summed up towards the end of the *Wake* in the pithy '[o]urselves, oursouls alone' (*FW* 623.28–9). Shaun, like de Valera, manipulates rurality in outlining his narrow vision of Irishness, gesturing towards 'the soil'. He tells the girls to '[b]e mackinamucks of yourselves', which might be translated from this pseudo-Irish as 'be sons of pigs of yourselves' (*mac*: 'son'; *muc*: 'pig'), reducing Irish aspiration to nothing beyond the farmyard. This vision of rural life is one that is closed off to the external world and utterly individualistic ('for the self alone'), in marked contrast to the internationalism and collectivism that rural Ireland had demonstrated previously. With such a perspective, Shaun can distort Hamlet and Ophelia, synonymous with the Englishness (or perhaps even the universality) of Shakespeare, into the rural Irish county of Offaly and nothing more than a small village. Everything, in such a myopic worldview, must become local, parochial, Irish. This is an uncritical provincialism to counterpoint an uncritical cosmopolitanism – where one globalises, the other localises, but both efface.

Shaun's regressive nationalism and his embrace of racist tropes stands in contrast to the distinction that Benedict Anderson draws between nationalism and racism. Anderson writes that despite the tendency for 'cosmopolitan intellectuals' to insist upon the racist character of nationalism, 'it is useful to remind ourselves that nations inspire love, and often profoundly self-sacrificing love'.[79] Unlike racism, which Anderson suggests 'dreams of eternal contaminations, transmitted from the origins of time', 'nationalism thinks in terms of historical destinies'.[80] Historical destinies are by definition a dream of the future, an attempt to grapple with modernity and shape its trajectory. Shaun, as a post-independence nationalist, working to cement the status quo rather than upend it, no longer dreams of

future destinies, instead focusing too heavily on the 'eternal contaminations'. As Platt notes, 'it is a specific version of republicanism and
nationalism that is being attacked here, rather than republicanism
and nationalism *per se*'.[81] In contrast to a figure such as Molly Ivors,
who is attempting to secure a concept of nationhood not yet in existence, Shaun embodies a state-sanctioned official nationalism that
secures its dominance through the denial of outside influence. In contrast even to the likes of the Citizen, who at least nominally speaks
of setting his 'eyes [. . .] on Europe' (*U* 12.1296), Shaun primarily
looks inwards and seeks to entrench a carefully edited version of the
national past and the rural present.

This obsession with the past is noted by the girls at the end of the
chapter, as they wish 'rural Haun' well as he sets off on his 'photo-
phoric pilgrimage to your antipodes in the past' (*FW* 472.17–18).
This pilgrimage to the past is in marked contrast to the peregrinations of Shaun's cosmopolitan brother, Shem.[82] Throughout the
Wake, Shaun lambasts Shem's worldliness by calling him a 'Euro-
pasianised Afferyank', as though Shem's cosmopolitanism has made
him a citizen of everywhere *but* Ireland (*FW* 191.4). Shaun lauds his
own rooted rurality in contrast to Shem's wandering around Europe,
saying '[m]y ruridecanal caste is a cut above you peregrines' (*FW*
484.28–9). Here, Shaun imagines himself as a rural dean, affirming
the twin idealisation that post-independence nationalism has made
of rural Ireland and the Church. By contrast, Shem is a peregrine, a
wanderer or foreigner.[83] The etymological root of 'peregrine' is the
Latin *peregrinus*, which referred to a free provincial subject who was
not from Rome, and therefore did not hold Roman citizenship.[84]
'Peregrine', as it is used in English, therefore makes a cosmopolitan
out of the provincial – a neat description for how Shaun views Shem.
Ireland's provincialism is the reason for Shem's exile, as we are told
that 'provencials drollo eggspilled him out of his homety dometry
narrowedknee domum (osco de basco de pesco de bisco!) because
all his creature comfort was an omulette finas erbas in an ark finis
orbe' (*FW* 230.5–8). This interpretation sees Shem being expelled
('eggspilled') out of his 'homety dometry' by 'provencials'. It is a
'domum' (from the Latin *domus*, meaning 'home') that is 'narrowedknee' in its outlook, with Shem finding more 'creature comfort' in
cities ('ark' echoes the Latin *arx* meaning 'citadel') at the end of the
world ('finis orbe') than in Ireland.[85] The provincial nature of Ireland
is emphasised by the number of words here that come from Pro-
vençal: 'drollo' (from *drola*) meaning 'girl'; 'osco' meaning 'bravo';
'basco' meaning 'Basque'; 'pesco' meaning 'to fish'; 'bisco' meaning

'soup' or 'ill humour'; and 'erbo' meaning 'herb'.[86] The use of the Humpty Dumpty metaphor – complete with the 'eggspilled' imagery – suggests that Shem has in some sense been broken by his exile (at least according to Shaun).

The typically contradictory Joycean notion that Shem's exile was embraced as an escape from Ireland while also being something that Ireland forced upon him against his will is clear from this passage. And yet, for all this, Shem is never fully removed from Ireland: Shaun likes to point out the hypocrisy he sees in Shem's homesickness, particularly when he returns 'home to mourn mountains from his old continence', a reference to the Mourne Mountains in County Down (*FW* 462.32–3). Meanwhile Issy, in the footnotes to the Night Lessons chapter, mocks Shem by noting that 'we float the meditarenias and come bask to the isle we love in spice' (*FW* 263.F2). Coming from Issy's more neutral point of view, this reveals that for all Shem's exilic wandering, there remains a love in spite of all for his home.

It is important not to dismiss Shaun as nothing more than a conservative, nationalist yin to Shem's progressive, cosmopolitan yang; in fact, Joyce blurs the distinction between the two when we are told that '[t]he gist is the gist of Shaum but the hand is the hand of Sameas' (*FW* 483.3–4). Often, Shaun acts the part of Shem's consciousness which is still unsure of the validity of the decisions he has made, the voice of guilt that plagues him 'about why he left Dublin [. . .] as an Inishman was as good as any cantonnatal' (*FW* 91.21–3). The question is posed again when Shem (as Glugg) asks himself '[w]as liffe worth leaving?' (*FW* 230.25). This is not just the fundamental question of whether life is worth living, but also whether the Liffey (Irish: *An Life*), and therefore Dublin, was worth leaving all those years before – to which he immediately provides his own emphatic answer in the (Danish) negative: 'Nej!' (*FW* 230.25). Shem, for all his worldly wanderings, remains something of a provincial – he is not entirely the 'Sameas' Shaun, but he is not totally different either.

Forget, Remember

Anderson, in *Imagined Communities*, draws attention to an Ernest Renan quotation regarding the need for the people of a nation to 'forget' many things. Renan writes that 'the essence of a nation is that all the individuals have many things in common and also have forgotten many things . . . Each French citizen *is required to have forgotten* Saint-Barthélemy, the massacres of the South in the thirteenth century.'[87] Renan takes as a given that for a nation to have any sense of togetherness, these past intra-national conflicts *need* to be forgotten by the people. This communal amnesia is certainly vital for nationalism to take hold, but it is equally true that nations exist in a constant state of flux between remembering and forgetting. As James Clifford writes:

> Living traditions must be selectively pure: mixing, matching, remembering, forgetting, sustaining, transforming their senses of communal continuity [. . .] Moreover, in a context of decolonizing tribal activism, it becomes easier to recognize that native societies have always been both backward and forward looking. Loyalty to a traditional past is, in practice, a way ahead, a distinct path in the present.[88]

Ireland, at the turn of the century, as an emerging decolonising nation, existed in this state between constant remembrance and forced forgetting of the past. Indeed, Deane writes that 'Joyce's Ireland was a perfect example of this dual state of remembering and forgetting everything'.[89] Deane sees Revivalist Ireland as engaged in an act of rewriting the past, but even without fabrication or invention – if that were possible – the turn towards a traditional past raises its own problems. To remember everything is to be stuck in a state of stasis, unable to move forward; to forget one's past is ultimately to create a false future. The act of nation-building evidently requires a constant flitting between the two.

Towards the end of the *Wake*, Joyce gestures one final time towards these plaguing issues. In the final *ricorso*, Part IV, following the debate between St Patrick and the archdruid and just before ALP reveals the contents of the letter, there is a brief interlude filled with references to questions of the past, nationality and rural matters. Previous sections of the *Wake* are briefly referenced, such as the Ondt and the Gracehoper, which now become '[o]wned or grazeheifer, ethel or bonding' (*FW* 613.36–614.1). This appears to nod to the land issues that dominated rural Ireland, such as the larger, grazier farmers mentioned in the previous chapter, as well as the Revivalist dream of an alliance between the aristocracy and the peasantry – 'ethel' and 'bonding' reference the Danish *ædel*, 'nobleman', and *bonde*, 'peasant'.[90] The notion of traditional, rural Ireland being worshipped with a kind of religious devotion by the likes of Russell is alluded to with the prayer offered, 'for the farmer, his son and their homely codes' (*FW* 614.31–2). But such fixations on the past leave no room for life in the present or the future, as highlighted by the line: 'Since ancient was our living is in possible to be' (*FW* 614.9–10). To be fixated on the past is to make living in the present 'in possible'. Joyce instead places emphasis on the need to strike a balance between past and present, remembering and forgetting:

> What has gone? How it ends?
>   Begin to forget it. It will remember itself from every sides, with all gestures, in each our word. Today's truth, tomorrow's trend.
>   Forget, remember! (*FW* 614.19–22)

Though we are encouraged to '[b]egin to forget it', there is a realisation here that the past can never fully be erased. Instead, '[i]t will remember itself', embodied by our 'gestures, in each our word'. That which seems novel and modern now ('Today's truth') becomes hackneyed and passé later ('tomorrow's trend'). This final exhortation to '[f]orget, remember' in some way counteracts the danger inherent in giving oneself over to one side of the binary. It recommends instead the necessary Janus-faced perspective, the eyes that look both to the past and to the future, internally and externally, the circularity embodied by Anna Livia herself as she flows out to the sea and rises into the clouds to fall again. Such is the circularity inherent in how decolonising nations negotiate questions of cosmopolitanism and provincialism. Joyce's reflections on the political debates in the Ireland of his youth caution against the denial of either half of the many binaries that dominated the country – modernity and tradition, cosmopolitanism and provincialism, urbanity and rurality. Instead, his writings imagine a more inclusive dream of nationhood, one that encourages the Irish citizen to both remember and forget, to be both 'ruric' *and* 'cospolite'.

Notes

1. McHugh, *Annotations*, 309.
2. Vincent J. Cheng, '"Terrible Queer Creatures": Joyce, Cosmopolitanism, and the Inauthentic Irishman', in Michael Patrick Gillespie (ed.), *James Joyce and the Fabrication of an Irish Identity* (Amsterdam: Rodopi, 2001), 12.
3. Mathews, *Revival*, 4.
4. Ibid., 11.
5. Wim Van Mierlo, *James Joyce and Cultural Genetics: The Joycean Genome* (London: Bloomsbury Academic, 2023), 24.
6. Ibid., 30.

7. Ezra Pound, '"Dubliners" and Mr. James Joyce', *The Egoist* 1/14 (1914), 267.
8. Van Mierlo, *James Joyce and Cultural Genetics*, 30.
9. Ibid., 30.
10. Stephanie Boland makes this point in an article on Joyce's interaction with Cornish motifs in *Finnegans Wake*, writing that the national versus cosmopolitan debate in Joycean criticism has 'led critics largely to overlook the specificity of the rural, regional locations featured in his writing'. Stephanie Boland, 'The "Cornish Tokens" of *Finnegans Wake*: A Journey Through the Celtic Archipelago', *James Joyce Quarterly* 54/1 (2016), 106.
11. Seamus Deane, 'Joyce the Irishman', in Derek Attridge (ed.), *The Cambridge Companion to James Joyce*, 2nd edn (Cambridge: Cambridge University Press, 2004), 39.
12. Pheng Cheah, 'Introduction Part II: The Cosmopolitical – Today', in Pheng Cheah and Bruce Robbins (eds), *Cosmopolitics: Thinking and Feeling Beyond the Nation* (Minneapolis, MN: University of Minnesota Press, 1998), 22.
13. Kevin Whelan, 'The Memories of "The Dead"', *The Yale Journal of Criticism* 15/1 (2002), 65.
14. John Eglinton, W. B. Yeats, Æ and William Larminie (eds), *Literary Ideals in Ireland* (London: T. Fisher Unwin, 1899), 5.
15. For an outline of the overall critical context in which the *Express* debates took place in Revivalist Ireland, see Gerry Smyth, 'Irish Literary Criticism During the Revival', in Marjorie Elizabeth Howes (ed.), *Irish Literature in Transition, 1880–1940*, IV (Cambridge: Cambridge University Press, 2020), 339–55.
16. Eglinton et al., *Literary Ideals*, 9.
17. John Eglinton, *Anglo-Irish Essays* (Dublin: The Talbot Press, 1917), 4.
18. Ibid., 4.
19. Ibid., 5–6.
20. Cuguan [Arthur Griffith], 'Our Living Irish Writers,' *United Irishman*, 5 October 1901, 3, cited in Bonnie Kime Scott, 'John Eglinton: A Model for Joyce's Individualism', *James Joyce Quarterly* 12/4 (1975), 347.
21. Ellmann, *Consciousness of Joyce*, 107.
22. Scott, 'John Eglinton', 347.
23. Eglinton et al., *Literary Ideals*, 27.
24. Ibid., 42.
25. Ibid., 80.
26. Ibid., 82.
27. Ibid., 85.
28. Ibid., 82.
29. Æ, *Imaginations and Reveries*, 20.
30. Ibid., 20.

31. Ibid., ix–x.
32. Giuseppe Mazzini, *The Duties of Man*, extracted in Omar Dahbour and Micheline R. Ishay (eds), *The Nationalism Reader* (Atlantic Highlands, NJ: Humanities Press, 1995), 91–4, cited in Cheah, 'Introduction Part II', 25.
33. Sun Yat-sen, *San Min Chu I: The Three Principles of the People*, trans. Frank Price (Shanghai: China Committee, Institute of Pacific Relations, 1927), 89, cited in Cheah, 'Introduction Part II', 30.
34. Eglinton et al., *Literary Ideals*, 12.
35. Indeed, Eglinton's initial article appears to cast a long shadow over Joyce's career, with echoes of it to be found years later in *Ulysses*. For example, Eglinton concludes his article by proclaiming that '[i]n all ages poets and thinkers have owed far less to their countries than their countries have owed to them' (ibid., 13), a sentiment that Stephen Dedalus repeats in 'Circe' when he says to Private Carr: 'You die for your country [. . .] But I say: Let my country die for me' (*U* 15.4471–3).
36. Eglinton et al., *Literary Ideals*, 42.
37. T. S. Eliot, '*Ulysses*, Order and Myth', in *Selected Prose of T.S. Eliot*, ed. Frank Kermode (San Diego, CA: Harcourt, 1975), 178.
38. Margot Norris, '*Finnegans Wake*', in Derek Attridge (ed.), *The Cambridge Companion to James Joyce*, 2nd edn (Cambridge: Cambridge University Press, 2004), 172.
39. Cheah, 'Introduction Part II', 22.
40. Ibid., 25.
41. Ibid., 25.
42. Bruce Robbins, 'Introduction Part I: Actually Existing Cosmopolitanism', in Pheng Cheah and Bruce Robbins (eds), *Cosmopolitics: Thinking and Feeling Beyond the Nation* (Minneapolis, MN: University of Minnesota Press, 1998), 2.
43. Cheah, 'Introduction Part II', 25–6.
44. Tom Nairn also uses the metaphor of Janus to describe the way in which nationalism navigates the passage into modernity, looking into the past in order to gather strength for its future development, though he writes that '[i]n reality, this threshold of modernity has been a prolonged, dark passage for most of the world' (85). I treat the term here with more emphasis on its emancipatory, even cosmopolitan potential. See Tom Nairn, *The Break-Up of Britain: Crisis and Neo-Nationalism*, 2nd edn (1977; London: Verso, 1981), 329–63.
45. Louis de Paor, 'Réamhrá | Introduction', in Louis de Paor (ed.), *Leabhar na hAthghabhála: Poems of Repossession* (Hexham: Bloodaxe, 2016), 20.
46. Ibid., 21.
47. Scarlett Baron, '*Strandentwining Cable': Joyce, Flaubert, and Intertextuality* (Oxford: Oxford University Press, 2012), 180–1.

48. 'Gléo na gCath', *An Claidheamh Soluis*, 22 August 1903, cited in Philip O'Leary, *The Prose Literature of the Gaelic Revival, 1881–1921: Ideology and Innovation* (University Park, PA: Pennsylvania State University Press, 1994), 56.

49. Ibid., 56.

50. Walter Mignolo, 'The Many Faces of Cosmo-polis: Border Thinking and Critical Cosmopolitanism', *Public Culture* 12/3 (2000), 722.

51. Ibid., 722.

52. Ibid., 722.

53. Ibid., 723.

54. Ibid., 722–3.

55. Ibid., 723.

56. Ibid., 744.

57. E. A. Boyd, *Appreciations and Depreciations* (Dublin: The Talbot Press, 1918), 157, cited in Kiberd, *Inventing Ireland*, 160.

58. Mathews, *Revival*, 13.

59. McHugh, *Annotations*, 488.

60. Nels Pearson, *Irish Cosmopolitanism: Location and Dislocation in James Joyce, Elizabeth Bowen, and Samuel Beckett* (Gainesville, FL: University Press of Florida, 2015), 5.

61. Ibid., 8.

62. Whelan, 'The Memories of "The Dead"', 66.

63. Ibid., 66–7.

64. Owens, 'The Mystique of the West', 82.

65. Joyce wrote at least twenty reviews for the unionist-leaning *Daily Express* between December 1902 and November 1903. Kevin Barry writes that '[t]he few years that separate Joyce, the reviewer of the *Daily Express*, from Joyce, the lecturer and journalist in Trieste, display a reversal in his argument with Irish nationalism' (*OCPW* ix).

66. For a complication of the notion of Gabriel as a modern counterpart to Ivors's traditionalism, see Anne Fogarty, '"I Think He Died for Me": Memory and Ethics in 'The Dead"', in Oona Frawley and Katherine O'Callaghan (eds), *Memory Ireland: James Joyce and Cultural Memory*, IV (Syracuse, NY: Syracuse University Press, 2014), 46–61. Fogarty notes that the speech Gabriel gives is laden with references to Ireland's antiquity and traditions, writing that '[a]lthough Gabriel might present himself as urban, European, and cosmopolitan, his discourse belies this image as it indicates that he too is caught up with "sad memories" of a past that he has difficulty in keeping at bay' (53).

67. This theory is, unsurprisingly, not accepted among historical linguists today. For more on Joyce's interest in the Phoenicians, see Elizabeth Butler Cullingford, 'Phoenician Genealogies and Oriental Geographies: Joyce, Language and Race', in Marjorie Howes and Derek Attridge (eds), *Semicolonial Joyce* (Cambridge: Cambridge University Press, 2000), 219–39.

68. Joyce is in fact quoting himself here from a letter he sent to Nora in November 1909 (*L2* 266). He returns to this image at several points over this period, drawing an implicit association between Nora and rurality/nature. In a letter on 22 December he writes that 'I would pray that my soul be scattered in the wind if God would but let me blow softly for ever about one strange lonely dark-blue rain-drenched flower in a wild hedge at Aughrim or Oranmore' (*L2* 278).

69. Howes, '"Goodbye Ireland"', 65.

70. See Emer Nolan, '"Talking about Injustice": Parody, Satire and Invective in *Ulysses*', in *James Joyce and Nationalism* (London: Routledge, 1995), 85–119.

71. Pearson, *Irish Cosmopolitanism*, 29.

72. The names themselves are the first clue: Shem is a shortened form of Séamus, the Irish form of James, while Shaun is an anglicised spelling of Seán, the Irish form of John (Stanislaus's full name, like his father, was John Stanislaus Joyce). Stanislaus, however, at no point appeared to indulge in the kind of nationalism espoused by Shaun – if anything, Stanislaus was arguably even more of a committed cosmopolitan (or at least a more hostile opponent of an Irish-centred view of the world) than his brother. Speaking of his brother's interest in Gaelic bardic poetry, Stanislaus writes that 'Jim was not limitary in his sympathies as I was; they extended in Ireland from Mangan and Yeats to the unlettered poets of the rugged glens' (*MBK* 133–4).

73. McHugh notes that this is likely a reference to Ferrier, Pollock and Company, which manufactured textiles in Dublin from the nineteenth century (McHugh, *Annotations*, 404).

74. Hugh Trevor-Roper, 'The Invention of Tradition: The Highland Tradition of Scotland', in Eric Hobsbawm and Terence Ranger (eds), *The Invention of Tradition* (Cambridge: Cambridge University Press, 1983), 22, 24.

75. Timothy O'Neill, *Life and Tradition in Rural Ireland* (London: Dent, 1977), 44.

76. Len Platt, *Joyce, Race and 'Finnegans Wake'* (Cambridge: Cambridge University Press, 2007), 64.

77. Cheng, '"Terrible Queer Creatures"', 35. For Moran's use of the term, see *The Philosophy of Irish Ireland*, 7. Meanwhile the narrator of 'Cyclops' discusses how the barspongers 'started about Irish sports and shoneen games the like of lawn tennis and about hurley and putting the stone and racy of the soil and building up a nation once again and all to that' (*U* 12.889–91).

78. McHugh, *Annotations*, 108.

79. Benedict Anderson, *Imagined Communities: Reflections on the Origin and Spread of Nationalism* (1983; London: Verso, 2016), 141.

80. Ibid., 149.

81. Platt, *Joyce, Race and 'Finnegans Wake'*, 66.

82. Shem's cosmopolitanism is obliquely noted in the Ondt and Gracehoper section of the *Wake*, where Shem, as Ondt, is described as a 'weltall fellow' (*FW* 416.3), *weltall* being the German for 'universe' or 'cosmos' (McHugh, *Annotations*, 416).

83. Two of the Four Masters who compiled the *Annals of the Four Masters* that feature so prominently in the *Wake* anglicised their first names to Peregrine: Peregrine O'Clery and Peregrine O'Duignan. That both took on a name that lays emphasis on travelling attests to an easy cosmopolitanism at the core of Gaelic Ireland. The Four Masters will be discussed in further detail in Chapter 6.

84. A. N. Sherwin-White and Andrew William Lintott, 'peregrini', in *The Oxford Classical Dictionary* (Oxford: Oxford University Press, 2005), https://www.oxfordreference.com/view/10.1093/acref/9780198606413.001.0001/acref-9780198606413-e-4859 (accessed 20 April 2020).

85. McHugh, *Annotations*, 230.

86. Ibid., 230.

87. 'l'essence d'une nation est que tous les individus aient beaucoup de choses en commun et aussi que tous aient oublié bien des choses . . . Tout citoyen français *doit avoir oublié* la Saint-Barthélemy, les massacres du Midi au XIIIe siècle.' Ernest Renan, 'Qu'est-ce qu'une nation?', in *Œuvres Complètes*, I (Paris: Calmann-Lévy, 1947–61), 892, cited in Anderson, *Imagined Communities*, 199. (My translation.)

88. James Clifford, 'Traditional Futures', in Mark Salber Phillips and Gordon Schochet (eds), *Questions of Tradition* (Toronto: University of Toronto Press, 2004), 156.

89. Seamus Deane, 'Introduction', in James Joyce, *Finnegans Wake* (1939; London: Penguin, 2000), xviii.

90. McHugh, *Annotations*, 614.

Chapter 3

'Sing the peasantry': Joyce's Peasantry from *Stephen Hero* to *A Portrait of the Artist as a Young Man*

In 'Under Ben Bulben', one of the last poems W. B. Yeats wrote before his death in 1939, the old Revivalist commands the coming generations of Irish poets to '[s]ing the peasantry'.[1] This line comes in the poem's fifth section, which is a rallying cry to uphold the values and ideals of the Irish Literary Revival, among the most conspicuous of which was the idealisation of the Irish peasantry. Located typically in the rural west of Ireland and heralded for their romantic poverty and supposed folk spirituality, the peasantry represented the last repository of a glorious Gaelic past, while also providing a blueprint for the ideal citizen in a new Ireland yet to be realised. Almost every Revivalist in some way set out to 'sing the peasantry', with Revivalist plays at the height of the movement often judged by the degree of their 'PQ', or peasant quality.[2] Indeed, Len Platt describes the Revival as encompassing 'a culture of peasant worship'.[3]

One writer who is generally seen to have represented the antithesis of this culture is James Joyce, whom Ezra Pound described as being unique among Irish writers in *not* being 'an institution for the promotion of Irish peasant industries'.[4] From his earliest writings Joyce rejected the literary idealisation of the Irish peasantry, and even as late as *Finnegans Wake* he continued to describe Ireland as 'Emeraldilluim, the peasant pastured', with a populace composed of 'helotsphilots', or serf-lovers (*FW* 62.11–16).[5] Joyce's fraught relationship with the Revival has had the unfortunate result of encouraging readers to oversimplify – or outright ignore – his portrayal of the peasantry throughout his writings. This chapter seeks to correct this by delving into that most Revivalist of criteria in his work – his level of 'PQ'. Joyce's peasant characters bear little resemblance to the 'airish pleasantry' found in most Revivalist texts, as he offers a depiction of this social group that eschews facile idealisation (*FW* 344.18). In particular, I will focus here on the development between the posthumously published surviving manuscript of *Stephen Hero* and *A Portrait of the Artist as a Young Man*, as Joyce composes his own unique song of the peasantry.

Before going any further, it is important to acknowledge that the term 'peasant' is inherently problematic. It was used to refer to the impoverished tenant farmers by those outside this group, usually middle- or upper-class observers. Coming from the Latin *pagensis*, meaning 'the country or a country district', the *OED* notes that in addition to its primary definition of '[a] person who lives in the country and works on the land', the word has also acquired the pejorative sense of 'a person of low social status; an ignorant, stupid, unsophisticated, or (formerly esp.) unprincipled person; a boor, a lout; (also more generally) a person who is regarded with scorn or contempt, esp. by members of a particular social group' (*OED*, 'peasant, *n*. and *adj*.', 1a, 2). Unsurprisingly, therefore, Irish tenant farmers were unlikely to refer to themselves by such a term. In an essay on literary depictions of the Irish peasantry, Edward Hirsch notes that in Seumas O'Kelly's 1922 novel *Wet Clay*, one old woman is referred to as a 'peasant' by a visiting American, to whom she responds with mock incredulity: 'Faith, I never knew that until you came across the ocean to tell us' and affirms that '[w]e never call ourselves peasants'.[6] Another character remarks that '[i]t is only writers of books who have insisted upon our peasantry under all conditions'.[7] Leaving aside the obvious irony that a writer of fiction is putting these words into this particular 'peasant's' mouth, the general point made here by O'Kelly is important: the 'Irish peasantry' is more truthfully an aesthetic rather than a social category. Indeed, Hirsch refers to the creation of the literary peasantry as the '"aestheticizing" of the Irish country people', noting that '[s]uch aestheticizing takes place whenever a complex historical group of people is necessarily simplified by being collapsed into one entity'.[8] The fact that so many writers – and indeed critics – refer to 'the peasant' in the singular is proof of this continued collapsing into one unindividualised entity. Certainly, the more accurate term to use, from a sociological and historical perspective, would be 'tenant farmers' or 'landless labourers'; however, as this chapter is primarily focused on the aesthetic and literary depictions of this social group, it makes sense to continue to refer to 'the peasantry'.

It is important to bear in mind that all of the portrayals of the peasantry discussed in this chapter are necessarily rooted in aestheticisation, including the more unromanticised versions provided by Joyce. John Wilson Foster has argued that Joyce can be viewed as 'a realist doing the dirty work for romantics', and, while over-simplified as a general description, this seems to be particularly relevant to his portrayal of the peasantry.[9] While living in Paris, Joyce remarked to Arthur Power that 'one of the things I could never get accustomed to in my youth was the difference I found between life and literature',[10] while his brother Stanislaus reflected that James often said that 'literature provided men and women with false consciences, literary consciences' (*MBK* 106). In his depiction of the Irish peasantry, we can detect Joyce's aestheticised response to the perceived falsities of previous aestheticisations, founded often on colonial and primitivist clichés.

This chapter will argue that Joyce's peasantry, while necessarily another literary caricature, cannot be fully understood without considering the *idées reçues* against which he was reacting. It will do so by first delving into the nineteenth-century colonial and primitivist stereotypes of the Irish peasantry, before going on to examine Joyce's portrayal of individual peasant characters, such as Davin/Madden, and charting the development in his depictions of the peasantry in terms of smell and sexuality. In conclusion I will argue that Joyce provides the reader with a representation of the peasantry that is profoundly modern and essential to any understanding of Ireland or, indeed, as Stephen might put it, the conscience of the Irish race.

The Primitivisation of the Peasantry

The Revival's idealisation of the Irish peasantry can be read as a reaction against the negative depictions of the peasantry found throughout British colonial writing, most especially from the mid-nineteenth century, following the devastation wreaked by the Great Famine. The Irish peasantry's impoverished state provided colonialists with an easy target in emphasising their right to rule over a supposedly debased race. For example, Platt quotes from the English historian James Anthony Froude, who characterised the people of Catholic Ireland as 'more like tribes of squalid apes than human beings'.[11] Vincent Cheng's *Joyce, Race, and Empire* (1995) provides a useful background to this dehumanisation, with Cheng noting how nineteenth-century accounts give witness to a colonial rendering of the Irish peasantry as 'anthropoid apes'.[12] For Cheng, such accounts show the influence of Darwin, as the Irish peasantry is increasingly viewed as the 'missing link' between humans and apes.[13] Cheng's reading is heavily influenced by the work of L. Perry Curtis, who first drew attention to the simianisation of the Irish peasantry in his 1971 work *Apes and Angels: The Irishman in Victorian Caricature*. Curtis examines cartoons from Victorian periodicals, in particular *Punch*, noting how they transformed 'peasant Paddy into an ape-man or simianized Caliban'.[14] Political agitation in nineteenth-century rural Ireland resulted in an increased tendency in the English press to morph the formerly obedient Irish peasantry into simian vandals. Marion H. Spielmann writes that Victorian periodicals began to 'picture the Irish political outrage-mongering peasant as a cross between a garrotter and a gorilla',[15] while Curtis describes the typical Irish caricature in English periodicals as having a 'simous nose, long upper lip, huge projecting mouth, and jutting lower jaw as well as [a] sloping forehead'.[16] One typical character was called 'Mr. MacSimius', who made clear his animal origins by claiming that his 'progenitors were all educated in the hoigher branches'.[17] In *Stephen Hero*, Madden, representative of the Irish peasantry, is intimately aware of such dehumanising stereotypes, and challenges Stephen's criticism of the peasantry by claiming that he is 'simply giving vent to old stale libels – the drunken Irishman, the baboon-faced Irishman that we see in *Punch*' (*SH* 62). As Hirsch writes, '[t]o the English public the peasant incarnated the barbarism and savagery of Irish rural life, becoming an emblem of the Irish national character itself'.[18] This tendency to take one social group as emblematic of Irish people in general meant that the peasantry could not be ignored by the urban, middle-class, Catholic Irish, or even indeed the Anglo-Irish. The Revival must be understood as partly a reaction against such dehumanising accounts of the Irish peasantry – if the peasantry were already symbolic of the Irish people in general, then it was essential for middle-class self-esteem that they be idealised. With such a context in mind, it is important to state from the start, as Hirsch does, that '[n]o dramatization or portrayal of Irish peasant life could ever be wholly free of the looming shadow and presence of the English colonizer'.[19]

The transformation of the Irish peasant from chimpanzee to champion of an ancient, idealised vision of Ireland was itself founded on the concept of primitivism. In *Primitivism, Science, and the Irish Revival* (2004), Sinéad Garrigan Mattar argues that three of the key figures of the Revival – Yeats, Lady Gregory and Synge – were all heavily influenced by European traditions of Celtology and 'comparative science', which Mattar defines as 'the scientific, comparative study of Celtic culture, language, and literature'.[20] The result of this new interest was that these writers became fascinated by so-called 'primitive' groups, most especially the Irish peasantry. Mattar defines primitivism quite simply as 'the idealization of the primitive', but notes that it 'is always more reflective of the person or society doing the idealizing than it is of the people or culture being idealized'.[21] Just as with the simian caricatures in British colonial discourse, 'primitive' was another identity foisted upon the rural Irish without their say. Mattar does make the point, however, that not all versions of Revivalist primitivism were the same. For example, she argues that Yeats's Celticism followed a 'deeply Arnoldian' trajectory, leading to a view of the peasantry that is anachronistic and rooted in colonial cliché.[22] Yeats's peasantry therefore exist 'in a pre-Industrial time-warp' and are deeply spiritual, rather than religious.[23] Mattar is keen to highlight how inconsistent this is with the reality of life for the peasantry, noting that '[t]he peasant of the West whom [Yeats] denied had fought in the Land Wars and was religiously orthodox; his children were intent on leaving the fireside, discontent with the benefits of a fairy "swoon", to seek material comfort elsewhere'.[24] The reality of the peasantry's material concerns is also ignored by Lady Gregory, in Mattar's account, as her vision of the 'primitive remains always the projected image of an idealized past in a sanitized present; her mythologies have no more wildness than a walled garden'.[25] As Mattar describes it, no matter how much Gregory desired to build a relationship with the peasantry, as a member of the landed gentry 'she never ceased to be the Lady from the Big House, and her tenantry never ceased to be her tenantry'.[26]

It could be argued that this view of Revivalism is overly critical of its Anglo-Irish founders, though Mattar is much more sympathetic to Synge, given his emphasis on a more academic approach to primitivism. She argues that Synge's familiarity with the literature on 'comparative science' and Celtology meant that he 'was able to view the western peasantry with one eye fixed firmly on the social and economic conditions determining their character'.[27] This ability to remove the peasantry – if even momentarily – from the mythology surrounding them was a unique skill among Revivalists, and this arguably places Synge closer to Joyce in his portrayal of them. Joyce got to know Synge while living in Paris in 1903, though he was initially dismissive of his play *Riders to the Sea* (1904), set on the Aran Islands, informing his brother Stanislaus that it had not a single 'sound spot' (*L2* 35). Arthur Power claims that until the 1920s Joyce continued to believe that Synge's peasants spoke a 'fabricated language as unreal as his characters were unreal', and that their characteristics did not resemble the peasants that Joyce had met, whom he summarised as being 'a hard, crafty and matter-of-fact lot'.[28] Nevertheless, as early as 1907 Joyce's sympathy for Synge appears to have increased when *The Playboy of the Western World* found itself the subject of nationalist consternation during its opening night as a result of its portrayal of a sexually unrestrained peasantry. Joyce predicted that Synge would be 'condemned from the pulpit, as a heretic: which would be dreadful' (*L2* 208–9) and, reflecting now on *Riders to the Sea*, speculated that it might have had 'merit' all along and that Synge might in fact 'know[] and understand[] the Irish peasant, the backbone of the nation' (*L2* 212).[29] A year later Joyce translated *Riders to the Sea* into Italian in collaboration with his Triestine friend Nicolò Vidacovich (*L3* 195n3), while in 1918 he convinced Nora to play a minor role in a production of the play in Zurich (*JJII* 440). He appears to have been especially proud of this, writing that '[a]s she was born within sight of Aran I think Synge's words were spoken with the genuine brogue' (*L1* 118). Ellmann writes that Joyce's 1912 articles on Galway and the Aran Islands show that he 'came round to sharing Ireland's primitivism' (*JJII* 325), while John McCourt expresses the belief that 'Joyce, to some extent, can be said to have followed, however polemically, the primitive turn, and thus the reader can only benefit from reading him both in tandem with and in opposition to the openly primitivist writers of the revival'.[30] I would argue that this 'primitive turn' did not happen belatedly for Joyce, as primitivist tropes are present in some of his earliest writings.

This turn towards primitivism is evident most especially in the Mullingar section of *Stephen Hero*, when Stephen visits his godfather Mr Fulham in the provincial town. This section of the novel will be examined under different headings throughout this chapter, but initially it is worth pointing out elements that are quite explicitly primitivist and/or colonialist in tone. Stephen begins by observing – and noting the smells of – the peasants on the train to Mullingar, and on his arrival he remarks on the 'drowsy' and idle nature of the peasants along the road (*JJA* 8: 7).[31] In expressing this notion that the peasants are idle, Stephen parrots many of the observations made by colonial visitors to Ireland. David Lloyd interprets this 'idleness' as a refusal to engage in the colonial capitalist system, writing that along with 'commentary on Irish misery is the back-handed observation of Irish contentment, their lack of interest in material progress, their idleness, but also their vivacity and pleasure, qualities that grate on the Protestant sensibility of the English capitalist and administrator'.[32] Indeed, Stephen's similarity here to the Protestant gentry is emphasised when the occasional 'peasant plodding along the road' deems 'Stephen worthy of the honour [of] fumbl[ing] at his hat' (*JJA* 8: 7). We are told quite explicitly that '[m]ost of Mr Fulham's neighbours were primitive types' (*SH* 211), and when Mr Fulham declares that '[o]ur Irish peasantry [. . .] is the backbone of the nation', the authorial aside lays further emphasis on Stephen's primitivist voyeurism: 'Backbone or not, it was in the constant observance of the peasantry that Stephen chiefly delighted' (*SH* 213).

What follows this aside is a strikingly physiognomic description of the peasantry:

> they were almost Mongolian types, tall, angular and oblique-eyed. Stephen whenever he walked behind a peasant always looked first for the prominent cheek-bones that seemed to cut the air and the peasants in their turn must have recognised metropolitan features for they stared very hard at the youth as if he were some rare animals [*sic*]. (*JJA* 8: 27)

Here, not only are the peasantry collapsed into one indistinguishable whole, but all those peoples deemed 'primitive' by the middle-class urban observer – whether they be from Mullingar or Mongolia – are apparently identical. The sharp features of the peasantry – the cheek-bones that 'seemed to cut the air' – appear to be symbolic of their rough-hewn nature in general. This section would evidently not be out of place in a pseudoscientific, colonialist account of rural Irish people, only marginally less othering than the simian depictions of the peasantry quoted earlier. However, what is most fascinating about this brief aside is Stephen's awareness that he, too, is being judged in a similar manner by the passing peasantry. He imagines that they will identify in his physiognomy features of metropolitanism – a further underlining of the rural/urban binarism evident throughout this section – and indeed equate him with 'some rare animal'. This is an example of the 'primitive' subject performing their own ethnographic 'reading'. Indeed, by equating Stephen with an animal, they subject him to what the Victorian periodicals had been doing to the peasantry with their many simianised depictions. Joyce's account of the peasantry here borrows elements from both colonial and primitivist depictions, without the attendant idealisation of the latter. However, even if the peasantry in *Stephen Hero* do not represent an idealised version of Irishness, neither do they sit back and provide comforting images of spirituality and obedience. Unlike Yeats's peasants, Joyce's clearly have experienced the Land War and are not afraid to stare back at – and cause discomfort to – their supposed superiors.

The idealisation of the peasantry via primitivism was always going to be problematic. Declan Kiberd writes that Revivalist discourse often accepted the clichés developed by colonialists but attempted to reclaim them as positive attributes. However, as Kiberd notes, '[t]*he danger was that, under the guise of freedom, a racist slur might be sanitized and worn with pride by its very victims*'.[33] The employment of primitivist tropes, without the accompanying idealisation, means that Joyce's depiction of the peasantry in *Stephen Hero* remains clouded in a sense of colonial shame. McCourt posits that Joyce was incapable of idealising the peasantry as they could never represent a vision of the future for him, but rather remain 'an embarrassing reminder of a terrible past'.[34] McCourt explains this by virtue of Joyce's uncomfortable proximity to the peasantry, writing that, '[l]ike most Dubliners, Joyce is only a generation or two away from the soil'.[35] While Joyce was clearly conscious of his provincial roots through his Cork father, it had been a number of generations, at least on his father's side, since any Joyces had worked on the land. His great-grandfather, also named James Joyce, was a lime burner and a member of the Whiteboys, a secret and violent organisation that acted to defend the rights of tenant farmers. While James Joyce senior might have had strong sympathies with the peasantry, he was clearly well and truly above such a lowly station by the early nineteenth century, going on 'to establish himself as a successful building contractor'.[36] Joyce's mother, Mary Jane Murray, was born in the rural county town of Longford in 1859 before moving to Dublin; her father was from Leitrim, but it is not clear at what point her paternal ancestors left the land for a more urbanised existence.[37] In any case, it is clear that while Joyce had rural connections in his family, it had been some time since anyone had tended to the soil and paid rent for the privilege of doing so.

This does not negate the point made by McCourt, however, that many Catholic Dubliners saw themselves as fairly recent urbanites in the grand scale of their familial history, Joyce included. In *Finnegans Wake*, Joyce writes that 'every tim, nick and larry of us' are 'sons of the sod, sons, littlesons, yea and lealittlesons', with 'lea' being a reference to land that has been laid down for pasture (*FW* 19.27–9; *OED*, 'lea, n.1', a). With this emphasis on rurality, particularly ground and grassland, Joyce reminds the general reader of their rural origins; but this takes on an added significance in an

Ireland fixated on its peasantry as both noble ancestor and ideal future citizen. There may also have been a gnawing fear – realistic or not – that their recent urbanity and middle-class comfort (for those lucky enough to have made the leap into the middle class) was fragile, and that there was no guarantee that they would not regress to their former mud-cabin state if things did not go their way. Foster writes that, where it existed, '[m]iddle class disdain for peasant lore rests as much on close and uncomfortable succession in time, and sometimes proximity in space, as on difference in class, wealth or attitude'.[38] Such proximity in time was not something that the Anglo-Irish Revivalists had to worry about, and thus idealisation of the peasantry's impoverished state came more easily to them. Indeed, Foster again notes that some Protestant Revivalists lamented that they had not been born peasants, while 'James Stephens recalled hearing Yeats and AE actually express the desire to be reincarnated as such'.[39] The Revivalist romanticisation of the peasantry's poverty can be strikingly contrasted with Stephen's fear of the countryside in *A Portrait*, as he tells Cranly that among the things he fears are 'the country roads at night', believing 'that there is a malevolent reality behind those things I say I fear' (*P* 243). Indeed, when Stephen looks at the 'peasant student' Davin, he immediately sees in him 'the terror of soul of a starving Irish village in which the curfew was still a nightly fear', referring here to the Famine and also, as Seamus Deane notes, to the curfews imposed in rural areas by successive Coercion Acts (*P* 180).[40] It is clear that whatever else rural Ireland and its peasantry might have represented for Joyce, a reassuring sense of bucolic bliss was not part of it. Instead, Joyce sees only the reality of a recent history of starvation and misery.

The colonial and later primitivist accounts of the Irish peasantry certainly influenced Joyce's depictions, particularly in *Stephen Hero*, but the hangover of colonial shame that manifests itself as mockery in this early work develops instead into a more nuanced portrayal in *A Portrait*, where the peasantry become vital to an understanding of the country. In the latter work, Joyce continues to refute the notion of an idealised peasantry, but where they might have been dismissed as an embarrassing remnant of a feudal Ireland in *Stephen Hero*, in *A Portrait* they become as emblematic of Ireland's experience of modernity as Stephen's generation of Catholic undergraduates. Indeed, one of those very undergraduates – Davin – is of a peasant background himself, and the complexity of his character provides a fascinating insight into the place of the peasantry in a modern Ireland.

'The peasant student': Madden, Davin and Clancy

Among all the peasant characters that appear in Joyce's work, perhaps what they have most in common is their namelessness. We come to know them by epithets such as 'the milkwoman' in *Ulysses*, or in large anonymous groups, such as the foul-smelling peasants that Stephen meets on a train in *Stephen Hero* or the peasant women standing at the doors near Clane in *A Portrait*. This namelessness does not, however, set Joyce apart from the major Revivalist writers, for whom there was sometimes a tendency to keep the peasantry anonymous even while idealising them. For example, in Yeats's *The Countess Cathleen* (1892), some of the characters are listed simply as first, second and third peasant.[41] This namelessness means that the peasantry struggle to be anything more than a literary type – in Stephen's words, they often look 'as like one another as a peascod is like another peascod' (*SH* 53).

There is, however, one important exception to this trend in Joyce: Madden in *Stephen Hero*, or as he becomes in *A Portrait*, Davin. Madden/Davin is among the most significant characters in both works, helping to draw out many of Stephen's most memorable reflections on Irish nationalism and the peasantry. While Madden and Davin are broadly the same character, there are important differences between them, differences that lay bare much of the development between *Stephen Hero* and *A Portrait*. Both iterations of this character are based on Joyce's close university friend, George Clancy. Clancy was born in County Limerick in what appears to have been an Irish-speaking household based on the 1901 census return.[42] The same census shows that Clancy's father was a carpenter, and therefore not exactly the stereotype of the Irish peasant farmer; nevertheless, Clancy and his fictional iterations become synonymous with the peasantry for Joyce. Clancy was an enthusiast for the revival of the Irish language – it was apparently he who convinced Joyce to attend Irish-language classes – and for nationalism in general, going on to be elected Mayor of Limerick before being murdered by the Black and Tans during the Irish War of Independence (*JJII* 61). Clancy is described as having given life to the Gaelic League on his arrival at University College, while 'his lovable character equally with his athletic record and gift for organization gave him an exceptional influence over his contemporaries'.[43]

Stanislaus Joyce later wrote that his brother and Clancy 'had very little in common except the mutual attraction of brilliance on one side and of plain honest intelligence on the other, of city-bred and country-bred' (*MBK* 175). Despite what might appear to be Madden/Davin's superficial simplicity, Joyce clearly had a close relationship with Clancy; he was the only friend to address Joyce by his first name, as Madden and Davin also do with Stephen. Joyce reflected on this in mournful tones to his son Giorgio and daughter-in-law Helen in 1935:

> The only person who ever addressed me so (of my companions or friends) was my poor friend George Clancy (Davin in the *Portrait*). This is carefully pointed out in the book. He was afterward Mayor of Limerick and was dragged out of bed by the Black and Tans in the night and shot in the presence of his wife. (*L1* 357)

While Clancy represented much that Joyce was reacting against during the composition of *Stephen Hero*, by the time he was writing *A Portrait* his views had acquired more nuance, and this is particularly evident in the development of the character of Madden into that of Davin.

In *Stephen Hero*, Madden is portrayed as a type of rural stooge to Stephen as urban intellectual. On first meeting Madden we are told that 'he seemed grateful for Stephen's attentions', and just as with the physiognomic descriptions of the peasantry remarked upon earlier, so too does Stephen observe 'the peasant strength of his jaws' here (*SH* 28). Madden mostly basks in Stephen's reflected glory, as 'the rustic mind of one was very forcibly impressed by the metropolitanism of the other' (*SH* 51). Their conversations are apparently 'rarely serious', and when Madden does begin to speak about the subjects close to his heart, namely nationalist revival, we are told that 'Stephen allowed his critical faculty a rest' (*SH* 52). Some of their most engaging debates surround the significance of the Irish peasantry. Madden is a fervent defender of the peasantry, and deems that Stephen 'despise[s] the peasant because [he] live[s] in the city' (*SH* 53). Madden's defence of the peasantry has elements of primitivism – he notes, for example, that they live 'a simple life' that rejects English 'gross materialism' – but his idealisation is mostly a defensive reaction to what he perceives as Stephen's urban sense of superiority (*SH* 53). Stephen encourages such a view, claiming that the 'intelligence of an English city is not perhaps at a very high level but at least it is higher than the mental swamp of the Irish peasant' (*SH* 53). Despite Stephen's haughty dismissal of Madden's nationalist arguments, he ultimately begs Madden not to 'ask me such questions [. . .] You can use these phrases of the platform but I can't' (*SH* 54). This oblique mocking of the nationalists' platform clichés is also something of an admission of defeat on Stephen's part. Clearly his personal philosophy is not yet as defined as the nationalists' perhaps more simplified alternative. By the end of *Stephen Hero*, Madden comes to represent what the young Joyce saw as the dead end of nationalism and Revivalism. Before Stephen leaves for Paris, he meets Madden walking in the street, and we are told that the young Limerick man gave Stephen the kind of 'salute which [one] a friend who has failed gives to a friend who has succeeded' (*SH* 191).[44] Madden is clearly set up for a life of dull routine, 'sampling and discussing *camàns* [*sic*], smoking very heavy tobacco and speaking Irish with [one] newly arrived provincials' (*SH* 191).[45] There is no sense here that Madden's vision of national revival has any future in it, and we might even suspect that he will end up resembling an embittered and frustrated old nationalist akin to the Citizen of *Ulysses*.

Ultimately, however, for all their differences, the two have a relationship 'of affectionate familiarity' (*SH* 52). As pointed out by Joyce to his son Giorgio, the use of Stephen's first name takes on a special significance in both *Stephen Hero* and *A Portrait*. Madden in fact calls him 'Stevie', which is explained by the fact that Madden also has a brother named Stephen and so 'he sometimes used this familiar form' (*SH* 76). The two develop a quasi-fraternal relationship, and this sense that Madden is part of the family is further underscored by the fact that he is one of only three people to get an advance view of Stephen's university paper, the others being his actual brother Maurice and his mother (*SH* 76). It is this softer, fraternal aspect to their friendship that is most carried through to the character of Davin in *A Portrait*. Davin also calls Stephen by his first name, but where in *Stephen Hero* this is merely alluded to, in *A Portrait* Stephen appears to be emotionally moved by this familiarity: 'The homely version of his christian name on the lips of his friend had touched Stephen pleasantly when first heard for he was as formal in speech with others as they were with him' (*P* 180). Davin remains similar to Madden in many regards – he is still adamant in his support for Irish nationalism and the revival of the Irish language – but Stephen is not quite as acerbic with Davin during their debates as he is with Madden. Stephen likes to jokingly refer to Davin as 'the peasant student', but Davin is little bothered by such jibes; we are told that it was 'a jesting name between them but the young peasant bore with it lightly', daring Stephen to '[c]all me what you will' (*P* 180). Stephen retains a certain sense of superiority over Davin as we are told that he had a 'rude Firbolg mind', a reference to one of the legendary, primitive inhabitants of Ireland, the Firbolgs (*P* 180). The implication here appears to be that Davin's mind – and that of the peasantry in general – has not developed beyond that of the pre-historic settlers. Nevertheless, Stephen gradually comes to suspect that Davin's supposed simplicity is in fact a crafty way of hiding a 'plain honest intelligence', as Stanislaus described Clancy. This is particularly to the fore in his reflections on Davin's manner of speaking, when Stephen asks himself if Davin is really *'as innocent as his speech'* (*P* 202).[46] However, this is not to say that Stephen is won over by Davin's arguments in a way that he is not by Madden. He still views Davin as being overly wedded to 'the broken lights of Irish myth' and being blindingly hostile towards '[w]hatsoever of thought or of feeling came to him from England or by way of English culture' (*P* 180). However, Stephen engages Davin in debate with more honesty and less conde-scension than he does with Madden – at no point does he allow his 'critical faculty a rest' – and it is testament to Davin's intelligence that their debates in *A Portrait* draw out some of Stephen's most memo-rable and quotable lines: it is to Davin that he proclaims that 'Ireland is the old sow that eats her farrow', as well as his intention to fly by the nets of 'nationality, language, religion' (*P* 203).

Perhaps the most telling indication of the difference between Madden and Davin, as well as the development of Stephen's charac-ter between *Stephen Hero* and *A Portrait*, is in the final meeting of the two:

> *3 April:* Met Davin at the cigar shop opposite Findlater's church. He was in a black sweater and had a hurley stick. Asked me was it true I was going away and why. Told him the shortest way to Tara was *via* Holyhead. Just then my father came up. Introduction. Father polite and observant. Asked Davin if he might offer him some refreshment. Davin could not, was going to a meeting. When we came away father told me he had a good honest eye. (*P* 250)

Comparing this to Stephen's final meeting with Madden, there is not much difference in terms of the facts of what Davin is doing: he is in a cigar shop and evidently smoking 'very heavy tobacco'; he is hold-ing a 'hurley stick', just as he is sampling *'camàns'* in *Stephen Hero*, though the use of English rather than Irish seems to lend the activity a greater legitimacy here, or at least less of the ironic exoticism that it had in the previous draft. Davin cannot stay as he is on his way to a meeting, probably of some Revivalist organisation, whether the Gaelic Athletic Association or the Gaelic League. Most importantly, there is no mention here of Davin having 'failed' in comparison to Stephen who has 'succeeded'. Instead, when Stephen confirms that he is leaving the country, he explains it by reference to Tara, the seat of the ancient High Kings of Ireland, and Holyhead, the Welsh port synonymous with emigration from Ireland. Despite their differences, Stephen makes it clear that both he and Davin want to arrive at the same destination: the symbolic site of a free Ireland. For Davin, this will be brought about through national revival in Ireland; for Stephen, one must exile oneself first and achieve independence of the individual spirit. The arrival of Simon Dedalus as father figure again encourages us to view Stephen and Davin as having a fraternal relationship, and Simon's estimation of Davin as having 'a good honest eye' might be attributed to a sense of connection between these two provincials in Dublin, Simon being of course a migrant to the city himself. One is even tempted to speculate as to whether Davin might represent what Stephen would have been had his father not left Cork all those years before. At this point, Davin and Stephen represent two alternative ways of achieving freedom, but it would be wrong to think of them as antagonistic figures. Instead, we should view each, in his own way, as contributing to the emergence of a new Ireland.

Other named peasant characters come and go in Joyce's writing, such as Temple, another university student who is an incoherently loquacious presence in both *Stephen Hero* and *A Portrait* and an easy target for Stephen's ridicule. In *Stephen Hero* Temple is described as a 'raw Gipsy-looking youth with a shambling gait and a shambling manner of speaking' from the 'West of Ireland' (*SH* 98). His speeches fade into 'indistinct mutterings' (*SH* 99), and at points his mouth is 'flecked with a thin foam as it strove to enunciate a difficult word', underscoring the notion – recurrent through *Stephen Hero* – that the English language exists on a plane above the capacity of peasants such as Temple (*SH* 199). In spite of this supposed simplicity, he is also 'known to be very revolutionary' and rejects religion, though in a markedly less intellectual fashion than Stephen (*SH* 98). In *A Portrait* he remains an unsophisticated, 'emotional' character who blurts out questions at Stephen and tries to showcase his reading of Rousseau and Marx, while he attempts to ingratiate himself with Stephen by declaring him to be 'the only man I see in this institution that has an individual mind' (*P* 200). Cranly is particularly embarrassed by Temple, perhaps because Cranly himself might be considered a 'half-peasant', in that his father was a farmer, and Cranly remains very proud of his connection to Wicklow.

However, Davin is by far the most individualised peasant character in Joyce's work, the one most capable of self-expression and willing to debate with Stephen on close to equal terms. Gregory Castle rightly notes that Stephen's relationship with Davin 'is not simply the "affectionate familiarity" he felt for Madden but something closer to confessional intimacy'.[47] Davin primarily functions as a bridge between Stephen's mind and 'the hidden ways of Irish life', namely peasant life, and thus he is an essential informant if Stephen is to forge the uncreated conscience of his race (*P* 181). Davin is evidently a Revivalist in his cultural and political outlook and a believer to some degree at least in the myth of the idealised peasant, yet he himself has little in common with the primitive peasant as propounded by Revivalists. He will not spend his time trudging through fields and telling folk tales in a mud cabin. As an eventual university graduate, he can expect a prominent position in a new Ireland – as indeed Clancy himself achieved before his murder. Foster believes that Davin's status as a Dublin university student makes him 'a former not a genuine peasant', but I would argue instead that Davin is in fact the epitome of the modern peasant, adapting to an Ireland that is rapidly changing.[48] His very existence is a refutation of the clichés propagated by primitivist writers and a more accurate depiction of the type of citizen who would go on to dominate in an independent Ireland – for good or ill.

'Paddy Stink and Micky Mud'

Odour has long been recognised as an important feature of Joyce's work, especially in *A Portrait*. Early reviewers of the novel were, in Crispian Neill's words, keen to 'identify odor – or more specifically, the malodorous – as a conspicuous feature of the text'.[49] Among these early reviewers was H. G. Wells, who remarked upon Joyce's apparent 'cloacal obsession', while a review for the *Manchester Guardian* in 1917 notes Stephen Dedalus's 'passion for foul-smelling things'.[50] In his survey of olfactory perception in literature, Hans Rindisbacher identifies Joyce as one of the few modernist writers in whose work 'the olfactory element cannot be overlooked'.[51] Neill speculates that Joyce's privileging of the olfactory might be tied to his failing eyesight at this time,[52] while Christine O'Neill has examined the influence of what she calls the 'scentscapes of Dublin' on Joyce's writing.[53] Here, I intend to add to this olfactory tradition in Joycean criticism by examining the conspicuous references to smell in Joyce's depiction of the Irish peasantry. The use of smell further undermines the Revivalist idealisation of the peasantry, but it also necessarily draws attention to the dangerous colonial stereotypes that Irish Catholics had internalised at this point.

Along with taste, smell is the sense that is perhaps most difficult to separate from one's subjective experience, with the result that it becomes an extremely effective discriminatory tool. Mark M. Smith writes that throughout history, '[s]mell, more than any other sense perhaps, served to create and mark the "other," at once justifying various forms of subjugation and serving as a barrier against meaningful integration into host or dominant societies'.[54] Smith notes George Orwell's belief that class distinctions could be summarised by the notion that the working class smelled, while by contrast the middle and upper classes believed themselves to be entirely odourless – or, if possessing odours, having only those that were desirable, often acquired artificially through perfumes, an important contrast to the putrid smells that the lower classes and/or races supposedly produced naturally.[55] Following the industrial revolution, smell became an important signifier of changing priorities. The smells of the countryside, despite being 'natural', become synonymous with dirt and a lack of sophistication among the rural population. Smith highlights an example from 1930s China where garlic became a differentiating smell between urban and rural dwellers: 'To the Chinese farmer,' he writes, 'garlic was the signature smell of home and working with the land; to the Chinese urbanite in the 1930s, it was a mark of inferiority, something to be avoided and ridiculed.'[56] Max Horkheimer and Theodor Adorno argued that smell is unique among the senses in that it marks the person doing the smelling through identification, wanted or unwanted, with those being smelled. They wrote: 'When we see we remain who we are, when we smell we are absorbed entirely. In civilisation, therefore, smell is regarded as a disgrace, a sign of the lower social orders, lesser races, and baser animals.'[57] Smell, in Joyce's work, manages to unite these three categories in relation to the peasantry, emphasising their low social position, racial otherness and apparent animal-like nature.

While the prevalence of the olfactory has been well noted in *A Portrait*, it is also to the fore in *Stephen Hero*, particularly in the section where Stephen journeys out of Dublin and into the countryside. Stephen's time in Mullingar did not survive into the final draft of *A Portrait*, and the editors Slocum and Cahoon speculate that it was because 'the role of Stephen showing off against the provincials had something disagreeable in it' (*SH* 9). This is perhaps putting it mildly, as is clear from the beginning of Stephen's train journey, where we are given a description of the pungent company he keeps in the carriage:

> Mullingar, the chief town of Westmeath, is the midland capital and there is a great traffic of peasants and cattle between it and Dublin.

This fifty-mile journey is made by the train in about two hours and you are therefore to conceive Stephen Daedalus packed in the corner of a third-class carriage and contributing the thin fumes of his cigarettes to the already reeking atmosphere. The carriage was inhabited by a company of peasants nearly every one of whom had a bundle tied in a spotted handkerchief. The carriage smelt strongly of peasants (an odour the debasing humanity of which Stephen remembered to have perceived in the little chapel of Clongowes on the morning of his first communion) and indeed so pungently that the youth could not decide whether he found the odour of sweat [unpleasant] offensive because the peasant sweat is monstrous or because it did not now proceed from his own body. He was not ashamed to admit to himself that he found it [unpleasant] offensive for both of these reasons. (*SH* 209)

Certainly, as regards a literary depiction of the Irish peasantry, this is about as striking a rejection of Revivalist idealisation as it is possible to conceive. The narratorial voice is unique here in its direct address to the reader – 'you are therefore to conceive Stephen Daedalus' – which underlines the apparent absurdity of Stephen's position among the peasantry. The narrative tone borders on the kind used in a travelogue, spelling out for the reader exactly how to envision such strange and exotic circumstances. Stephen views himself as removed from the peasants in much the same way that the privileged Anglo-Irish Revivalists were, but where they were willingly interacting with the peasant population in search of literary material, Stephen is confronted with them because he can only afford a third-class ticket. This is revealing in itself of the social proximity between Stephen and the peasantry – though he might look down on them, his family's dwindling finances mean that he now occupies a social position not much higher than theirs. Stephen's lexical choice reveals this shame when he refers to the peasants' smell as 'offensive' – in fact, as the square brackets signify here, Joyce had originally described the peasants' smell as simply 'unpleasant', a relatively mild aesthetic judgement, before crossing it out and replacing the two instances of the word with 'offensive'. This is an important change as it shows that the peasantry's rusticity is an affront to Catholic Dubliners and their sense of self, dragging them back to the earth from which they notionally came. Horkheimer and Adorno's idea that smell results in us 'los[ing] [ourselves] in identification with the Other' appears particularly relevant here, as it seems to be just such an unwelcome identification that so unsettles Stephen.[58]

Throughout this passage, the peasants are both unindividualised – 'every one of [them] had a bundle tied in a spotted handkerchief' – and dehumanised, being grouped together with the cattle and having their sweat described as 'monstrous'. Where the peasants' humanity is acknowledged, it is only as a 'debasing humanity'. Such dehumanisation and animalisation forms part of a long tradition of colonial depictions of the peasantry, as evinced by the cartoons in Victorian periodicals. Lloyd draws attention to this passage in a discussion of the peasantry, noting that it is 'all too familiar in its representation of the uncouth peasant, odorous and heavy, ill-mannered and "offensive" to the urban sensibility'.[59] Lloyd also makes reference to Alain Corbin's notion of 'l'hommerde', or the dung-man, of nineteenth-century imagination, usually a peasant who is 'seen as inseparable from the odours of dung and thus opposed to the more hygienic and modern urban dweller'.[60] Such traditions, along with the broader colonial stereotypes of the peasantry, weigh heavily on passages such as this. Lloyd argues that what is most striking about the passage, 'with the hindsight of Joyce's mature style, is the rigidity of the boundaries established between Stephen and the material he reflects on, the sheer externality of the peasants as representatives of an unrefined backwardness'.[61] While it is certain that Stephen works hard to establish boundaries in his own mind between himself and the peasantry, one can argue that the very circumstances of his pecuniary situation – and thus his having to share the third-class carriage with the peasants – undermine such boundaries even as he sets about constructing them.

While passages such as this did not reappear during the drafting of *A Portrait*, the prevalence of smell did. The word 'smell' or its verbal variants occurs forty-three times in the text, while 'odour' occurs in some form twenty-three times. Meanwhile, 'stink(s)' appears twelve times, while 'perfume', 'reek' and 'stench' all occur in some form five times each. From the very first page of the novel, the young Stephen notices the 'queer smell' of the oilsheet put on his bed, as well as the 'nicer smell' of his mother compared to his father (*P* 7). One of the first scenes in which Stephen reflects on different kinds of smells occurs during his schooldays in Clongowes, when he is brought face-to-face with the peasantry living in the countryside nearby who travel to the school's chapel for Mass. The young Stephen has absorbed the dominant narrative of the holy, priest-fearing peasant, but even as a child he notes that the smell associated with them is not the same as the 'holy smell' of the chapel, even if they themselves are 'very holy' (*P* 18). Instead, the peasantry at the back of the chapel are described as smelling 'of air and rain and turf and corduroy' (*P* 18). Using imagery that could have been lifted from a Revivalist text, Stephen thinks of the peasants he has seen in Clane and imagines that '[i]t would be lovely to sleep for one night in that cottage before the fire of smoking turf, in the dark lit by the fire, in the warm dark, breathing the smell of the peasants' (*P* 18). Later, when the students are going home for the holidays, they meet the peasants again as they pass through Clane, with Stephen remarking once again that there was a 'lovely smell [. . .] in the wintry air: the smell of Clane: rain and wintry air and turf smouldering and corduroy' (*P* 20). The village of Clane clearly has the same smell as the peasants who inhabit it – or perhaps it is vice versa – as the peasants cannot be separated from the countryside that defines them. A Dubliner might have any number of individual, unique smells, but a ruralite must reek of rurality.

At this early stage, the smell of the peasants and the countryside is largely a positive one in Stephen's mind, even if the sensation of them 'breath[ing] behind him on his neck' suggests a certain discomfort and sense that these same peasants are watching over him (*P* 18). As the novel progresses, the homely imagery and comforting smells give way to a more unpleasant vision of rural life. At the beginning of the second chapter, Stephen is shocked by the foul odour of the cows once the relative cleanliness of summer has ended:

> But when autumn came the cows were driven home from the grass: and the first sight of the filthy cowyard at Stradbrook with its foul green puddles and clots of liquid dung and steaming bran troughs, sickened Stephen's heart. The cattle which had seemed so beautiful in the country on sunny days revolted him and he could not even look at the milk they yielded. (*P* 63–4)

This change in attitude towards the cows is a harbinger of Stephen's change in attitude towards the peasantry and rural life in general – where before the odours of the countryside were perceived as 'lovely', they now gradually incite a sickening feeling in him. The syntax becomes more extreme and overwhelmingly negative, with words such as 'filthy', 'foul', 'dung', 'steaming', 'sickened' and 'revolted' leaving little doubt in the reader's mind as to the effect such scenes have on the growing Stephen.

Perhaps the best example of the cognitive dissonance in urban minds towards the rural peasantry comes from Stephen's father, who revels in his identity as a Corkman, but who is also capable of showing disdain for those from beyond the Pale. When diminishing finances mean that the Dedaluses can no longer afford to send Stephen to Clongowes, Mr Dedalus is determined that he will continue to receive a Jesuit education as opposed to the more common – and sometimes free – tuition provided by the Christian Brothers teaching order: 'Christian brothers be damned! said Mr Dedalus. Is it with Paddy Stink and Micky Mud? No, let him stick to the Jesuits in God's name since he began with them' (P 71). A Christian Brothers education would necessarily place Stephen on the same level as the peasants of the country – the so-called Paddy Stinks and Micky Muds of the world. As the Christian Brothers order was originally founded to serve Ireland's provincial poor, Simon's nomenclature for them may be a reference to both the students and the teachers themselves, rural upstarts who despite their learning could never compare to the supposed sophistication of the Jesuits.[62] Regardless, Simon's monikers are revealing: these uncouth individuals have their debased odour and rustic dirt inbuilt into their very identities. Statements such as this make clear that, contemporaneous idealisations of the peasantry notwithstanding, new Dubliners such as Simon Dedalus still recoil in horror at the idea of being associated with rural peasants in any way.

The foul smells and attendant animalisation of the peasantry is, arguably, the underlying subtext to one of *A Portrait*'s most famous passages: its depiction of hell. During a school retreat, Stephen is subjected to a fire-and-brimstone sermon by a preacher, and critics such as James R. Thrane and Elizabeth F. Boyd have noted how faithfully this vision of hell accords with Jesuit teachings, most notably those of Giovanni Pietro Pinamonti in the 1688 work *Hell Opened to Christians, To Caution Them from Entering into It*. Joyce copies whole sections from this work, including a striking passage on the 'stench' of hell (P 120).[63] Following the preacher's sermon, Stephen experiences his own vision of hell, located in '[a] field of stiff weeds and thistles and tufted nettle-bunches' (P 137). Among the vegetation are 'clots and coils of solid excrement' (P 137), which create '[a]n evil smell, faint and foul as the light' (P 138). This contrasts with Pinamonti's vision, where the foul odours emanated from the damned and the burning brimstone. Instead, Joyce's hellish stench has a much more rustic source, coming from a field of 'stale crusted dung' (P 138). Next, Stephen notices strange, hybrid 'creatures' in the field: they are described as '[g]oatish creatures with human faces, hornybrowed, lightly bearded and grey as indiarubber', while the 'malice of evil' glitters in their eyes (P 138). One of them clasps 'a torn flannel waistcoat', further emphasising the hybridity of these depraved animal-like creatures decked in human clothing. While such imagery could simply be the result of Stephen's hyperactive religious fervour, it is striking that these hybrid creatures – half-animal, half-human, wandering around a dung-filled field – correspond almost too well with the animalised peasantry found in the cartoons of Victorian periodicals. Like the rural peasantry, the creatures here have a unique accent, described by Stephen as a 'soft language' (*P* 138). This hell – 'stinking, bestial, malignant, a hell of lecherous goatish fiends' (*P* 138) – seems specifically constructed to represent the insecurities and figures of repulsion that are specific to middle-class Dubliners at the turn of the century. This is their collective hell as much as it is Stephen's, filled with the sights and smells of the peasant farmsteads so many of them had only recently left behind.

Joyce's use of smell to frame depictions of the peasantry is an important signifier of their social position at this time in Ireland, and especially of the attitudes of the middle-class urban Catholics towards their rural counterparts. Odour, inextricably tied as it is to emotions and prejudice, is effective at stripping away the cultural and political efforts to idealise the peasantry, but it always risks simply reverting back to familiar, pejorative stereotypes as promulgated by colonial commentators. In *A Portrait*, the peasantry are portrayed with more empathy, but Joyce does not neglect to depict the subtle prejudices that result in Stephen's cavalier attitude towards the peasants on his train journey to Mullingar in *Stephen Hero*. Even as Joyce rows back on this explicit othering of the peasantry, smell nevertheless continues to trail after them, a persistent reminder of their social position in the eyes of the urbanite.

The Peasantry's Court of Love

In Chapter II.3 of *Finnegans Wake*, HCE laments 'those hintering influences from an angelsexonism' upon the nation's women (*FW* 363.34–5). '[A]ngelsexonism' appears to be a clear reference to Anglo-Saxon influences on sexuality, though this is not necessarily to suggest that such influences increased promiscuity, as HCE is primarily – and contradictorily – interested in 'unlifting upfallen girls' (*FW* 363.33). The Anglo-Saxon influence might in fact be a reference to Victorian prudishness, while 'angel' might nod towards the Church's prurience. As the Anglo-Irish Protestants and conservative Catholic nationalists idealised the Irish peasantry in terms they found congenial, one of the results was to utterly desexualise them. This was especially the case with regard to the peasant women portrayed in Revivalist literature, acting as they did as symbols of national purity. However, such notions of peasant purity born out of piety were not necessarily accurate. Declan Kiberd argues that Gaelic writers of the seventeenth and eighteenth centuries were preoccupied with 'denounc[ing] the new Anglicization of sexuality in rural Ireland'.[64] The writer Kiberd marks out for most attention is Brian Merriman. Merriman was born in rural County Clare in the mid-eighteenth century, and is most famous for his comic masterpiece *Cúirt an Mheán Oíche* (*The Midnight Court*). Kiberd writes that Merriman's poem was 'based on the idea of a court of love ruled by women'.[65] The poem is a vociferous attack on men who refuse to marry until they are old, lambasting the new conservative sexuality that was taking hold in rural Ireland. The so-called 'Anglicization' of Irish sexuality would ensure that notions such as Merriman's were gradually censored out.

In the 1930s the anthropologists Arensberg and Kimball carried out an influential survey of life in rural Ireland in which they noted that the conservative sexuality of the peasants was in fact a recent development that had its source in urban life:

> Certain observers profess to find the puritanical outlook on sexual matters on the increase in the countryside. The country people themselves purport to see a change in their own outlook. And it may be that the last generation has brought a considerable spread of Catholic moral standards with the spread of education and the opening of the countryside to urban influence.[66]

It is of note here that Arensberg and Kimball do not attribute sexual puritanism to traditional beliefs, but rather to symbols of modernity: education and influence from urban centres. For all their harking back to peasant traditions and folklore, the major figures of Revivalism were, in general, happy to have their peasants conform to this urbanised sexuality. Foster notes that Lady Gregory found 'overt sexual references' to be 'distasteful',[67] while Kiberd writes that Revivalism would prove to be 'rigidly selective of that which was worthy to be revived and translated into popular versions. Sexuality, it seemed, was not to be deanglicized.'[68] Even in contemporary literature written in Irish by the inhabitants of the Blasket Islands, the urge to censor overtook the desire for original material written in the language. Two of the most famous writers in Irish, Tomás Ó Criomhthain and Peig Sayers, had their manuscripts purged of all sensuality and controversial material.[69] Sexuality, perhaps more than any other factor, demonstrated that if the peasantry were to be depicted as an ideal, then this would be determined by what the urban commentator and editor considered to be ideal, not the peasantry themselves.

There is, however, one notable and significant exception to this trend within Revivalism. Synge's drama courted some of the greatest controversy of the Revival in its depiction of a sexually uninhibited peasantry, particularly with regard to women. In doing so, Synge was not simply undercutting the mythology built up by nationalists, but was crucially showing loyalty to the anthropological sources that he had used to inform his portrayals of Irish peasant life. Mattar notes that Synge's drama is marked by a '[s]avage paganism, savage violence, and savage, especially female, sexuality'.[70] These were, in Mattar's words, 'the three elements Celtology had revealed in the ancient texts'.[71] As a result, 'instead of the idealized and desexualized figures of nineteenth-century Celticism, [Synge] introduces women whose physicality, in terms of both strength (often translated to violence) and sexuality, is paramount'.[72] This is apparent in Synge's travelogue account *The Aran Islands* (1907), most especially the picture he gives us of the women on the islands. He writes: 'Quiet as these women are on ordinary occasions, when two or three of them are gathered together in their holiday petticoats and shawls, they are as wild and capricious as the women who live in towns', later going on to state that '[t]he direct sexual instincts are not weak on the island'.[73] This is a clear rejection of the nationalist view of the chaste and comely maiden, a view that would become dominant and defining following Irish independence.

Apart from the manuscript of *Riders to the Sea* that Synge let him read in Paris in 1903, it appears that Joyce did not read Synge's writings on the peasantry until 1907 (*JJII* 124). Each copy of Synge's works that Joyce owned in Trieste was published in that year, just when Joyce was abandoning *Stephen Hero*.[74] Between 1907 and the eventual publication of *A Portrait*, Joyce's depiction of peasant women changed dramatically. While he evidently read widely during this time, it seems very likely that Synge's accounts of the peasantry, fictional or otherwise, had an influence on his own portrayals of peasant women and sexuality. Although in *Stephen Hero* the eponymous character is eager to dismiss Revivalist discourse surrounding the peasantry, he is still prey to the notion of their purity. When Madden argues that the peasantry are 'chaste' Stephen does not disagree: 'I fully recognize that my countrymen have not yet advanced [to] as far as the machinery of Parisian harlotry' (*SH* 54). He does, however, speculate that the peasantry only remain chaste 'because they can do it by hand' (*SH* 54). Almost as though in answer to Stephen's contrast between peasant piety and Parisian harlotry, Synge in *The Aran*

Islands writes that '[t]he women of this island are before convention-ality, and share some of the liberal features that are thought peculiar to the women of Paris and New York'.[75] Far from being sexually repressed, Synge's peasants possess all the characteristics and urges found among urbanites.

Synge's 1903 play *In the Shadow of the Glen* probably influenced one of Joyce's most striking depictions of a peasant woman in *A Portrait*. Synge's play, his first to be performed, features a tramp who asks a woman, Nora Burke, if he can take shelter in her cottage. On entering he sees that there is a dead man laid out on the table – Nora's husband, Dan. When Nora exits, the husband rises off the table and reveals to the tramp that he has not been dead all this time. Rather, he suspects that his wife is being unfaithful with a young neighbour, Michael Dara, and he has set up this ruse to reveal her infidelity. When Nora returns with Michael we are given a picture of what life has been like for this young woman married to an old man in a remote part of the country:

> MICHAEL: I'm thinking it's a power of men you're after knowing if it's a lonesome place you live itself.
>
> NORA *giving him his tea*: It's a lonesome place you do have to be talking with someone, and looking for someone, in the evening of the day, and if it's with a power of men I'm after knowing they were fine men, for I was a hard child to please, and a hard girl to please (*she looks at him a little sternly*), and it's a hard woman I am to please this day, Michael Dara, and it's no lie I'm telling you.[76]

The suggestion that Nora has 'known' these men in a biblical sense is hardly subtle, and her warning to the feeble Michael Dara that she is a hard woman to please presents us with a woman capable of taking control of this extramarital courting process. Dan eventually rises from the table once again and revels in his proof of Nora's infidelity. She is told to leave his house, but rather than this being a victory for Dan, she does so willingly, taking off with the tramp, saying: 'you've a fine bit of talk, stranger, and it's with yourself I'll go'.[77]

Later, in *The Playboy of the Western World*, Synge presents us with another assertive peasant woman in Pegeen Mike, who, along with a cast of local women, falls in love with a man who claims to have killed his father. The rioting that followed the first performance of the play was a result of many factors, such as the peasantry's seeming glorification of violence and their unrestrained sexuality. However, what eventually set off the crowd was a rather harmless reference to a woman's undergarment.[78] This was symbolic of so much of Synge's overall project, revealing to the metropolitan audience what they would rather keep hidden about the peasantry.

As noted, Joyce followed these controversies with great interest, and it would appear that they led him to reassess his own depictions of the peasantry in *Stephen Hero*. The most explicitly Syngean scene in *A Portrait* is one recounted by Davin of a meeting with a peasant woman on his way home from a hurling match in Buttevant, County Cork:

> After a while a young woman opened the door and brought me out a big mug of milk. She was half undressed as if she was going to bed when I knocked and she had her hair hanging and I thought by her figure and by something in the look of her eyes that she must be carrying a child. She kept me in talk a long while at the door, and I thought it strange because her breast and her shoulders were bare. She asked me was I tired and would I like to stop the night there. She said that she was all alone in the house and that her husband had gone that morning to Queenstown with his sister to see her off. And all the time she was talking, Stevie, she had her eyes fixed on my face and she stood so close to me I could hear her breathing. When I handed her back the mug at last she took my hand to draw me in over the threshold and said: '*Come in and stay the night here. You've no call to be frightened. There's no one in it but ourselves. . . .*' I didn't go in, Stevie. I thanked her and went on my way again, all in a fever. At the first bend of the road I looked back and she was standing at the door. (*P* 182–3)

This young peasant woman is a far cry from the peasantry of *Stephen Hero* who had not advanced as far as Parisian harlotry. Like Synge's Nora Burke, she is suffering from the loneliness of a remote life and is not afraid to beckon the young man into her house. Unlike the desexualised peasantry of much Revivalist literature, this young woman is described in explicitly sexual terms: half undressed, with her breast and shoulders bare, Davin thinks that she is pregnant 'by her figure and by something in the look of her eyes' (*P* 182). Quite how Davin would know this by the 'look of her eyes' is difficult to say; rather, it would appear that the fact of 'carrying a child' is proof that one is a sexual being, and it is this that Davin thinks he sees in the glint of her eye. The gendered power relations, as in Synge's plays, undergo a reversal of sorts here, with the young woman dictating matters, standing uncomfortably close to Davin so that he can hear her breathing, even reassuring him not to be frightened. This is a rejection of Anglicised sexuality in favour of an older form of courting that afforded more power to women, such as is seen in Merriman's *Cúirt an Mheán Oíche*.

Davin's story marks Stephen, as he reflects on what he has just been told:

> The last words of Davin's story sang in his memory and the figure of the woman in the story stood forth reflected in other figures of the peasant women whom he had seen standing in the doorways at Clane as the college cars drove by, as a type of her race and of his own, a bat-like soul waking to the consciousness of itself in darkness and secrecy and loneliness and, through the eyes and voice and gesture of a woman without guile, calling the stranger to her bed. (*P* 183)

It is perhaps peculiar that this young woman should recall to his mind the other peasant women he had seen standing in doorways as a child in Clane. These women had had children in their arms and fitted with the Revivalist image of an idealised female peasantry that dutifully served their husbands and families. It is such propaganda that he was reacting against in *Stephen Hero*, but in *A Portrait*, Stephen is awakening to the realisation that the supposedly pious peasantry possess the same urges that he does. This is clear when he describes the young woman as 'a type of her race and his own'. No longer an alien and/or inferior race, Stephen realises that he and the peasant woman are both on the same journey of self-discovery, 'waking to the consciousness' of themselves. Where Davin reacts in horror and confusion at something that does not align with dominant tropes regarding the peasantry, Stephen sees in this young woman something that is more recognisable.

These women without guile in Synge and Joyce, calling strangers to their beds, stand in contrast to the image of the priest-fearing, pious peasantry that Revivalism and conservative nationalism demanded. However, they still fall within the general parameters of Revivalism in that they are examples of primitivism. Maria McGarrity and Claire A. Culleton write that

> Too often in discussions of primitivist discourse, women are theorized as objects onto which primitive impulses are projected rather than being identified as agents who use and exploit the tropes themselves. They are often viewed as repositories of a primeval, emotional existence that is somehow inherently less 'civilized' because although it seems closer to a time-honoured and traditional past, it also manifests a wild, untamed aspect.[79]

While Nora Burke and the young peasant woman in *A Portrait* have significantly more agency than women often have in Revivalist literature, there is still a sense of titillation at these so-called primitive women presenting the perhaps presumed male reader or audience member with their 'wild, untamed aspect'. The line between striving for unshackled modernity and indulging in exoticised primitivism is therefore a thin one in Synge and Joyce. Nevertheless, peasant women, struggling to survive in mud cabins, often lonely and/or unhappily married, clearly did exist in rural Ireland, and by giving voice to them, Synge and Joyce dismantled one of the core totems of the idealised peasantry. This portrayal of a sexualised peasantry is non-judgemental – like the young woman to Davin, it holds a hand out to those Irish who would deny this reality, as if to say: '*You've no call to be frightened. There's no one in it but ourselves*' (P 182).

A Modern Peasantry

In his essay on literary depictions of the Irish peasantry, Hirsch notes that the peasantry 'no longer existed as such by the time they were being fiercely "discovered" and portrayed by Irish antiquarians and imaginative writers', arguing that this shows that 'what mattered to those writers and their urban audiences was not so much what peasants were but what they represented'.[80] The newly urbanised Catholic was caught between two sources of shame at the turn of the twentieth century: one being their low rustic roots, and the other being their gradual disavowal of this Gaelic past for a future that necessitated increased Anglicisation. Therefore, there was a deep need among the urban Irish of the time for an idealised peasantry with an uninterrupted link to a glorious past, without the taint of British influence, and most especially without the taint of British collusion. This view is epitomised in the writings of D. P. Moran, especially in *The Philosophy of Irish Ireland*, where he writes:

> The ignorant peasants are the most interesting portion of the population. In them are yet to be seen, undeveloped and clouded perhaps, the marks of the Gaelic race. An impassable gulf separates them from any type to be met with in England. They still possess the unspoiled raw material for the making of a vigorous and a real Irish character. The moment we mount up the social scale, the prospect is less pleasing. Teach the peasant to read and write in English, put a black coat on him and let him earn his living in some 'genteel' fashion, and what does he become? Well – they call him Irish.[81]

This passage illustrates – perhaps unwittingly – the bind that the peasantry are caught in: in order to constitute an ideal, they must be unmaterialistic, illiterate, pre-modern; but being these things means that they will always on some level also be 'ignorant' and a source of shame. The educated peasant, leaving behind the mud cabin, suddenly ceases to be a model for the nation, becoming modern Irish as opposed to ancient Gaelic – and thereby another source of shame.

While Revivalists' depictions of the peasantry responded to what they knew their metropolitan audiences demanded, it is also arguable that, for those from Anglo-Irish backgrounds, the image of a loyal tenantry was particularly comforting.[82] This flew in the face of real, lived experience for most of the Anglo-Irish, who had just experienced the full force of the peasantry's wrath during the Land War. Indeed, Yeats himself acknowledged the invented nature of this idealised peasantry in his 1919 poem 'The Fisherman', when he wrote that the peasant figure is 'A man who does not exist, / A man who is but a dream'.[83] Read favourably, such statements make the Revivalists' idealisation of the peasantry seem an innocent form of primitivism; read more cynically, however, the Revivalist peasant figure can be viewed as a deliberate invention designed to keep social hierarchies intact.

In 1902 Yeats wrote to Joyce, telling him that in the countryside 'you find people who are hardly individualized to any great extent. They live through the same round of duty and they think about life and death as their fathers have told them' (qtd. in *JJII* 103). These unindividualised peasants, who ape the lives and manners of their forefathers, are not just pre-modern, but fundamentally at odds with the practical realities of the modern world. Lady Gregory believed that as she spent more time with the peasantry, she began to lose 'the practical side of memory that is concerned with names and dates and the multiplication table, and the numbers on friends' houses in a street'.[84] Perhaps nowhere is this pre-modern simplicity more apparent than in the peasantry's attitude to money as portrayed by Revivalists. In *The Countess Cathleen*, a group of assorted, nameless peasants express wonder at this utterly foreign concept, describing it as '[t]he most beautiful thing under the sun, / That's what I've heard'.[85] This notion of an Irish peasantry expressing wonderment at the idea of money is vehemently refuted in *Stephen Hero* when Stephen describes the average peasant as being 'as cute as a fox – try to pass a false coin on him and you'll see' (*SH* 53). The peasantry's 'life of dull routine' in Stephen's eyes is primarily taken up with 'the calculation of coppers' (*SH* 53), while later he outlines what he sees as the peasantry's 'compensative system' whereby '[t]he old peasant down the country [. . .] counts over his greasy notes and says "I'll put the priest on Tom an' I'll put the polisman on Mickey"' (*SH* 62). This is a complete rejection of the Revivalists' view of the peasantry as existing in a pre-modern, non-materialist world. Instead, the peasantry in *Stephen Hero* know exactly how to cleverly use what few 'greasy notes' they have to put their children into positions of authority and thereby ensure that they can 'balance[] the priest against the polisman' (*SH* 62). This, Stephen states, is 'Irish peasant wisdom' (*SH* 62).

Indeed, this is a view of the peasantry that Joyce appears to have maintained, as the milkwoman in *Ulysses* shows a similarly practical attitude towards pecuniary matters, totting up the amount that the men in the Martello tower owe her in lightning-quick time:

> Well, it's seven mornings a pint at twopence is seven twos is a shilling and twopence over and these three mornings a quart at fourpence is three quarts is a shilling. That's a shilling and one and two is two and two, sir. (*U* 1.442–5)

While the milkwoman is often spoken of as a 'Shan Van Vocht', the 'poor old woman' representing old Gaelic Ireland, in fact she is utterly modern in her sensibilities. She appears at first to represent the peasantry, though she is never referred to as such, and as an inhabitant of southern County Dublin she would certainly be a different type of peasant to the western variant so lauded by Revivalists. This is apparent in her inability to recognise Irish when it is spoken to her, something that would be highly unlikely for a member of the western peasantry. In truth, it is only in the minds of the men in the Martello tower – and of overly impressionable readers perhaps – that she has any relevance as a primitive figure. It might not even be a stretch to say that she has more in common with Stephen than with the peasants of the western coast.

Indeed, this latter point is worth dwelling upon, for to speak of a uniform peasantry in Joyce is inherently flawed. Where most Revivalists, when they spoke of the peasantry, meant those people living along the western coast, in Joyce we are given a fuller spectrum of the Irish peasantry. Given that, etymologically, 'peasant' means simply a country-dweller, the farmers that Stephen encounters near Mullingar in *Stephen Hero* and near Clane in *A Portrait* evidently fit this description, but these midland communities by the late nineteenth century no longer had many Irish speakers left, and so they too would not fit the clichéd vision of the Revivalist peasantry. In truth, only the peasant man whom Mulrennan meets at the end of *A Portrait* accords most fully with the stereotype, living as he does in a mountain cabin in the west and speaking fluent Irish:

> John Alphonsus Mulrennan has just returned from the west of Ireland. European and Asiatic papers please copy. He told us he met an old man there in a mountain cabin. Old man had red eyes and short pipe. Old man spoke Irish. Mulrennan spoke Irish. Then old man and Mulrennan spoke English. Mulrennan spoke to him about universe and stars. Old man sat, listened, smoked, spat. Then said:
> —Ah, there must be terrible queer creatures at the latter end of the world. (*P* 251–2)

However, even this figure does not align completely with the primitive stereotype. Far from being lost in the world of fairy, this is a man grappling with the modern world. Though he speaks to Mulrennan in Irish, he is evidently fluent in English and realises the comparative ease of switching to this language once he has performed the necessary touristic services for the visitor. Rather than viewing this as Joyce pointing out the uselessness of the revival of the Irish language, as some have been wont to see it, this scene instead portrays a truly hybrid figure, moving between the worlds of tradition and modernity. The old man's comment on the 'terrible queer creatures at the latter end of the world' is not proof of his ignorance but rather his realisation of his place in the world (*P* 252). There is also the irony that for most Revivalists indulging in primitivism, old men like him were examples themselves of such 'terrible queer creatures'. The old man's comment implicitly rejects the exoticisation he has been subjected to by reversing the perspective.

This is not the first time Joyce has performed such a reversal, as can be seen in the manuscript of *Stephen Hero* where the peasant man subjects Stephen to physiognomic interrogation. Indeed, Nels Pearson describes the effect of the *Portrait* scene as 'the old man returning the anthropologist's gaze, refusing assimilation into an abstract of Celtic tradition, remaining unexplained'.[86] Stephen's first reaction to this figure is one of fear and hostility, before eventually realising that he need no longer struggle with him.

> I fear him. I fear his red-rimmed horny eyes. It is with him I must struggle all through this night till day come, till he or I lie dead, gripping him by the sinewy throat till. . . Till what? Till he yield to me? No. I mean no harm. (*P* 252)

The image of Stephen's hands loosening themselves from the 'sinewy throat' of the peasant is, arguably, one of the most important in the novel, and brings a sense of closure to the struggle with the peasantry from *Stephen Hero* through to *A Portrait*. Later, in *Ulysses*, Bloom underlines this idea of coexistence between urban intellectuals such as Stephen and the rural peasantry: 'You have every bit as much right to live by your pen in pursuit of your philosophy as the peasant has. What? You both belong to Ireland, the brain and the brawn. Each is equally important' (*U* 16.1157–9). This sense of reconciliation continues into the *Wake* with the proposal to '[b]ring lolave branches to mud cabins' (*FW* 244.4–5). McHugh notes the apparent reference here to the *lulav* branches of the Jewish festival of Sukkot, but there is also the idea of offering an olive branch to the peasantry in their mud cabins, a peace offering after years of suspicion.[87] However, we might add to this interpretation the 'eye-echo' that 'lolave' invites with the Spanish verb *lavar*, 'to wash', with the phrase *lo lavé* meaning 'I washed it'. Such an interpretation would appear to make this a reference to the supposed filthiness of peasant life from Joyce's urban perspective. As with so much of the *Wake*, every interpretation seems to contain within it its own contradiction. In many ways, however, it is an appropriately double-edged note on which to end this account of Joyce's portrayal of the Irish peasantry, a portrayal that vacillates between shame and sympathy, primitivism and realism, but that is at all times unique in the context of Revivalist literature.

Notes

1. Yeats, 'Under Ben Bulben', in *Yeats's Poems*, 451.
2. Lyons, *Ireland Since the Famine*, 231.
3. Len Platt, *Joyce and the Anglo-Irish: A Study of Joyce and the Literary Revival* (Amsterdam: Rodopi, 1998), 173.
4. Pound, '"Dubliners" and Mr. James Joyce', 267.
5. McHugh, *Annotations*, 62.
6. Seumas O'Kelly, *Wet Clay* (Dublin: The Talbot Press, 1918), 246, cited in Hirsch, 'The Imaginary Irish Peasant', 1123.
7. O'Kelly, *Wet Clay*, 247.
8. Hirsch, 'The Imaginary Irish Peasant', 1117.
9. John Wilson Foster, *Fictions of the Irish Literary Revival: A Changeling Art* (Syracuse, NY: Syracuse University Press, 1987), 154.
10. Arthur Power, *Conversations with James Joyce*, ed. Clive Hart (London: Millington, 1974), 34.

11. J. A. Froude, untitled, *The Times*, 3 December 1880, 3, cited in L. H. Platt, 'The Buckeen and the Dogsbody: Aspects of History and Culture in "Telemachus"', *James Joyce Quarterly* 27/1 (1989), 79.

12. Vincent Cheng, *Joyce, Race, and Empire* (Cambridge: Cambridge University Press, 1995), 37. Cheng borrows this term from Stephen Dedalus in 'Circe' (*U* 15.2590).

13. Cheng, *Joyce, Race, and Empire*, 37.

14. L. Perry Curtis, *Apes and Angels: The Irishman in Victorian Caricature*, 2nd edn (Washington, DC: Smithsonian Books, 1996), 2.

15. Marion H. Spielmann, *The History of 'Punch'* (London: Cassell, 1895), 106, cited in Curtis, *Apes and Angels*, 31.

16. Curtis, *Apes and Angels*, 29.

17. Ibid., 57.

18. Hirsch, 'The Imaginary Irish Peasant', 1119.

19. Ibid., 1119.

20. Sinéad Garrigan Mattar, *Primitivism, Science, and the Irish Revival* (Oxford: Oxford University Press, 2004), 10.

21. Ibid., 3.

22. Ibid., 73. Matthew Arnold's *On the Study of Celtic Literature* (London: Smith, Elder, 1867) interprets the Celt as poetic but incapable of self-rule. 'The Celtic genius' has, he argues, 'sentiment as its main basis, with love of beauty, charm and spirituality for its excellence, ineffectualness and self-will for its defect' (115).

23. Mattar, *Primitivism*, 98.

24. Ibid., 98.

25. Ibid., 239.

26. Ibid., 237.

27. Ibid., 171.

28. Power, *Conversations*, 33.

29. The phrase 'the backbone of the nation', or slight variants thereof, occurs a number of times in Joyce's work in relation to the peasantry, usually with a heavy dose of irony attached (see *SH* 213 and *U* 16.1022). It should therefore be treated with some suspicion here.

30. John McCourt, 'Queering the Revivalist's Pitch: Joycean Engagements with Primitivism', in Maria McGarrity and Claire A. Culleton (eds), *Irish Modernism and the Global Primitive* (New York: Palgrave Macmillan, 2009), 21.

31. Some pages from the Mullingar section were missing when *Stephen Hero* was first posthumously published, and are still not included in most subsequent versions. These missing pages can, however, be read in the eighth volume of *The James Joyce Archive*, edited by Michael Groden et al., and are cited here as *JJA* 8, followed by page number.

32. Lloyd, *Irish Times*, 45.

33. Kiberd, *Inventing Ireland*, 32.

34. McCourt, 'Queering the Revivalist's Pitch', 32.

35. Ibid., 32.
36. Gordon Bowker, *James Joyce: A New Biography* (New York: Farrar, Straus and Giroux, 2011), 12.
37. Ibid., 16.
38. Foster, *Fictions of the Irish Literary Revival*, 302.
39. Ibid., 206.
40. Seamus Deane, 'Notes', in James Joyce, *A Portrait of the Artist as a Young Man* (London: Penguin, 2000), 309 n.31.
41. William Butler Yeats, *The Countess Cathleen*, in David R. Clark and Rosalind E. Clark (eds), *The Collected Works of W.B. Yeats, Volume II: The Plays* (London: Palgrave, 2001), 52.
42. 1901 Census of Ireland, Limerick, District Electoral Division (DED) Grange, Grange Lower, House 15, John Clancy Household; digital image, 'Household Return (Form A)', The National Archives of Ireland, http://www.census.nationalarchives.ie/ (accessed 19 January 2022).
43. Fathers of the Society of Jesus, *A Page of Irish History: Story of University College, Dublin, 1883–1909* (Dublin: The Talbot Press, 1930), 477.
44. Theodore Spencer used square brackets in his original edition of *Stephen Hero* to indicate a word that was deleted by Joyce in the manuscript; I have retained them in my quotations.
45. A *camán* is the Irish word for a hurley, the ash-stick used for playing hurling, one of the ancient Irish sports being codified at this time by the Gaelic Athletic Association.
46. For an examination of the rural dialect in *Stephen Hero* and *A Portrait*, see Niall Ó Cuileagáin, '"Is he as innocent as his speech?": Rural Hiberno-English in *Stephen Hero* and *A Portrait of the Artist as a Young Man*', in Serenella Zanotti (ed.), *Joyce Studies in Italy 21: Language and Languages in Joyce's Fiction* (Rome: Anicia, 2019), 113–26.
47. Gregory Castle, *Modernism and the Celtic Revival* (Cambridge: Cambridge University Press, 2001), 196.
48. Foster, *Fictions of the Irish Literary Revival*, 313.
49. Crispian Neill, 'The Afflatus of Flatus: James Joyce and the Writing of Odor', *James Joyce Quarterly* 53/3 (2016), 307.
50. H. G. Wells, 'James Joyce', *Nation*, 24 February 1917, 710, and A.M., 'A Sensitivist', *The Manchester Guardian*, 2 March 1917, 3, cited in Neill, 'The Afflatus of Flatus', 307.
51. Hans J. Rindisbacher, *The Smell of Books: A Cultural-Historical Study of Olfactory Perception in Literature* (Ann Arbor, MI: University of Michigan Press, 1993), 143, cited in Neill, 'The Afflatus of Flatus', 322–3 n.5.
52. Neill, 'The Afflatus of Flatus', 310.
53. Christine O'Neill, '"A Faint Mortal Odour": The Elusive World of Smell in *A Portrait of the Artist as a Young Man*', *Dublin James Joyce Journal* 5 (2012), 82.

54. Mark M. Smith, *Sensing the Past: Seeing, Hearing, Smelling, Tasting, and Touching in History* (Berkeley, CA: University of California Press, 2007), 59.

55. Ibid., 66.

56. Ibid., 70.

57. Max Horkheimer and Theodor Adorno, *Dialectic of Enlightenment: Philosophical Fragments* (1944; Stanford, CA: Stanford University Press, 2002), 151.

58. Ibid., 151.

59. Lloyd, *Irish Times*, 88.

60. Ibid., 88 n.42.

61. Ibid., 88.

62. This sense of the inferiority of a Christian Brothers education is alluded to in the Night Lessons chapter of *Finnegans Wake*, when a footnote to a passage mimicking the Hiberno-English accent begs us to '[e]xcuse theyre christianbrothers irish' (*FW* 301.F2).

63. See James R. Thrane, 'Joyce's Sermon on Hell: Its Source and Its Backgrounds', *Modern Philology* 57/3 (1960), 172–98; and Elizabeth F. Boyd, 'James Joyce's Hell-Fire Sermons', *Modern Language Notes* 75/7 (1960), 561–71. For a translation of the original passage, see Giovanni Pietro Pinamonti, *Hell opened to Christians, to caution them from entering into it, or, Considerations on the infernal pains: proposed to our meditation to avoid them: and distributed for every day in the week* (Derby: Thomas Richardson & Son, 1845), 19–20.

64. Kiberd, *Inventing Ireland*, 177.

65. Ibid., 177.

66. Conrad Maynadier Arensberg and Solon Toothaker Kimball, *Family and Community in Ireland*, 2nd edn (Cambridge, MA: Harvard University Press, 1968), 199.

67. Foster, *Fictions of the Irish Literary Revival*, 28.

68. Kiberd, *Inventing Ireland*, 182.

69. Paul O'Brien, 'Primitive Communism and The Blasket Islands', *Irish Marxist Review* 4/12 (2015), 36.

70. Mattar, *Primitivism*, 173.

71. Ibid., 13.

72. Ibid., 176.

73. John Millington Synge, *The Aran Islands* (1907; Oxford: Oxford University Press, 1995), 47, 122.

74. Ellmann, *Consciousness of Joyce*, 129–30.

75. Ibid., 121.

76. John Millington Synge, 'In the Shadow of the Glen', in *The Complete Plays* (London: Methuen Drama, 1990), 89.

77. Ibid., 94.

78. Kiberd, *Inventing Ireland*, 183.

79. Maria McGarrity and Claire A. Culleton, 'Introduction', in Maria McGarrity and Claire A. Culleton (eds), *Irish Modernism and the Global Primitive* (New York: Palgrave Macmillan, 2009), 3.
80. Hirsch, 'The Imaginary Irish Peasant', 1118.
81. Moran, *The Philosophy of Irish Ireland*, 4.
82. This image of a peasantry loyal to their superiors can be seen at the beginning of Yeats's *The Countess Cathleen*, when the peasant wife welcomes the Countess into her house saying: 'For my old fathers served your fathers, lady, / Longer than books can tell – and it were strange / If you and yours should not be welcome here' (Yeats, *The Countess Cathleen*, 31).
83. Yeats, 'The Fisherman', in *Yeats's Poems*, 252.
84. Lady Gregory, *Visions and Beliefs in the West of Ireland* (1920; Gerrards Cross: Colin Smythe, 1970), 16, cited in Foster, *Fictions of the Irish Literary Revival*, 211.
85. Yeats, *The Countess Cathleen*, 52.
86. Pearson, *Irish Cosmopolitanism*, 7.
87. McHugh, *Annotations*, 244.

Part II

Place and Peregrinations

Chapter 4

Rus in Urbe: Where Rural Meets Urban in Joyce's Dublin

In 'Ithaca', Leopold Bloom states that his 'ultimate ambition' (*U* 17.1497) is 'to purchase by private treaty in fee simple a thatched bungalowshaped 2 storey dwellinghouse of southerly aspect' (*U* 17.1504–5) located 'not less than 1 statute mile from the periphery of the metropolis, within a time limit of not more than 15 minutes from tram or train line' (*U* 17.1514–16). From his rural home Bloom would have views 'over unoccupied and unoccupyable interjacent pastures' (*U* 17.1510–11), even entertaining the idea of becoming a 'gentleman farmer' (*U* 17.1603). Bloom imagines himself dressed '[i]n loose allwool garments with Harris tweed cap', while working outside 'planting aligned young firtrees, syringing, pruning, staking, sowing hayseed, trundling a weedladen wheelbarrow without excessive fatigue at sunset amid the scent of newmown hay, ameliorating the soil' (*U* 17.1582–6). Much of Bloom's rustic dream involves contradiction or at the very least betrays a desire to have one's cake and eat it too. The traditional countryside bungalow by definition only has one storey, and therefore Bloom's desire to have a larger, though still superficially rustic home means that it will be 'bungalowshaped' rather than a bungalow *tout court*. Although Bloom might see himself as a 'gentleman farmer', he envisions having no more than '1 or 2 stripper cows' (*U* 17.1604). A 'stripper cow' is one that is not in calf and giving very little milk, and so these cows seem more ornamental than of the cash variety.[1] Meanwhile, whatever work Bloom will do in the fields will crucially not involve 'excessive fatigue' (*U* 17.1585). Despite his notions of modesty, Bloom's rural dream is clearly modelled more on the lives of the landlords of rural Ireland than the peasants who toiled in the fields.

In imagining his 'bungalowshaped' house, Bloom dismisses other forms of residence, such as the excess of 'an extensive demesne' (*U* 17.1500), the more working-class 'terracehouse', and the 'semi-detached villa' with pretensions to grandeur, signified by lofty descriptions such as '*Rus in Urbe* or *Qui si sana*' (*U* 17.1503–4). Despite Bloom's dismissal, these overblown inscriptions – *Rus in Urbe* coming from the Latin for 'the country in the city' and *Qui si sana* from the Italian for 'here one is healed' – quite accurately describe what he is looking for in his ideal home: somewhere that can lend the salubriousness of the countryside, while remaining within easy reach of the city centre.

As critics such as William J. Kupinse and Liam Lanigan have shown, Bloom's attitude bears all the hallmarks of the 'Garden City' movement established by Ebenezer Howard in late nineteenth-century Britain, which was based upon a 'utopian commitment to a "town-country" that is "free from the disadvantages" of either the urban or the rural'.[2] Despite being very much a British phenomenon to begin with, Lanigan demonstrates how the ideals of the Garden City movement were eagerly seized upon by nationalist urban planners in the context of Revivalist Ireland. Lanigan argues that the development of the Garden City allowed the 'emergent urban middle class' to identify with 'the pastoral and mythic symbolism through which Irish nationalism had identified itself in opposition to English cultural identity'.[3] In truth, Bloom is looking for a middle-class suburban ideal, one that would become a reality in the twentieth century for thousands of Dublin families and that would ensure that the rural villages Bloom has his eyes on – Dundrum and Sutton (*U* 17.1516–17) – were subsumed into suburbia. In seeking a rural haven within a short distance of the city, Bloom and his middle-class peers ironically would enact what *Finnegans Wake* describes as an '*Urbs in Rure*' (*FW* 551.24), resulting in 'the cit [. . .] leaking asphalt like a suburbiaurealis in his rure' (*FW* 332.33–4). This is the gradual sprawl east to west of the urban area into the rural – the same trajectory taken by Aurora, goddess of dawn in Roman mythology, hinted at in 'suburbiaurealis'. This is in many ways the traditional hierarchical view of urban–rural relations, as the rural area gets gradually subsumed into the urban. However, as this chapter will show, this simplified vision is consistently undercut in Joyce's works, as the rural and the urban are shown to exist in a much more interconnected way than is often acknowledged.

The likes of Bloom did not have to go very far to feel the influence of the rural in urban Dublin. In fact, the border between rural and urban in Joyce's works is rarely neat and more often porous, as rural influences filter into the city. In this chapter, I will focus on two examples of this: people, via internal migration, and cattle, as part of the agricultural economy. I will also examine the liminal zones along the edge of the city where rural and urban interconnect and coexist. As a phrase, *rus in urbe* is usually used in reference to aspects of the urban environment that create the illusion of the countryside, such as parks. Here, I will show that Joyce in his fiction enacts a literary *rus in urbe*, presenting a modern metropolis that is never untethered from its rural surroundings and at times seems to blend into them.

A number of critics have claimed that Irish writers found it difficult to give expression to the urban experience in forms that were not tied to those used to describe rural, peasant experience during the Revival. Lanigan comments, for example, that 'when writing about the city Irish writers adopted rural forms, depicting small, knowable communities and relatively contained settings, so that, for instance, [Seán] O'Casey's tenement blocks essentially transplant a village community into a superficially urban milieu'.[4] Meanwhile, Luke Gibbons cites the late nineteenth-century writer May Laffan, whose urban slum district of Commons-lane depicts a society where '[p]rivate life hardly exists [. . .] in keeping with its rural counterpart'.[5] However, rather than dismissing this as a failure of imagination on the part of these writers, one should investigate to what extent the Dublin of the late nineteenth and early twentieth centuries found itself existing in a kind of halfway zone between the rural countryside and the modern European metropolis, a cliché that has survived in the idea of Dublin-as-village. Fredric Jameson famously described Joyce's Dublin as an 'underdeveloped village',[6] a view that Andrew Thacker accords with, writing that the Dublin of *Ulysses* 'has something of the quality of a busy village on market-day, where everyone is familiar with everyone else'.[7] There is certainly some truth in this: Joyce, for all that he is credited with giving expression to the modern metropolis, nonetheless depicts a city that feels more like a small country town, a place where 'everyone knows everyone else's business' (*D* 49). There are strikingly few strangers on the streets of Joyce's Dublin; when strangers do appear, such as the figure of 'M'Intosh', it becomes a major event in the day, something to plague the mind. Declan Kiberd describes Joyce's Dublin as 'a classic example of a periphery-dominated-centre, that is to say, a conurbation dominated by the values and mores of the surrounding countryside'.[8] The fluid intermingling of rural and urban life is a key aspect of Joyce's conception of Dublin as metropolis and contradicts the notion of the islanded city cut off from the countryside, so dominant in modernist literature, and of particular resonance in an Irish context where the Pale had attempted to cut Dublin off from the rest of the country during the Middle Ages.

This view of the modern city as existing independently of the surrounding countryside can be felt in much European writing contemporary to Joyce. The German historian Oswald Spengler described the development of the modern city in the first volume of *The Decline of the West* (1918) as constituting *'a place from which the countryside is henceforth regarded, felt, and experienced as "environs,"* as something different and subordinate'.[9] Following the development of the early modern European city, Spengler argued that 'there are two lives, that of the inside and that of the outside', to the point that these two existences become unintelligible to each other: 'The man of the land and the man of the city are different essences. First of all they feel the difference, then they are dominated by it, and at last they cease to understand each other at all.'[10] Similarly, Georg Simmel, in 'The Metropolis and Mental Life' (1903), draws a clear distinction between the psychological make-up of urban and rural people:

> The metropolis exacts from man as a discriminating creature a different amount of consciousness than does rural life. Here the rhythm of life and sensory mental imagery flows more slowly, more habitually, and more evenly. Precisely in this connection the sophisticated character of metropolitan psychic life becomes understandable – as over against small town life which rests more upon deeply felt and emotional relationships.[11]

Simmel goes so far as to posit that 'the metropolitan type of man [. . .] develops an organ protecting him against the threatening currents and discrepancies of his external environment'.[12] People dwelling in rural or small-town areas, however, do not stop themselves from reacting emotionally to each person they meet, given that in these places 'one knows almost everybody one meets'.[13] However, as Joyce's Dublin is a city where people are intimately connected and strangers are few, disconnecting oneself emotionally risks social ostracism.

Henri Lefebvre's writings on the transition to an urban-dominated West are also useful for conceptualising Dublin's status as an urban centre at this time. As discussed in Chapter 1, Lefebvre began his career as a rural sociologist, before gaining fame for his Marxist critiques of urban life and the everyday. However, even in the works that are more focused on urbanity, the rural is rarely far from view, with Lefebvre placing emphasis on the interconnectivity of urban and rural life. In *The Urban Revolution* (1970), Lefebvre notes that with the development of the first major cities there remained a clear distinction between city and countryside, and that it was in the rural areas that economic power was concentrated through property and the products of the land. However, Lefebvre writes,

> [a]t a given moment, these various relationships were reversed; the situation changed [. . .] From this moment on, the city would no longer appear as an urban island in a rural ocean, it would no longer seem a paradox, a monster, a hell or heaven that contrasted sharply with village or country life in a natural environment. It entered people's awareness and understanding as one of the terms in the opposition between town and country. Country? It is now no more than – nothing more than – the town's 'environment,' its horizon, its limit. Villagers? As far as they were concerned, they no longer worked for the territorial lords, they produced for the city, for the urban market. And even though they realized that the wheat and wood merchants exploited them, they understood that the path to freedom crossed the marketplace.[14]

Like Spengler, Lefebvre retains this hierarchical structure between urban and rural, seeing the rural as relegated to the position of mere environs to the city, but for Lefebvre this power-reversal has the result of bringing the countryside and the city into closer collaboration, as the products of the rural space must pass into the urban marketplace. As such, urban and rural people are brought into closer contact as Europe moves from being a feudal to an industrial society. Lefebvre describes this progression in terms of three 'fields': the rural, the industrial and finally the urban.[15] However, he also theorises that there exists a 'point of transition between two periods'.[16] These Lefebvre designates as '*blind fields*', writing that '[i]n the past there was a field between the rural and the industrial – just as there is today between the industrial and the urban – that was invisible to us'.[17] Lefebvre's theory is not neatly applicable to Dublin in 1904, given that Dublin never attained a position as Ireland's industrial powerhouse – that would be occupied instead by Belfast – but the idea that Dublin occupies a 'blind field' between the rural and urban 'fields' is persuasive in the context of Joyce's writing. Indeed, Richard Lehan goes so far as to argue that Joyce's Dublin 'was closer to a peasant than an industrial world', with Joyce sharing 'the concern of late nineteenth-century realism with the transition from an agrarian/landed to a commercial/urban world'.[18]

In *The Production of Space* (1974), Lefebvre emphasises the inter-connectivity that exists between different types of space. In particular, he conceives of 'social space', whereby space takes on more than just a 'geometrical meaning'.[19] Andrew Thacker writes that Lefebvre's theory of social space insists on space as 'inherently composite, mingling heterogenous spaces together in one physical location'.[20] Lefebvre's theory argues for the porousness of boundaries, writing that

> *Social spaces interpenetrate one another and/or superimpose themselves upon one another.* They are not things, which have mutually limiting boundaries and which collide because of their contours or as a result of inertia [. . .] Visible boundaries, such as walls or enclosures in general, give rise for their part to an appearance of separation between spaces where in fact what exists is an ambiguous continuity.[21]

If we conceive of the rural and the urban as separate social spaces with their own unique ideological and sociological characteristics, we must also be open to acknowledging how these spaces 'interpenetrate' each other, forming an 'ambiguous continuity'. Rather than focusing on purely hierarchical accounts of the relationship between the rural and the urban, this chapter proposes a relationship founded instead upon interconnectivity.

Certainly, Dublin is not the kind of 'urban island in a rural ocean' that European modernists and social theorists saw around them when they examined other metropolises. Nevertheless, much criticism has treated Joyce's Dublin as emblematic of the European metropolis of the time. The earliest propagandist for this view of Joyce was, once again, Ezra Pound, who wrote of *Dubliners*:

> He gives us things as they are, not only for Dublin, but for every city. Erase the local names and a few specifically local allusions, and a few historic events of the past, and substitute a few different local names, allusions and events, and these stories could be retold of any town.[22]

Pound was one of the most determined of the early critics in championing Joyce as a European writer, but, as his almost comically long list of required erasures shows, this could only be achieved by significantly writing out Joyce's Irishness. The aim of this chapter is to show that the stories and novels produced by Joyce could not be of 'any town' but are very specifically of Dublin, and a Dublin in constant contact with its rural surroundings at that. In looking at rural migration, cattle, and the liminal spaces between rural and urban in *Dubliners*, *A Portrait* and *Ulysses*, this chapter will show how Joyce emphasises the unique, semi-rural character of Dublin as Hibernian metropolis.

'Bostoons' and 'country cute': Joyce's Rural Migrants

It has become something of a critical mainstay to claim that early twentieth-century Dublin was a city 'overrun by unplanned migrations of rural folk'.[23] These rural migrants are then credited – or blamed – with 'sentimentaliz[ing] the rhythms of a country life which they ha[d] not yet, in their minds, completely abandoned', turning Dublin into an overly provincialised capital city ripe for Revivalist cliché.[24] The idea of rural migrants in the city became a convenient explanation for many of Ireland's ills following independence. For example, we read that a 'rural mind-set expanded outwards into towns and cities creating the strangling conservatism that characterised Irish society in the second half of the nineteenth century and the first half of the last'.[25] First, given the very well-documented migrations of rural people to major cities across Europe in the nineteenth century, one must question why other countries did not see the kind of nation-defining peasant worship and conservatism associated with Revivalist and post-independence Ireland, if this can be primarily attributed to the presence of country people in the city. Secondly, and most importantly, Dublin did not in fact see large inmigration of rural people in the nineteenth century. As in other European countries, people were fleeing the countryside, and in alarming numbers, particularly following the Famine; but these people were largely not becoming urbanised in Ireland, with Timothy W. Guinnane noting that 'to become urban most Irish left their country'.[26] While Dublin did see some significant population growth in the first decades of the nineteenth century, this dramatically slowed after the Famine.[27] Between 1851 and 1911, Dublin's population grew from 247,000 to just 305,000.[28] Compared with other cities in Europe, this is remarkably low. Guinnane notes that, over the same period, 'Düsseldorf increased its population by nearly eight times, Hamburg by over five times', while even more established cities such as London and Paris more than doubled their populations.[29] During this time Belfast's population also exploded due to its importance as an industrial centre for linen production, expanding from a town of little more than 30,000 people in 1815 to a city approaching 400,000 in 1911.[30]

Those who did migrate to Dublin often found themselves struggling to survive in insalubrious conditions. Joseph V. O'Brien gives an account of what a typical family migrating to Dublin might have had in store for them:

> Sad stories were repeated of the results in the familiar one-room tenements: healthy families migrating from country to city to take up residence in undisinfected quarters having a continuous history of inhabitants dying from consumption – hardly a member of the family would be alive in five years; daughters nursing consumptive mothers and both dying within months of each other; young adults in the last stages of consumption sleeping in the same bed with healthy siblings; the poor and unemployed living largely on bread, porter, and tea and unable to withstand the ravages of the disease when contracted.[31]

Dublin was therefore not an attractive destination for the majority of rural migrants in late nineteenth-century Ireland. Those few who did migrate were unlikely to see themselves occupying a position of power or even middle-class comfort, let alone as defining the brand of politics that would come to dominate Irish public life.

However, facts are one thing, perceptions quite another; and it was the perception of Dublin being overrun by rural migrants that would gain dominance in cultural discourse. Indeed, Dublin Corporation, the city's government and administrative organisation, 'was blamed for not deterring the alleged influx of rural laborers and their families into the city' and in 1906 inserted a clause into its contracts 'making two years' residence in the city a condition of employment, only to have it disallowed by the Local Government Board'.[32]

Such notions of the extent of rural migration to Dublin are clearly to the fore in Joyce's works, with rural characters, or characters of recent rural origins, over-represented. Biographical realities might also explain Joyce's tendency to overpopulate his works with rural and provincial migrants, given that his father was an arrival from Cork. Joyce always emphasised this aspect of his family origins, most notably when correcting a biographical entry in the Revd Stephen Browne's work *Ireland in Fiction* (1916), which mistakenly suggested that his family came from Galway.[33] Joyce instead noted: 'My father is from Cork city, his father from Fermoy, county Cork. The family comes, of course, from the west of Ireland (Joyce's country) but mine is a southern offshoot of the tribe' (*L1* 115). When organising his father's gravestone inscription, Joyce made sure to note these roots, including 'OF CORK' below his father's name (*L3* 263n1).

This insistence on his father's Cork background is transferred to Simon Dedalus, who, it is noted in *Ulysses*, is 'of Cork and Dublin' (*U* 17.538). The double allegiance, to both place of birth and place of long-term residence, is revealing of the split identity of the migrant to the city. In *A Portrait*, Simon says that he has been 'trying for thirty years to get rid of his Cork accent up in Dublin', as though trying to shake off the Cork aspect of his identity and fully embrace the Dublin half (*P* 93). This is, however, only partially true: at every opportunity that presents itself, Simon is on the hunt for information about life down in Cork. 'How are all in Cork's own town?' he asks Ned Lambert, who has just come back from the southern city (*U* 6.558). Ned shares stories about old acquaintances in Cork – namely Dick Tivy, suddenly bald (*U* 6.562–3) – showing the close bonds that still exist between migrants and their former social worlds, as gossip only works when these ties remain strong. Simon's association with Cork is made most explicit during his appearance in 'Circe', where he assumes the role of a cardinal with 'a rosary of corks ending on his breast in a corkscrew cross' hanging around his neck (*U* 15.2659–60). The 'rosary of corks' and 'corkscrew cross' are references to Simon's proclivity for consuming alcohol, but given Joyce's own propensity for drawing a punning association between cork as material and Cork as county – during a visit to Joyce in Paris, Frank O'Connor noted a map of Cork surrounded by a frame made of cork (*JJII* 551) – it is also quite clearly another nod to Simon's origins.

Joyce's correction to Revd Browne is notable not just for emphasising his father's links to Cork, but also for neglecting to affirm his own identity as a born-and-bred Dubliner. This might be because he too was, to a certain degree, a migrant to the city proper. The Joyce family's first home was, after all, in the Dublin suburb of Rathgar, and at the age of five the young Joyce was not even living in the county of Dublin, let alone the city, but instead in Bray, County Wicklow. Ellmann explains the move as being due to the fact that 'John Joyce longed to live closer to water and farther from his wife's relatives'; however, the move was also a signifier of the family's middle-class comfort at this time, as Ellmann acknowledges when he refers to Bray as being 'a fashionable neighbourhood' and a short train journey from Dublin city (*JJII* 24). Joyce's early life in Bray was surrounded by other Munster migrants like his father, with Mrs Hearn Conway and his father's uncle, William O'Connell, joining them from Cork, and Mr John Kelly of Tralee, County Kerry, also often staying with them (*JJII* 24–5). Scenes of this life in Bray, featuring Mrs Conway ('Dante') and Mr Kelly ('Mr Casey'), make it into the early narrative of *A Portrait*, as noted by Joyce's brother Stanislaus (*MBK* 30–1, 34–5). Stanislaus's account of this time emphasises their proximity to nature, describing the family home at Bray as being 'within a stone's throw of the sea', while behind their terrace 'were lanes and fishermen's cottages and a long strand reaching to Killiney' (*MBK* 27–8). Joyce was 10 years old when the family's failing fortunes forced them away from Bray and back into Dublin, though even then it was at first to the relatively leafy suburb of Blackrock (*JJII* 35). The next move, to Fitzgibbon Street, brought the 11-year-old Joyce into the city for the first time (*JJII* 35).

Stephen, like Joyce, spends most of his childhood years living outside the city, in a house dominated by people from Cork and Kerry. Little wonder, then, that when Stephen finds himself making a similar move to the city, he registers Dublin as 'a new and complex sensation' (*P* 66). Stephen is, therefore, something of a half-migrant to the city, or a second-generation migrant who, like the first generation, knows what it is to have lived elsewhere. Stephen largely comes to reject the idea of borrowing from his father, like an ill-fitting suit, an inauthentic Cork identity, especially during the journey they take there together in *A Portrait*. Stephen's friend Cranly is also the son of a rural migrant; however, unlike Stephen, Cranly wholly identifies himself with the county where his father was born rather than with Dublin. Cranly is based on Joyce's acquaintance John Francis Byrne, born in Dublin to an erstwhile farmer from County Wicklow. Ellmann writes that every summer Byrne 'disappeared into Wicklow, where his activities were so unaffectedly rural as to puzzle his city friend' (*JJII* 64).[34] In *Stephen Hero*, Cranly frequently speaks about Wicklow and makes his allegiance clear by referring to it as 'his part of the country' (*SH* 125). Meanwhile, in *A Portrait*, we meet him reading a book entitled *Diseases of the Ox*, which, though further underlining his interest in rural life, does also seem to suggest that he remains removed from the reality of agricultural matters, having to learn about them in the library rather than in the field, so to speak (*P* 227).

Cranly's accent is also revealing, as, unlike the 'peasant student' Davin, he

> had neither rare phrases of Elizabethan English nor quaintly turned versions of Irish idioms. Its drawl was an echo of the quays of Dublin given back by a bleak decaying seaport, its energy an echo of the sacred eloquence of Dublin given back flatly by a Wicklow pulpit. (*P* 195)

Cranly's accent is a strange commixture of Dublin and Wicklow – there is no suggestion that either one is dominant or that the Wicklow component is necessarily a forced affectation – and so he appears to represent the hybridity of the second-generation migrant. Cranly presumes himself an authority on all things to do with 'Wickla', informing his listeners that yellow bees are called '[r]ed-arsed bees' in that part of the country (*SH* 118). Such tendencies might be what marks Cranly out from actual migrants such as Davin/Madden and Simon Dedalus, who never speak of home in terms of ironic bemusement. That Joyce has the spelling of Wicklow disfigured in Cranly's speech hints perhaps at a similar disfigurement of reality as well. Cranly would seem to be a good example of what Kiberd terms the 'citified children' of rural migrants to Dublin who view the countryside 'through a haze of sentiment and nostalgia'.[35]

The emphasis on Cranly's accent is significant, for when rural and provincial characters appear in Joyce's work they are often set apart by their accents, especially in *Dubliners*, a collection of stories preoccupied with accent types. Ulster accents are typically described negatively, with Farrington's superior in 'Counterparts' having 'a piercing North of Ireland accent' (*D* 66). Flat accents are also frequently remarked upon, with the snobbish and ambitious Mrs Kearney in 'A Mother' quick to notice Mr Fitzpatrick's flat accent, which she rewards 'with a quick stare of contempt' (*D* 108). When Fitzpatrick mentions the Committee, Mrs Kearney mimics him by replying '[a]nd who is the *Cometty*, pray?' (*D* 110). By contrast, the man from the *Freeman's Journal* is approved of, given his 'plausible voice and careful manners' (*D* 112). Fitzpatrick's accent might be a sign that he is from the midlands, a part of the country whose accent is often described as 'flat', though he might also be a North Dubliner and therefore associated with the kind of working-class background of which Mrs Kearney disapproves. Another interesting clash of accents occurs in 'Counterparts' when Farrington arrives home drunk and primed for violence. After his son informs him that his wife is at the chapel, Farrington begins 'to mimic his son's flat accent, saying half to himself: *At the chapel. At the chapel, if you please!*' (*D* 75). It seems strange for a father to mimic his son's manner of speech, given that one might expect them to share an accent. The fact that Farrington does so suggests that they do not share an accent, and that Farrington may in fact be a migrant to Dublin himself, while his son, growing up in Dublin, has acquired its flat accent.[36] The exposure to an accent deemed to be different to his own seems to recall in Farrington's mind the humiliation he had experienced earlier in the day with his superior from Ulster. Accent, and its capacity for marking one out as different, inferior or out of sync with one's place of habitation, becomes one of the factors that erodes Farrington's sense of self-worth throughout the day, with his son eventually suffering the consequences.

An even more explicit linguistic differentiation occurs in 'Eveline' in the mother's infamous and enigmatic dying words of 'Derevaun Seraun!' (*D* 28). I do not intend to add to the theories already proffered regarding what this exclamation might mean, but its quite clear phonetical similarity to the Irish language does heavily imply that Eveline's mother is a migrant to the city, probably from the west of Ireland. Another potential link to the west lies in Eveline's first name: the Irish name Eibhlín, usually anglicised as 'Eileen' in accordance with its pronunciation in Munster Irish, is in fact pronounced as 'Eveline' in Connacht Irish, suggesting that Eveline's mother might have come from an Irish-speaking area in the west. In any case, the old woman's rural origins appear to resurface in this final utterance, transporting the reader out of this otherwise urban deathbed scene.

One of the more extended discussions of rural people in the city is found in 'Grace', after Tom Kernan, most likely as the result of too much alcohol, collapses in the lavatory of a pub. A young police constable is called to the scene, where he takes notes and speaks in 'a suspicious provincial accent' (*D* 118). Later in the narrative, a convalescing Kernan, surrounded by his friends, first remembers the policeman as a '[d]ecent young fellow', but gradually grows affronted 'by those whom he called country bumpkins' (*D* 125). This leads to a discussion about rural police officers in the city that it is worth quoting in full.

– Is this what we pay rates for? he asked. To feed and clothe these ignorant bostoons . . . and they're nothing else.

Mr Cunningham laughed. He was a Castle official only during office hours.

– How could they be anything else, Tom? he said.

He assumed a thick provincial accent and said in a tone of command:

– 65, catch your cabbage!

Everyone laughed. Mr M'Coy, who wanted to enter the conversation by any door, pretended that he had never heard the story. Mr Cunningham said:

– It is supposed – they say, you know – to take place in the depot where they get these thundering big country fellows, omadhauns, you know, to drill. The sergeant makes them stand in a row against the wall and hold up their plates'. He illustrated the story by grotesque gestures.

– At dinner, you know. Then he has a bloody big bowl of cabbage before him on the table and a bloody big spoon like a shovel. He takes up a wad of cabbage on the spoon and pegs it across the room and the poor devils have to try and catch it on their plates: 65, *catch your cabbage*.

Everyone laughed again: but Mr Kernan was somewhat indignant still. He talked of writing a letter to the papers.

– These yahoos coming up here, he said, think they can boss the people. I needn't tell you, Martin, what kind of men they are.

Mr Cunningham gave a qualified assent.

– It's like everything else in this world, he said. You get some bad ones and you get some good ones.

– O yes, you get some good ones, I admit, said Mr Kernan, satisfied.

– It's better to have nothing to say to them, said Mr M'Coy. That's my opinion! (*D* 125–6)

Kernan's indignant outbursts are partly a result of his sense of humiliation, while Cunningham's story is born out of a desire to get Kernan to agree to go on a retreat where, he hopes, Kernan will change his ways. However, the story only works because it confirms many of the attitudes held by Dubliners such as Kernan towards arrivals from rural Ireland to the city, particularly those who had joined the Dublin Metropolitan Police. Kernan displays a suspicion of the young police officer who hailed from the country that was in fact quite common among Dubliners at the time. In her history of the Dublin Metropolitan Police, Anastasia Dukova writes of the scepticism that existed towards the new force due to the fact that the 'majority of the policemen in Dublin were the sons of tenants and farmers, or otherwise working men'.[37] Dukova argues that the 'crumbling of the existing social structure', and the nature of the work, led to many of their peers viewing 'these freshly minted members of the force as traitors'.[38] Fitzgerald and Lambkin note, however, that joining the police was one of the few options available to the non-inheriting sons of farmers if they wished to remain in Ireland.[39] For Kernan, someone 'of Protestant stock', the rural policeman represents the upending of a social structure that had for so long favoured his own class and religion (*D* 122). Even Catholics such as Cunningham – who also benefits from the present social hierarchy, most noticeably in his work for the 'Castle' – look down on these country constables as social upstarts. However, while Cunningham's bias is mostly expressed in what for him is an outlandish, cliché-confirming anecdote, Kernan's hostility towards these rural arrivals goes deeper. He resents the idea that his taxes are used to 'feed and clothe these ignorant bostoons', while the fact that they are now in a position to 'boss the people' of Dublin is felt as an especially bitter insult.

Kernan's use of language, as well as the other men's, is also interesting here, as the words they use to describe these country people are often borrowed from Irish. One of Kernan's favourite insults is to dismiss country people as 'bostoons'; in addition to the above example, Kernan in 'Wandering Rocks' sees a horse and cart left 'without fare or jarvey' and immediately presumes that it belongs to '[s]ome Tipperary bosthoon endangering the lives of the citizens' (*U* 10.775–7). 'Bost(h)oon' comes from the Irish *bastún*, meaning a 'lout' (*FGB*, 'bastún'). In the example from 'Wandering Rocks', it is placed in direct contrast with the 'citizens' of Dublin, a term that emphasises their urbanity through its original meaning: '[a]n inhabitant of a city or town' (*OED*, 'citizen, n. and adj.', 1a). Cunningham also falls back on insults from the Irish language when telling his story, describing the rural policemen as 'omadhauns', an anglicisation of *amadán*, meaning a 'fool' (*FGB*, 'amadán'). This tendency to use Irish terms might be a deliberate attempt to associate these country people with a language often seen by socially ambitious middle-class Catholics as stuck in the past and linked with poverty and shame. However, it is also possible to read the use of insults from Irish as an attempt by Joyce to undercut the sense of superiority felt by these men towards the rural characters, by highlighting the fact that their recourse to such terms betrays their own Irish-speaking roots from only a few generations back.

Like Farrington in 'Counterparts', Kernan's humiliation results in a feeling of self-loathing which he then turns on the easiest available target – in this case, rural migrants in Dublin. The attitudes of the other men, however, being Catholic Irish and therefore supposedly of the same 'tribe' as these rural policemen, seem to require further comment. While Cunningham shows himself to be a decent character in *Ulysses*, particularly in 'Hades' where he steers the conversation away from topics that might be upsetting to Bloom, here he is content enough to regale the room with this story, assuming a mock-provincial accent while doing so and generalising all rural policemen as 'thundering big country fellows, omadhauns'. However, when the story incites Kernan's anger, Cunningham attempts to cool him down by acknowledging that '[y]ou get some bad ones and you get some good ones'. In fact, Cunningham does not seem to intend to tell the story until M'Coy feigns ignorance and encourages him to do so. This appears to be simply the effort of a hanger-on trying to ingratiate himself with the other men, but M'Coy's final word on the matter is still revealing of his own attitudes towards rural people: '[i]t's better to have nothing to say to them'. It is possible that a certain amount of the men's disdain for the rural policeman lies in his being a representative of the British Empire, though given Cunningham's job at Dublin Castle, this is hardly something he can be overly judgemental about. Perhaps most noteworthy in this passage is the relative silence throughout of the fourth character in the room, Mr Power. While one might read his silence as complicity – and it is not complete silence, for we are twice told that '[e]veryone laughed' at Cunningham's story – when we examine appearances by Power in *Ulysses* we find a character who is often thinking about the affairs of rural Ireland. In 'Hades', when drops of rain begin to fall, Cunningham laments the change in the weather, but Power notes that it is '[w]anted for the country', by which he means the country-*side*, which has been going through a period of drought (*U* 6.134). This contrasts with Kernan's appearance later, when we get snippets of a conversation that he has: 'Lovely weather we are having. Yes, indeed. Good for the country. Those farmers are always grumbling.' (*U* 10.723–4). Unlike Kernan, Power shows a greater sympathy towards the dependency of farmers and the agricultural economy on meteorological variations, and therefore his relative silence throughout Cunningham's story is quite likely a sign of mild disapproval of its general tenor.

The attitudes expressed by Kernan and implied by Cunningham's story are familiar ones regarding any migrant group, be they internal or external. The arrivals from rural Ireland are seen as simpletons – or bostoons – who, even when they have full-time jobs, are still viewed as leeching from the born-and-bred Dubliners, who apparently 'feed and clothe' them through their rates. However, this is only one half of the stereotype, with the other cliché being in many ways its exact opposite: when these migrants are not idiotic and a drain on the urbanites, they are suspiciously successful. Even Bloom displays this type of suspicion when in 'Calypso' he thinks about the kind of rural migrant who arrives in the city to work as a bartender – or 'curate' – before suddenly going on to form their own establishment: 'Where do they get the money? Coming up redheaded curates from the county Leitrim, rinsing empties and old man in the cellar. Then, lo and behold, they blossom out as Adam Findlaters or Dan Tallons'

(*U* 4.126–8). Bloom crafts an image of a stereotypically rural figure, 'redheaded' for good measure, who goes on to become successful like Adam Findlater, a major wine merchant and grocer who had several branches of his company throughout Dublin, or Dan Tallon, a successful publican who went on to become Lord Mayor of Dublin.[40] Bloom's imagined trajectory of the rural migrant to Dublin, though certainly exaggerated, might be based to some degree in fact. The sociologists Arensberg and Kimball note that it was common for rural people to be given jobs as shop assistants or pub 'curates' by businessmen who were originally from the same part of the country as themselves, thus facilitating their move to the city.[41] After a few years working as a bartender or shop assistant and having learned the tricks of the trade, the rural migrant could then set up a business under their own name. This solidarity among people of rural origin seems to have given the new arrivals something of an advantage over those born in the city. This is not to suggest that such routes to success awaited all arrivals in the city – O'Brien's earlier outline of the usual penurious fate of rural migrants shows that it was far from a given – but it is possible that it happened sufficiently often for urbanites to feel that rural people had the game rigged in their favour. Such attitudes resulted in the rural migrant being caught in something of a bind: wallow in poverty and be dismissed as a simpleton and a leech, or become successful and be suspected of cheating one's way to the top.

This sense that the rural arrival is suspiciously shrewd is apparent also in 'The Dead', when Gabriel Conroy reflects on his mother's snobbish attitude towards his wife Gretta, whom she dismisses as 'country cute' (*D* 147). '[C]ute' is employed here to mean overly cunning and is yet another instance of rural people being deemed crafty by urbanites. Gabriel tries to overcome his anxiety about Gretta's rural background by de-ruralising her: when Molly Ivors notes that Gretta is from Connacht, he replies that '[h]er people are' (*D* 148). Gretta, by contrast, feels no such shame about her roots. When she hears about Ivors's plan to go to the Aran Islands, she is immediately enthusiastic about the idea: 'O, do go, Gabriel, she cried. I'd love to see Galway again' (*D* 150). Gabriel's shame contrasts with Gretta's willingness to embrace her background (or at least not deny it). To a degree this shame might spring from Gabriel's knowledge that at some point 'his people' were also from the west of Ireland. Gabriel's surname of Conroy comes from the Irish *Ó Maol Chonaire*, a surname traditionally common in Connacht.[42] In fact, John V. Kelleher has noted that Lily's accent, which he presumes to be 'Dublin lower-class', actually serves to emphasise the Gaelic sound of the original surname, as she gives 'Conroy' an extra third syllable, rendering it 'Connery', and thus returning it to the approximate sound of the Irish 'Conaire'.[43] The 'three syllables she had given his surname' thus act as an example of a subtle *rus in urbe*, the third syllable appearing to ruralise and Gaelicise Gabriel's carefully crafted urban identity (*D* 139).

This instance is but the first of many such rural infiltrations into the story which destabilise the urban setting. Ivors's lambasting of Gabriel's cosmopolitanism is another, and though it provokes irritation in Gabriel, it does not unsettle him to the same degree as later, more subtle instances do. The next most explicit example is when Bartell D'Arcy sings 'The Lass of Aughrim', introducing the musical airs of the west into the house, and bringing with them images of rural desolation – '*O, the rain falls on my heavy locks / And the dew wets my skin, / My babe lies cold. . .*' – and transporting Gretta back to memories of her childhood in Galway (*D* 166). When Gabriel first hears the notes of the song, he is standing at the bottom of the staircase and looks up to see that '[a] woman was standing near the top of the first flight, in the shadow also' (*D* 165). Gabriel at first does not recognise her, as '[h]e could not see her face', but slowly he makes out the colours of the skirt she is wearing and can affirm that '[i]t was his wife' (*D* 165). Gretta in this moment appears unrecognisable to Gabriel as she is transported by the music back to her life before coming to Dublin. This is not a Gretta that Gabriel has ever known, for it is a Gretta not of the big city, but of the provincial town. Gabriel thinks that she must be 'a symbol of something' but is not sure what 'a woman standing on the stairs in the shadow, listening to distant music, [is] a symbol of' (*D* 165). To the likes of Ivors and her clique, it would seem quite clear what Gretta is a symbol of here, as in this moment she falls into the old Gaelic trope of the *spéirbhean* of *aisling* poetry, a beautiful woman who appears to the poet in a dreamlike vision representing Ireland. Gabriel clearly does not want to humour this thought for too long, and instead he looks at his wife and decides that if he were a painter he would paint her thus and title it '*Distant Music*' (*D* 165). The music – 'The Lass of Aughrim' – is distant not only because it emanates from another room but also because it comes from a cultural context far from the urban centre: the village of Aughrim in county Galway and the rural hierarchies of landlords and tenants.[44] However, even in Gabriel's efforts to have his wife symbolise something beyond her western background, he cannot avoid partially ruralising her, as the distant music that floats into the scene both witnessed and imaginatively 'painted' by him is yet another instance of *rus in urbe*. This music will eventually lead to Gabriel's notion of his wife's past and identity being overturned, culminating in the last rural infiltration into the story through the ghost of Michael Furey, as Gabriel imagines 'the form of a young man standing under a dripping tree' outside (*D* 176).

Finally, beckoning taps on the windowpane draw Gabriel's attention to the snow falling and set him on his imaginative 'journey westward' across the breadth of rural Ireland (*D* 176). While Gabriel's realisation of the need to travel west comes late in the story, rural references have been infiltrating the urban setting throughout, like strains of faint, distant music, from Lily's pronunciation of Conroy to Michael Furey's ghost. The rural reality of Gretta's background that Gabriel has been at pains to deny can no longer be kept at bay as he is forced to come to terms not just with his wife's past, but also that of his country. At last we move from successive instances of *rus in urbe* to an ultimate *urbs in rure* as the urban Conroy figuratively leaves the city.

Cowtown: Cattle in the Joycean City

Joyce's fiction is filled with migrants coming to the city from the countryside, but it is not just human characters who make this journey. In 'Hades', as Bloom and the other men in the funeral cortege move towards Glasnevin cemetery on the edge of the city, they are forced to pause momentarily on the North Circular Road as another group of rural migrants pass through the streets in a remarkable instance of *rus in urbe*:

> A divided drove of branded cattle passed the windows, lowing, slouching by on padded hoofs, whisking their tails slowly on their clotted bony croups. Outside them and through them ran raddled sheep bleating their fear.
> – Emigrants, Mr Power said. (*U* 6.385–9)

As has been alluded to already, Power is perhaps the character most sensitive to matters relating to rural Ireland, and his labelling of the cattle and sheep as '[e]migrants' is a just one, as the cattle are on their way to the quays to be shipped off to Britain. In the decades following the Great Famine, Ireland's population, especially its rural population, was decimated by successive waves of emigration. Power's description of the cattle as 'emigrants' is apt, therefore, as for those reared in the fields of rural Ireland, be they people or cattle, there was a certain inevitability about leaving. In his 1907 lecture 'Ireland: Island of Saints and Sages', Joyce lamented the seemingly predestined nature of Irish emigration, writing that 'there has to be something inimical, ill-fated and despotic about [Ireland's] present condition that her sons cannot lend their skills to their native land' (*OCPW* 124). Just as Ireland lost some of its most talented people to emigration, so too does Bloom bemoan how Britain 'buy[s] up all the juicy ones' while looking at the cattle (*U* 6.394). Later, Murphy in the cabman's shelter makes a similar point when he complains that England 'gobbl[es] up the best meat in the market' (*U* 16.992–3).

It is tempting, therefore, to see the animals as existing simply as an allegory for Irish emigration in general, but it is important to consider them first and foremost as what they are: cattle. At this time, Ireland's economy was heavily dominated by its agricultural sector, which in turn was dominated by its cattle trade with Britain. The 1901 census states that agriculture was 'the staple industry of Ireland',[45] while in Arensberg and Kimball's study of early twentieth-century rural Ireland, they write that '[c]attle, of course, are the Irish "money crop"'.[46] Ireland's cattle industry was overly reliant on access to the British market, to the extent that Ireland's economy became defined by its dependence on the meat consumption of its nearest neighbour. This relationship was a profoundly unequal one, as Ireland lost out on many of the potential by-products of cattle, while their husbandry greatly reduced the amount of land dedicated to tillage growth. This section will show how the appearance of cattle on the streets of Dublin, as well as the preponderance of bovine imagery throughout *Ulysses*, emphasises the central place of cattle in Ireland's history, economy and society.

The cattle in 'Hades' are on their way from the Dublin cattle market, which was located near Stoneybatter on the north-western edge of the city. This was hardly the most convenient location, given that the cattle then had to be led to the quays on the eastern side of the city. To get there, they had to walk along the busy North Circular Road. Liam Clare, in his account of the history of the market, notes that

[m]any older Dubliners' sole memory of the cattle market is the driving of cattle down the North Circular Road. As early as 1870, there were complaints of 'great inconvenience and danger' arising from the practice. In 1895 and again in 1902, the City Council considered the regulation of cattle traffic, but the police responded that they could not send a policeman to accompany every drove of cattle.[47]

Such accounts of the impracticalities of leading cattle to the quays explain Bloom's enthusiasm for a tramline that would take the cattle directly there: 'I can't make out why the corporation doesn't run a tramline from the parkgate to the quays, Mr Bloom said. All those animals could be taken in trucks down to the boats' (*U* 6.400–2). This is an idea to which Bloom's thoughts turn at many points throughout the day (*U* 4.108–10, 15.1367–8, 17.1726–43). It is, in many ways, typical Bloom: empathy balanced with practicality, for the tramline would lessen the suffering of the animals as much as it would the 'blocking up [of] the thoroughfare' (*U* 6.403). Bloom, of course, is intimately familiar with the cattle market itself, having worked there as a clerk between 1893 and 1894 (*U* 17.483–6).

Clare goes on to note that the Stoneybatter area around the cattle market became known to Dubliners as 'cowtown'.[48] This humorous appellation is a neat summation of the *rus in urbe* that pervaded this part of Dublin, the stereotypically rural ('cow') meshed together with the urban ('town'). The existence of this nickname shows just how much the rural could infiltrate the urban, to the point that it could define its identity, and also makes clear how economically dependent these two worlds were on one another. Writing about the market town of Ennis in County Clare, Arensberg and Kimball note that 'the town is impossible to visualize apart from the rural hinterland that it serves'.[49] Similarly, here, in this part of Dublin so dominated by the presence of its cattle market, the rural surroundings are impossible to ignore, as the boundaries and hierarchies that divide town from country blur and break down.[50]

Once the cattle got to the quays they were transported by ship to Britain; in 1917, when the cattle trade was reaching its peak, there were thirty-six weekly sailings.[51] However, this booming trade in cattle was not an utterly modern phenomenon, as Irish society had been unusually centred around cattle long before British colonisation. Patrick Cunningham writes that 'Ireland [. . .] throughout its history represents the more extreme end of the spectrum of dependency on cattle'.[52] In fact, 'cattle were the primary measure of wealth and of exchange' in Gaelic society, while the ramparts of the Pale were 'designed primarily to prevent cattle raiding'.[53] Following the consolidation of British interests in Ireland, the agricultural make-up of the country became even more dramatically cattle-based and pastoral. Joyce notes this change in 'Ireland: Island of Saints and Sages' when he writes that, 'by introducing a new system of agriculture' – by which he means a system based on pastureland – '[England] reduced the power of the native leaders and granted huge estates to her soldiers' (*OCPW* 119). Cunningham notes that by the time Sir William Petty carried out his survey of Ireland in the mid-seventeenth century, the island's human population of 1.3 million was dwarfed by its cattle population of three million.[54] As time went on, British demand for Irish beef meant that increasing swathes of land were converted to pasture. Ireland's stereotypical image as the emerald isle can be attributed to this enforced 'greening' of the land through the conversion of arable acreage into pasture. Michael Turner outlines the dramatic upheavals that took place in the agricultural sector in the nineteenth century by tracking this change:

> The hay and pasture acreage combined increased from 9.995 million acres in 1851, to 12.08 million acres in 1881, and 12.42 million acres by the Great War. The arable acreage declined from 4.6 million acres in 1851, to 3.2 million acres in 1881, and 2.3 million acres by 1911.[55]

The result of such dramatic changes, carried out to accommodate the tastes of the neighbouring island, was that '[t]he market for Irish produce continued to be, or became even more, dependent on Britain'.[56] Statistics regarding meat consumption also show a striking difference between the two islands. In 1889, for example, the average British person consumed 118 pounds of meat per year, while the average Irish person consumed 56 pounds; of the meat consumed in Britain, 13.5% was Irish in origin, while no British meat of statistical significance was consumed in Ireland.[57] The dependence upon such trade resulted in Ireland becoming, in the words of Jeremy Rifkin, 'a giant cattle pasture to accommodate the English palate'.[58]

In an article on agriculture in Joyce's work, Caitlin McIntyre argues that 'Joyce is demonstrably critical of the effect that British colonial control had on Irish land, space, and animals', writing that '[a]griculture ultimately is the way in which colonialism exerts its power'.[59] McIntyre goes on to cite Timothy Morton's term 'Agrilogistics' as a description of the colonial approach to agriculture, paraphrasing this concept as follows:

> Agrilogistics denotes a conquering of land, through the violent removal of other inhabitants, and the imposition of private ownership to increase profit-oriented efficiency. Agrilogistics is also then the central focus of imperial excursions, the means of subjugating and displacing indigenous communities, animals, and ecosystems.[60]

The transformation of the Irish landscape into one dominated by pastureland is agrilogistics in action, prioritising the needs of the colonial neighbour over the ecological balance of the island of Ireland. One symbol of this agrilogistical transformation was the deforestation of the island from the Elizabethan plantations onwards.[61] The cattle roaming through the streets of Dublin, on their way to England, are simply another reminder of the agrilogistics that have utterly transformed Ireland's society, economy and ecology.

For all that Ireland depends upon it, the cattle trade is still seen as an inherently unequal deal, as Bloom looks out at the drove of cattle in 'Hades':

> Thursday, of course. Tomorrow is killing day. Springers.[62] Cuffe sold them about twentyseven quid each. For Liverpool probably. Roastbeef for old England. They buy up all the juicy ones. And then the fifth quarter lost: all that raw stuff, hide, hair, horns. Comes to a big thing in a year. Dead meat trade. Byproducts of the slaughterhouses for tanneries, soap, margarine. (*U* 6.392–7)

Here Bloom bemoans a trading relationship that transports cattle to England 'on the hoof' (i.e. alive). Because the animals are then slaughtered in Britain, Ireland loses out on the potential by-products of the dead animals. Wim Van Mierlo shows that in earlier sketches for this scene, Bloom's point is made with more force: 'Cattle trade less good / than agriculture & °rob country of raw stuffs (bones & hoofs for / combs) hides for shoes, tanners, fallow, bones etc for manure / Slaughtered meat trade better°'.[63] In this earlier version, the trading relationship between Ireland and Britain is presented as clearly exploitative, with Bloom's use of the word 'rob' to describe British policy towards Ireland noticeably more explicit than the final version, where Bloom designates the 'fifth quarter' – that is, the by-products – as merely 'lost'. In the earlier draft this policy is viewed as a deliberate act of draining the country of resources, as opposed to simply an accidental side effect. Robert Brazeau argues that Joyce uses animals throughout *Ulysses* to underline Ireland's subservient colonial position in relation to Britain, as opposed to the idyllic, pastoral image of Ireland as propounded by Revivalists.[64] Brazeau emphasises how the colonial capitalist structure exploited Ireland, writing that

> the animal as commodity is not simply caught in the ambit of capital, culture, and domination that writes colonial authority into the

spaces of Irish life but is centrally figured in how the Irish economy is ensnared in the perpetual trap of derivativeness and dependence that renders it a hinterland for English needs and wants.[65]

The readings proposed by Brazeau and McIntyre rightly draw attention to the dependent economic model that Ireland found itself in at the turn of the twentieth century, but the idea that Ireland's farmers existed only as victims of this model is perhaps overly simplified and denies agency to those very farmers. It is, of course, important to emphasise that Irish farmers were not a monolithic group, and there were evidently many farmers – particularly of the grazier class – who stood to profit handsomely from the trading relationship with Britain. David Jones writes that nationalists were hostile towards graziers precisely because of 'the perception that they played a vital role in meeting the food needs of Britain'.[66] Peter Adkins argues that Bloom's recalling of '[r]oastbeef for old England' is an acknowledgement of 'Ireland's unwitting complicity in the process [of British imperialism] as it literally sustains the colonial center with an unremitting flow of hoofed "emigrants"'.[67] It is possible that this uneasy sense of contributing to the colonial system partly influences Bloom's desire to have a tramline take the cattle directly to the quays and thereby keep the reality of Ireland's 'complicity' out of sight. Like so many aspects of colonialism, the cattle trade is a murky admixture of those who suffered under an exploitative system and those who found a way to manipulate it to their relative advantage.

The reliance of the Irish economy on its cattle trade is best demonstrated by the reaction of the Dubliners of *Ulysses* to the outbreak of foot-and-mouth disease. Foot-and-mouth is a highly infectious viral disease affecting almost all cloven-hoofed animals, including cattle. It spreads rapidly through contact, including by humans and farm equipment, leading foot-and-mouth to be considered 'the most economically devastating livestock disease in the world'.[68] Once an outbreak of the disease is discovered on a farm, '[t]he premises are quarantined, and all infected and susceptible animals on the premises frequently are euthanized and their carcasses buried or cremated'.[69] In *Ulysses*, Deasy, an Ulster unionist, solicits Stephen's help in having a letter regarding the so-called 'Styrian cure' for foot-and-mouth published in the papers. Stephen, despite his hesitancy at being involved with such earthy matters, agrees to help Deasy, and the letter is eventually published in the evening paper. The instance of foot-and-mouth in *Ulysses* is, however, one of the few ahistorical events in the novel. While there was no outbreak of the disease in 1904, there was a serious epidemic in 1912.[70] Joyce was in Ireland during the 1912 outbreak and received a letter from Henry Blackwood Price, an Ulsterman with whom he was acquainted in Trieste, containing information regarding the Styrian cure for foot-and-mouth disease, which he forwarded on to William Field, the MP and president of the Cattle Traders' Society (*L2* 300).[71] Terence Killeen has recently argued that an unsigned sub-editorial in *Freeman's Journal* from 6 September was written by Joyce, a theory backed up by a letter that Joyce's brother Charles wrote to Stanislaus on the same day reporting that 'Jim wrote a sub-editorial today for the *Freeman* about the Styrian cure for the foot-and-mouth disease' (*L2* 318).[72] The sub-editorial from 6 September explains the Styrian cure and refers to the efforts of Blackwood Price to prevent the 'wholesale slaughter' of the animals.[73] Killeen argues that the content of the short piece aligns with what we garner from Stephen's speed-reading of Deasy's letter and concludes that any future collections of Joyce's journalistic writings 'would be fully justified in including the "sub-editorial"'.[74]

In addition to the aspects of Deasy's letter that parrot the *Freeman* sub-editorial, it is also worth noting the elements that go beyond this and that tackle a number of separate political themes. While both the sub-editorial and Price's letter to Joyce are taken up with the specifics of the veterinary treatment in question, Deasy's letter mentions topics that might seem surprising for a unionist: 'That doctrine of *laissez faire* which so often in our history. Our cattle trade. The way of all our old industries. Liverpool ring which jockeyed the Galway harbour scheme' (*U* 2.324–6). Here, Deasy makes a number of arguments that would not be wholly dissimilar to those put forward by a Sinn Féin nationalist. The reference to the 'doctrine of *laissez faire*' recalls a familiar criticism of British governmental inaction during the Famine, while the death of Irish industry is bemoaned by the Citizen in 'Cyclops' (see *U* 12.1241–55) and by Joyce himself in 'Ireland: Island of Saints and Sages':

> Ireland is poor because English laws destroyed the industries of the country, notably the woollen one; because, in the years in which the potato crop failed, the negligence of the English government left the flower of the people to die in hunger [. . .] (*OCPW* 119)

Likewise, the reference to the failed Galway harbour scheme recalls the main purpose of Joyce's 1912 piece of journalism, 'The Mirage of the Fisherman of Aran'. This melding of parody and self-parody necessarily implicates Joyce in the question of foot-and-mouth, making Deasy's letter more difficult to dismiss as simply the ramblings of a busybody. Though Stephen knows that helping Deasy is likely to result in Mulligan dubbing him 'a new name: the bullockbefriending bard', he still agrees to 'help him in his fight' (*U* 2.430–1). The extent of the Irish economy's dependence on its cattle trade with Britain means that even urbanites such as Deasy and Stephen feel themselves compelled to help solve the crisis. The cattle trade, then, is a thread that helps to unite urbanites and ruralites, unionists and nationalists, as well as bullocks and bards.

Talk of foot-and-mouth disease dominates many thoughts and conversations across Dublin on 16 June 1904. In 'Lestrygonians', Bloom looks at the gulls and thinks '[t]hey spread foot and mouth disease too' (*U* 8.84–5), while later in 'Cyclops', Joe Hynes appears fresh from the meeting of the cattle traders who have been discussing the foot-and-mouth disease in the City Arms Hotel in order 'to give the citizen the hard word about it' (*U* 12.62–3). In 'Oxen of the Sun', the narrator reports his concern for the welfare of the affected cattle: 'will they slaughter all? I protest I saw them but this day morning going to the Liverpool boats, says he. I can scare believe 'tis so bad, says he' (*U* 14.567–8). Given its title and allusions to Homer's Cattle of Helios, 'Oxen of the Sun' unsurprisingly features much discussion of the 'Kerry cows that are to be butchered along of the plague' (*U* 14.546–7). However, the young men's boisterous disregard for the welfare of the animals – 'But they can go hang, says he with a wink, for me with their bully beef, a pox on it [. . .] *Mort aux vaches*, says Frank' (*U* 14.547–52) – is in marked contrast to Bloom's concern and Stephen's action earlier in the day. While there are any number of micro-level personal events unfolding throughout the day in *Ulysses*, the main macro-level political affair is the foot-and-mouth crisis.

The section of most interest in 'Oxen of the Sun', in terms of bovine imagery, is that where Joyce performs a parody of the writing style of Jonathan Swift (*U* 14.581–650), particularly as found in *A Tale of a Tub* (1704). Swift's allegorical work is a satire on the Catholic Church, most especially in Part IV, where he uses the metaphor of Peter's bulls to satirise the 'papal bulls' of the Catholic Church.[75] Swift's extended bovine metaphor references everything from excommunications to papal pardons; however, what Swift neglects to reference is that it was just such a papal bull that provided England with permission to colonise Ireland, as the English Pope Adrian IV, or Nicholas Breakspear, bestowed the overlordship of Ireland on Henry II in 1155 through a papal bull known as *Laudabiliter*. Using the stylistic and allegorical model provided by Swift, Joyce offers the reader a crash course in Irish history, most particularly regarding the forms of colonisation – English and ecclesiastical – that took place on the island. In Joyce's 'Oxen', Pope Adrian is given the moniker 'farmer Nicholas' and is described as 'the bravest cattlebreeder of them all' (*U* 14.582–3). By designating Adrian as a cattle breeder, Joyce is once again playing on contemporary attitudes to the big cattle breeders in Ireland, the graziers, who profited from the work of smaller tenant farmers. By doing this, Joyce roots this seemingly outlandish metaphor for English colonisation in the politics of rural Ireland. In addition, the bull also represents the primacy of cattle in the agricultural economy following English colonisation. Nicholas sends his bull to Ireland with devastating consequences for the landscape: the bull grows fatter and permits 'nought to grow in all the land but green grass for himself' (*U* 14.610–11). Lord Harry – who flits between the various monarchical Henrys of English history, though Don Gifford posits that on this occasion he would appear to be Henry VII, who applied English land-use laws to Ireland – has a board erected in the middle of the island declaring: 'Green is the grass that grows on the ground' (*U* 14.613).[76] In fact,

> if ever he got scent of a cattleraider in Roscommon or the wilds of Connemara or a husbandman in Sligo that was sowing as much as a handful of mustard or a bag of rapeseed out he run amok over half the countryside rooting up with his horns whatever was planted and all by lord Harry's orders. (*U* 14.614–18)

Britain's use of Ireland as its own 'giant cattle pasture', to again cite Rifkin, is here emphasised in the bull only allowing green grass to grow for himself. Meanwhile, the Gaelic Irish – significantly they are viewed pejoratively as cattle raiders as opposed to legitimate farmers, the kind of people that the ramparts of the Pale were designed to keep out – are forbidden to use their land for arable farming. While the agricultural imagery used by Joyce is an effective way of parodying the twin colonisers of Ireland, it is also apposite in terms of colonisation's impact on the Irish landscape and the agricultural economy.

For all that it is tempting to read the cattle of *Ulysses* as allegories, during their appearances Joyce also encourages the reader to reflect on the actual place of cattle in Ireland's contemporary political and economic situation. While the cattle that walk down the North Circular Road are among the most explicit examples of *rus in urbe* in *Ulysses*, this is not the only time that cattle infiltrate the urban space, consuming the thoughts of headmasters and would-be artists, as well as taking over the identities of historical figures. To trace the route of the cattle, from the small fields of the west, through lush pasturelands and down the North Circular Road to the quays, is to see how interconnected and interdependent the rural periphery and urban centre are, breaking down notions of hierarchy between the two. It would be easy to dismiss the cattle as a remnant of a past society, but in fact they represent a modern Ireland implicated in the larger colonial capitalist system. In the end, cattle occupy not only the streets of Joyce's Dublin but also the minds of his Dubliners, at times rendering the whole city one vast 'cowtown'.

'Between two roaring worlds': Liminal Zones Between Rural and Urban

When Bloom dreams of his ideal property location, he states that it must be at least '1 statute mile from the periphery of the metropolis' (*U* 17.1514–15). This is most likely to ensure that, even allowing for urban sprawl, Bloom will remain beyond the encroachment of the urban area and will be allowed to enjoy his semi-rural existence. Of course, Bloom was not to know the dramatic changes that Dublin would experience over the following century, and his preferred locations of Dundrum and Sutton are now certainly part of suburbia. In 1904, however, Bloom could have made the reasonable assumption that he would be safe from such suburbanisation, given that one did not have to go very far from the centre of Dublin to find oneself surrounded by green fields.[77] Dublin for a long time was considered enclosed by the North and South Circular Roads, making these roads the city's effective periphery.[78] On numerous occasions Joyce's characters cross this periphery and enter transitional zones, located in a hazy middle ground between rurality and (sub)urbanity. Indeed, it is easily overlooked that Joyce's great masterpiece of the city, *Ulysses*, begins in leafy Sandycove, sufficiently rural for Buck Mulligan to demand 'Sandycove milk' from the local cows for his tea (*U* 1.342–3). In this section, I will examine these in-between zones in *Dubliners*, *A Portrait* and *Ulysses*, focusing in particular on how their liminality can often be linked to transgression.

Enda Duffy has written that 'the place most obsessively attended to in James Joyce's writing is not Dublin'.[79] Instead, Duffy argues, '[t]hat place is the northern suburb of Drumcondra'.[80] The Joyces first moved to Drumcondra in 1894, living on Millbourne Avenue – Ellmann mistakenly calls it Millbourne Lane, but no such address exists (*JJII* 39). Even in the Ordnance Survey carried out in 1907, this address was surrounded to the north by green fields and to the south by suburban housing. This, therefore, is life on the edge of suburbia, a kind of transitional zone between the suburban and rural. The strangeness of Drumcondra is highlighted in *A Portrait*, when Stephen crosses the bridge over the River Tolka and looks down on the 'encampment of poor cottages' which do not seem to belong in an urban, or even a suburban setting (*P* 162).

> The faint sour stink of rotted cabbages came towards him from the kitchen gardens on the rising ground above the river. He smiled to think that it was this disorder, the misrule and confusion of his father's house and the stagnation of vegetable life, which was to win the day in his soul. Then a short laugh broke from his lips as he thought of that solitary farmhand in the kitchen gardens behind their house whom they had nicknamed the man with the hat. A second laugh, taking rise from the first after a pause, broke from him involuntarily as he thought of how the man with the hat worked, considering in turn the four points of the sky and then regretfully plunging his spade in the earth. (*P* 162–3)

Duffy draws attention to this passage and notes the cottages as 'an uncanny rural intrusion, like an image of a Famine village fifty years earlier', though the uncanniness is tempered somewhat by Stephen's laughter.[81] Here we have another case of *rus in urbe*, complete with typically rural characters (the farmhand) and smells (rotting cabbages) which seem out of place on the edge of the city. The seemingly anachronistic farmhand treats this small patch of suburban garden space like a field, working it with the spade. He does so 'regretfully', however, as though all too aware that his efforts are pointless in a space that is no longer made for such work, the absurdity of which draws Stephen's laughter. The scene recalls his prior encounters with the peasants outside Clane in its emphasis on smells and the manual work involved in extracting food from the earth – after all, one of the potatoes Stephen was given at Clongowes still 'had the mark of the spade in it' (*P* 53).

Duffy describes the scene as being located in 'the liminal wasteland between suburb and country'.[82] The half-rural disorder of Drumcondra acts as a symbolic depiction of the Dedalus family's fall from grace, a far cry from the salubrious order of the suburbs or the grandeur of central city life. Duffy is right that this scene feels like a 'rural intrusion', though perhaps it would be more accurate to frame it as a remnant of rurality, as in this case it is more truly the urban that is intruding upon the rural. Nevertheless, the rural is felt as a destabilising force here, upturning the Dedaluses' former position and bringing them dangerously close to their ancestral rural origins. The half-development of this scene recalls Eveline's memories of her childhood setting in *Dubliners* when she laments the 'new red houses' that have recently been built where once 'there used to be a field' (*D* 25). Eveline remembers how she and the other children used to play there every evening until 'a man from Belfast bought the field and built houses in it' (*D* 25). Though her father forbade her to play in the field – linking rurality with transgression – Eveline still thinks that he 'was not so bad then; and besides, her mother was alive' (*D* 25). The innocence of her childhood ends, therefore, with the (sub)urbanisation of this rural space. Her family's happiness appears tied up with the rural surroundings, and the half-development that results from this partial sprawling of the urban space ends her bucolic bliss. In both examples, the rapid changing of a space's identity – from rural to suburban – is felt as a wound inflicted on the landscape by those who knew it differently, be it Eveline as a child or the farmhand. The result is, as Duffy notes, a 'liminal wasteland', a place without a defined purpose.

This is but one of numerous journeys into the liminal zones found along the northern periphery of the city in Joyce's work. The sense of being 'between things' is most to the fore, however, in the 'Hades' episode of *Ulysses*. It is not difficult to ascertain why Joyce would emphasise liminality here. This episode follows the classical tradition of katabasis, wherein the still-living protagonist enters the world of the dead. In Joyce's modern-day retelling it is not quite so neat, for instead of fully journeying to the world of the dead, we enter a halfway zone between life and death: this world is Glasnevin cemetery. What is striking about Joyce's narrative, however, is how the sense of entering this liminal, half-dead zone is signalled by an increasing emphasis on rurality and, in particular, on field, earth and the pastoral. A quick look at the Ordnance Survey map for Glasnevin cemetery shows that in 1907 it was very much on the edge of the city, with fields stretching out beyond it to its north and west (fig. 4.1). This sense of leaving the urban area is first indicated in the narrative by the appearance of the aforementioned drove of cattle passing in front of the funeral cortege, just as it rounds the corner of the North Circular Road, the city's theoretical periphery. We have already noted how this signals a sudden intrusion of rural and agricultural life into the city space, but it is also a deathly intrusion: the whole purpose of these cattle lies in their death, noted by Bloom almost immediately when he thinks '[t]omorrow is killing day [. . .] Dead meat trade' (*U* 6.392–6). The cattle themselves are already considered half-dead, their date of execution so near.

The carriage turns north, up Phibsborough Road, until it reaches the Crossguns Bridge over the Royal Canal. At this point, the men in the carriage notice a bargeman bringing turf into the city from the boggy midlands. This figure becomes another instance of *rus in urbe*, and his journey from rural to urban space is first outlined by the narratorial voice and then immediately reflected upon in Bloom's interior monologue:

> On the slow weedy waterway he had floated on his raft coastward over Ireland drawn by a haulage rope past beds of reeds, over slime, mudchoked bottles, carrion dogs. Athlone, Mullingar, Moyvalley, I could make a walking tour to see Milly by the canal [. . .] Come as a surprise, Leixlip, Clonsilla. Dropping down lock by lock to Dublin. With turf from the midland bogs. (*U* 6.442–51)

Athlone, often considered the centre of Ireland, is imagined by Bloom as the originating point of this bargeman's journey, emphasising that this figure has travelled to Dublin from deep in the heart of Ireland. The fact that the bargeman is bringing turf, the product of bogs, is also significant. As Alison Lacivita notes, '[b]ogs are neither land nor water, solid nor liquid; they occupy a transitional space, both geographically and culturally'.[83] Similarly, James Fairhall examines the significance of the Bog of Allen at the close of 'The Dead' and notes that 'the geographical and biological properties of bogs mark them as liminal territories that subvert boundaries and categories [. . .] Mirages of apparent solidity, bogs are deceptive crossroads where earth merges with water, life with death.'[84] The man's identity as a boatman immediately casts him as the classical figure of Charon, ferrying souls across the Styx, from the world of the living to the world of the dead; but in addition to this, his identity as bringer of turf from the boggy midlands serves to further underscore his association with liminality, occupying the zone between life and death. Turf is itself an image of death and decay, the accumulation of millennia's worth of vegetation and organic matter decomposing.

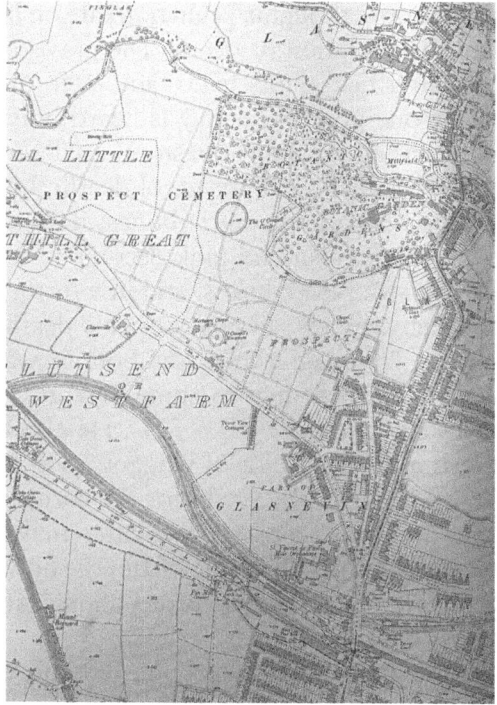

Figure 4.1   Glasnevin and Drumcondra, including Glasnevin (Prospect) Cemetery in the top left. Ordnance Survey, *Dublin, Castleknock, Coolock,* sheet XVIII.3, 25 inches to 1 mile, Dublin, 1911.

When the men finally get to Glasnevin cemetery, Bloom speculates on the uncanny nature of the graveyard and imagines what it must be like for the caretaker to live there. Bloom even conjures up an image of '[w]ill o' the wisp' hovering over the graveyard, produced by the '[g]as of graves' (*U* 6.752–3). Will-o'-the-wisp, also known as jack-o'-lantern or *ignis fatuus,* is a phenomenon associated with bogland, whereby a strange light 'appear[s] to hover over the bog and move ever ahead, enticing travelers to their doom'.[85] In Irish folklore, the lights are thought to be 'carried by the Water Sheerie or Bog Sprite, a relative of the Sowlth, a solitary fairy ghost who wanders about in search of rest' – a figure, therefore, stuck in its own liminal zone.[86] In reality, the light is caused by 'the spontaneous combustion of peat gas', a result of decaying organic matter.[87] By imagining the gas from the dead bodies as forming will-o'-the-wisp over the graves, Bloom in fact renders Glasnevin cemetery a quasi-bog.

Following this, Bloom's thoughts begin to fixate on matters relating to earth, soil, and their relation to death. The graveyard is ruralised by becoming 'field after field. Holy fields' and later 'dismal fields' (*U* 6.763–4, 6.877). At one point a donkey is heard braying in the distance, further emphasising the almost pastoral quality of the scene (*U* 6.837). The soil itself is filled with images of death: 'I daresay the soil would be quite fat with corpsemanure, bones, flesh, nails. Charnel-house. Dreadful. Turning green and pink decomposing. Rot quick in damp earth' (*U* 6.776–8). Nevertheless, and in a further insistence on the graveyard's in-betweenness, Bloom sees this deathly soil as also being a source of life. He imagines that the Botanic Gardens, located beside the graveyard, must benefit in some way as '[i]t's the blood sinking in the earth gives new life' (*U* 6.771). He also thinks that the corpses 'must breed a devil of a lot of maggots. Soil must be simply swirling with them' (*U* 6.783–4). Earth, for the corpse, is both friend and enemy: Bloom notes how a person will often make requests such as '[l]ay me in my native earth. Bit of clay from the holy land', and yet also desire to be placed in a coffin '[t]o protect him as long as possible even in the earth' (*U* 6.819–21).

As he watches the gravediggers working, Bloom's thoughts fixate on the earth: 'Clay, brown, damp, began to be seen in the hole. It rose. Nearly over. A mound of damp clods rose more, rose, and the gravediggers rested their spades. All uncovered again for a few instants' (*U* 6.906–8). Joyce's insistence on the clay *rising* out of the hole is important here, as it is wrenched out of the realm of the dead and back up into that of the living – however, the only resurrection happening here is a temporary one of the earth, as it gets lifted up for its next inhabitant. The opening up of the earth – '[a]ll uncovered again for a few instants' – provides a view down into the underground, brown and damp. Unsurprisingly, Bloom is eager to remove himself from this liminal zone when he gets sight of the gates: 'Back to the world again. Enough of this place. Brings you a bit nearer every time' (*U* 6.995–6). For Bloom, Glasnevin cemetery is an uncanny in-between zone: neither rural nor urban, dead nor alive, a place where '[b]oth ends meet' (*U* 6.760). Bloom's escape from the cemetery is both a return to the city and to 'warm fullblooded life' (*U* 6.1005).

If 'Hades' is an episode wherein the characters are brought out of the city centre and into a liminal zone, 'Wandering Rocks' occupies a liminal zone within the very structure of *Ulysses* as narrative itself. The episode, though technically the first of the second half of the book, is more often considered as a 'pivot' in the novel, with Steven Morrison noting that 'just because it stands at the opening of the second part of *Ulysses* does not mean that it has crossed over the threshold entirely'.[88] This sense of in-betweenness is also apparent in the allusion to the treacherous moving rocks, or Symplegades, that Jason and the Argonauts were forced to navigate their way between.[89] The reader, like Jason, is therefore also navigating their way between the two halves of *Ulysses* in 'Wandering Rocks', as well as between the various mini-episodes and characters in the episode itself. The notion of liminality is built into the micro-level structure of this episode, as well as its place within the macro-level structure of *Ulysses*. Stephen, as he watches the '[b]eingless beings' around him, feels himself having to navigate opposing forces: 'I between them. Where? Between two roaring worlds where they swirl, I' (*U* 10.822–4).

The very first vignette of 'Wandering Rocks' features a character who is leaving the stable micro-universe of the city for the liminal zone between city and countryside. Father Conmee has been tasked by Martin Cunningham with approaching Brother Swan of the O'Brien Institute for Destitute Children to see if the young Patrick Dignam might be admitted into their care following the death of his father. This involves a journey in the direction of the then-village of Artane, with the Ordnance Survey maps showing the O'Brien Institute in 1907 to have been located in the middle of fields outside the city (fig. 4.2). While 'Hades' associated an increasing rurality with the cycle of life and death, in 'Wandering Rocks' the move towards the countryside is linked in Conmee's mind with a move back into the past and a static notion of tradition. The episode opens with what Clive Hart famously termed one of Joyce's 'reader traps', whereby Conmee 'reset[s] his smooth watch', leading us to imagine him changing the time on his watch (*U* 10.1–2).[90] Conmee, however, is in fact putting his watch back into his pocket, not changing the time. Nevertheless, the sense of Conmee's outlook being linked with a temporal shift remains throughout this vignette, as the Jesuit priest dwells on rural Ireland and the past, as he 'walk[s] and move[s] in times of yore' (*U* 10.174).

Conmee is based on a real-life figure from Joyce's schooldays at both Clongowes and Belvedere College. Indeed, it was Conmee who 'saved' Joyce from a Christian Brothers education when he arranged for him to attend Belvedere without fees after Joyce's father had to remove him from Clongowes (*JJII* 35). Joyce's feelings towards the real-life Conmee are hard to ascertain from the 'Wandering Rocks' vignette, since the fictionalised Conmee is a somewhat supercilious figure, whose romanticised view of the world is parodied by Joyce. Conmee's generosity

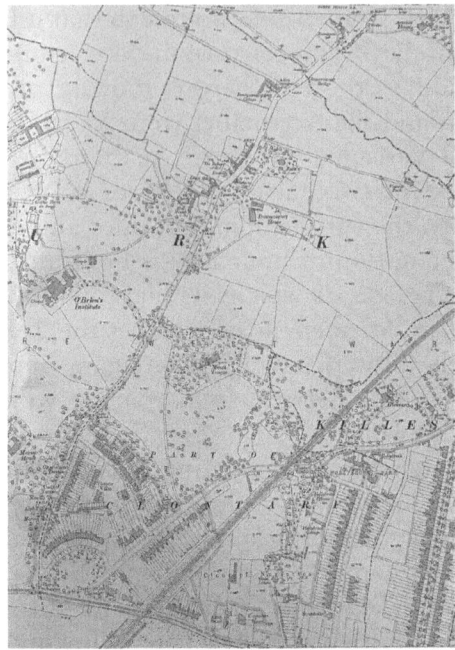

Figure 4.2   Semi-rural area of north Dublin, with the O'Brien
Institute to the left of centre. Ordnance Survey, *Dublin, Coolock*,
sheet XVIII.4, 25 inches to 1 mile, Dublin, 1911.

towards Joyce is mirrored, however, in his effort to find a place in the
O'Brien Institute for Patrick Dignam, even if this is carried out more as
a matter of duty – indeed, Conmee is trying to 'oblige' Cunningham as
he might be 'useful at mission time' – than as something Conmee cares
deeply about (*U* 10.5–6).

The fictional Conmee's tendency to romanticise a pastoral vision
of the past is a nod towards the historical Conmee's authoring of a
pamphlet entitled *Old Times in the Barony* (1895), as noted by Anne
Fogarty:

> [Conmee's] study is an idiosyncratic but heartfelt meditation on a tra-
> ditional rural world in the vicinity of 'Luainford,' the author's designa-
> tion for Athlone. Conmee depicts this forgotten locality in idyllic terms
> as a self-sufficient feudal economy, an epitome of Celtic civilization,
> and an organic community undisturbed by class divisions [. . .][91]

Joyce refers to the pamphlet when he has Conmee nostalgically reflect
that '[t]hose were old worldish days, loyal times in joyous townlands,

old times in the barony' (*U* 10.159–60). Fogarty notes that while Conmee's tendency to romanticise aristocratic figures such as Lord Talbot de Malahide and Mary, the first countess of Belvedere, 'might seem to indicate his Anglocentrism', this is balanced against his insistence on 'a return to native, Gaelic values'.[92] Fogarty sees Conmee as not all that different from the kind of politically active 'Gaelic League priest' who was springing up around the country at this time.[93] In *Old Times in the Barony*, Conmee claims that in former times there was 'the complete absence of any contention between classes or creeds' and that 'the resident gentry of the Barony were not so far removed from the farming classes, either by wealth or social position'.[94] In many ways, Conmee's romanticisation of both the aristocracy and the traditions of rural, Gaelic Ireland puts him in step with many of the leading figures in Revivalism and their '[d]ream of the noble and the beggar-man'.[95] Len Platt is less forgiving towards both the fictional and the historical Conmee, describing the world his pamphlet conjures up as a 'sickly idyll' where 'the past is robbed of its dynamic and resistance to authority is silenced'.[96] However, this is only partially true, as the real Conmee peppers his romanticism with realism, drawing attention, for example, to the blight of emigration which has 'decimated and desolated the land', as well as the cruel life of the 'Spalpeen', a labourer who had to travel yearly for work in England.[97] Meanwhile, the fictional Conmee, even during his rural reveries, is not blind to the modern reality of what is going on around him, as we shall see.

Just as the world of 'Hades' is increasingly ruralised as the funeral cortege slowly makes its way to Glasnevin, so too is Conmee's world as he walks towards the city's periphery. The first indication of this occurs when Conmee remembers that he must send a letter to the 'father provincial' (*U* 10.39). This is not, however, a reference to a provincial priest, but rather to the '[t]he authority to whom Conmee was accountable, the provincial of the Jesuits in Ireland, who would, in turn, report back to Rome'.[98] This passing thought, while not so much a 'reader trap', does at least plant in the reader's mind an association between Conmee and the provincial. Conmee walks along the North Circular Road, on to Portland Row, and turns northward up the North Strand road, thus going beyond the traditional periphery of the city. Despite the fact that this part of Dublin was well and truly suburbanised by the early twentieth century, Conmee's mindset begins to alter at this point, with rural references gathering apace. As he comes to the Newcomen Bridge over the Royal Canal, Conmee sees Corny Kelleher chewing 'a blade of hay' (*U* 10.97–8). Next he notices a police constable – whose rural connotations have already been discussed – followed by the pig's puddings in the butcher's shop, products of agricultural Ireland. At this point Conmee sees

> a turfbarge, a towhorse with pendent head, a bargeman with a hat of dirty straw seated amidships, smoking and staring at a branch of poplar above him. It was idyllic: and Father Conmee reflected on the providence of the Creator who had made turf to be in bogs whence men might dig it out and bring it to town and hamlet to make fires in the houses of poor people. (*U* 10.101–6)

It seems almost certain that this is the same bargeman noticed by Bloom in 'Hades', whom he imagines as having come from Athlone, the focal point for Conmee's meditations on a rural ideal in *Old Times in the Barony*. Conmee's notion of the origins of turf contains none of the sinister, deathly connotations associated with turf and bogs in 'Hades'; instead, he views turf as something provided in its present form by God, rather than as the product of millennia of decay. Conmee sees the relationship between rural and urban life as one in which the rural world provides for the needs of the town, in what is a fairly reductive view of rural life. However, there is still a sense of co-dependency and interconnectivity here, for as the urban depends on the rural for its turf, so too does the rural depend on the metropolis for its market. Each sod of turf, burning in the houses of the urban poor, is an example of *rus in urbe* for Conmee.

Following these meditations on the rural ideal, Conmee finds himself getting near the end of the urban space when he makes what would appear to be a surprising decision: he takes the tram. The reason for this is even more surprising: he does so because 'he disliked to traverse on foot the dingy way past Mud Island' (*U* 10.114). Mud Island was the name of a marshy area on Dublin Bay which has since been reclaimed.[99] Despite Conmee's valorisation of rural life, his first encounter with a genuine unurbanised, natural setting is passed over because it does not meet the image he has of pastoral beauty. While sitting on the tramcar, Conmee thinks about the other people on the tram, the older Mass-goers who receive Communion from him, and the souls of unbaptised races; but not once does he look out and reflect upon the mud flats passing by outside the tram window. By contrast, he shows a remarkable ability to transform the most mundane things into images of rurality. For example, he describes the clouds in the sky as a 'flock', and notes the French verb *moutonner*, meaning to appear fleecy, coming from the word for sheep, *mouton*. As Conmee leaves the tram and walks further out of the urban area, nature is imagined as something grand yet subordinate to him, and he even goes so far as to convince himself that the cabbages he sees in a field are 'curtseying to him' (*U* 10.181). The aforementioned clouds cause Conmee to be lifted out of the present and into his past at Clongowes, watching the clouds over nearby Rathcoffey while '[h]is thinsocked ankles were tickled by the stubble of Clongowes field' (*U* 10.185–6). Nature, in Conmee's carefully curated world, is a benign presence, one that curtseys and tickles and bends to the will of man.

Conmee, however, is rudely awoken from his anachronistic rural daydream by the reality of the rural present:

> A flushed young man came from a gap of a hedge and after him came a young woman with wild nodding daisies in her hand. The young man raised his cap abruptly: the young woman abruptly bent and with slow care detached from her light skirt a clinging twig. (*U* 10.199–202)

Here Conmee is confronted with how young couples put the relative wilderness provided by the semi-rural areas on the edge of the city to use. Nature itself clings to the couple – the daisies in the young woman's hand and the twig attached to her skirt – making it impossible to remove their actions from the space in which they are carried out, and complicating the notion of the rural space as a pure idyll. Conmee might romanticise his surroundings when it suits him, but he is not blind to the reason for the young couple's presence in this semi-rural zone. Rather than ignoring them, he blesses them 'gravely' and looks to the next page of his breviary, which conveniently is headed with the Hebrew letter *Sin* (*U* 10.203–4). Here is another 'reader trap', the pun suggesting that the semi-rural liminal zone is a site of sexual transgression. While this act is not 'transgressive' in quite the same way as other instances described in Joyce, clearly it transgresses Conmee's sense of Catholic morality.

Later we learn that the young man in question was Vincent Lynch, a character based on Joyce's acquaintance and one-time friend, Vincent Cosgrave (*JJII* 160). During Joyce's return to Dublin in 1909, Cosgrave claimed that while Joyce was courting Nora, she had also been seeing Cosgrave every second night (*JJII* 279). The thought of Nora having been unfaithful overwhelmed Joyce, with one particular detail sticking out in his mind and which he repeated in a bitter letter to her: 'Tell me. When you were in that field near the Dodder (on the nights when I was *not* there) with that other (a "friend" of mine) were you lying down when you kissed?' (*L2* 232). Joyce clearly imagines Nora's supposed infidelity as having occurred in a field on the southern edge of the city, near the River Dodder – evidently it must have been where Joyce took Nora, given the first parenthesis. Joyce therefore had his own reasons for associating the semi-rural zone with sexual trysts and transgression.

Even before this scene in *Ulysses*, Joyce had portrayed the fields on the edge of the city as sites of transgression. The most explicit example of this is in the short story 'An Encounter', in which two schoolboys decide to skip school in order to seek adventure. Their plan of escape from the stifling world of Dublin is to go to the docks and watch the boats from far-off places come and go. The quays themselves are evidently another liminal zone, existing between the static urban world of Dublin and the imagined excitement of foreign lands, as they also do in 'Eveline'. The boys eventually decide to move on from the quays and continue south into Ringsend, which, as Jeri Johnson notes, was then 'a small working-class village'.[100] The narrator's companion, Mahony, chases a cat until it escapes 'into a wide field' (*D* 14). At this point, the two boys grow tired and decide to take a break: 'when we reached the field we made at once for a sloping bank over the ridge of which we could see the Dodder' (*D* 14). The *rus in urbe* scene has now been set: the boys are located in a field, beside the Dodder, very similar to the description Joyce gives of the place he used to take Nora. Soon, the field's semi-rurality becomes the site of transgression:

> There was nobody but ourselves in the field. When we had lain on the bank for some time without speaking I saw a man approaching from the far end of the field. I watched him lazily as I chewed one of those green stems on which girls tell fortunes. He came along by the bank slowly. He walked with one hand upon his hip and in the other hand he held a stick with which he tapped the turf lightly [. . .] He walked towards us very slowly, always tapping the ground with his stick, so slowly that I thought he was looking for something in the grass. (*D* 15)

Joyce here emphasises the semi-rural location, twice noting that the boys and the stranger are in a field, having the narrator chew on a bit of grass and the stranger repeatedly tap the 'turf' of the field, almost as though he is 'looking for something in the grass'. This last point is significant, for it reminds us that the narrator hid his schoolbooks 'in the long grass near the ashpit at the end of the garden' earlier in the morning, the day's first transgressive act (D 12). The man approaches the boys and engages them in friendly, if peculiar conversation. Finally, the narrator notes that he walked 'slowly away from us towards the near end of the field' (D 16). Once there, the man engages in something which the narrator chooses not to look at and which causes Mahony to exclaim 'I say . . . He's a queer old josser!' (D 16). The man's transgressive act can only happen because the field offers him a space where he is unlikely to be seen by others, barring the two boys. The narrator feels a profound sense of unease when the man returns and his escape from this situation is only made possible by running back up the slope and out of the field itself (D 18). What might have been a pleasant and relaxing instance of *rus in urbe* on the edges of the city instead becomes a place where transgression occurs and the schoolboys' innocence is broken.

These examples from 'Wandering Rocks' and 'An Encounter' are not the only such instances of sexual trysts and transgressions occurring in liminal, semi-rural settings. In 'Two Gallants', Corley talks about 'a fine tart' whom he brought to Donnybrook and 'into a field there' (D 37). Donnybrook, then a suburban village south of the city of Dublin, is often associated in Joyce's works with the Donnybrook Fair, a lively, often riotous event that took place in the village up until the mid-nineteenth century. Fairs held a central place in Ireland's agricultural society, and this association is further underlined by the fact that the girl told Corley that 'she used to go with a dairyman' (D 37). Joyce follows this fact with an ellipsis, after which Corley says '[i]t was fine, man', leaving us in little doubt as to what has happened in the field near Donnybrook (D 37). Not far from Donnybrook is the Royal Dublin Society's grounds where Bloom suspects that Molly may have had some kind of amorous encounter with 'a farmer' at the Horse Show (U 17.2135).

Returning to 'Hades', Bloom wonders how the Glasnevin caretaker could possibly convince a woman to '[c]ome out and live in the graveyard' (U 6.747–8). Nevertheless, he thinks that the graveyard's very status as a taboo-laden zone might in fact arouse sexual excitement:

> You might pick up a young widow here. Men like that. Love among the tombstones. Romeo. Spice of pleasure. In the midst of death we are in life. Both ends meet. Tantalising for the poor dead. Smell of grilled beefsteaks to the starving. Gnawing their vitals. Desire to grig people. Molly wanting to do it at the window. Eight children he has anyway. (U 6.757–62)

Bloom's notion of '[l]ove among the tombstones', a reference to Robert Browning's poem 'Love Among the Ruins', also calls to his mind the final scene in *Romeo and Juliet.*[101] Just as the love of the eponymous couple is itself transgressive in the context of the play, so too here is the emphasis on sex of a transgressive or at least risqué nature. This is clear in Bloom's imagined couples being filled with the '[s]pice of pleasure', and he thinks of the dead jealously watching the sexual encounters taking place above them, which are like the smell of 'grilled beefsteaks to the starving'. He thinks that such a desire for half-public amorous encounters comes from this '[d]esire to grig people', 'grig' coming from the Irish *griog*, meaning to 'tease' or even 'titillate' (*FGB*, 'griog'). This is a desire that Molly herself displayed when she wanted 'to do it at the window'. Whatever reluctance Bloom might have imagined women feeling about living in the graveyard is seemingly refuted by the simple fact of the caretaker's large family: 'Eight children he has anyway.'

Bloom's reference to Molly's proclivity for risqué sexual encounters is also underscored by the location of the love scene that closes *Ulysses*. Molly and Leopold are, after all, 'lying among the rhododendrons on Howth head' when she utters her famous 'Yes' (*U* 18.1572–3). Bloom, too, appears to be more inclined to sexual fantasy when in semi-rural spaces, given that Sandymount Strand is the location of his surreptitious masturbation in 'Nausicaa'. Indeed, Thacker hints at this when noting how striking it is that 'this voyeuristic fulfilment occurs in a quite separate space, outside of the boundary of the city'.[102] It might seem strange to speak of an association in *Ulysses* between semi-rural, liminal zones and the flouting of sexual restrictions, especially when the most explicit and prolonged examples of this take place in 'Nighttown' in the centre of Dublin. However, it is worth noting that in the introductory 'stage directions' at the start of 'Circe', the entrance to Nighttown is coloured by 'red and green will-o'-the-wisps' (*U* 15.2–3). As described above, will-o'-the-wisps are observed primarily in marshy areas, briefly setting up Nighttown as a bog-like liminal zone. Of course, it remains very much an urban setting, but it is not insignificant that Joyce uses a staple of rural folklore to introduce this phantasmagorical, transgressive space. Finally, it is important to remember that while there is much uncertainty about the details of the 'sin' committed by HCE in *Finnegans Wake*, the one thing that is sure is that it was committed 'opposite a pair of dainty maidservants in the swoolth of the rushy hollow' in that most conventional example of *rus in urbe* in Dublin: Phoenix Park (*FW* 34.19–20).[103]

Where All Ends Meet: Joyce's Exurban, Exilic Endings

For a writer who set all of his major works primarily in the city of Dublin, it is striking that none of them end there, at least in the imagination. *Dubliners* famously ends with Gabriel Conroy mentally soaring over the central plains of Ireland, embarking upon his 'journey westward' (*D* 176). In *A Portrait*, Stephen's final diary entries are taken up with images of far-off lands, 'the black arms of tall ships that stand against the moon, their tale of distant nations', but also of old peasants in mountain cabins along Ireland's western edge (*P* 252). *Ulysses*, meanwhile, ends not in the city where we have passed the majority of the day but in one of the semi-rural zones on its edge: Howth. Howth was – and is – ideally located for Dubliners as a quick escape to a semi-rural setting, and Molly's memories of the day she said 'Yes' to Bloom are resurrected following her rumination on nature:

> theres nothing like nature the wild mountains then the sea and the waves rushing then the beautiful country with the fields of oats and wheat and all kinds of things and all the fine cattle going about that would do your heart good to see rivers and lakes and flowers all sorts of shapes and smells and colours springing up even out of the ditches primroses and violets nature it is (*U* 18.1558–63)

If Bloom is mostly a man of the urban pavement, Molly is more attuned to nature – in this they mirror Joyce's next couple of HCE and ALP – and Bloom's description of her as 'a flower of the mountain' appears to have been perhaps the most flattering thing Molly could have wished for: 'that was the one true thing he said in his life' (*U* 18.1576–7). Molly's memories of that day become intertwined with her memories of Gibraltar, so that the rustic images of her childhood interlace with her account of the day on Howth. The last lines feature 'poor donkeys slipping half asleep' and 'big wheels of the carts of bulls', scenes of Gibraltar but which could also believably be of Howth (*U* 18.1590–2). *Ulysses* begins in a semi-rural setting, looking out at the 'snotgreen [. . .] scrotumtightening sea [. . .] *Thalatta! Thalatta!*' (*U* 1.78–80); it ends in the semi-rurality of Howth/Gibraltar, looking out through Molly's eyes at 'the sea the sea crimson sometimes like fire' (*U* 18.1598–9). While the narrative begins with Buck's ironic fetishisation of rural Ireland through the character of the milkwoman and the dairy produce she brings with her, finally through Molly we witness a more genuine embrace of nature, rural and natural life on its own terms rather than as a grand symbol of something else.

Joyce ends his masterpiece of the day on Howth, and begins his masterpiece of the night there too, as he weaves his riverine opening sentences 'from swerve of shore to bend of bay' around 'Howth Castle and Environs' (*FW* 1.1–3). Though still primarily set in Dublin, *Finnegans Wake* – to the extent that it has a setting – makes perhaps the greatest number of journeys of any Joyce work out of the city and into rural Ireland. In keeping with the trends of his other works, the end of the *Wake* also involves a departure from Dublin, as we follow the river Liffey on its journey into the Irish Sea, 'pass[ing] through grass behush the bush to [. . .] A way a lone a last a loved a long the / riverrun' (*FW* 628.12–16, 3.1).

Appropriately for a writer so keen on his status as a voluntary exile, each of Joyce's works ends with an imaginative departure from Dublin. Most significant, however, is how Joyce incorporates the exurban as a signifier of this exile, a final *rus* in the predominant *urbs* of the works. Like the Revivalists, Joyce's liberation also involved a move away from the city of Dublin, even if unlike them Europe was to be the ultimate destination. The first step of this exile is, nevertheless, a step into the semi-rural natural spaces on the edges of the city: the bogs, the fields, the rivers and the seas.

Notes

1. Slote et al., *Annotations*, 1218.
2. Lanigan, *James Joyce*, 8. See also William J. Kupinse, 'Private Property, Public Interest: Bloom's Ecological Fantasy in "Ithaca"', *James Joyce Quarterly* 52/3–4 (2015), 593–621.
3. Lanigan, *James Joyce*, 26.
4. Ibid., 39.
5. Luke Gibbons, *Joyce's Ghosts: Ireland, Modernism, and Memory* (Chicago: University of Chicago Press, 2015), 94.
6. Fredric Jameson, *Modernism and Imperialism*, Field Day Pamphlet 14 (Derry: Field Day, 1988), 22.
7. Andrew Thacker, *Moving Through Modernity: Space and Geography in Modernism* (Manchester: Manchester University Press, 2003), 130.
8. Kiberd, *Inventing Ireland*, 484–5.
9. Oswald Spengler, *The Decline of the West: Form and Actuality*, trans. Charles Francis Atkinson (New York: Alfred A. Knopf, 1926), 91.
10. Ibid., 91. Spengler sees this unequal relationship between city and country as contributing to his reactionary notion of the 'decline of

the west', as 'the giant city sucks the country dry, insatiably and incessantly demanding and devouring fresh streams of men, till it wearies and dies in the midst of an almost uninhabited waste of country' (102).

11. Georg Simmel, 'The Metropolis and Mental Life', in *The Sociology of Georg Simmel*, ed. and trans. Kurt H. Wolff (Glencoe, IL: Free Press, 1950), 410.
12. Ibid., 410.
13. Ibid., 415.
14. Henri Lefebvre, *The Urban Revolution*, trans. Robert Bononno (Minneapolis, MN: University of Minnesota Press, 2003), 11.
15. Ibid., 28.
16. Ibid., 28.
17. Ibid., 29. 'Field' in Lefebvre is a temporal rather than a spatial category, though its use – it is a literal translation of *champ* in the original – may suggest a blurring of these time-space categories, particularly as Lefebvre's theory applies to the development of a space in time. For the original, see Henri Lefebvre, *La révolution urbaine* (Paris: Gallimard, 1970), 41–2.
18. Richard Lehan, 'Joyce's City', in Bernard Benstock (ed.), *James Joyce: The Augmented Ninth* (Syracuse, NY: Syracuse University Press, 1988), 249.
19. Henri Lefebvre, *The Production of Space*, trans. Donald Nicholson-Smith (Oxford: Blackwell, 1991), 1.
20. Thacker, *Moving Through Modernity*, 18.
21. Lefebvre, *The Production of Space*, 86–7.
22. Pound, '"Dubliners"', 267.
23. Kiberd, *Inventing Ireland*, 492.
24. Ibid., 485.
25. Margaret Murphy and Matthew Stout, 'Introduction', in Margaret Murphy and Matthew Stout (eds), *Agriculture and Settlement in Ireland* (Dublin: Four Courts Press, 2015), xxix.
26. Timothy Guinnane, *The Vanishing Irish: Households, Migrations, and the Rural Economy in Ireland, 1850–1914* (Princeton, NJ: Princeton University Press, 1997), 124.
27. Joseph V. O'Brien, *'Dear, Dirty Dublin': A City in Distress, 1899–1916* (Berkeley, CA: University of California Press, 1982), 7 n.
28. Guinnane, *The Vanishing Irish*, 121.
29. Ibid., 122.
30. Patrick Fitzgerald and Brian Lambkin, *Migration in Irish History, 1607–2007* (London: Palgrave Macmillan, 2008), 186.
31. O'Brien, *'Dear, Dirty Dublin'*, 112.
32. Ibid., 155.
33. Stephen J. Browne, *Ireland in Fiction: A Guide to Irish Novels, Tales, Romances, and Folklore* (Dublin: Maunsel, 1916), 123.

34. For a detailed account of Byrne and Joyce's connection, see Ken Hannigan, '"Up In His Hat": Joyce and John Francis Byrne: The Wicklow Connections', *Dublin James Joyce Journal* 11 (2018), 47–72.
35. Kiberd, *Inventing Ireland*, 481.
36. Simon Dedalus displays a similar attitude to Stephen during their journey to Cork when he dismisses his son as 'only a Dublin jackeen' (*P* 93). 'Jackeen' is a derogatory term used in reference to someone from Dublin city (*OED*, 'jackeen, n.').
37. Anastasia Dukova, *A History of the Dublin Metropolitan Police and its Colonial Legacy* (Dublin: Palgrave Macmillan, 2016), 33.
38. Ibid., 33.
39. Fitzgerald and Lambkin, *Migration in Irish History*, 190.
40. Slote et al., *Annotations*, 113.
41. Arensberg and Kimball, *Family and Community in Ireland*, 344.
42. Owens, 'The Mystique of the West', 88.
43. John V. Kelleher, 'Irish History and Mythology in James Joyce's "The Dead"', in Charles Fanning (ed.), *Selected Writings of John V. Kelleher on Ireland and America* (Carbondale, IL: Southern Illinois University Press, 2002), 44, cited in Gibbons, *Joyce's Ghosts*, 253 n.17.
44. While the version sung here easily overlaps with themes of cruel landlords in rural Ireland, the original version of this song is in fact of Scottish origin, as Jeri Johnson points out in her 'Explanatory Notes', *Dubliners* (Oxford: Oxford University Press, 2008), 277. For an extended discussion of the significance of the song and Aughrim itself in Joyce and Irish history, see Shovlin's chapter '"Their friends, the French": Joyce, Jacobitism and the Revival', in *Journey Westward*, 62–121.
45. Thomas E. Jordan, *The Census of Ireland, 1821–1911: General Reports and Extracts*, III (Lewiston, NY: Edwin Mellen Press, 1998), 577.
46. Arensberg and Kimball, *Family and Community in Ireland*, 21.
47. Liam Clare, 'The Dublin Cattle Market', *Dublin Historical Record* 55/2 (2002), 174–5.
48. Ibid., 178.
49. Arensberg and Kimball, *Family and Community in Ireland*, 310.
50. 'Hades' is not the only occasion in Joyce's works when we see cattle being 'driven' down a road on the periphery of the city. An early Joyce poem entitled 'Ruminants', later rewritten as 'Tilly' and included in the collection *Pomes Penyeach*, features a farmer '[u]rging the cattle along a cold red road' near Cabra, in Joyce's time a rural area just north of Phoenix Park (*PSW* 51).
51. Clare, 'The Dublin Cattle Market', 174.
52. Patrick Cunningham, 'The Evolution of Cattle and Cattle Farming Systems: The Genetic Evidence', in Margaret Murphy and Matthew Stout (eds), *Agriculture and Settlement in Ireland* (Dublin: Four Courts Press, 2015), 9.

53. Ibid., 10, 11.

54. Ibid.,11.

55. Michael Turner, *After the Famine: Irish Agriculture, 1850–1915* (Cambridge: Cambridge University Press, 1996), 15.

56. Ibid., 62.

57. W. G. Mulhall, *Dictionary of Statistics* (London: George Routledge and Sons, 1892), 286, cited in Forrest Capie and Richard Perren, 'The British Market for Meat, 1850–1914', *Agricultural History* 54/4 (1980), 505.

58. Jeremy Rifkin, *Beyond Beef: The Rise and Fall of the Cattle Culture* (New York: Dutton, 1992), 57.

59. Caitlin McIntyre, '"We Are All Animals:" James Joyce, Stephen Dedalus, and the Problem of Agriculture', *Humanities* 6/3 (2017), para. 2, https://doi.org/10.3390/h6030072 (accessed 23 February 2024).

60. Ibid., para. 11.

61. For more on how Joyce addressed the deforestation of Ireland, see James Fairhall, 'Eco-criticism, Joyce, and the Politics of Trees in the "Cyclops" Episode of *Ulysses*', *Irish Studies Review* 20/4 (2012), 372; Katherine O'Callaghan, 'Joyce's "treeless hills": Deforestation and Its Cultural Resonances', in Oona Frawley and Katherine O'Callaghan (eds), *Memory Ireland: James Joyce and Cultural Memory*, IV (Syracuse, NY: Syracuse University Press, 2014), 95–111; and Yi-Peng Lai, 'The Tree Wedding and the (Eco)Politics of Irish Forestry in "Cyclops": History, Language and the Viconian Politics of the Forest', in Robert Brazeau and Derek Gladwin (eds), *Eco-Joyce: The Environmental Imagination of James Joyce* (Cork: Cork University Press, 2014), 91–110.

62. A springer is a cow or heifer that is close to calving. 'Cuffe's prime springers' are again mentioned by the narrator in 'Cyclops' (*U* 12.105). While it would not be unusual to sell springers at the cattle market, it would be quite peculiar to send them to England for slaughter.

63. Wim Van Mierlo, 'The Greater Ireland beyond the Sea: James Joyce, Exile and Irish Imagination', in Andrew Gibson and Len Platt (eds), *Joyce, Ireland, Britain* (Gainesville, FL: University Press of Florida, 2006), 188.

64. Robert Brazeau, '"The Sassenach wants his morning rashers": The Colonial Market and the Commodified Animal in "Telemachus"', *James Joyce Quarterly* 58/1–2 (2020), 19–20.

65. Ibid., 32.

66. David Jones, 'The Issue of Land Distribution: Revisiting *Graziers, Land Reform and Political Conflict in Ireland*', in Fergus Campbell and Tony Varley (eds), *Land Questions in Modern Ireland* (Manchester: Manchester University Press, 2013), 139.

67. Peter Adkins, 'The Eyes of That Cow: Eating Animals and Theorizing Vegetarianism in James Joyce's *Ulysses*', *Humanities* 6/3 (2017), para. 13, https://doi.org/10.3390/h6030046 (accessed 23 February 2024).

68. 'Foot-and-mouth disease (FMD)', *Britannica Academic*, Encyclopædia Britannica, 3 February 2012, https://www.britannica.com/science/foot-and-mouth-disease (accessed 14 September 2024).

69. Ibid.

70. Turner notes that there had been outbreaks of foot-and-mouth in Ireland in 1869, 1871, 1872 and again in 1884, demonstrating the regular threat posed by the disease (*After the Famine*, 61).

71. Blackwood Price's letter to Joyce is reproduced by Ellmann – see *JJII* 326–7 n.

72. For many years it was thought that an unsigned editorial from 10 September entitled 'Politics and Cattle Disease' was written by Joyce; however, it has since been convincingly shown that this attribution is incorrect and the piece could not possibly have been written by him – see Terence Matthews, 'An Emendation to the Joycean Canon: The Last Hurrah for "Politics and Cattle Disease"', *James Joyce Quarterly* 44/3 (2007), 441–53.

73. *Freeman's Journal*, 6 September 1912, p. 6, The British Newspaper Archive, https://www.britishnewspaperarchive.co.uk/viewer/BL/0000056/19120906/072/0006 (accessed 20 January 2022).

74. Terence Killeen, 'On the Authorship of a *Freeman* Sub-Editorial', *James Joyce Online Notes*, para. 9, https://www.jjon.org/joyce-s-environs/price (accessed 19 January 2022).

75. Slote et al., *Annotations*, 786.

76. Don Gifford and Robert J. Seidman, *'Ulysses' Annotated: Notes for James Joyce's Ulysses*, 2nd edn (Berkeley, CA: University of California Press, 1988), 424.

77. For information regarding the boundaries between the urban and the rural in Joyce's Dublin, I have referred to the 1911 edition of the 25-inch Ordnance Survey maps for Dublin, whose unparalleled level of detail makes them by far the most useful tool for consultation. All of the maps that I have used here were revised in 1907, making them an accurate point of reference for the Dublin of Joyce's fiction.

78. O'Brien, *'Dear, Dirty Dublin'*, 12.

79. Enda Duffy, 'Drumcondra Modernism: Joyce's Suburban Aesthetic', in Marjorie Elizabeth Howes (ed.), *Irish Literature in Transition, 1880–1940*, IV (Cambridge: Cambridge University Press, 2020), 229.

80. Ibid., 230.

81. Ibid., 241.

82. Ibid., 241.

83. Lacivita, *The Ecology of 'Finnegans Wake'*, 134.

84. James Fairhall, 'The Bog of Allen, the Tiber River, and the Pontine Marshes: An Ecocritical Reading of "The Dead"', *James Joyce Quarterly* 51/4 (2014), 587.

85. Dianne Meredith, 'Hazards in the Bog: Real and Imagined', *Geographical Review* 92/3 (2002), 328.

86. Ibid., 329.
87. Ibid., 329.
88. Steven Morrison, 'Introduction', in Steven Morrison and Andrew Gibson (eds), *Joyce's 'Wandering Rocks'* (Leiden: Brill, 2002), 3.
89. Slote et al., *Annotations*, 436.
90. Clive Hart, 'Wandering Rocks', in Clive Hart and David Hayman (eds), *James Joyce's 'Ulysses': Critical Essays* (Berkeley, CA: University of California Press, 1977), 196.
91. Anne Fogarty, 'States of Memory: Reading History in "Wandering Rocks"', in Ellen Carol Jones and Morris Beja (eds), *Twenty-First Joyce* (Gainesville, FL: University Press of Florida, 2004), 68–9.
92. Ibid., 68.
93. Ibid., 68.
94. John S. Conmee, *Old Times in the Barony* (1895; Dublin: Catholic Truth Society of Ireland, 1911), 12.
95. Yeats, 'The Municipal Gallery Revisited', in *Yeats's Poems*, 439.
96. Len Platt, 'Moving in Times of Yore: Historiographies in "Wandering Rocks"', in Steven Morrison and Andrew Gibson (eds), *Joyce's 'Wandering Rocks'* (Leiden: Brill, 2002), 151.
97. Conmee, *Old Times in the Barony*, 13, 30.
98. Slote et al., *Annotations*, 441.
99. Ibid., 445.
100. Johnson, 'Explanatory Notes', 204.
101. Robert Browning, 'Love Among the Ruins', in *The Major Works*, ed. Adam Roberts (Oxford: Oxford University Press, 2005), 157–9.
102. Thacker, *Moving Through Modernity*, 143.
103. For a detailed account of the transgression in Phoenix Park, see Alison Lacivita, 'Trouble in Paradise: Violence and the Phoenix Park in *Finnegans Wake*', *James Joyce Quarterly* 51/2 (2014), 317–31.

Chapter 5

Journeys Westward: Travel Writing, Geography and Joyce's Cultural Landscapes

In July 1905 Joyce wrote to his brother Stanislaus to update him on his progress with writing what would become *Dubliners*. In the letter, Joyce states: 'It is my intention to complete "Dubliners" by the end of the year and to follow it by a book "Provincials"' (*L2* 63). That Joyce intended to follow his portrayal of Ireland's capital city with one focused by contrast on Irish provincial life complicates the stereotypical image we have of a writer whose gaze did not go beyond the metaphorical city walls. It also suggests that Joyce himself was aware that *Dubliners* could not claim to be a definitive depiction of the country as a whole given the overbearing focus on its eponymous city. This anxiety regarding the rest of the country is perhaps most evident at the end of 'The Dead' as Gabriel Conroy determines to set out on a 'journey westward' (*D* 176). In this initial notion to write a provincial sequel to *Dubliners*, Joyce similarly seems to have felt a need to go on his own 'journey westward' in his writing.

Provincials never came into being, but this does not mean that Joyce did not hold good to his promise, albeit in a less obvious way. This chapter will argue that following the completion of 'The Dead', Joyce set off on a journey westward in his writing that impacted each of his subsequent works. It is important to state at this point that by speaking of journeying 'westward', I am not limiting this study to the west coast of Ireland, though it plays a significant part in this chapter. Instead, I will be more generally examining Joyce's literal and literary 'journeys' beyond Dublin. Given that the majority of Ireland lies somewhere west of Dublin, 'the west' can therefore be conceived of as a metonym for the rest of Ireland. This chapter will, however, limit its focus to the works before the *Wake*, with the following chapter dedicated to that final work's engagement with Irish settings beyond Dublin.

The idea that landscapes beyond Dublin are missing from Joyce's work has been effectively challenged by a wave of ecocritical writing, most notably in Robert Brazeau and Derek Gladwin's edited collection *Eco-Joyce: The Environmental Imagination of James Joyce* and in Alison Lacivita's *The Ecology of 'Finnegans Wake'*, as well as in numerous other articles and individual chapters. From its roots in biology, 'ecology' has taken on numerous adapted significations in various fields of study, including literary studies.[1] Cheryll Glotfelty gave an early definition of ecocriticism as 'the study of the relationship between literature and the physical environment', while noting that 'nature per se is not the only focus of ecocritical studies of representation'.[2] Indeed, while the first 'wave' of ecocriticism focused primarily on the 'natural environment', subsequent waves have broadened this focus to encompass both 'natural and built environments', with increasing emphasis on urban ecology.[3] While ecocriticism has by now moved well beyond signifying simply 'nature', in this chapter I am deliberately focusing on how the natural and the human/cultural intertwine in Joyce, particularly in depictions of the landscape. Indeed, Malcolm Sen, in his introduction to *A History of Irish Literature and the Environment* (2022), notes that this interrelationship between culture and nature has not always been acknowledged in Irish Studies, with criticisms often 'segregating them into distinct categories, as if one is not integrally a part of the other'.[4] The development of 'cultural ecology', which studies how human culture adapts to its ecological setting, specifically emphasises this interrelationship, by considering 'the sphere of human culture not as separate from but as interdependent with and transfused by ecological processes and natural energy cycles'.[5] Hubert Zapf, a leading theorist of cultural ecology, nevertheless argues that this brand of ecological thought 'resists the tendency in recent versions of ecotheory to abolish all boundaries', instead highlighting the 'fundamental relation between culture and nature, which are seen to be inextricably interconnected but are also irreducible to each other'.[6]

Throughout this chapter I use the term 'geography', given its emphasis on the intersection between the human and the natural, particularly the physical features of the landscape.[7] Geography as a field of study specifically situates the natural and physical environment within the cultural, political and sociological environments that envelop it (or that are enveloped by it). Cultural geography – with its focus on how human culture makes sense of its physical environment – and cultural ecology naturally share many of the same concerns. One term that has had a long history of use in cultural geographic studies is the 'cultural landscape'.[8] The term (*Kulturlandschaft*) was first employed by the German geographer Friedrich Ratzel in the late nineteenth century and became current among German geographers in the years that followed, before being introduced to the English-speaking world by the American geographer Carl O. Sauer in 1925.[9] Sauer described the idea of the cultural landscape in the following terms:

> The cultural landscape is fashioned out of a natural landscape by a culture group. Culture is the agent, the natural area is the medium, the cultural landscape is the result. Under the influence of a given culture, itself changing through time, the landscape undergoes development, passing through phases, and probably reaching ultimately the end of its cycle of development. With the introduction of a different – that is, an alien – culture, a rejuvenation of the cultural landscape sets in, or a new landscape is superimposed on remnants of an older one. The natural landscape is of course of fundamental importance, for it supplies the materials out of which the cultural landscape is formed. The shaping force, however, lies in culture itself.[10]

The cultural landscape refers, in short, to landscapes 'that have been modified or influenced by human activity'.[11] This can be both in physical terms – 'traces of human activity in the landscape as humans have influenced and modified "nature" through time' – and in cognitive terms – 'the cultural meanings that humans attached to their physical surroundings'.[12]

The idea of the cultural landscape has to its advantage and detriment a certain vagueness, in that it is arguable that there are few if any landscapes left on Earth that have not in some way been 'modified' by humans physically or cognitively.[13] Michael Jones describes Harald Plachter's attempt to better define the concept by dividing landscapes into four categories: '*natural and semi-natural landscapes*' where human influence is lacking or minimal; traditional landscapes 'where humans are dependent on the limits of the natural system while shaping the landscape'; modern agricultural landscapes, 'which depend on huge imports of resources and energy'; and finally, urban landscapes.[14] As Jones writes, '[t]he implication is that only the second category should be considered as cultural landscape'.[15] In employing this term, I have broadly followed Plachter's outline and limited my focus to those aspects of the landscape where 'culture and nature have shaped one another, where human influence was consciously creative, and where ecological mechanisms are still at work in interaction with humans'.[16]

Human culture and influence are never far removed from Joyce's portrayals of the rural Irish landscape, and therefore it seems more accurate to speak of 'cultural landscapes' in his work than simply 'natural' landscapes in and of themselves. Even those landscapes that seem closest to a 'natural' state in Joyce are usually endowed with centuries of cultural meaning; for example, the mountain Croagh Patrick, which features repeatedly throughout the *Wake*, is impossible to imagine divorced from its central place in Irish spirituality, both pagan and Christian.[17] Throughout this chapter, therefore, there is an emphasis on how landscapes and humans interact and define each other, a relationship that goes beyond the ecological domain to incorporate the cultural, political and sociological realms as well.

'The lazy Dubliner': Joyce and Travel Writing

In *Structure and Motif in 'Finnegans Wake'* (1962), Clive Hart offers what remained for a long time the traditional view of Joyce's relationship with nature and Ireland beyond Dublin:

> Joyce was essentially an indoor man, a city dweller. All his books before *Finnegans Wake* are urban. Nature in the Wordsworthian sense seems to have meant little to him, and although in *Finnegans Wake* river and mountain, flower and tree are for the first time used as major recurrent symbols, they are little more than stylised icons which rarely develop into sensuous, living images. In *A Portrait* the rural setting of Clongowes Wood College is barely mentioned and fulfils no important function as it might have done in, say, a Lawrence, while the more recently published pages from *Stephen Hero*, dealing with rural Mullingar, show how out of touch Joyce felt when he attempted to write naturalistically about events in settings outside his native city. The biographies have little to say about holidays spent away from city life, and the Letters contain very little mention of the natural world (except, of course, for the frequent allusions to the Liffey, which formed an essential part of Joyce's urban Dublin).[18]

While Hart acknowledges that nature plays a role in *Finnegans Wake* – albeit never developing into 'sensuous, living images' – he does not accord much significance to rurality and nature in Joyce's other works. However, the plethora of recent ecological readings of

Joyce have by now demonstrated the centrality of nature in his work, while, as Chapter 3 set out to show, the rural backdrop of Clane and its peasant population plays an important role in Stephen's development in *A Portrait*, and the surviving chapters of *Stephen Hero* set in Mullingar demonstrate Stephen's self-fashioning as a cosmopolitan man above what is viewed as rustic naivety.

Hart's claim that the 'biographies have little to say about holidays spent away from city life' is also suspect; Ellmann, though generally keen to emphasise Joyce's urbanity, does provide short accounts of childhood journeys to Cork and Mullingar. In February 1894 Joyce was taken by his father to Cork, where John Joyce was to sell off his remaining properties to pay off his increasing debts. Ellmann writes that the week spent in his father's hometown left a lasting impression on Joyce, as '[i]n later life he always showed a fellow feeling for Cork men, and would ask them about the Imperial Hotel, where he stayed, about the Mardyke, a fine promenade, and about the special Cork dish, drisheens' (*JJII* 37).[19] Evidently the journey left enough of an impact to make its way into *A Portrait* many years later, as we shall explore. An affinity for Cork *city*, of course, does not contradict Hart's insistence on an urban Joyce, notwithstanding the fact that the Cork that Joyce visited would have been a more provincial setting than Dublin or Belfast at the time, its population in 1901 being only 76,000, significantly less than Dublin's 350,000 and Belfast's 349,000.[20]

However, Joyce's numerous trips to Mullingar would certainly have exposed him to a much more rural setting. In the summer of 1900, John Joyce was tasked with 'straighten[ing] out the voting lists in Mullingar', taking his children, including James, along with him (*JJII* 77). Ellmann interprets Joyce's experience of Mullingar through the lens of *Stephen Hero*, particularly in relation to his attitude towards the locals. Indeed, Mullingar provides the setting for two of Joyce's Epiphanies, numbers 9 and 15, the first featuring advice to marry young and the latter involving a beggar threatening young children with a stick (*PSW* 169, 175).[21] It would seem that Mullingar proved a conducive setting for getting work done, as Joyce wrote his first play there, *A Brilliant Career*, and on another trip to Mullingar in summer 1901 he would complete translations of Hauptmann's *Vor Sonnenaufgang* and *Michael Kramer* (*JJII* 77–8, 87). According to his brother Stanislaus, *A Brilliant Career* – described by Joyce in his dedication to the play as 'the first / true work of my / life' – concerns a provincial doctor who goes on to become mayor of a small town, leading it through a plague (*JJII* 78).

Joyce destroyed the play in 1902, leaving behind only one four-line fragment from a gypsy song:

We will leave the village behind,
Merrily, you and I,
Tramp it smart and sing to the wind,
With the Romany Rye. (*JJII* 78)

From Stanislaus's description, it is clear that Joyce's 'first true work' was a provincial drama, most likely inspired by the setting of its composition, and not an urban piece. Even the fragment that survives from the gypsy song is clearly concerned with life in a 'village' rather than that of an urban metropolis, even if only to leave it behind.

In autumn 1912 Joyce made his first forays into travel writing with a pair of articles for the Triestine newspaper *Il Piccolo della Sera*. Joyce, however, differs significantly from the majority of other travel writers of the time in that rather than going abroad to describe the strange ways of foreign lands, he returned to Ireland to do his travel writing. Yet while Joyce might have returned home, he did not write about the Ireland he knew intimately – the city of Dublin – but rather, like most travel writers, about somewhere unfamiliar: Galway and the Aran Islands. It is important to bear in mind that in these articles Joyce was writing for an Italian audience, and as such might have somewhat cynically spotted an opportunity to capitalise on what might be deemed the most marketable region of Ireland. Joyce's depiction of Galway and the western isles that lie off it is noticeably sanguine, however, and suggests a genuine fascination with the region in which his partner Nora had grown up. Ellmann's account of Joyce's time in Galway in 1912 presents an idyllic summer in which 'Joyce took up rural sports; he rowed and one Sunday bicycled forty miles' (*JJII* 324). This was not, however, Joyce's first trip to Galway; three years earlier he had visited Nora's mother and had spent most of the weekend with her, asking her to sing verses of 'The Lass of Aughrim' (*JJII* 286). When Mrs Barnacle died many years later, Joyce was said to have 'wept like a child' (*JJII* 737). Joyce's early associations with Galway therefore appear to have been resoundingly positive, though it is important to state that this was not always the case, particularly after Nora, Giorgio and Lucia were caught up in Civil War crossfire during a trip there in 1922, with Joyce referring to the town as Nora's 'native dunghill' in a letter to his Aunt Josephine (*L1* 191). However, even in this letter Joyce acknowledges the potential restorative nature of Galway – 'The air in Galway is good but dear at the present price' (*L1* 191) – and it is this image of the town that is conveyed in his early journalism.

The first sentence of 'The City of the Tribes: Italian Memories in an Irish Port' condemns the 'lazy Dubliner who does not travel much' and presents Galway almost as an Irish Venice – hardly a coincidence given the article's Italian audience – as Joyce describes the city 'lying over countless little islands [. . .] veined in all directions by small rivers, cataracts, ponds, and canals' (*OCPW* 197). Galway does not seem to contain any of the emotional stasis of Joyce's early depictions of Dublin; instead, it is a place in which 'reign the passions of pride and lust' (*OCPW* 200). Joyce positions himself as a typical travel writer, a stranger in a strange land, a position that is only heightened in the final paragraph of the article as the supposed foreignness of Galway's natural and human culture combine in a dizzying mix:

> The evening is silent and grey. From afar, from beyond the falling waters, comes a humming sound. It is like the buzzing of bees around their hive. It comes nearer. Seven young men come into sight, bagpipe players, at the head of a train of people. They pass proud and martial, heads uncovered, playing a music that is vague and strange. In the uncertain light the green plaids hanging from their right shoulders and their saffron kilts are just distinguishable. They turn into the road to the Presentation Convent and, while the vague music permeates the twilight, in the windows of the convent appear, one by one, the white wimples of the nuns. (*OCPW* 200)

The bagpipe players are at first confused with their natural surroundings, mistaken for humming bees, an error that only serves to bind them even more determinedly to the ecological backdrop of the west of Ireland. This is a typically Revivalist technique – Synge describes the people of the Aran Islands as having retained 'the agile walk of the wild animal' while they share a 'charm [. . .] with the birds and flowers'.[22] When the bagpipers come into view, they do not in any sense become any clearer; the music emanating from them is 'vague and strange', while they stand in an 'uncertain light' that renders their kilts only 'just distinguishable'. As they turn towards the convent, they merge once again with their surroundings, as their 'vague music permeates the twilight'. Joyce's repeated emphasis on all that is 'vague', 'strange' and 'uncertain' renders Galway suitably exotic for the travel writer passing through. Despite this seeming remove from the norms of western Europe, Joyce leaves us with the peculiar image of the 'white wimples of the nuns' appearing at the convent window, a recognition of Ireland's deep connection to Europe through Christianity. This final paragraph manages to balance Galway's links to Europe, something Joyce has insisted upon throughout the article, with its sense of being the gateway to one of the remaining geographical spaces of Gaelic Ireland.

During this same summer in Galway, Joyce had another idea for an article for *Il Piccolo della Sera*, this time journeying out to the Aran Islands, the fabled site of Gaelic culture in its supposedly most undiluted form. By going to the Aran Islands, Joyce was undertaking a journey that Gabriel Conroy, in his most cosmopolitan guise, had rejected. John Wilson Foster writes that '[u]ntil well into the twentieth century, the Aran Islands [. . .] were rarely visited by ordinary tourists: a journey there was an earnest of one's cultural commitment to the new Ireland'.[23] Of course, the fact of Joyce's journey to the largest of the islands, Árainn – or Aranmor as he terms it – does not mean that he was culturally committed to the 'new Ireland' under construction, but it does suggest a deep desire to discover an Ireland he had not hitherto experienced, especially as this was not an easy part of the tourist trail as it is today. Joyce's main journalistic purpose was to write about the Galway harbour scheme, a plan to transform Galway into a major transatlantic port, though this quickly took a secondary position to a cultural exploration of the islands and islanders themselves.

While Joyce's Galway articles were primarily written to make some quick and easy money, they nonetheless reveal his complex engagement with rural Ireland. Throughout the Árainn article, Joyce stresses the inherent strangeness of the place, as is clear from the subordinate part of the title: 'The Mirage of the Fisherman of Aran'. The 'mirage' is a reference to Hy-brasil, the mythical island which was supposed to be located off the west coast of Ireland, 'vague and tremulous on the mirror of the ocean' (*OCPW* 203). As he had done with the bagpipers of Galway, Joyce again emphasises the 'vague' quality of this part of Ireland. The sense of it being set apart culturally from the rest of Ireland is underlined before the journalist has even left Galway, with the nearby village of the Claddagh described as '[a] cluster of cabins, and yet a kingdom' (*OCPW* 201). Joyce notes that up until quite recently the Claddagh had 'elected its own king, had its own style of dress, made its own laws and lived apart' (*OCPW* 201).[24] This strangeness is only heightened on Árainn itself, as Joyce meets a young islandman who claims that 'Aran [. . .] is the strangest place in the world', a perhaps peculiar comment to make about the place one has grown up in (*OCPW* 204). Another islander's psyche seems to meld with his ecological surroundings: 'Around the shrubs growing with difficulty on the hillocks of the island, his imagination has woven legends and fables that reveal the hereditary taint of his psyche' (*OCPW* 204). What exactly Joyce means by the 'hereditary taint' of this islander's psyche is hard to say. In the Italian original, Joyce writes this as 'la tara della sua psiche' (*OCPW* 232). *Tara*, the Italian for 'taint', seems hardly accidental in this context, with Joyce potentially punning on the Hill of Tara, seat of the High Kings of ancient Ireland, which comes to stand as a symbol of a future, if differently idealised, version of Ireland for both Davin and Stephen in *A Portrait*. The interlingual wordplay here draws a link between the islander as a repository of Gaelic Ireland's 'legends and fables' and one of the most important of its ancient sites, present throughout so many of those tales. Most importantly, the psychological impact of the place the islander inhabits clearly filters into the stories he tells, emphasising a deep connection between place and narrative for Joyce. The island's shrubby hillocks stand as monuments around which an islander must structure their sense of the world, just as the streets of Dublin shaped many of Joyce's own narratives. In his investigation of Joyce as a travel writer, Derek Gladwin argues that he uses 'a spatial and ecocritical practice called place-attachment: accessing place through personal and cultural experience in a landscape'.[25] Regarding the above passage, Gladwin argues that Joyce shows how the islander 'accesses the cultural memory of his people "woven" through legends and deposited in his psyche [. . .] Landscape, therefore, is both external, as a spatial jurisdiction, and internal, as an emotional register of place-attachment.'[26]

Gladwin's application of the theory of place-attachment in relation to Joyce's travel writing has much in common with the older Gaelic tradition of *dinnseanchas*.[27] This term, which in modern Irish dictionaries is translated as 'topography' (*FGB*, 'dinnseanchas'), is primarily used to describe what Gerry Smyth calls 'both a general tendency in early Gaelic literature and (when prefixed with "the") a body of Middle-Irish toponymic literature known as *Dinnshenchas Erenn* assembled during the twelfth century'.[28] Mac Giolla Léith translates this sense of the term as 'the traditional, legendary lore of notable places'.[29] *Dinnseanchas* is therefore a form of literary practice that emphasises place and landscape, being especially concerned with the etymological roots of place names, with Seán Ó Tuama writing that '[no] poet was accounted educated if he was not fully acquainted with the *dinnsheanchas*'.[30] That Joyce was particularly concerned with toponymy is clear from Stanislaus's description of the Joyce family's move to Glengariff Parade. He writes that on hearing a butcher boy outside their house singing a rhyming verse, James described him as a poet of 'the rugged glen', a translation of the original place name *Gleann Garbh* (*MBK* 123). In addition to this, Joyce's Paris library contained the third volume of P. W. Joyce's *The Origin and History of Irish Names of Places* (1920), while *Finnegans Wake* includes relentless punning on the roots of Irish place names.[31] Maria Tymoczko argues that P. W. Joyce's work 'is a likely source for some of James Joyce's knowledge of the Irish tradition of dindsenchas', suggesting that Joyce 'was aware of the ways in which his own work fit into this aspect of Irish literary tradition'.[32] The cartographer Tim Robinson writes that '[p]lacenames are the interlock of landscape and language',[33] and indeed this is something that is apparent throughout Joyce's work, leading to the inevitable melding of the two in the *Wake* as 'landuage' and 'landeguage' (*FW* 327.20, 478.9–10).

However, while etymological concerns might lie at the heart of *dinnseanchas*, it would be wrong to see its influence on Irish literature as stopping there. Smyth concludes that *dinnseanchas* 'reflects an understanding in which place and identity are inseparable'.[34] Such an understanding is clear in Joyce's travels to Galway and Árainn, where the people's psyches are shaped by the local topography. *Dinnseanchas* at its core is an insistence on the need to understand one's location if one is to understand oneself. As such, Joyce in his travel writing begins what will become a general trend in his works, connecting place with identity, and thus follows in a literary practice that is as deeply embedded in the national tradition as it is in the soil itself.

Name, Nation, Dwellingplace: Place and Identity in *A Portrait*

The relationship between identity and place is brought to the fore from near the beginning of *A Portrait*, most clearly in the passage where Stephen studies his geography book. Stephen's book is filled with 'different places that had different names. They were all in different countries and the countries were in continents and the continents were in the world and the world was in the universe' (*P* 15). Stephen's geographical layering or scaling of existence is mirrored in what he has written on the flyleaf of his book:

> *Stephen Dedalus*
> *Class of Elements*
> *Clongowes Wood College*
> *Sallins*
> *County Kildare*
> *Ireland*
> *Europe*
> *The World*
> *The Universe* (P 15–16)

Jon Hegglund writes that 'Stephen understands his relationship to space in terms of a neatly ordered hierarchy in which each geographical scale is enfolded within another, larger scale', eventually reaching 'the blurry area between physical and metaphysical geographies'.[35] Hegglund sees this list as bespeaking 'a post-Enlightenment hierarchical arrangement of knowledge'.[36] Certainly, this arrangement is far from innocent; it is noticeably a scaling that aligns to *geographical* realities rather than political ones. Stephen does not locate Ireland in the political realm of the United Kingdom, but instead in the geographical and cultural setting of Europe. This scaling also insists on one's temporary location in time, with even the Class of Elements acting as a location just as more conventional ones such as Sallins, Kildare or Ireland do. It is also easy to forget that not every element of this list is spatial in nature, as 'Stephen Dedalus' hovers above the locations. The inclusion of Stephen's name brings the question of identity into what might otherwise be simply read as geographical scaling – one's personal name being the most conventional marker of identity – and so also encourages the reader to question how the places mentioned impinge upon one's sense of self.

The relation between place and identity is also apparent in the parody scrawled on the opposite page by Stephen's classmate Fleming:

> *Stephen Dedalus is my name,*
> *Ireland is my nation.*
> *Clongowes is my dwellingplace*
> *And heaven my expectation.* (P 16)

This ditty echoes the scales that Stephen has adumbrated on the other page but relates them explicitly to the question of identity. Fleming draws a distinction between Ireland, which is bound up with nationality and therefore identity, and Clongowes, which is merely a 'dwellingplace'. Fleming's rhyme differentiates between the locations that had simply been listed out by Stephen by injecting the notion of meaning and identity into Ireland, which Clongowes appears to lack. By contrast, Hegglund sees Stephen's list as a demonstration that 'the nation is but one geographical scale among many that press their claims to shape individual and cultural identities'.[37] Indeed, Stephen scales up and down the list, as though in an attempt to extract meaning from these geographical locations, though in vain: 'he read from the flyleaf from the bottom to the top till he came to his own name. That was he: and he read down the page again. What was after the universe? Nothing' (*P* 16). The '[n]othing' that Stephen is left with following this scaling suggests a difficulty in anchoring his identity to any of the places mentioned, a difficulty that Fleming does not appear to understand in his quick designation of Ireland as betokening an identity.

Stephen later looks at the first page of his geography book with 'the green round earth in the middle of the maroon clouds' (*P* 16). We might interpret this as Stephen choosing the world, and all of humanity, over just Ireland; but immediately Stephen's thoughts turn to 'which was right, to be for the green or for the maroon', a reference to Irish political conflict over the Parnell affair (*P* 16). Even as he attempts to scale out towards the world, Stephen is dragged back to the local and national. Hegglund reads Fleming's doggerel as 'render[ing] Ireland with an affective quality that the other scales lack', an interpretation that appears to be validated by Stephen's thoughts turning to Parnell and Ireland despite his looking literally at the world.[38] However, we might also view Fleming's verse as a – perhaps unintended – acknowledgement that one's identity is a composite of grander national ties and the micro-geographical reality of one's location in time. Stephen's temporary location in Clongowes will remain part of his identity no matter where he moves around 'the green round earth'.

At its most fundamental level, Stephen's geographical list is notable for placing him outside Dublin. For much of the first section of *A Portrait*, Stephen is located firmly in the Irish countryside – albeit cocooned somewhat within the walls of Clongowes – and it is this rural landscape that colours his cultural imagination in his early years. As noted previously, Stephen struggles to separate the potatoes he eats from the soil, with one still having 'the mark of the spade in it' (*P* 53). Stephen's familiarity with the rural landscape therefore creates an uneasy link between the ordinary habits of everyday life, such as consuming food, and the reality of its production. Stephen's early experiences are heavily influenced by his temporary dwelling in rural Ireland, to such an extent that when he eventually does move back to Dublin, it registers as 'a new and complex sensation' (*P* 66).

Ireland beyond Dublin is a constant presence in Stephen's life through the influence of his father, Simon, and his constant 'evocation of Cork and of scenes of his youth' (*P* 87). It is with Simon and Stephen Dedalus that Joyce takes his readers on his next 'journey westward' – or south-westward, to be more precise. This journey is quite clearly based on Joyce's own trip to Cork with his father. As in Joyce's own life, Stephen accompanies his father, whose 'property was going to be sold by auction' (*P* 87). The train journey begins unremarkably: Stephen describes the train and watches the telegraph poles pass by outside his window, while listening 'without sympathy' to his father's nostalgic memories of Cork. At Maryborough (now Port Laoise), Stephen falls asleep and does not wake until the train has passed Mallow, not too far from their destination. However, something strange has happened in the meantime. The carefree attitude of earlier has given way to something more sinister that seems to emanate from the landscape itself.

> The cold light of the dawn lay over the country, over the unpeopled fields and the closed cottages. The terror of sleep fascinated his mind as he watched the silent country or heard from time to time his father's deep breath or sudden sleepy movement. The neighbourhood of unseen sleepers filled him with strange dread, as though they could harm him, and he prayed that the day might come quickly. His prayer, addressed neither to God nor saint, began with a shiver, as the chilly morning breeze crept through the chink of the carriage door to his feet, and ended in a trail of foolish words which he made to fit the insistent rhythm of the train; and silently, at intervals of four seconds, the telegraph-poles held the galloping notes of the music between punctual bars. This furious music allayed his dread and, leaning against the windowledge, he let his eyelids close again. (*P* 87–8)

The rural Irish landscape immediately instils a sense of dread in Stephen. This dread is tied to the emptiness of the 'silent' countryside, the 'unpeopled fields and the closed cottages', its 'unseen sleepers'. It is a well-worn trope of rural Ireland that emigration following the Famine reduced a once-teeming population to miles of 'unpeopled fields'. Such an image dominates George Moore's influential short story collection, *The Untilled Field* (1903); Moore's fields are of course untilled because they have been abandoned. This emptiness is also the dominant image in Gabriel Conroy's reflections towards the end of 'The Dead', as he pictures the snow falling over Ireland. Conroy might conclude that it is falling on 'all the living and the dead', but it is specifically the latter that he emphasises with the images of 'crooked crosses and headstones', as we are guided through a barren landscape that is empty save for the corpses lying within it (*D* 176).

Similarly, there is no waking life in the landscape Stephen views from his carriage window – the 'unseen sleepers' appear a source of danger, malevolent beings caught somewhere between life and death. The journey Stephen has undergone during his sleep seems to have transported him, like Bloom in the 'Hades' episode of *Ulysses*, into a perilous liminal zone – he is caught somewhere between night and day, sleep and wakefulness, life and death, city and village. The strangeness of the landscape appears to be echoed in the 'insistent rhythm of the train', which Stephen finally forces through concentration into fitting the more regular rhythm of the passing telegraph poles, moving 'at intervals of four seconds' and eventually holding the 'music' of the train to more 'punctual bars'. It is probably no accident that this accords with most conventional Western music, which has four beats in a bar. Though the music remains 'furious', its irregular rhythm has now been stabilised, and Stephen can relax and 'let his eyelids close again'.

Tobias Boes argues that in this scene, 'it is precisely the recognition of an Irish landscape outside that allows Stephen to arrive at a sense of who he is'.[39] Rather, I would argue that it is not the recognition of the Irish landscape but its reshaping – or even unqueering – to adhere to what Stephen deems to be familiar that allows him to settle back into a sense of self that he finds familiar and comfortable. Stephen finds solace in the 'music' of the train's machinery, which if anything is antithetical to the natural landscape they are traversing. Stephen has been presented with a literal window into an aspect of his family's past – the landscape of Cork – but it is one for which he is not yet prepared. Later, in a slightly more familiar urban setting, he will be told by friends of his father that they 'have unearthed traces of a Cork accent in his speech' and will be made to 'admit that the Lee was a much finer river than the Liffey' (*P* 94). The syntax here is important, as the accent of his forefathers is 'unearthed', tying it to the very landscape that Stephen now treads upon, again drawing a link between place and identity. Stephen is made to 'admit' that the Lee – as a river, another important geographical feature and influence on the identity of Cork city itself – is finer than the Liffey, suggesting that Stephen does so reluctantly. The sense that this journey to Cork is a journey back to Stephen's origins is underlined also during the visit to the anatomy theatre where Stephen's father studied for a time, and where Stephen sees the word '*Foetus*' etched into the desk (*P* 90).

Such is the identity crisis at play throughout this time in Cork that Stephen is forced at one point to repeat to himself:

> I am Stephen Dedalus. I am walking beside my father whose name is Simon Dedalus. We are in Cork, in Ireland. Cork is a city. Our room is in the Victoria hotel. Victoria and Stephen and Simon. Simon and Stephen and Victoria. Names. (*P* 93)

The emphasis on names here is intricately bound up with place and identity. Stephen attempts to anchor himself to his own name, to his father, to the place where they are, and its relation to the world. By listing what appear to be irrefutable declarations – 'I am Stephen Dedalus [. . .] We are in Cork [. . .] Cork is a city' – Stephen looks for certainty within himself and his sense of identity. But even in attempting this, names have a strange way of rejecting the certainty they seem to promise. Cork might be geographically in Ireland, but the hotel in which they are staying is clearly named after an English queen, underlining Cork's place in the political domain of the British Empire. We can take this even further by investigating the name 'Cork', which is a translation of the name that this place was originally given. *Corcaigh*, coming from *corcach*, meaning a marsh, describes the nature of the land that the city rests on and so provides an insight into the place's identity (*FGB*, 'corcach'). The translation 'Cork' evidently distances the name of the place from its identity, particularly given that the word 'cork' has its own separate meaning in English; indeed, Cork might be said to be having as much of an identity crisis as Stephen is. Stephen's surname, meanwhile, elicits suspicion from his peers, due to its un-Irish-sounding nature: 'What kind of a name is that?' (*P* 9). The emphasis on names, whether they be of people or places, returns us to a question at the heart of the *dinnseanchas* tradition: how to make a name fit the identity of that which carries it.

Overall, the journey to Cork, though framed by his father as a journey 'home', is manifestly incapable of providing such solace to the young Stephen. Katherine O'Callaghan argues that following sustained ecological estrangement, often brought about by colonialism, such searching-in-vain for a notion of 'home' is intrinsic to Irish, and particularly Joycean, modernism. For Irish modernists, '[t]he concept of home which has been created by a form of collective imagining, that place which might provide solace and nourishment, does not correspond with the physical reality of their surroundings'.[40] In *A Portrait*, Stephen rejects the identity passed down to him by his father through their common surname for the identity that he can create from it for himself by reference to the Dedalus of Greek myth. This is a rejection – or denial – of his paternal and south-western, rural origins for self-created ones – eastwards – in Europe and its mythology. This process will always have a limited success, however, as the Stephen of *A Portrait* and *Ulysses*, like his younger self looking at the picture of the world and seeing only the colours of Irish politics, will always be forced to reckon with the country of his birth.

The Joggerfry of *Ulysses*

Stephen's journey to Cork would appear to be the last straight-forward excursion out of Dublin in Joyce's work before the more abstract journeys in *Finnegans Wake*. While the characters of *Ulysses* do skirt the edges of the city, at no point do they leave the county of Dublin. However, this does not mean that the rest of Ireland is not present in the novel, or that the reader is not guided through it at various points. While the Citizen and other cultural nationalists might see in the Irish countryside a cause for national pride – the line between countryside and country being rendered as thin as possible – for Bloom, the Irish landscape provides an excellent opportunity for touristic pursuits for the tired urban dweller. One of the earliest references in *Ulysses* to rural Ireland comes when Bloom overhears a group of schoolchildren studying 'joggerfry' by rote-learning the names of a trinity of islands located off the west coast: 'Inishturk. Inishark. Inishboffin' (*U* 4.138). Located to the west of Galway, these remote islands did not acquire quite the same lofty place in the Irish cultural imagination that the more famous Aran Islands did, and the degree to which these young Dubliners would have known anything about them is perhaps debatable. The distortion of 'geography' to 'joggerfry' might suggest that the students are not in fact being taught geography at all, but are rather being inculcated with the growing cultural nationalism that emphasised the western isles as the last bastions of Gaelic culture in Ireland. This 'geography' is of a type that consists merely in reeling off the names of places, rivers and mountains in a wheeling tour of Ireland. However, Joyce does exactly this on several occasions in *Ulysses*, taking the reader on a number of 'Grand Tours' of Ireland.

Given its thematic preoccupation with cultural nationalism and its stylistic flair for absurd parodic lists, it is perhaps no surprise that 'Cyclops' should feature many of these 'tours'. The first such instance occurs early on in the episode when the narrator parodies James Clarence Mangan's poem 'Prince Aldfrid's Itinerary through Ireland', a translation of an Irish poem attributed to the Northumbrian king Aldfrith, which takes the reader on a tour through the country.[41] The poem notes that the prince 'travelled its fruitful provinces round', going from 'Armagh, the splendid' to 'Munster, unfettered' and 'Connaught the just'; from 'the noble district of Boyle' to 'Leinster the smooth and sleek'; '[f]rom Dublin to Slewmargy's peak'; and finally from 'the broad rich country of Ossorie' to 'Meath's fair principality'.[42] Mangan emphasises the values, both moral and topographical, of the places he travels through, describing each province's landscape and the products thereof, particularly the food. The parody contained in 'Cyclops' goes even further in praising the ecological marvels of the strangely exotic Irish landscape. The reader soars through the provinces of Ireland as Mangan's prince does, as we move 'from Eblana to Slievemargy, the peerless princes of unfettered Munster and of Connacht the just and of smooth sleek Leinster and of Cruachan's land and of Armagh the splendid and of the noble district of Boyle' (*U* 12.83–6).[43] Coming as this does a mere two pages into the episode, this parody of Mangan sets up the reader for the numerous tours of Ireland they are about to experience.

Just a few paragraphs later, and following a description of the Dublin cattle market, the narrator expounds on the many types of farm animals residing in Ireland. The sudden introduction of the sounds of the farmyard – 'trampling, cackling, roaring, lowing, bleating, bellowing, rumbling, grunting, champing, chewing' (*U* 12.108–10) – immediately ruralises this scene, which is otherwise taking place in an inner-city public house. In a parody of the kind of rural-idolising writings of Revivalist literature, such as those featured in *The Irish Homestead*, the narrator describes the

> sheep and pigs and heavyhooved kine from pasturelands of Lusk and Rush and Carrickmines and from the streamy vales of Thomond, from M'Gillicuddy's reeks the inaccessible and lordly Shannon the unfathomable, and from the gentle declivities of the place of the race of Kiar, their udders distended with superabundance of milk and butts of butter and rennets of cheese and farmer's firkins and targets of lamb and crannocks of corn and oblong eggs in great hundreds, various in size, the agate with the dun. (*U* 12.110–17)

This agrarian tour takes the reader from Dublin – albeit rural Dublin: Lusk, Rush and Carrickmines were all still predominantly rural areas outside the city at this point in time – to the famous pasturelands of Munster, with emphasis on the dairy products associated with this region. Geography is again emphasised in this tour of Ireland and, again, parodically distorted to fit in with a particular narrative. The need for the pasturelands of Ireland to be peaceful results in County Kerry ('the race of Kiar') becoming a place of 'gentle declivities', something it is emphatically not. Indeed, such a view is contradicted in the very same sentence by the narrator drawing attention to the 'M'Gillicuddy's reeks [*sic*]', a mountain range in Kerry which includes Ireland's highest point, Carrauntoohil. The River Shannon is here presented as 'unfathomable' in scale, which is in keeping with the image of the 'dark mutinous Shannon waves' at the end of 'The Dead' (*D* 176). John Brannigan notes that the Shannon is not tidal beyond Limerick and so would only 'generate waves of small proportions, perhaps, in stormy conditions'.[44] The Shannon, therefore, can hardly be considered a mysterious or perilous feature in the Irish landscape. What it most certainly can be considered, however, is a major dividing line between east and west, and the description of it as 'mutinous' likely nods towards the notion of the rural west as being historically rebellious. The Shannon is also the longest river in either Ireland or Britain, flowing through or between a third of the counties in Ireland. To be west of the Shannon is to be physically separated from the rest – and the most prosperous part – of Ireland. Brannigan argues that by giving it 'waves' in 'The Dead', Joyce turns the Shannon into a mirror of the Irish Sea, 'a boundary to mark out the west as a different country, a place apart, while the east slides imperceptibly towards a borderless England'.[45] More than anything else, the Shannon's 'waves' exist in the cultural nationalist imagination as a barrier between the west and outside influence. By distorting geographical features in contradictory ways, Joyce creates a vision of the west of Ireland as set apart.

Similar tours of Ireland continue to proliferate as we move through 'Cyclops'. Later, the Citizen praises the 'potteries and textiles' of Ireland, taking us from the 'looms of Antrim' to 'Limerick lace', before going on to include 'Foxford tweeds', 'Connemara marble' and 'silver from Tipperary' (*U* 12.1241–52). The Citizen is, however, adamant in emphasising the European connections of these rural Irish products, with references to trading with the Huguenots, Greek merchants and King Philip of Spain. But undoubtedly the most emphatic tour of Ireland is offered by the

fantastical 'embroidered ancient Irish facecloth', which is in reality a presumably plain handkerchief (*U* 12.1438–9). The facecloth
is attributed to the authors of the fourteenth-century Irish manuscript, *The Book of Ballymote*, and shares some of the same tropes
later found throughout the *Wake*, which was heavily inspired by
another Irish manuscript, *The Book of Kells*. For example, it features 'each of the four [. . .] presenting to each of the four masters his evangelical symbol, a bogoak sceptre, a North American
puma [. . .] a Kerry calf and a golden eagle from Carrantuohill'
(*U* 12.1443–6).[46] The coming together of the four evangelists and
the four masters, authors of the eponymous *Annals*, will go on to
be one of the major recurring tropes of *Finnegans Wake*. Though
there is no suggestion just yet that the four also represent the four
provinces as they do in the *Wake*, their appearance is immediately
followed by a journey through the Irish landscape, as it almost
always is in the *Wake*. The first descriptions we have are of those
aspects of the landscape that have come under the influence of a
human hand: 'our ancient duns and raths and cromlechs and gri-
anauns and seats of learning and maledictive stones' (*U* 12.1447–
8). Dating primarily from pre-Christian Ireland, sites such as these
have occupied a part of the landscape for so long that their human
shaping has ceased to be apparent, often existing as tree-filled hillocks or crumbling circles of stone that to the untrained eye might
appear 'natural'; as such these are good examples of the 'cultural
landscape' of Ireland. Writing of the rural Irish landscape, F. H. A.
Aalen notes that 'natural landscapes, the product of geological, cli-
matic and biological processes unaffected by humans, are already
rare, perhaps non-existent'.[47] He goes on to note that even the likes
of the pasturelands of rural Ireland, mentioned earlier, 'seemingly
so obvious a natural product, are in fact a cultural artefact pains-
takingly created and maintained by many generations of farming
people'.[48]

The facecloth next takes us on a whistle-stop tour of some of
Ireland's most famous tourist sites, though the stylistic distortion
of the episode results in more unexpected inclusions:

> Glendalough, the lovely lakes of Killarney, the ruins of Clonmacnois,
> Cong Abbey, Glen Inagh and the Twelve Pins, Ireland's Eye, the Green
> Hills of Tallaght, Croagh Patrick, the brewery of Messrs Arthur
> Guinness, Son and Company (Limited), Lough Neagh's banks, the
> vale of Ovoca, Isolde's tower, the Mapas obelisk, Sir Patrick Dun's
> hospital, Cape Clear, the glen of Aherlow, Lynch's castle, the Scotch

house, Rathdown Union Workhouse at Loughlinstown, Tullamore jail, Castleconnel rapids, Kilballymacshonakill, the cross at Monasterboice, Jury's Hotel, S. Patrick's Purgatory, the Salmon Leap, Maynooth college refectory, Curley's hole, the three birthplaces of the first duke of Wellington, the rock of Cashel, the bog of Allen, the Henry Street Warehouse, Fingal's Cave [. . .] (*U* 12.1451–61)

This section was originally added during the proof stage, to what are known as the first placards, and featured a relatively short list of the more traditional sites: 'Glendalough, the lovely lakes of Killarney, the ruins of Clonmacnoise [*sic*], Cong Abbey, Glen Inagh and the Twelve Pins, the rock of Cashel, the bog of Allen' (*JJA* 19: 172). In the second placards, Joyce added most of the other sites, which, though primarily based on real places, also featured more eye-catching 'locations' such as 'Kilballymacshonakill' and 'the three birthplaces of the first duke of Wellington' (*JJA* 19: 181–2).[49] In the fourth placards, Joyce added 'S. Patrick's Purgatory', 'the Salmon Leap' and 'Fingal's Cave' (*JJA* 19: 197). Finally, in the fifth page proofs, he added 'Rathdown Union Workhouse at Loughlinstown' and 'the Henry Street Warehouse' (*JJA* 25: 166). Clearly, Joyce began this section by focusing on sites that are evidently quite traditionally touristic. Some of these would fall into that narrow category that Aalen deems to be of the 'natural' landscape, such as the Lakes of Killarney, Glen Inagh and the Twelve Pins, and the Bog of Allen, while others have a clear human influence, but are still long-standing tourist sites: Glendalough, Clonmacnois, Cong Abbey and the rock of Cashel. By the second and fourth placards, we have sites that are fundamentally untouristic – Sir Patrick Dun's hospital, Tullamore jail and Jury's Hotel – as well as places that do not even 'exist' in a manner that can be depicted (the three birthplaces of the first duke of Wellington), do not exist in Ireland (Fingal's Cave) or do not exist at all (Kilballymacshonakill). From the beginning Joyce includes sites which seem to exist on the periphery between nature and human culture, such as Croagh Patrick, the Vale of Ovoca and the Bog of Allen; these are geological creations that have had significance bestowed on them through their closely entwined history with human settlement and culture. By including Fingal's Cave, located off Scotland, the list also shows that Ireland's cultural landscape does not end at its own frontier. Neither does it stop at the boundary of reality, as the facecloth includes places that only exist in theory, such as S. Patrick's Purgatory or Kilballymacshonakill. Joyce's drafting of this passage steadily moves the tour away from the physical landscape and into the cultural imagination. Although primarily a piece of comedic parody, the seemingly arbitrary nature of the facecloth's tour nevertheless manages to suggest that one cannot possibly understand Ireland if one only visits sites such as the Lakes of Killarney and the Rock of Cashel, but overlooks Rathdown Union Workhouse and Tullamore jail.

Although the facecloth's 'tour' incorporates many of the most famous sites in Ireland, it is hardly touristic, given the inclusion of some of its more unconventional locations. A more stereotypical version of Irish tourism is provided by Bloom in 'Eumaeus', appropriate given this episode's parody of clichéd writing styles. Bloom's tour of Ireland is designed specifically for the tired urbanite who requires a break from 'the grind of city life in the summertime for choice when dame Nature is at her spectacular best' (*U* 16.545–6). The capitalisation of 'Nature' makes evident that Bloom's tour will be a decidedly more conventional and romantic one than that provided by the facecloth earlier, as the style echoes that of a tourist's guidebook:

> There were equally excellent opportunities for vacationists in the home island, delightful sylvan spots for rejuvenation, offering a plethora of attractions as well as a bracing tonic for the system in and around Dublin and its picturesque environs even, Poulaphouca to which there was a steamtram, but also farther away from the madding crowd in Wicklow, rightly termed the garden of Ireland, an ideal neighbourhood for elderly wheelmen so long as it didn't come down, and in the wilds of Donegal where if report spoke true the *coup d'œil* was exceedingly grand though the lastnamed locality was not easily getatable so that the influx of visitors was not as yet all that it might be considering the signal benefits to be derived from it [. . .] Because of course uptodate tourist travelling was as yet merely in its infancy, so to speak, and the accommodation left much to be desired. (*U* 16.547–65)

This is a tour of Ireland curated by a Dubliner, for a Dubliner. Only those parts of Ireland that are within easy access of Dublin are discussed – the wilds of Donegal are lauded for their majestic views, though the fact that this area is 'not easily getatable' means that it is not given much further consideration – and emphasis is placed on the modern transportation, such as the 'streamtram' to Poulaphouca, that renders these areas attractive to the Dubliner. This is a vision of rural Ireland that sees its merits only in the potential it provides for spiritual and physical 'rejuvenation' for the tired city-dweller. This version of rural Ireland is also one that prioritises a very traditional view of the 'natural' landscape: Bloom admires the 'delightful sylvan spots', the 'picturesque environs', Wicklow's fame as the 'garden of Ireland'. Always one to spot an opportunity for commercial gain,

Bloom laments the fact that the tourism industry is not yet 'uptodate' and lacks the kind of accommodation required for the travelling Dubliner. Donegal's remote location and difficulty of access means that 'the influx of visitors was not as yet all that it might be' – though of course, Donegal's attractive wilderness would very quickly cease to be quite so wild if hordes of tourists began to arrive.

Ultimately Bloom's view of rural Ireland is that of a place to visit, not to actually inhabit – rural Ireland as theme park. This is in keeping with the style of a typical tourist guidebook, where places are valued for what they can give the tourist temporarily located there, rather than for how they function as places to inhabit. Roland Barthes highlights this in his essay 'The *Blue Guide*', a comment on the famous guidebooks of the same name. Barthes, for example, writes that the *Blue Guide* 'hardly knows the existence of scenery except under the guise of the picturesque', which 'is found any time the ground is uneven'.[50] Barthes sees this promotion of the rugged mountainous landscape as appealing to a sense of 'Helvetico-Protestant morality' and functioning 'as a hybrid compound of the cult of nature and of puritanism (regeneration through clean air, moral ideas at the sight of mountain-tops, summit-climbing as civic virtue, etc.)'.[51] Barthes notes that plains are rarely included for consideration, as '[o]nly mountains, gorges, defiles and torrents can have access to the pantheon of travel, inasmuch, probably, as they seem to encourage a morality of effort and solitude'.[52] This comment is in keeping with Bloom's selection of areas which are known for being mountainous or appealing in some sense to the sublime: Poulaphouca, Wicklow, Donegal, and also later Howth, which it is noted 'had its own toll of deaths by falling off the cliffs by design or accidentally' (*U* 16.561–2). Barthes continues to note that '[j]ust as hilliness is overstressed to such an extent as to eliminate all other types of scenery, the human life of a country disappears to the exclusive benefit of its monuments'.[53] Barthes describes this as a tendency in tourism and its guidebooks to 'suppress at one stroke the reality of the land and that of its people', leading to the guidebook becoming 'the very opposite of what it advertises, an agent of blindness'.[54] As a form of mythology, therefore, the guidebook 'reduc[es] geography to the description of an uninhabited world of monuments'.[55] Though it would be harsh to accuse Bloom of engaging in a deliberate erasure of the inhabitants of these rural settings, this is the inevitable result of the stylistic mimicking of the clichéd tourist guidebook. Even the facecloth of 'Cyclops' at least suggested some inhabitants – or perhaps more correctly 'inmates' – with its inclusion of the hospital, workhouse and jail.

The Bloom of 'Eumaeus' is driven to excessive cliché out of exhaustion, and so it is somewhat unfair to judge his view of the rural Irish landscape based just on this passage. He does, indeed, provide the reader with one more tour of Ireland in 'Ithaca' when prompted to outline the most 'attractive [. . .] localities' in Ireland (*U* 17.1969), for which he offers the following list:

> The cliffs of Moher, the windy wilds of Connemara, lough Neagh with submerged petrified city, the Giant's Causeway, Fort Camden and Fort Carlisle, the Golden Vale of Tipperary, the islands of Aran, the pastures of royal Meath, Brigid's elm in Kildare, the Queen's Island shipyard in Belfast, the Salmon Leap, the lakes of Killarney. (*U* 17.1974–8)

This is our last so-called tour of Ireland in *Ulysses*, and it is by far the most succinct and conventional. Three of the localities (Lough Neagh, the Salmon Leap and the Lakes of Killarney) are also mentioned on the facecloth, but in general this is a tour more grounded in reality than the cultural nationalist version or Bloom's nature-exploring Dubliner. Nevertheless, Bloom's list is noteworthy for being an all-Ireland account – unlike in 'Eumaeus', ease of access is not a determining consideration here – and for offering a view of Ireland that takes in both the 'natural' and the 'human'. The natural, geological beauty of the likes of the Cliffs of Moher and the Giant's Causeway is contrasted with modern sites such as the Queen's Island shipyard in Belfast, while the Golden Vale and the pasturelands of Meath are examples of subtle cultural landscapes. Even though this list is typical of the scientific reasoning of 'Ithaca', it also has some room for 'places' that exist only in the cultural imagination, such as the 'submerged petrified city' supposedly lying in Lough Neagh. Bloom's list is carefully curated to present Ireland at its most conventional and tourist-pleasing, but it remains a more complete tour than the one imagined in 'Eumaeus', if a slightly less immersive experience than that which the facecloth provides of modern Ireland. Ever the pragmatist, Bloom's list of localities is the one that Tourism Ireland is still most likely to lean upon today.

Joyce's Cultural Landscapes

In the Mullingar scenes of *Stephen Hero*, an iconoclastic Stephen Daedalus deliberately irks the nationalist Heffernan by declaring that '[m]y own mind [. . .] is more interesting to me than the entire country' (*SH* 216). Whatever the truth of such statements for the Daedalus of *Stephen Hero*, the entire country would appear to have gradually become of more interest for the mature Joyce who wrote *A Portrait* and *Ulysses* – and certainly also *Finnegans Wake*, the subject of the following chapter. With each work, the landscape of Ireland begins to merge with the landscape of the mind, suggesting that to understand the individual or national psyche, one must also understand the surrounding geography. Joyce portrays a cultural landscape in his works, where the geographical and the cultural must always be considered in tandem. To separate the natural from the human is to run the risk of fabrication, for there are few if any geographical entities that have not felt a human influence in Ireland's history. Aalen underlines this by describing the 'cultural landscape' as 'our major and most productive creation; it is both an artefact, based on foundations of geology and climate, and a narrative, layer upon layer of our history and nature's history intertwined'.[56] Instead of accepting the notion of Joyce as an uninterested urbanite, or a 'lazy Dubliner', we must be willing to peel back the narrative layers of his work by beginning 'in medias reeds', as the *Wake* has it, to understand how he actively engaged with the landscape beyond Dublin (*FW* 158.7).

Notes

1. For a synopsis of general trends in ecocriticism, see Lawrence Buell, 'The Emergence of Environmental Criticism', in *The Future of Environmental Criticism* (Oxford: Blackwell, 2005), 1–28; and Ursula K. Heise, 'The Hitchhiker's Guide to Ecocriticism', *PMLA* 121/2 (2006), 503–16.
2. Cheryll Glotfelty, 'Introduction: Literary Studies in an Age of Environmental Crisis', in Cheryll Glotfelty and Harold Fromm (eds), *The Ecocriticism Reader: Landmarks in Literary Ecology* (Athens, GA: University of Georgia Press, 1996), xviii.
3. Buell, *The Future of Environmental Criticism*, 21–2.
4. Malcolm Sen, 'Introduction: Culture, Climate, Capital, and Contagion', in Malcolm Sen (ed.), *A History of Irish Literature and the Environment* (Cambridge: Cambridge University Press, 2022), 1.
5. Hubert Zapf, 'Ecocriticism, Cultural Ecology, and Literary Studies', *Ecozon@* 1/1 (2010), 137.
6. Hubert Zapf, 'Cultural Ecology of Literature – Literature as Cultural Ecology', in Hubert Zapf (ed.), *Handbook of Ecocriticism and Cultural Ecology* (Berlin: De Gruyter, 2016), 138.

7. The *OED* defines 'geography' as '[t]he field of study concerned with the physical features of the earth and its atmosphere, and with human activity as it affects and is affected by these, including the distribution of populations and resources and political and economic activities' (*OED*, 'geography, n.', 2a).
8. For a thorough history of this term and its employment in geographical studies, see Michael Jones, 'The Concept of Cultural Landscape: Discourse and Narratives', in Hannes Palang and Gary Fry (eds), *Landscape Interfaces: Cultural Heritage in Changing Landscapes* (Dordrecht: Springer, 2003), 21–51.
9. Ibid., 21.
10. Carl Ortwin Sauer, 'The Morphology of Landscape', in Carl Ortwin Sauer and John Leighly (eds), *Life and Land: A Selection of the Writings of Carl Ortwin Sauer* (Berkeley, CA: University of California Press, 1967), 343.
11. Jones, 'The Concept of Cultural Landscape', 32.
12. Ibid., 32.
13. It should be noted that Sauer's definition of the cultural landscape has also come under criticism for creating a reified concept of culture that exists somehow externally to individual human beings, as well as its supporting of the dominance of a landscape tradition in cultural geographical studies. See Richard H. Schein, 'Cultural Traditions', in James S. Duncan, Nuala C. Johnson and Richard H. Schein (eds), *A Companion to Cultural Geography* (Oxford: Blackwell, 2004), 14–16.
14. Jones, 'The Concept of Cultural Landscape', 43.
15. Ibid., 43.
16. Ibid., 42.
17. For an analysis of the importance of Croagh Patrick in the *Wake*, see O'Callaghan, 'The Riddle of the Broken Spectre', 133–53.
18. Clive Hart, *Structure and Motif in 'Finnegans Wake'* (Evanston, IL: Northwestern University Press, 1962), 185–6.
19. In a 1913 letter to Geoffrey Molyneux Palmer, Joyce responded enthusiastically to Palmer having been to visit Cork: 'I am glad you like the South of Ireland. My father is a Munsterman and my people came from Fermoy. I know only Cork and Youghal – and like Youghal very much. I should be glad to have some cards of Mallow' (*L1* 74).
20. Thomas A. Welton, 'Notes on the Census of Ireland, 1911', *Journal of the Royal Statistical Society* 77/2 (1914), 205.
21. The latter scene also features in the unpublished pages from the Mullingar section of *Stephen Hero* (*JJA* 8: 27, 29).
22. Synge, *The Aran Islands*, 24, 86.
23. Foster, *Fictions of the Irish Literary Revival*, 96.
24. The tradition of having a 'king' was in fact relatively common on islands off Ireland until well into the twentieth century. Joyce references this again in *Finnegans Wake* when he refers to 'kings of the

arans and the dalkeys, kings of mud and tory' (*FW* 87.25–6). These places – the Aran Islands, Dalkey Island, Mud Island and Tory Island – continued to have kings by this point, except for Aran.

25. Derek Gladwin, 'Joyce the Travel Writer: Space, Place and the Environment in James Joyce's Nonfiction', in Robert Brazeau and Derek Gladwin (eds), *Eco-Joyce: The Environmental Imagination of James Joyce* (Cork: Cork University Press, 2014), 177.

26. Gladwin, 'Joyce the Travel Writer', 191.

27. There are many varying spellings of this tradition, such as 'dinnshenchas', 'dindsenchas' or 'dindshenchas'. I have chosen to use the official modern spelling as per Niall Ó Dónaill's *Foclóir Gaeilge-Béarla* (*Irish–English Dictionary*).

28. Gerry Smyth, *Space and the Irish Cultural Imagination* (London: Palgrave Macmillan, 2001), 47.

29. Caoimhín Mac Giolla Léith, 'Dinnseanchas and Modern Gaelic Poetry', in Gerald Dawe and John Wilson Foster (eds), *The Poet's Place: Ulster Literature and Society* (Belfast: Institute of Irish Studies, 1991), 158, cited in Smyth, *Space and the Irish Cultural Imagination*, 47.

30. Seán Ó Tuama, 'Stability and Ambivalence: Aspects of the Sense of Place and Religion in Irish Literature', in Joseph Lee (ed.), *Ireland: Towards a Sense of Place* (Cork: Cork University Press, 1985), 24, cited in Smyth, *Space and the Irish Cultural Imagination*, 48.

31. Thomas E. Connolly, *The Personal Library of James Joyce: A Descriptive Bibliography*, 2nd edn (1955; Buffalo NY: University of Buffalo, 1957), 21.

32. Maria Tymoczko, *The Irish 'Ulysses'* (Berkeley, CA: University of California Press, 1994), 291. An extended exploration of Joyce's employment of *dinnseanchas* in *Ulysses* can be found in Tymoczko, *The Irish 'Ulysses'*, 153–9, as well as Frawley, *Irish Pastoral*, 106–21.

33. Tim Robinson, *Setting Foot on the Shores of Connemara and Other Writings* (Dublin: Lilliput, 1996), 155, cited in Smyth, *Space and the Irish Cultural Imagination*, 41.

34. Smyth, *Space and the Irish Cultural Imagination*, 48.

35. Jon Hegglund, *World Views: Metageographies of Modernist Fiction* (Oxford: Oxford University Press, 2012), 22.

36. Ibid., 22.

37. Ibid., 22.

38. Ibid., 22.

39. Tobias Boes, *Formative Fictions: Nationalism, Cosmopolitanism, and the 'Bildungsroman'* (Ithaca, NY: Cornell University Press, 2012), 136.

40. O'Callaghan, 'Solastalgic Modernism', 160.

41. Slote et al., *Annotations*, 557–9.

42. James Clarence Mangan, 'Prince Aldfrid's Itinerary through Ireland', in *Selected Poems of James Clarence Mangan*, ed. Jacques Chuto, Rudolf

Patrick Holzapfel, Peter van de Kamp and Ellen Shannon-Mangan (Dublin: Irish Academic Press, 2003), 218–21.

43. Eblana was an ancient Irish settlement that appears in Ptolemy's *Geographia*, traditionally thought to be the same site as present-day Dublin. 'Cruachan's land' is another direct quote from Mangan's poem. Cruachan was the capital of the prehistoric rulers of Connacht, identified as present-day Rathcroghan in County Roscommon, and can be considered the western equivalent of the Hill of Tara. See the entries for 'Eblana' and 'Cruachain' in James MacKillop, *A Dictionary of Celtic Mythology* (Oxford: Oxford University Press, 1998), 148, 101.

44. John Brannigan, *Archipelagic Modernism: Literature in the Irish and British Isles, 1890–1970* (Edinburgh: Edinburgh University Press, 2015), 74.

45. Ibid., 74.

46. The evangelists appear in biblical order here as Matthew, Mark, Luke and John, the same order that they appear in throughout the *Wake*. They are identifiable by their symbols: Matthew (winged man with pen or book) holding a sceptre; Mark (winged lion) represented by a puma; Luke (winged ox) by a Kerry calf; and John (eagle) by a golden eagle (Slote et al., *Annotations*, 639).

47. Aalen, 'The Irish Rural Landscape', 5.

48. Ibid., 5.

49. Slote et al. explain this by noting how the exact place of the Duke of Wellington's birth was a matter of debate in Dublin (*Annotations*, 643).

50. Roland Barthes, 'The *Blue Guide*', in *Mythologies*, trans. Annette Lavers (New York: Farrar, Straus and Giroux, 1972), 74.

51. Ibid., 74.

52. Ibid., 74.

53. Ibid., 75.

54. Ibid., 76.

55. Ibid., 76.

56. Aalen, 'The Irish Rural Landscape', 5.

Chapter 6

The 'Geoglyphy' of *Finnegans Wake*: Provincial Division and Unity atop the Hill of Uisneach

Louis O. Mink writes that Joyce's last work 'has its own geography, and a very queer geography it is too, since it violates the geographical postulate of identification by fixed coordinates'.[1] Mink notes that while *Ulysses* is 'precisely mapped by exactly the same maps which represent the "real" Dublin', by contrast '[n]o one can tour the world of *Finnegans Wake* except in imagination'.[2] Critics have, however, attempted to map out the world of the *Wake* on real-world maps. John Bishop most notably sketches out a phenomenally detailed map of Dublin, with HCE's prostrate body stretching 'from the Hill of Howth [. . .] westward to Castle Knock'.[3] In Bishop's 'Relief Map B', HCE's head corresponds to Howth Head, while one must go 'well to the west in quest of his tumptytumtoes', which Bishop interprets as the western edge of Phoenix Park (*FW* 3.21).[4] Bishop's map therefore conspicuously stops at the edge of Dublin city, thus denying any Wakean representation of the rest of the country. Katherine O'Callaghan has offered another interpretation, hearing instead an echo of the 'journey westward' at the end of 'The Dead' in Joyce's sending the reader 'well to the west', thus establishing the west of Ireland as part of the *Wake*'s geography.[5]

While Bishop's map is no doubt ingenious, Mink's warning remains a fair one: to speak of a Wakean geography that corresponds with any degree of fidelity to that found on maps is to ignore much of the time-space bending that Joyce deliberately inflicts on his account of the world. To add to this tradition of 'mapping' the *Wake*, I wish to suggest that, rather than geography's more banal 'earth description', what Joyce provides us with is closer to what he calls in the *Wake* a

'Geoglyphy' (*FW* 595.7). A geoglyph, literally an 'earth-carving', is a 'large-scale image or design produced in the natural landscape by techniques such as aligning rocks or gravel or removing soil or sod, the complete form of which is visible only aerially or at a distance' (*OED*, 'geoglyph, n.', 2). Prominent examples include the Nazca Lines in Peru and the Cerne Abbas Giant in Dorset, with the land-scape itself appearing alive. Where the mapmaker looks down from above and attempts a fixed definition of the land, Joyce instead carves out a seemingly living landscape throughout the *Wake*. Here I will examine how Joyce does this through the provincial personalities of the Four Old Men and the 'landshape' that Shaun/Yawn forms atop the Hill of Uisneach, ancient centre of Ireland, surrounded by the provinces (*FW* 474.2–3).

The 'untired world of Leimuncononnulstria': The Provinces of Ireland in the *Wake*

As discussed in the previous chapter, the 'Cyclops' episode of *Ulysses* features a fantastical facecloth that links the four evange-lists with the four masters, writers of the *Annals of the Four Mas-ters* (1632–36), an exhaustive chronicle of medieval Irish history. '[T]hose four fellows', as Joyce referred to them in a 1923 letter, go on to have a central role in the *Wake*'s narrative (*L1* 203). While their first names immediately echo the evangelists – Matt Gregory, Mark Lyons, Luke Tarpey and Johnny MacDougall – they also rep-resent any number of other quartets. According to Adaline Glasheen, in addition to the evangelists, they at various points represent the four masters, the four provinces of Ireland, the four compass points, the four winds, the four dimensions, the four elements, Paracelsus' four parts of the human body, the four classical ages, the four ages of man, 'and doubtless many another four'.[6] Nevertheless, Anne L. Cavender states that '[c]onsistently throughout the *Wake*, the Four are associated with space, with a desire for order and fixity'.[7] It is this spatial component of the Four that I am going to focus on here, though the question of fixity is a more complicated one, as I will show. Specifically, I will focus on their representation of the four provinces of Ireland, peppered as it is – often unexpectedly and not always evidently – throughout the *Wake*. Most often this is signalled through an echo or pun on the names of the provinces – Ulster, Munster, Leinster and Connacht, usually in that order, to align with the four 'characters' – such as 'used her, mused her, licksed her and cuddled' (*FW* 96.16–17) or through referencing counties, towns or even personalities from each province: 'our quadrupede island, bless madhugh, mardyk, luusk and cong!' (*FW* 325.31–2). Here the references are to Hugh O'Neill, the Earl of Tyrone (Ulster); the Mardyke in Cork (Munster); Lusk in Dublin (Leinster); and Cong in Mayo (Connacht).[8] By emphasising the Four's symbolisation of the provinces, Joyce continually takes his reader on a tour of the 'untired world of Leimuncononnulstria' – the entire world being, as ever in the *Wake*, Ireland (*FW* 229.17–18).

In their primary roles as annalists, the Four are mostly associated with history, but, as we shall see, their concomitant allegorisation of the provinces means that they are also geographers in the *Wake*. This geographical aspect of the Four is clear when they examine Yawn in III.3, as a 'map of the souls' groupography rose in relief within their quarterings' (*FW* 476.33–4). Another early reference to the Four – 'all that farfath'd and peragrine or dingnant or clere' – specifically alludes to the Anglicised names of the annalists: Fearfeasa O'Mulconry, Peregrine O'Clery, Peregrine O'Duignan and Michael O'Clery. This is followed by a lush description of an idyllic rural Irish landscape: 'how paisibly eirenical, all dimmering dunes and gloamering glades, selfstretches afore us our fredeland's plain!' (*FW* 14.28–31). This is a peaceful Irish landscape (paisibly [*paix, paysage*] eirenical [*Éire*, irenical]) that glosses over the past one thousand years of war as 'the Formoreans have brittled the tooath of the Danes and the Oxman has been pestered by the Firebugs' (*FW* 15.5–7). Joyce's description of events spans 'a chiliad' (*FW* 15.4–5), a term for a group of one thousand that also evidently echoes Homer's bellicose *Iliad* (*OED*, 'chiliad, n.', 1a). He follows this with references to the waves of invasions of the island of Ireland: the mythical Formorians, Tuatha Dé Danaan ('tooath of the Danes') and Firbolgs, as well as the much more demonstrably real Vikings, founders of Oxmantown in Dublin.[9]

The Four as provinces, and the landscape they convey, manage at one and the same time to insist upon the island of Ireland as a complete, totalised whole, but also one that is in a perennial state of division. The peaceful pastoral image portrayed above is undercut at every point by Joyce reminding the reader that these 'four fellows' have spent most of history at each other's throats: 'these paxsealing buttonholes have quadrilled across the centuries and whiff now whafft to us, fresh and made-of-all-smiles as on the eve of Killallwho' (*FW* 15.9–11). Despite the desire to convey an image of Ireland's provinces as being 'paxsealing' and 'made-of-all-smiles', this is juxtaposed against one of the most infamous periods of Irish men fighting Irish men, with the obvious violence of 'Killallwho' also being a reference to Killaloe, the birthplace of Brian Boru, High King of Ireland, who led his troops to victory at the Battle of Clontarf in 1014, only to be slain after the battle itself. While the above section was first drafted in 1926, the recent history of the Irish Civil War (1922–23) and the partition of the island continued to colour Joyce's thinking about the extent to which the country could ever have truly been considered 'united'. John Nash writes that Joyce's first *Finnegans Wake* notebook (VI.B.10) from 1922 is 'often more concerned with recent Irish events rather than with a "universal history"', and, quoting Vincent Deane, he notes that 'the founding of the Free State and the consequent Civil War "form a constant background to Joyce's notes in this period"'.[10] In a similar fashion, Emer Nolan views 'the fact of partition' being 'treated in tones of apparent regret and lament throughout *Finnegans Wake*'.[11] Nolan interprets the Four as signalling 'a drive towards integration and unification',[12] an interpretation that Nash rejects, instead viewing the Four's 'squabbling incohesion' as illustrating 'an Irish readership that is always inevitably split'.[13]

There is, however, an argument to be made for viewing the Four as encompassing both the fact of partition/division but also the potential for a political and spiritual unity to match geographical unity. To fully understand the Four and their significance in the *Wake* we must first acknowledge that the Four are never just four, but five. Matt, Mark, Luke and Johnny are always followed by a donkey, whose presence is usually alluded to with a bray: 'Hear the four of them! Hark torroar of them! I, says Armagh, and a'm proud o'it. I, says Clonakilty, God help us! I, says Deansgrange, and say nothing. I, says Barna, and whatabout it? *Hee haw!*' (FW 57.7–10, my emphasis). The donkey is normally paired with Johnny MacDougall, probably because he represents Connacht, the poorest and most rural province. Ancient Ireland was traditionally composed of five provinces rather than four – in fact, the word for province in Irish is *cúige*, coming from *cúig* for 'five' – with the royal province of Meath being the central province where the High King sat and where the leaders of the other provinces converged. The donkey, then, comes to stand for the ancient fifth province of Ireland, but also for the notion of a missing 'fifth' in post-partition Ireland, something that is alluded to early in the *Wake* when Joyce refers to 'the five pussyfours green of the united states of Scotia Picta' (FW 43.29–30). The Romans referred to Ireland as *Scotia* (*Scoti* being the Latin term used for Gaels) while 'Picta' is a reference to the Picts of Scotland. As unionists in the north of Ireland were generally of Scottish extraction, coming to Ireland during the Ulster Plantation of the early seventeenth century, 'the united states of Scotia Picta' might be interpreted as the union of Gaels with those whose ancestry goes back to Scotland. Therefore, while the fifth element of 'the Four' would appear to disrupt the neat square they form and therefore suggest division, it also speaks to a potential for unity in a partitioned Ireland. It is for this reason that Joyce did not represent 'the Four' with a square but rather a quincunx (*L1* 213).[14]

Joyce's interest in the idea of a missing fraction of a whole is not something new to the *Wake* and is present in some of his earliest writing. The most famous example is the reference to the 'gnomon' on the first page of 'The Sisters', the opening story of *Dubliners* (*D* 3). Scarlett Baron notes the word's 'connotative density' but writes that '[t]he meaning foregrounded by the text' – that is, 'The Sisters' – is that 'of the Euclidian gnomon as "the part of a parallelogram which remains after a similar parallelogram is taken away from one of its corners"'.[15] Baron therefore writes that as '[a]n image of both partial presence and partial absence [. . .] the geometrical gnomon stands for incompleteness and lack'.[16] Though *Dubliners* was published almost a decade before partition became a political reality, the north-east of Ireland had long been culturally set apart from the rest of the country. Ireland had for many years therefore existed as a sort of gnomon; the establishment of Northern Ireland simply sought to make a permanent political fact of it. The Four, followed around by the 'missing' fifth in the donkey, exist as another Joycean gnomonic structure, a structure which seems to underpin so much of past and present political realities in Ireland for the writer. There seems little doubt that Joyce took a negative view of partition, writing elsewhere in the *Wake* of the country being 'bowed and sould [. . .] for a price partitional of twenty six and six' (*FW* 264.20–3).[17] While Joyce seems determined to acknowledge the political reality of partition – the latest iteration in a long line of division on the island – he nevertheless highlights the paradox of trying to chop up the geographical reality into two statelets. There remains, despite everything, the potential that Ireland might, like the Four forming a quincuncial unity with the donkey, eventually live out the reality of its geographical unity and, in Baron's words, 'box' itself again.[18] Joyce's view of Ireland is thus at one and the same time embedded in contemporary reality while also gesturing towards the nationalist notion of unity: 'partitioned Irskaholm, united Irishmen' (*FW* 132.33–4).[19]

One of the most explicit instances of the provinces being compared, contrasted and ultimately cobbled together in an effort at
unity comes during the radio quiz of I.6. The quiz features twelve
questions, the fourth of which asks what should be some relatively
simple questions regarding Ireland's 'capitol city (a dea o dea!) of two
syllables and six letters, with a deltic origin and a nuinous end' (*FW*
140.8–9). The 'deltic origin' (the letter 'D') and the 'nuinous end'
(*nuin* being the letter 'N' in the Ogham alphabet) evidently point to
Dublin.[20] The answerers are then asked to 'harmonise' the responses
(*FW* 140.14). However, an otherwise simple question is rendered
complex by the intrusion of the Four into the proceedings, as each
makes the case for his own province to contain the capital city of
Ireland. The Four engage in a kind of flirtation whereby they present
themselves as potential suitors to a young woman – perhaps a female
personification of Ireland, a familiar trope in Irish literature – while
the descriptions they offer tell us much about how the provinces are
portrayed in the *Wake*.

Matt Gregory presents 'Delfas' (i.e. Belfast) as his favoured capital city of Ireland (giving it a 'deltic origin' though not a 'nuinous
end'). The description of 'Delfas' abounds with references to Ulster,
from the industrial sounds of its shipyards ('gould hommers [. . .]
bingbanging' and the 'tenderbolts of my rivets' [*FW* 140.15–17]) to
the province's involvement with the linen/flax industry ('my floxy
loss' [*FW* 140.16]). This section is also notable for its emphasis on a
harsh-sounding Northern accent ('ye'll be sheverin wi' all yer dinful
sobs' [*FW* 140.18]).[21] References to 'yer orange garland' (*FW* 140.19)
call to mind unionist Orangemen and the orange sashes they wear
when marching, while the 'greaseways' appears to be a reference to
the Giant's Causeway (*FW* 140.20). However, these references aside,
what is most striking about this passage is the quite sinister tone in
which Matt makes his case as a potential suitor. Matt might try to
describe his love in emphatic terms, but the result is threatening rather
than romantic, his heart 'bingbanging again the ribs of yer resistance
and the tenderbolts of my rivets working to your destraction' (*FW*
140.16–18). The 'destraction' here is as much a 'destruction' of the
potential lover as it is a 'distraction', leading to her 'sheverin wi'' all
yer dinful sobs'. The two eventually go riding along the 'greaseways
of rollicking into the waters of wetted life' (*FW* 140.20–1) – more an
image of a couple sliding off the Giant's Causeway and falling head-
first into the sea, as opposed to head over heels in love.

In contrast, Mark Lyons of Munster presents his suitability as lover
in more dulcet tones, with 'Dorhqk' (i.e. Cork) portrayed here through

mellifluous musicality, echoing the 'chimes' of the Shandon bells (*FW* 140.21–2). 'The Bells of Shandon' is a poem by Francis Sylvester Mahony about the chiming bells of St Ann's Church in Cork, whose rhythm is echoed just prior to this in answer to Question 2, as noted by Joseph Campbell.[22] Joyce presents the musicality of this speech in wholly positive terms – it is 'descanting' (*FW* 140.24), for example, a verb meaning 'to sing harmoniously' (*OED*, 'descant, v.', 1a) – noting the 'plovery soft accents' (*FW* 140.23–4) of the people of Cork and their so-called gift of the gab, a gift apparently bestowed by kissing the Blarney stone, leading to a 'soapstone of silvry speech' (*FW* 140.27). Mark appears more confident in his wooing abilities than Matt, promising to take his potential lover 'on the Mash' (*FW* 140.22), which McHugh notes is an expression meaning to be 'in constant pursuit of women' but also a reference to the Marsh district in Cork.[23]

Luke Tarpey of Leinster follows with what should be the simplest answer to the question, yet he manages to somehow make Dublin appear the wrong answer by instead proffering 'Nublid' as the capital of Ireland (*FW* 140.27). Luke, as Dubliner, offers a tale of potential economic comfort to his beloved, though it is notably not going to be brought about by any work he carries out himself. Instead, Luke envisages their fortune coming from 'the mills'money he'll soon be leaving you' – 'he' probably being the girl's own father (*FW* 140.28–9). Luke offers an idealised image of upper-middle-class Dublin life, with ownership of a Georgian mansion, far from his previous regrettable arrears ('errears' [*FW* 140.32]) and drunken errors ('erroriboose' [*FW* 140.33], a combination of the Latin *erroribus* and 'booze') around his city's 'combarative embottled history', a history of battles and bottles of alcohol (*FW* 140.33).[24] Luke's idyllic future involves his belle 'churning over the newleaved butter' (*FW* 140.34) all day long while he sleeps in the garden – again, like Ulster's Matt, this does not appear quite so appealing to the other half involved. Curiously, perhaps, the Dublin accent presented here is replete with phrases from Irish: 'Isha' from *muise*, an exclamatory phrase meaning 'indeed!', and 'avourneen' from *a Mhuirnín*, meaning 'my darling' (*FW* 140.27, 140.28; *FGB*, 'muise', 'muirnín'). One could speculate as to whether this character is a relatively recent Dubliner, perhaps having moved from rural Ireland, while his dream future of a wife churning butter might in fact link him with Cork, the butter capital of Ireland, and therefore with Joyce's father. Whatever the story of his origins, Luke cannot offer his lover financial comfort at present, but instead can only offer her the dream of someday making it big in the metropolis.

Fourthly, to Connacht, and Johnny MacDougall, who makes his 'argument' as follows:

> Dalway. I hooked my thoroughgoing trotty the first down Spanish Place, Mayo I make, Tuam I take, Sligo's sleek but Galway's grace. Holy eel and Sainted Salmon, chucking chub and dace, Rodiron's not *your* aequal! says she, leppin half the lane. (*FW* 140.36–141.4)

Replete with references to fishing (trout, eel, salmon, chub and dace), the counties of Connacht, and the cosmopolitan history of Galway ('Spanish place'), Johnny's account of himself is noticeably the most relaxed and confident.[25] He presents himself as having already 'hooked' his lover, just as easily as catching a fish, and having brought her for an easygoing stroll through Galway. This already won-over lover sees him as even greater in stature than Roderick O'Connor ('Rodiron'), the last king of Ireland, also from Connacht – evidently this also has phallic connotations implied by the iron rod used to 'hook' her. Where the others make promises of what *will* happen if they are chosen as a lover, Johnny points to his Casanova past as proof of his romantic attributes.

Finally, as the question demanded, the answers offered by the Four are harmonised as follows:

> A bell a bell on Shalldoll Steepbell, ond be'll go massplon pristmoss speople, Shand praise gon ness our fayst moan *neople*, our prame *Shandeepen*, pay name muy *feepence*, moy nay non *Aequalllllll!* (*FW* 141.4–7)

This harmonisation of the responses chimes with the Shandon bells, with McHugh noting that the eight 'l's in '*Aequalllllll*' match the eight bells in the bell tower at Shandon.[26] Despite the apparent harmonisation or (a)equalisation of the provinces, this emphasis on Shandon would appear to suggest a preference for Cork, and Munster, over the others. Perhaps given the musicality of the Cork accent, it makes sense that it would dominate a 'harmonised' response. Indeed, Joyce credited his 'good tenor voice' as having come to him from his Cork father (*L1* 312) and remarked that the Irish tenor John Sullivan was, like his father, both 'a Cork man and a tenor', drawing a seeming association between the two (*L1* 313). Bloom in 'Sirens' also attributes Simon Dedalus's fine voice to the 'Cork air softer also their brogue' (*U* 11.695).

The answers outlined here seem to clearly delineate a degree of judgement towards the provinces, from the harsh, somewhat threatening Ulster and the drunken chancery of Leinster, to the confident, womanising Connacht and the melodious Munster. The provinces might try to make an '[a]*equalllllllll*' claim to being the rightful capital of the country, but by bitterly contesting this prize, they lose all claims to being truly united. This quiz question, and the answers that follow, demonstrate how division and partition are hardwired into the Irish provincial structure, making unity nigh-on impossible. Such discord would be impossible to make harmony of, and so one must win out in the end. When it comes to attempting a harmonisation of the provinces on '[a]*equalllllllll*' terms, Joyce does not seem to have been able to shake off the memory of the 'silvry speech' of his 'corked father' (*FW* 155.1).

'The knoll Asnoch': The *Wake* on the Hill of Uisneach

How, then, to render united what appears to all purposes to be so divided? Is partition the inevitable state of being for an island that is at constant war with itself? Can the four bickering and senile old men ever truly come together in harmony? In III.3, Joyce takes the reader to the very centre of Ireland, the ancient *omphalos* of the Hill of Uisneach, in an effort to see at last if political and personal unity can mirror geographical unity. This journey to Uisneach is also in many ways a journey back to ancient Ireland itself and to the pentarchic structure of power on the island. Lying '[o]n the mead of a hillock' is 'pure' – in his own narrow racial sense, but also *poor* – Yawn (erstwhile Shaun), exhausted from his sermonising to the girls of St Bride's in the previous chapter (*FW* 474.1–2). Laying claim to the centre point of Ireland, Yawn quite literally inflates himself to cover as much of the country as he can: 'length by breadth nonplussing his thickness, ells upon ells of him, making so many square yards of him' (*FW* 475.4–6). Yawn stakes a claim for himself as representative of Ireland, the High King to whom the lesser regional kings must descend, as the Four, donkey in tow, converge upon him from their provincial homes (*FW* 476.5–6). However, Yawn's topographical throne cannot save him from the interrogation that follows from the Four, acting as senators. Before long, the Four inevitably turn on each other, and whatever semblance of unity that briefly existed breaks down. The beginning of III.3, set in the heart of rural Ireland, sets in motion a Viconian take on history that develops towards the citybuilder HCE boasting of his urban creations; but in this pastoral beginning lie the origins of so much of modern-day division. Part III, Chapter 3 condenses many of the ideas about Ireland's unity or lack thereof that run through the *Wake*. From its central vantage point, on 'the knoll Asnoch' (*FW* 476.5–6), III.3 demonstrates how the story of Ireland's history is ineluctably the story of Ireland's geography.

The Hill of Uisneach is located in present-day County West-meath (formerly part of the ancient fifth province of Meath, or *Mide*, meaning 'middle'), rising to a height of 180 metres above sea-level, and offering a panoramic view of hills and mountains in twenty other modern Irish counties.[27] As such, Uisneach pro-vides a sweeping view of nearly two-thirds of the Irish counties to the north, south, east and west, making it a logical centre point for the country. Uisneach holds an important place in early Irish literature, being identified as 'the umbilical centre of Ireland, the meeting place of the ancient provinces', and is in particular associ-ated with the pagan festival of *Bealtaine*, held on May Day.[28] Atop Uisneach stands the 'massive, conglomerate boundary stone [. . .] called *umbilicus Hiberniae* by Giraldus Cambrensis [. . .] and *Ail na Mireann* [*sic*] ('the Stone of Divisions') by Geoffrey Keating', author of *Foras Feasa ar Éirinn* (1634), a history of Ireland on the grandest of scales.[29] This stone is today most commonly known as the 'Catstone' and is, in Roseanne Schot's words, 'the most evoca-tive symbol of the *axis mundi*: an *omphalos* ("navel") comparable to Apollo's seat at Delphi'.[30] *Ail na Míreann*, referenced elsewhere in the *Wake* as the 'Mearingstone' (*FW* 293.14), emphasises the division of Ireland into five provinces (*mír* being the Irish for a 'segment' or 'portion'). The nearest sizeable town is Mullingar, and it is possible that Joyce might in fact have visited Uisneach dur-ing his summers there with his father.[31] Where Stephen in *Ulysses* searches for an *omphalos* and is offered the Martello tower by Buck Mulligan, here is a true *omphalos*, 'fixed by the Ice Age', as John Garvin notes, as though bestowed by a grander cosmological and ecological design.[32]

Joyce's knowledge of Uisneach does appear to go beyond what snippets he might have gleaned from a passing reference in a book – Alison Lacivita cites Stephen Gwynn's *The History of Ireland* (1923) as the source for some of Joyce's direct references to Uisneach, to which I will return later – making it quite likely that he had a deeper familiarity with the site.[33] Garvin speculates that Joyce acquired his ash-plant at Uisneach, which may be the 'staff of citron briar' that Yawn holds as he lies on the hill (*FW* 474.3–4).[34] If so, this was not an innocent act, for Uisneach was supposed to have been the site of a 'sacred ash tree, associated with the inauguration of kings',[35] known variously as *Bile Uisnig*[36] and *Craeb Uisnig.*[37] Joyce's namesake P. W. Joyce writes in the first volume of *The Origin and History of Irish Names of Places* (1869) that trees that were designated *bile* were 'regarded with intense reverence and affection; one of the greatest triumphs that a tribe could achieve over their enemies, was to cut down their inauguration tree'.[38] By snapping off a branch of an ash tree, Joyce would have been crowning himself to a degree and drawing a direct line between himself and ancient Irish royalty.

Of course, all this is mere conjecture, but more significant is how Joyce goes on to work this sacred ash tree into III.3. The motif of the tree and the stone is one of the more recurrent ones in the *Wake*; as quasi-religious images, they stand for all that is growing and mutable (the tree) and all that is eternal and unchanging (the stone) in the universe: 'A shrub of libertine, indeed! But that steyne of law indead what stiles its neming' (*FW* 505.21–2).[39] Uisneach as a site provided Joyce with ancient examples of both the free, libertine 'shrub' and the dead stone of law: the sacred *Bile/Craeb Uisnig* and *Ail na Míreann*. In III.3 Joyce dwells most on the ash tree, and from pages 503–6 offers the reader an extended description of an 'overlisting eshtree' that 'used to be [. . .] stuck up' at the site (*FW* 503.30). Over these few pages, Joyce does for trees what he does for rivers in I.8, peppering arboreal vocabulary throughout the narrative. Martin Brick writes that while the sacred tree might initially seem to point towards the Tree of Knowledge in the Garden of Eden, Joyce litters these pages with references to trees from Norse mythology, Celtic paganism and Ovid's *Metamorphoses*.[40] Brick, while acknowledging the possible Druidic connections to the maypole and the May Day festival of *Bealtaine*, does not make the connection with the location of Uisneach. I would argue that the sacred tree described by Joyce is at its most fundamental level that 'grawndest crowndest consecrated maypole' that stood at Uisneach, and under which Irish kings were crowned, which then becomes representative of all sacred trees in world culture, from the Tree of Knowledge to Yggdrasil, or 'eggdrazzles' (*FW* 503.33–4, 504.35).[41] Joyce establishes a 'fraternitrees' of trees in this section, underlining humanity's deep association with, and indeed reliance upon, our sylvan spaces (*FW* 504.21). As humans first took shelter in wooded environments – and indeed Ireland is noted for having been almost entirely covered in forests when people first arrived on the island – it makes sense that trees should have a central place in this Viconian story: 'For we are fed of its forest, clad in its wood, burqued by its bark and our lecture is its leave' (*FW* 503.36–504.1).

Proinsias Mac Cana writes that 'one of the most fundamental constituents of Irish, and, indeed of Celtic ideology [is] the cult of the centre'.[42] This 'cult of the centre', Mac Cana argues, suggests an 'encompassed unity' and was recreated by Celtic peoples 'wherever they established themselves as a distinct community or nation with reasonably well-defined borders'.[43] On the island of Ireland, this central assembly was *Mordháil Uisnigh*, held at Uisneach on *Bealtaine*.[44] During *Bealtaine* a great inferno was ignited on the Hill of Uisneach, followed by fires on the other hills of Ireland.[45] Joyce makes reference to this tradition when one of the Four notes that '[t]here were fires on every bald hill in holy Ireland that night' (*FW* 501.22–3). According to legend, Túathal Techtmar founded the site at Uisneach about AD 150, though it is likely that it was a ritual meeting spot long before this.[46] Túathal is said to have annexed portions from the four provinces of Ireland to create his own province in the centre of the country, Meath.[47] Thus the concept of the 'pentarchy', an Ireland divided into five provinces of more or less equal power, was established. Eóin MacNeill writes that this pentarchic division of the country is 'the oldest certain fact in the political history of Ireland'.[48] By dividing out power in this way, Mac Cana notes that the pentarchy had 'the effect of highlighting the underlying conceptual unity of the country'.[49] Mac Cana even posits a wider cosmological significance to this political power structure:

> The pattern of a central province enclosed by four others representing the cardinal points cannot be explained otherwise than as a historical reflex of an ancient cosmographic schema, and one which has striking analogues in several of the 'great traditions' of the world.[50]

It is clear that Joyce knew about the pentarchic division of ancient Ireland from a letter he sent to his son Giorgio and his wife Helen in 1935, though in this letter he places emphasis on the nearby Hill of Tara, rather than Uisneach:

> Tara was the Mecca and Jerusalem of the ancient Irish. The island was a pentarchy = 5 kings. One for each of the four provinces, Ulster, Munster, Leinster, Connaught and the fifth, the high king (ard ri [*sic*]), was crowned at Tara. (*L3* 346n1)[51]

It appears that Joyce's source for his information on Uisneach, and perhaps on the pentarchic structure in general, was Gwynn's aforementioned *The History of Ireland*, which stresses the equal nature of the division of power in Ireland among these five kingdoms. It is from Gwynn's account that Joyce read of Túathal extending his power 'across the Shannon to the Hill of Usnach, the central point of Ireland, about ten miles west of Mullingar',[52] a point which Joyce specifically noted down: 'Usnach hill / centre of I –' and '10 miles W of Mullingar'.[53]

The neat division of Ireland into five equal parts would appear not to have lasted very long, as Gwynn notes when he writes of Túathal's grandson Conn Cétchathach, or Conn of the Hundred Battles:

> Conn's great opponent in Ireland was Mogh Nuadat, and tradition relates that after many battles they decided on a division of Ireland, following the Esker Riada or line of gravelly hillocks (still called eskirs) which runs across the central boggy plain from near Dublin to Maaree on the bight of Galway Bay. From that time onward the northern half of Ireland, marked off by this natural way, along which ran the Slighe Mor, chief road from east to west, was called Leath Cuinn (Conn's Half), and the southern Leath Mogha.[54]

Ireland is thus divided in two, a northern half and a southern half, with the border running along the geological formation of the Esker Riada – the landscape itself seeming to bestow a natural division of the country. Joyce works this into the *Wake* as the Four arrive '[u]p to the esker ridge' (*FW* 475.22), while Yawn is sprawled atop Uisneach with 'one half of him in Conn's half but the whole of him nevertheless in Owenmore's five quarters' (*FW* 475.6–7).[55] The contradictions here – how can one half of Yawn be in Conn's half and yet the whole of him in Owenmore's five quarters? how can one even have five quarters? – mirror the contradictions at the heart of Ireland's composition following partition, as the country was once again divided into five portions: Munster, Leinster, Connacht, the three counties of Ulster in the Free State, and the six counties of Ulster that make up Northern Ireland. It had also been once again divided North and South. These ancient divisions of the country seem to have returned to Ireland following independence, but where before they might have notionally emphasised centrality and unity, now there is only fragmentary partition.

Wyndham Lewis criticised Joyce for being overly concerned with time rather than space in *Time and Western Man* (1927), grouping him together with Proust and Bergson as part of a '*time-cult*'.[56] Lewis's haranguing of Joyce was notoriously class- and race-inflected, and Joyce rewarded his diatribe by making Shaun a parody of Lewis in the *Wake*. This is most explicit in the Shaunian figure of Professor Jones, described as being 'so eminent a spatialist' (*FW* 149.18–19). Shaun, like Lewis, stands for space over time, but it would be a mistake to dismiss the spatial element of the *Wake* as a result. When Frank Budgen raised Lewis's criticisms with him, Joyce replied: 'Allowing that the whole of what Lewis says about my book is true, is it more than ten per cent of the truth?'[57] Joyce evidently saw space as playing more of a role in his writings than Lewis credited, a point that Clive Hart notes when he argues that '[i]n so far as he consistently organises his creations according to almost visible spatial patterns, Joyce is surely one of the most spatially conscious of writers'.[58] Uisneach and its position as *omphalos* allows Joyce the perfect vantage spot from which to dissect the impact of space on the Irish cultural imagination.

The idea of placing Yawn on this ideal vantage spot is important also in the context of British imperialism and Irish nationalism. Gerry Smyth discusses the 'monarch-of-all-I-survey' moment that occurs in many imperialist narratives, wherein 'the European traveller encounters a particular landscape or edifice, usually from a height, which somehow encapsulates the identity of the non-European other whose territory is being traversed'.[59] Smyth writes that such 'monarch-of-all-I-survey' moments occur repeatedly in eighteenth- and nineteenth-century accounts of Ireland, as 'the complete English subject encounters the finished Irish landscape and interprets it from a position of privilege and power, symbolised by his promontory location'.[60] The landscape is 'finished', brought into being, only at the moment of its being surveyed by the coloniser; as Smyth writes, 'the landscape *exists* only by virtue of the traveller's presence'.[61]

Yawn attempts to perform a reverse imperialist moment atop the Hill of Uisneach, but rather than as before claiming the landscape for colonialism, Yawn attempts to reclaim it for Irish nationalism. Such a reclaiming, however, requires the same 'finalisation' of the landscape, in the Bakhtinian sense; the space is removed from the flux of time and a stabilising, fixed definition is imposed. Writing of Dostoevsky's poetics, Bakhtin outlines his theory of 'unfinalizability':

> *Nothing conclusive has yet taken place in the world, the ultimate word of the world and about the world has not yet been spoken, the world is open and free, everything is still in the future and will always be in the future [. . .]*[62]

For Bakhtin, '[e]verything completed, fixed, or defined is declared to be dogmatic and repressive'.[63] In *Finnegans Wake*, Joyce has the rural Irish landscape reject Yawn's attempts at finalisation – the provinces of Ireland literally get up and converge upon Uisneach and Yawn to interrogate this self-proclaimed monarch. This is an unfinalised living landscape, one that reacts against definition.

In addition to the idea of unfinalisability, Bakhtin's theory of the 'chronotope' is also worth considering when analysing Joyce's depiction of Uisneach. Inspired by Einsteinian physics, Bakhtin 'give[s] the name *chronotope* (literally, "time space") to the intrinsic connectedness of temporal and spatial relationships that are artistically expressed in literature'.[64] Bakhtin goes on to explain that

> [i]n the literary artistic chronotope, spatial and temporal indicators are fused into one carefully thought-out, concrete whole. Time, as it were, thickens, takes on flesh, becomes artistically visible; likewise, space becomes charged and responsive to the movements of time, plot and history.[65]

Morson and Emerson write that chronotopic literature encourages 'seeing in apparently static objects or institutions the "congealed" activity of the past and everything that still "pulsates" in the present'.[66] To see time in such a way involves seeing what Bakhtin calls 'heterochrony', the many different layers of time across natural, human and historical cycles, 'the interactions of a world rich in temporalities'.[67] Throughout *Finnegans Wake*, and most especially in III.3, Joyce performs a chronotopic and heterochronic portrayal of Ireland, with time – in all its multifarious layers – and space fusing together to offer a more complete and unfixed vision of Irish history and society.

Heterochronies are often discussed in conjunction with heterotopias, an important concept in Michel Foucault's writings on space. In 'Of Other Spaces', Foucault conceives of unreal spaces that he calls heterotopias, and which, he argues, 'are absolutely different from all the sites that they reflect and speak about'.[68] One of the examples of a heterotopia that Foucault gives is the Persian garden:

> The traditional garden of the Persians was a sacred space that was supposed to bring together inside its rectangle four parts representing the four parts of the world, with a space still more sacred than the others that were like an umbilicus, the navel of the world at its center (the basin and water fountain were there); and all the vegetation of

the garden was supposed to come together in this space, in this sort of microcosm [. . .] The garden is the smallest parcel of the world and then it is the totality of the world.[69]

Foucault's description of the heterotopic Persian garden has some clear similarities with Uisneach. Rees and Rees write that '[t]he pillar-stone at Uisneach was five-ridged, symbolizing the five provinces at the centre. Around it was marked out a measure of land consisting of the portion of each province in Uisneach.'[70] As such, at Uisneach, 'the world was symbolized by a series of microcosms, each set within the other'.[71] Joyce portrays Uisneach as surrounded on all sides by the four quarters of Ireland, becoming akin to a Foucauldian garden: a small plot of land and yet also the totality of the land. Also like a Foucauldian garden, that most choreographed representation of nature, Uisneach becomes an 'unreal' space where stable conceptions of space and time blur.[72] Heterotopias, for Foucault, are linked to 'heterochronies', as heterotopias function most explicitly when 'men arrive at a sort of absolute break with their traditional time'.[73]

Joyce's portrayal of Uisneach has the heterochronic effect of extracting the reader out of our traditional sense of time. As the Four 'hop[] it up the mountainy molehill', they also seem to go back in time, 'traversing climes of old times gone by of the days not worth remembering' (*FW* 474.22–3). This is underscored again as we follow the senators walking along the 'esker ridge', particularly Gregory, trailing 'through the deep timefield' (*FW* 475.22–4). Again, the insinuation is that by entering this sacred *omphalos*, we are also entering a space where time functions heterochronically. The structure of ancient Ireland appears to take over despite contemporary debates over partition dominating the dialogue between the provinces. This is demonstrated in the following relatively throwaway line from Johnny MacDougall: 'Follow me up Tucurlugh! That's the place for the claire oysters, Polldoody, County Conway' (*FW* 479.5–7). Johnny is talking about the famous oysters from Pouldoody Bay, near Turlough ('Tucurlugh') in the Burren, County Clare.[74] Even though Johnny acknowledges that these are 'claire oysters', he still puts 'Polldoody' in 'County Conway', a seeming mix of Connacht and Galway. While County Clare is located in present-day Munster (and so would normally be the domain of Mark Lyons), this was not always the case, as in antiquity Clare, lying west of the Shannon like the rest of Connacht, was considered part of that province, as Joyce would have read in Gwynn.[75] In this otherwise innocuous sentence, Johnny of Connacht lays claim to Clare once again, seemingly reinstating this ancient division of the country. This chapter of the *Wake*, though it might appear to have spatial certainty in being located at Uisneach, is marked by temporal rupture, as Ireland exists in multiple states of time at once. Uisneach, as spatial Other or heterotopia, effects a heterochronic rift in linear temporal progression. Perhaps in response to Lewis's claims about *Ulysses*, Joyce here shows time and space to be in a reciprocal and dynamic relationship with each other.

Further underlining the heterochronic nature of Ireland's 'neverstop navel' (*FW* 475.14), Yawn ventriloquises characters from Irish history that, as Garvin writes, 'come up out of the historic hill on which he lies' and 'purport to represent the racial memory of the Irish and their leaders and conquerors'.[76] One of those summoned figures is St Patrick, or 'Trinathan partnick', with an emphasis on his teaching on the Trinity (*FW* 478.26). Patrick via Yawn speaks a form of 'mal prononsable' French-German-Irish as he references the legend of his teaching the Irish people about the Trinity through the use of the shamrock: '*Moy jay trouvay la clee dang les champs*' (*FW* 478.19–21).[77] Patrick finds the key to converting this country of pagans by searching in the landscape itself – *moy* (Irish: *maigh* or *má*, meaning 'plain' [*FGB*, 'má']), *clee* (German: *klee*, meaning 'clover' or 'shamrock') and *dang les champs* (French: *dans les champs*, meaning 'in the fields'). The suggestion here is that to find an explanation for the mysteries of the world – and indeed the history of Ireland – one must look to the land itself. This centrality of the landscape in human thought is inscribed into the very language that Yawn speaks – it is a 'landeguage' (*FW* 478.9–10) – while Yawn himself forms a 'landshape' on the Hill of Uisneach, that 'mountainy molehill' (*FW* 474.2–3, 474.22). In this way, Yawn resembles his father in his association with the stagnant mountain, rather than his mother, the flowing river. The Four, meanwhile, are referred to as 'four claymen', linking them with the earth also (*FW* 475.18).

However, Yawn differs from his father in one important aspect, in that rather than being associated with the urban space, Yawn ties himself to rural Ireland. This does not mean that Yawn – and more generally Shaun – is from rural Ireland. A representative of the most conservative form of Irish revolutionary nationalism, Yawn is Joyce's take on the growing number of politicians who were hugely influenced by the cultural nationalism of the Revival and its valorisation of rural Ireland, even if, in Declan Kiberd's words, '[t]hey were to a man the urbanized descendants of country people'.[78] Yawn, therefore, might be more accurately seen as a product of an urban Ireland in search of so-called 'rural authenticity'. He sees himself as the rightful heir to this culture, as he places himself in a sylvan setting:

> spancelled down upon a blossomy bed, at one foule stretch, amongst
> the daffydowndillies, the flowers of narcosis fourfettering his footlights,
> a halohedge of wild spuds hovering over him, epicures waltzing with
> gardenfillers, puritan shoots advancing to Aran chiefs. (*FW* 475.8–12)

Complete with spancel ('[a] rope or fetter for hobbling cattle, horses,
etc.' [*OED*, 'spancel, n.'], and also possibly a reference to another hill
in rural Ireland, Spancill Hill in County Clare), Yawn lies on a bed of
flowers, namely daffodils, which, being of the genus *Narcissus*, also
add to Yawn's stupor by causing 'narcosis'. Later, the Four find him
'laying too amengst the poppies' (*FW* 476.19–20). Meanwhile, the
'halohedge of wild spuds hovering over him' suggests that Yawn sees
himself as saint of the potato-eating peasantry. Joyce then lists a variety of potatoes, which he noted from an advertisement in the regional
newspaper, the *Connacht Tribune*.[79] While Joyce was dependent for
his newspaper sources on what Nora's uncle Michael Healy sent to
him in Paris, the fact that he regularly trawled through the pages of
the *Connacht Tribune* is proof of how immersed he was in Irish culture beyond Dublin when drafting this section.[80] Yawn's halo of spuds
illustrates the *décalage* between his notion of himself as representative of rural Ireland and the reality of rural life, potatoes being the
most explicit symbol of the Famine's devastation. Yawn's halo also,
of course, resembles a crown, suggesting that he sees himself as an
authoritarian High King, one man ruling over the entire island. Such a
position problematises the idealised notion of the pentarchic structure
of ancient Ireland, the equal division of power among the provinces.
Little wonder then, lying on his molehill in a self-congratulatory stupor, that Yawn should soon find himself being descended upon by four
provincial potentates, ready to hold him to account.

The Four arrive at Uisneach from their respective provinces, coming 'from the westborders of the eastmidlands, three kings of three
suits and a crowner, from all their cardinal parts' (*FW* 474.18–19).
The first hint of division is provided by their comparison to a pack of
cards, as three of the provinces are sovereign kings, different only in
their suit ('three kings of three suits'), while the other is a 'crowner'.
This is most likely Ulster, the part of the country most loyal to the
British crown. Joyce describes them as 'senators four', acting as public representatives on their way to the national assembly (*FW* 474.21).
'Shanator Lyons' follows Gregory of Ulster, 'trailing the wavy line of
his partition footsteps', meaning that Gregory is clearly more representative of Northern Ireland than he is of the province of Ulster itself
(*FW* 475.24–5). 'Dr Shunadure Tarpey' of Leinster and 'old Shunny

MacShunny, MacDougal the hiker', representing impoverished Connacht, make up the Four (*FW* 475.27–30). Of course, given that four
is always five in the world of the *Wake*, trailing behind MacDougall
of Connacht is the ass, 'their skygrey globetrotter, by way of an after-
thought' (*FW* 475.31–2). The ass as 'globetrotter' may be a nod to the
far-flung diaspora of Ireland; however, the ass primarily represents
the ancient fifth province of Ireland, Meath, where the Four are now
headed, and this would appear to be hinted at in Joyce's transcription
of Uisneach as 'the knoll *A*snoch', the ass as central province being
contained within the name Joyce gives the hill itself (*FW* 476.5–6, my
emphasis). As usual, the ass accompanies MacDougall of Connacht,
with Johnny referred to as 'Jonny na Hossaleen' or 'Jonny-of-the-
little-donkey' (*FW* 476.27–8).[81] Connacht's and the west's history of
poverty and misery is again to the fore when reference is later made
to 'that O'mulanchonry plucher you have from the worst curst of
Ireland' (*FW* 482.12–13).[82] The melancholic cough ('plucher' comes
from the Irish *plúchadh*, meaning a suffocating, asthmatic cough
[*FGB*, 'plúchadh']) is linked to the impoverished conditions of those
most cursed inhabitants on the west coast of Ireland. Hunger and
sickness are again emphasised when reference is made to MacDougall
'chuam and coughan' (*FW* 482.9–10) – chewing and coughing in the
Connacht town of Tuam and, seemingly less consistently, in the Ulster
county of Cavan.[83] However, similarly to Clare, Cavan was previously considered part of Connacht, and so another temporal rupture
might be in play here.[84] As the province most affected by the devastation of the Famine, it is clear that Connacht's history leaves an indel-
ible mark on its senatorial representative.

Mink dismisses the idea that the provinces the Four represent
have any impact on their personalities as characters, writing that 'on
the whole the provinces remain places rather than persons', but as
the above example regarding Johnny of Connacht shows, the Four's
characteristics are evidently impacted by their provinces.[85] Nowhere
is this clearer than when relations between the Four break down.
Roy Benjamin writes of the rivalry that existed in Ireland prior to
Henry II's annexation of the country, and argues that the ability of
the central province of Meath to bring the other provinces 'into har-
monious alignment' failed at this time, making Ireland susceptible
as a result to outside forces.[86] The growing impotence of Meath is
reflected by Yawn's stupor in III.3 and his inability to keep the four
provinces in a state of peace.

This interprovincial acrimony is most apparent in the relationship between Matt Gregory of Ulster and the rest. Gregory becomes

most irate with Mark Lyons of Munster when the latter refers to
Gregory as a 'Robman Calvinic', mocking this particular Ulster
unionist's fear of Roman Catholics while also referencing what
is seen by the Munsterman as the illegal theft of Irish land both
through the Ulster Plantations and the more recent partition of
the country (*FW* 519.26). An incensed Gregory responds with the
tried-and-trusted offer to take things outside:

> – Will you repeat that to me outside, leinconnmuns?
> – After you've shouted a few? I will when it suits me, hulstler.
> – Guid! We make fight! Three to one! Raddy? (*FW* 521.28–31)

Gregory lumps together the other three provinces as 'leinconnmuns',
while they view him as a hustler. They gently mock Gregory's (and,
by extension, Ulster unionism's) apparent proclivity for getting easily
incensed by sardonically coaxing him: 'Gently, gently Northern Ire!
Love that red hand!' (*FW* 522.4).[87] The Ulster accent is portrayed as
piercing, through rendering 'good' as '[g]uid' and 'ready' as '[r]addy',
while Gregory in turn mocks the tendency in the south of Ireland to
pronounce the voiced dental fricative in English with a 'd' ([d]) sound
rather than 'th' (/ð/): 'Dis and dat and dese and dose' (*FW* 528.27).
Indeed, the spelling of 'good' as '[g]uid' might also be a pun on the
Irish verb *goid*, meaning 'to steal', and thereby another reference to
Gregory as a '*Robman* Calvinic'.[88] Gregory underlines his sense of
Ulster (specifically Northern Ireland) as standing apart from the rest
of Ireland: 'there's all the difference in Ireland between your bordera-
tion, my chatty cove, and me' (*FW* 528.30–1). He then dismisses the
financial state of the other three provinces and predicts worse times to
come, all the while mocking the Irish language: 'The leinstrel boy to
the wall is gone and there's moreen storeen for Monn and Conn' (*FW*
528.31–3). '[M]oreen storeen' might be translated as '(little) Mary my
little darling' (*Máirín a stóirín*). This innocent term of endearment,
though, becomes a threat (i.e. 'there's more in store') as employed by
Gregory.

Matt Gregory's surname has puzzled Wakeans, with Glasheen
writing 'I cannot explain the surname. It ought to include Lady Gregory [. . .] but I don't see how.'[89] Glasheen is correct in making a link
between Lady Gregory and Ulster's Matt Gregory, though I would
argue that the reference is instead to her husband, William Henry
Gregory. This Gregory became infamous in Ireland for the 'Gregory Clause' during the Great Famine, which prevented tenants from
availing themselves of relief if they occupied more than one quarter

of an acre.[90] This had disastrous consequences for the starving Irish tenantry, and Gregory, though not blatantly hostile towards Irish Catholics in general, became associated with some of the worst characterics of unionist Anglo-Irish landlords. Joyce's Matt Gregory is linked with him most particularly through his attitude to Irish tenants when he exclaims that the other three senators have 'as much skullabogue cheek on you now as would boil a caldron of kalebrose' (*FW* 528.36–529.1). Joyce once again took this expression from a letter in the *Connacht Tribune*, in which the writer complained of tenants claiming certain conditions when purchasing their place of residence, writing that they had '[a]s much cheek as would boil a whole pot of cabbage'.[91] Gregory's phrase contains a reference to Scullabogue, the location of a massacre of Irish Protestants during the 1798 Rebellion, further emphasising the division between different groups.[92]

If the journey of Joyce's Four to the umbilical centre of Ireland is supposed to represent an attempt at unity and harmony, such an effort appears futile following Gregory's outburst. However, rather than putting all the blame on Gregory and Ulster, what we are witnessing, Joyce suggests, is not the sudden partition of a once holistic community, but the continuation of centuries of division. Yawn, as symbol of conservative Irish nationalism, recrowning itself at Uisneach, is as impotent as the final potentates of Meath just prior to the Norman invasion.

Chapter III.3 of the *Wake* is perhaps best known for its final section, *Haveth Childers Everywhere*, which Joyce first published in *transition* 15 in February 1929. In this section, which Joyce referred to as 'the city piece', HCE boasts of the many cities he has built where once there were merely fields: 'I built in *Urbs in Rure*' (*L1* 285; *FW* 551.24). From prehistoric mound to HCE's multifarious metropolises, this is a Viconian journey from humanity's rural beginnings to their supposedly inevitable urban endings. Beckett delineates this Viconian structure in 'Dante . . . Bruno. Vico . . Joyce' as follows: '"Forest-cabin-village-city-academy" is one rough progression. Another: "mountain-plain-riverbank".'[93] But in the Viconian schema there is always the *ricorso*, an inevitable starting over again, and so the urbanite never truly leaves behind their rural roots:

> the cave becomes a city, and the feudal system a democracy: then an anarchy: this is corrected by a return to monarchy: the last stage is a tendency towards interdestruction: the nations are dispersed and the phoenix of Society arises out of their ashes.[94]

The grand new capital city of Ireland is in reality a 'Nova Tara' (*FW* 535.8), a new take on the ancient seat of the High Kings, its concrete pavements merely a *nova terra*. By beginning III.3 on the Hill of Uisneach, Joyce enacts a return to the primordial centre, in an attempt to stymie the 'tendency towards interdestruction' that dominates Irish history. Ultimately, it appears to be yet another centre that cannot hold, and the divisions that define Ireland break through once again. In carving out the giant figure of Yawn atop the Hill of Uisneach, Joyce provides the reader with a geoglyph to decipher; but this is a landscape with an agency of its own, one which consistently reacts against attempts to define it. In a 1885 speech in Cork, Charles Stewart Parnell warned William Gladstone that 'no man has the right to fix the boundary to the march of a nation' – in the *Wake* this appears as 'no mouth has the might to set a mearbound to the march of a landsmaul' (*FW* 292.26–7). Here, 'mear' once again echoes *Ail na Míreann*, the stone of divisions on Uisneach, while 'landsmaul' is a reference to *Landsmål* or 'New Norse', which McHugh notes is based on rural dialects, literally 'land's language', and which Joyce echoes in his 'landeguage' (*FW* 478.9–10).[95] As the protean, living landscape speaks to us throughout the *Wake*, it makes clear that it is a foolhardy person indeed who attempts to fix any kind of boundary in this 'partitioned Irskaholm' (*FW* 132.33).

Notes

1. Louis O. Mink, *A 'Finnegans Wake' Gazetteer* (Bloomington, IN: Indiana University Press, 1978), xi.
2. Ibid., xi.
3. John Bishop, *Joyce's Book of the Dark: 'Finnegans Wake'* (Madison, WI: University of Wisconsin Press, 1993), 30.
4. Ibid., 34–5.
5. O'Callaghan, 'Solastalgic Modernism', 165.
6. Adaline Glasheen, *Third Census of 'Finnegans Wake'* (Berkeley, CA: University of California Press, 1977), 98.
7. Anne L. Cavender, 'The Ass and the Four: Oppositional Figures for the Reader in *Finnegans Wake*', *James Joyce Quarterly* 41/4 (2004), 665.
8. McHugh, *Annotations*, 325.
9. McHugh, *Annotations*, 15.
10. John Nash, *James Joyce and the Act of Reception: Reading, Ireland, Modernism* (Cambridge: Cambridge University Press, 2006), 134.
11. Nolan, *James Joyce and Nationalism*, 142.
12. Ibid., 142.

13. Nash, *James Joyce and the Act of Reception*, 137–8.

14. Brendan O Hehir also notes that the Preface to the *Annals of the Four Masters* 'lists six men as having had a hand in its production', though one of them 'is believed to have worked on the book for only one month, so he may perhaps be eliminated from the reckoning' (O Hehir, *A Gaelic Lexicon*, 384). Using this logic, O Hehir thus concludes that 'five "Four Masters" are left, a fact which may have attracted Joyce as a complement to the four "fifths" which constitute the number of Irish provinces' (384).

15. Baron, 'Strandentwining Cable', 61.

16. Ibid., 61.

17. Ireland's thirty-two counties, following partition, were divided up, with twenty-six going on to form the Free State and six forming Northern Ireland.

18. Baron, 'Strandentwining Cable', 66.

19. 'Irskaholm' being Danish for 'Irish islet' (McHugh, *Annotations*, 132).

20. This letter also appears written as *nin* in Old Irish and *nion* in Modern Irish, both meaning 'ash-tree' – 'beithe-luis(-nin)', *eDil*, dil.ie/5598 (accessed 19 November 2020).

21. Joyce in fact provided a schema to Harriet Shaw Weaver regarding the Four in which he specifically noted the accents of each 'character': Matt having that of Belfast, Mark that of Cork-Kerry, Luke that of Dublin and Johnny that of Galway-Mayo (*SL* 297).

22. Joseph Campbell and Henry Morton Robinson, *A Skeleton Key to 'Finnegans Wake': Unlocking James Joyce's Masterwork* (1944; Novato, CA: New World Library, 2005), 106.

23. McHugh, *Annotations*, 140.

24. Ibid., 140.

25. The references to fishing, salmon-fishing especially, echo Joyce's description of Galway in 'The City of the Tribes' where he notes how an Italian traveller in the sixteenth century saw 'a salmon killed by a spear' in Galway (*OCPW* 198). This is in fact referenced again earlier in this chapter of the *Wake*: 'who could see at one blick a saumon taken with a lance' (*FW* 139.2–3). One of the main bridges in Galway is the Salmon Weir Bridge, and the section of the river Corrib which flows under it is still described today by Salmon Ireland as 'one of the most prolific salmon fisheries in Ireland' ('River Corrib (Galway Fishery)', *Salmon Ireland*, https://salmonireland.com/rivers/western-rivers/river-corrib-galway-fishery/ [accessed 19 November 2020]).

26. McHugh, *Annotations*, 141.

27. Roseanne Schot, 'Uisneach Midi a medón Érenn: A Prehistoric "Cult" Centre and "Royal Site" in Co. Westmeath', *The Journal of Irish Archaeology* 15 (2006), 39.

28. Ibid., 39–40.

29. Ibid., 41.

30. Ibid., 41.
31. Leo Daly's *James Joyce and the Mullingar Connection* (Dublin: Dolmen Press, 1975) does not specifically mention a visit to Uisneach, but does make clear how familiar Joyce was with the area around Mullingar.
32. John Garvin, *James Joyce's Disunited Kingdom and the Irish Dimension* (Dublin: Gill and Macmillan, 1976), 155.
33. Lacivita, *The Ecology of 'Finnegans Wake'*, 234 n.1.
34. Ibid., 29.
35. Caroline Donaghy and Eoin Grogan, 'Navel-gazing at Uisneach, Co. Westmeath', *Archaeology Ireland* 11/4 (1997), 24.
36. Schot, 'Uisneach', 40.
37. Garvin, *James Joyce's Disunited Kingdom*, 155.
38. P. W. Joyce, *The Origin and History of Irish Names of Places*, I (Dublin: M.H. Gill & Son, 1869), 461.
39. Much has been written about the tree/stone motif in the *Wake*. See, for example, Moshe Gold, 'A Proverbial Tale of Tree or Stone: Joyce's Rewriting of Plato's Reminders', *Joyce Studies Annual* 11 (2000), 66–101; and Campbell and Robinson, *A Skeleton Key to 'Finnegans Wake'*, 308–9.
40. Martin Brick, 'Joyce's Overlisting Eshtree: A Genetic Approach to Sacred Trees in *Finnegans Wake*', *Genetic Joyce Studies* 12 (2012), para. 1, https://www.geneticjoycestudies.org/articles/GJS12/GJS12_Brick (accessed 19 November 2020).
41. In a felicitous coincidence, the modern Irish word for tree is *crann*, pronounced almost identically – in Munster Irish – to the English word 'crown', something that Joyce is probably playing on here.
42. Proinsias Mac Cana, 'Early Irish Ideology and the Concept of Unity', in Richard Kearney (ed.), *The Irish Mind: Exploring Intellectual Traditions* (Dublin: Wolfhound, 1984), 68.
43. Ibid., 68.
44. Ibid., 68.
45. For a history of the fire tradition at Uisneach, see Alwyn Rees and Brinley Rees, *Celtic Heritage: Ancient Tradition in Ireland and Wales* (London: Thames and Hudson, 1961), 156–8.
46. Bruce Stewart, 'Joyce at Tara', in Theo D'haen and José Lanters (eds), *Troubled Histories, Troubled Fictions: Twentieth-Century Anglo-Irish Prose* (Amsterdam: Rodopi, 1995), 84.
47. Ibid., 85.
48. Eoin MacNeill, *Phases of Irish History* (Dublin: M.H. Gill & Son, 1920), 101, cited in Mac Cana, 'Early Irish Ideology', 67.
49. Mac Cana, 'Early Irish Ideology', 67.
50. Ibid., 67.
51. Tara and Uisneach, though both located in Meath, performed different functions in ancient Ireland. Tara was the seat of political power, while Uisneach, as *omphalos*, was the site of spiritual power. If Yawn has

ambitions towards political power, in placing himself on Uisneach he has placed himself on the wrong hill. By comparing Tara to the spiritual centres of Mecca and Jerusalem, it is not exactly clear that Joyce was aware of the difference between the two, and so Yawn's positioning might be accidently ironic.

52. Stephen Gwynn, *The History of Ireland* (London: Macmillan, 1923), 13.

53. Vincent Deane, Daniel Ferrer and Geert Lernout (eds), *The 'Finnegans Wake' Notebooks at Buffalo* (Turnhout: Brepols, 2001), VI.B.6: 180–1, cited in Lacivita, *The Ecology of 'Finnegans Wake'*, 58. Citations of these notebooks take the form VI.B. followed by the notebook and page number.

54. Gwynn, *The History of Ireland*, 12–13.

55. Mug Nuadat (i.e. Gwynn's Mogh Nuadat) was also known as Eoghan Mór, anglicised to Owen Mor by Standish O'Grady in *Selected Essays and Passages* (1918), probably another source used by Joyce – see Mikio Fuse, Robbert-Jan Henkes and Geert Lernout, 'Emendations to the Transcription of *Finnegans Wake* Notebook VI.B.14', *Genetic Joyce Studies* 10 (2010), 2, https://www.geneticjoycestudies.org/static/issues/GJS10/GJS10_B14Word_errata.pdf (accessed 19 November 2020).

56. Wyndham Lewis, *Time and Western Man* (London: Chatto and Windus, 1927), 3.

57. Budgen, *James Joyce and the Making of 'Ulysses'*, 359.

58. Hart, *Structure and Motif*, 109.

59. Smyth, *Space and the Irish Cultural Imagination*, 26.

60. Ibid., 27.

61. Ibid., 27.

62. Mikhail Bakhtin, *Problems of Dostoevsky's Poetics*, ed. and trans. Caryl Emerson (Minneapolis, MN: University of Minnesota Press, 1984), cited in Gary Saul Morson and Caryl Emerson, *Mikhail Bakhtin: Creation of a Prosaics* (Stanford, CA: Stanford University Press, 1990), 37.

63. Morson and Emerson, *Mikhail Bakhtin*, 92.

64. M. M. Bakhtin, *The Dialogic Imagination: Four Essays*, ed. Michael Holquist, trans. Caryl Emerson and Michael Holquist (1981; Austin, TX: University of Texas Press, 2014), 84.

65. Ibid., 84.

66. Morson and Emerson, *Mikhail Bakhtin*, 416.

67. Ibid., 416. The term 'heterochrony' comes from biology, in which context it means 'the occurrence of a process, or development of a tissue, organ, or organic form, at an abnormal time' (*OED*, 'heterochronic, adj.', derivatives).

68. Michel Foucault, 'Of Other Spaces', trans. Jay Miskowiec, *Diacritics*, 16/1 (1986), 24.

69. Ibid., 25–6.

70. Rees and Rees, *Celtic Heritage*, 159.

71. Ibid., 159.
72. Foucault, 'Of Other Spaces', 24.
73. Ibid., 26.
74. 'Follow me up Tucurlugh' is a reference to the song 'Follow Me Up to Carlow', a rebel song written by Patrick Joseph McCall that Joyce was particularly taken by and described as a 'ferocious and exciting song' (*L3* 427). The song tells the story of Fiach MacHugh O'Byrne, who led a Gaelic army to victory against English forces at the Battle of Glenmalure in 1580 and conducted several raids into the Pale, as noted in the song: 'See the sword of Glen Imayle / Flashing o'er the English Pale! / See the children of the Gael / Beneath O'Byrne's banners!' Patrick Joseph McCall, *Songs of Erinn* (Dublin: M.H. Gill & Son, 1899), 23.
75. Gwynn, *The History of Ireland*, 16.
76. Garvin, *James Joyce's Disunited Kingdom*, 153.
77. Pseudo-French (or perhaps French with an Irish accent), which can be approximated to 'J'ai trouvé la clé dans les champs', meaning 'I found the key in the fields.'
78. Kiberd, *Inventing Ireland*, 481.
79. McHugh, *Annotations*, 475.
80. For more on how Joyce made use of the *Connacht Tribune* as a source for the *Wake*, see Vincent Deane, 'Sewing a Dream Together: "Work in Progress" 1923–4', *Dublin James Joyce Journal* 14–15 (2021–22), 102–25.
81. Pseudo-Irish: *Jonny na hasailín*. The grammatically correct version would read *Jonny an asailín*.
82. 'O'mulanchonry' seems to be a clear reference to one of the four masters, Fearfeasa Ó Maol Chonaire, whom Joyce links with Luke Tarpey of Leinster in his schema (see *SL* 297). In this instance, however, Ó Maol Chonaire is associated with the west, appropriate given that this surname – the Irish for Conroy, as noted in Chapter 4 – is traditionally linked with this part of the country.
83. McHugh, *Annotations*, 482.
84. 'Cavan', *Britannica Academic*, Encyclopædia Britannica, 8 April 2013, para. 3, https://www.britannica.com/place/Cavan-county-Ireland (accessed 14 September 2024).
85. Mink, *A 'Finnegans Wake' Gazetteer*, xxi.
86. Roy Benjamin, 'Waking the King: Faction and Fission in *Finnegans Wake*', *James Joyce Quarterly* 46/2 (2009), 309.
87. The red hand of Ulster is the heraldic symbol of the northern province, used by both nationalists and unionists.
88. In Munster Irish, *goid* was in fact spelled as *guid* in the early twentieth century, as can be seen in the works of the influential Munster writer Peadar Ua Laoghaire. An example of this spelling occurs on the first page of his 1907 novel *Niamh*. Peadar Ua Laoghaire, *Niamh* (Dublin: Irish Book Co., 1907), 7.

89. Glasheen, *Third Census of 'Finnegans Wake'*, 110.
90. Foster, *Modern Ireland*, 328.
91. McHugh, *Annotations*, 528.
92. Ibid., 528.
93. Samuel Beckett, 'Dante . . . Bruno. Vico . . Joyce', in *Our Exagmination Round his Factification for Incamination of Work in Progress* (1929; New York: New Directions, 1972), 10–11.
94. Ibid., 5.
95. McHugh, *Annotations*, 292.

Coda: Beyond the Pale, Beyond Joyce

In his contribution to *Writings on Joyce, UCD James Joyce 2012*, the Irish writer Patrick McCabe, in typically absurdist style, begins by bemoaning the lack of critical attention paid to James Joyce's 'mixing of tarmacadam in Athlone' one day 'in the late nineteen-eighties'.[1] McCabe recounts how, while discussing Joyce's work one day with an unnamed artist, he received a sudden blow to the back of his neck and turned around to find a roadworker, who bore a striking resemblance to Patrick Tuohy's painting of Joyce's father, shouting down at him: 'What are youse bastards saying about the Joyces? Hah?'[2] Following an explanation that McCabe and the artist are in fact *Joyceans*, rather than merely badmouthing this man's relatives, the roadworker calms down and they share a few beverages. While I am loath to begin the tiresome business of explaining the joke, McCabe's comedy here is grounded in the fantastical notion of meeting James Joyce in Athlone of all places, at the very centre of the country. The idea that Joyce, that most metropolitan of writers, should appear in small-town, provincial Ireland is absurd; and yet McCabe acknowledges in the same essay that Leo Daly's *James Joyce and the Mullingar Connection* (1975) had already shown that Joyce was no stranger to the midlands. Many Joyceans will have felt, like McCabe, that unfortunate tendency to see Joyce *everywhere*, in everything we hear or read; and so there is something profoundly strange about the collective difficulty of even imagining Joyce as a local figure, passing through the small towns and villages of provincial Ireland, cycling through Connemara, or getting the boat to the Aran Islands. And yet all of these things he did.

McCabe's short reflection on Joyce is just one of many by Irish writers, seemingly obliged as they are to make at least some reference to the master's influence upon their own work. As Derek Attridge writes, every English-language writer 'has to take account of *Ulysses*', and if they do not, then they 'will be taken to have *avoided* Joyce'.[3] While making the obligatory reference to Joyce is an international phenomenon by now, Attridge acknowledges that '[t]his syndrome is, of course, felt with especial force by the Irish writer'.[4] We might add that this is augmented even more so for writers who make Dublin their setting. This coda will instead briefly consider how those writers who hailed from rural and provincial Ireland navigated Joyce's influence.

While Joyce might have been a heroic figure to the generation that followed him, over time he began to seem emblematic of the kind of overbearing authority that he had determined not to serve in his own lifetime. The Cork writer Frank O'Connor famously declared that he 'almost said "Thank God" when Joyce died'.[5] Similarly, most writers, at some time, have probably empathised with Brian O'Nolan's assertion: 'If I hear that word "Joyce" again I will surely froth at the gob.'[6] O'Nolan (alias Flann O'Brien) had the (mis)fortune of seeing Joyce namechecked in discussions of his own work. While born in the provincial town of Strabane in County Tyrone, O'Nolan spent the majority of his life in Dublin. His first novel, *At Swim-Two-Birds* (1939), is most frequently associated with Joyce, though the rural hellscape of *The Third Policeman* (1967) is arguably Wakean in its playful use of the page itself through long footnotes and surrealist plot. Meanwhile *An Béal Bocht* (*The Poor Mouth* [1941]) – written in Irish under the pseudonym Myles na gCopaleen – takes much from Joyce in its unrelenting parody of Irish-language memoirs in the early twentieth century, though this is also counterbalanced with a genuine love for the subject of its irony even as it lampoons it. In fact, O'Nolan ultimately appears as an aberration in the course of twentieth-century rural Irish literature, as his flair for experimental playfulness is superseded over time by writing dominated by naturalism.

Joe Cleary identifies this tendency towards a naturalist aesthetic as an embrace by Irish writers of the early Joyce of *Dubliners* and *A Portrait*, and a rejection of the modernist experimentation of *Ulysses* and *Finnegans Wake* as unsuited to the rural writer's determination to unmask the social ills at the heart of rural Irish society.[7] Cleary argues that this vogue for early Joycean naturalism – he acknowledges that this term is not without complications in relation to Joyce – is born out of a frustration with modernism's seeming remoteness from 'social engagement'.[8] By contrast, naturalism 'remained admirably socially committed', but, Cleary argues, 'its aesthetic conservatism paradoxically replicated the dour conservatism of Irish society against which natural-ism had set itself'.[9] John McGahern might be considered emblematic of this generation of rural naturalists, writing in a style akin to the 'scru-pulous meanness' that Joyce acknowledged as characterising the stories of *Dubliners* (*L2* 134). Indeed, in his own critical writings, McGahern lauds *Dubliners*, writing that '[o]nly in the great passages of *Ulysses* was Joyce able to surpass the art of *Dubliners*'.[10] Meanwhile, another of the most celebrated authors of rural Ireland, Edna O'Brien – whom Cleary also designates as one of Ireland's great naturalists – was forth-right about the influence Joyce had on her writing, even going so far as to write a short biography of him, *James Joyce* (1999), and an extended essay on his marriage with Nora Barnacle, *James and Nora: A Portrait of a Marriage* (1981).

While Cleary's criticism might appear harsh, there is a certain truth that, as admirably engaged as it is, rural naturalism's deter-mination to lay bare the malignancies at the heart of rural Ireland runs the risk of failing to imagine an alternative rural future. Even the Wexford writer John Banville focuses his praise of *Dubliners* on how it seemed relevant to his negative experience of small-town, pro-vincial Ireland: 'The book [*Dubliners*] was a revelation to me – the idea that literature could be very elevated but still be about life as I knew it, about the rather grim, gray, mundane life I was living as a boy in Wexford in the fifties.'[11] Continuing, Banville describes the Wexford of his youth as one of his 'traumas', saying that he 'never even bothered to learn the street names, because I knew I was going to be out of there as soon as I possibly could. I hated it because it was boring and provincial.'[12] Banville's description of Wexford is familiar in its rolling out of the clichés of rural and provincial Ireland that any reader of twentieth-century Irish literature will be familiar with. Trapped in a crippling and bleak traditionalism, there is little sugges-tion here of the modernity that Joyce was fascinated by in his writing on rural Ireland.

Another of the major Joycean concepts found in such rural and provincial writers is the notion of exile. Examples include Edna O'Brien's country girls who leave first for Dublin and then Eng-land; McGahern's many male protagonists who depart, or are about to depart, Ireland; and the character of Máirtín in Breandán Ó hEithir's Irish-language novel *Lig Sinn i gCathú* (*Lead Us Into Temptation* [1976]). This latter work is as evocative a depiction of Galway (disguised as 'Baile an Chaisil' in the novel) as Joyce's works are of Dublin, and, in its portrayal of youthful, alcohol-fuelled disaffection, it is comparable to Stephen's scenes in *Ulysses*.

Like *A Portrait*, *Lig Sinn i gCathú* also ends with a flight from Ireland and a determination to live independently, free from the shackles put upon the individual by Ireland itself. The Irish here is strikingly similar to Joyce's 'nets', though more rural in flavour, with Máirtín encouraged to reject the 'crobhnasc', or 'horn-and-leg spancel', tied round the individual (*FGB*, 'cornasc').[13] This is as clear an echo of Stephen's *non serviam* as any to be found in twentieth-century Irish literature. Regarding this impulse towards exile, Cleary notes that '[i]n Irish naturalist fiction, protagonists usually survive their deathly social condition only if they can escape or emigrate; to remain within or committed to the local community is to atrophy with it'.[14] At times it might seem as though Irish naturalists took Stephen Dedalus's flight from Ireland as an end point, ignoring his determination to circle back eventually to Tara and create – or recreate – a national conscience.

It might be tempting to think, then, that most rural Irish writers, when they were not bemoaning the long shadow cast by Joyce on Irish literature, only found use for his early stylistic model, the naturalism of *Dubliners*. Such a view would align with that which sees rural life as caught in a stasis, incapable of making the leap into a truly modernist aesthetic. However, it is possible to point to a number of writers of rural Ireland who do not align with this trend. First, Flann and Edna were not the only O'Briens to be deeply influenced by Joyce – to this group we must also add Kate O'Brien. Born in Limerick, Kate O'Brien was forthright in her sense of indebtedness to Joyce, even if her writing might appear at first to be more in keeping stylistically with the realists already discussed. In her personal writings, O'Brien is explicit about the influence that Joyce had on her, describing him as 'the greatest Artist'[15] and a 'lonely genius'.[16] Meanwhile, in her 1938 novel *Pray for the Wanderer*, O'Brien has one character declare that 'we've only got Joyce to measure against the immortals'.[17] In her life, O'Brien seems to have followed a Joycean model, choosing exile in Europe over stagnation in Ireland, though she returned more often and for longer periods than Joyce ever did. Her Limerick roots remain the key common denominator of many of her works, with O'Brien admitting that 'wherever I am it is still from Limerick that I look out and make my surmises'.[18] In a comparison of both writers, Elizabeth Foley O'Connor acknowledges the 'deceptively simple, conventional style of many of [O'Brien's] novels', but insists on the 'deep ambiguity and modernist irresolution in her work'.[19] Indeed, O'Brien's greatest work, *The Land of Spices* (1941), a *bildungsroman* set in a convent school in rural Ireland, has been viewed as a feminist rewriting of *A Portrait*. O'Connor argues that 'O'Brien structures *Land of Spices* around several key reworkings of moments in *A Portrait*', while Aintzane Legarreta Mentxaka has posited that the principal character of Anna can be viewed as O'Brien imagining how Stephen's sister might have navigated the world, just as Virginia Woolf imagined Shakespeare's sister.[20] In her writings on sexuality, particularly homosexual and non-normative sexual relations, O'Brien certainly has much in common with Joyce. However, what is perhaps most interesting for the purposes of this study is the emphasis that both O'Brien and Joyce place on a modern and often cosmopolitan version of rural Ireland. O'Brien's novels are unique in the Irish literary canon for their treatment of a middle-class Catholicism that is in touch with European trends. Many of her principal characters who find themselves in rural Ireland in fact come from elsewhere in Europe, such as the English Mother Superior Helen in *The Land of Spices*, and the French actress Angèle Maury in *The Last of Summer* (1943), while Matt Costello in *Pray for the Wanderer* is a returned exile. The convent of La Compagnie de la Sainte Famille in *The Land of Spices* is quite evidently influenced by French Catholicism, and extended passages of the work are written in French. O'Brien's rural Ireland is therefore not one cast adrift from the continent but rather one with its 'eyes [. . .] on Europe', to quote the Citizen (*U* 12.1296).

Finally, any summary of rural Irish literature that offers the conclusion that it lacks a modernist figurehead can only do so by ignoring the writings of Máirtín Ó Cadhain. Born in 1906 in Cnocán Glas, part of the Irish-speaking area situated west of Galway city known as Cois Fharraige, Ó Cadhain is perhaps the most radical writer that rural Ireland has ever produced. An active member of the IRA, Ó Cadhain was imprisoned for almost all of the Second World War as part of an effort by the Irish government to prevent Irish republicans from disrupting Ireland's carefully balanced neutrality. Ó Cadhain was a committed socialist throughout his life, as well as a steadfast supporter of Irish language rights. He wrote in a style of Irish characterised by the dialect of west Galway and possessed an extraordinary breadth of vocabulary, with his writing noted for its dense quality. Ó Cadhain was a polyglot of Joycean proportions and, in addition to his native Irish, understood – with varying degrees of fluency – English, Scottish Gaelic, Welsh, Breton, Russian, Spanish, German, French and Italian.[21] He was a prolific writer of journalism, short stories and novels, only one of which was published in his lifetime, the modernist masterpiece *Cré na Cille* (1949), literally translated as 'Churchyard Clay'. The novel takes place underground, among the clay and the corpses, as instead of finding peace in death, the deceased continue their raucous bickering into the afterlife. The 'main character' is Caitríona Pháidín, who spews out a never-ending invective towards her still-living sister Nell, though over the course of the work dozens of characters enter the fray, as each fresh corpse brings news from above ground. The novel is composed solely of the characters' voices coming and going, each voice indicated by a dash, with the only clues as to who is speaking provided by repeated phrases or particular personal hang-ups. There is no plot to speak of, as the stream of new gossip provides little sense of an overall narrative arc or conclusion.

While the fact of Ó Cadhain's writing in Irish was always going to make his acceptance into the pantheon of European modernists unlikely, this was only exacerbated by his writing's notorious difficulty. As Ó Cadhain admitted late in life, 'I don't yield an inch to my readers but I have readers.'[22] Some of his later writings have been spoken of in reference to Joyce, particularly the short story 'A Simple Lesson' from *An tSraith ar Lár* (1967), and the difficult-to-classify *Barbed Wire* (unpublished until 2002), which both feature a very Joycean flair for multilingual wordplay. Ó Cadhain appears to have enjoyed cultivating comparisons with Joyce, with his contributions to IRA Council meetings 'recorded under the *nom-de-guerre* "Joyce"',[23] while during a 1969 lecture he recounted overhearing a conversation on the bus in which two fellow passengers discussed his writings, with one dismissing Ó Cadhain as nothing more than a 'Joycean smutmonger'.[24] Indeed, *Cré na Cille* had originally been refused publication by An Gúm, with the reason given that it was too long and too 'Joycean'.[25] Perhaps because of such notoriety, *Cré na Cille* went untranslated into English until 2015, with *The New Yorker* somewhat dramatically dubbing it 'The Irish Novel That's So Good People Were Scared to Translate It'.[26] In 2015 Alan Titley translated *Cré na Cille* under the title *The Dirty Dust*, while the following year saw its publication as *Graveyard Clay*, translated by Liam Mac Con Iomaire and Tim Robinson. The appearance of these translations saw Joyce namechecked in many reviews – indeed, it has become something of a commonplace in literary criticism to refer to *Cré na Cille* as the *Ulysses* of the Irish language. This could be seen as early as 1972, when David Greene wrote that 'Ó Cadhain's *Cois Fharraige* takes its place with Joyce's Dublin, and *Cré na Cille* is the only book by an Irishman which is worthy of comparison with *Ulysses*.'[27] Of all the writers under discussion here, it is Ó Cadhain who comes closest to providing us with a rural modernism to match the experimentation of Joyce's more urban variety.

This short coda has attempted to gesture towards the influence that Joyce had upon his rural inheritors, one that, while often based on his early naturalist style, goes beyond this to take in the more radical possibilities proffered by his modernist masterpieces. While I have focused on rural Irish writers of the twentieth century who were influenced by Joyce, writers in the twenty-first century have arguably been more keen to embrace Joycean stylistic experimentation. One oft-cited example is Eimear McBride's *A Girl is a Half-formed Thing* (2013), which has been noted for how it employs Joycean stream-of-consciousness to delve into the mind of a young girl coming of age in rural Ireland. Evidently, it is impossible to fully cover the scope of Joyce's influence upon writers from rural Ireland, though it seems clear that his emphasis on the particularity of place has been of especial importance to generations of rural writers. It remains important also to acknowledge that Joyce's pursuing of a literary style that had grander, cosmopolitan ambitions provided writers such as Ó Cadhain and Kate O'Brien with a path to follow for their own brands of modernism. Not only this, but for those writers who went looking, it was clear that Joyce had already delved into the modernity at the heart of rural Ireland.

* * *

To honour Joyce's fiftieth birthday in 1932, the artist César Abin drew a portrait of the writer in the form of a question mark. Following Joyce's strict instructions, Abin drew the point of the question mark as a globe, but with the outline of Ireland taking up all of its space. Within the contours of Ireland itself, an oversized map of Dublin was coloured in black, standing out from the rest of the country.[28] If Joyce-as-question-mark was supposed to underscore his enigmatic qualities, then there was little ambiguity regarding the point of the punctuation mark: in Joyce's universe, Ireland was the world, and Dublin was the highlighted centre of that world. While it might have taken a strangely long time for critics to accept Joyce's centring of Ireland in his work, mostly this correction has followed Abin's – and Joyce's – lead by putting Dublin in bold. The point of this book has not been to argue for Joyce as a predominantly rural writer, but rather, using the material provided to us by Joyce himself, to colour in the rest of this map of Ireland. By focusing the lens on the rural in Joyce, we come to a new understanding of his engagement with modernity, as well as an updated sense of rural Ireland within the scope of Irish literature. Too often discourse regarding rural Ireland has been dominated by a focus on stasis and conformity; by situating rural life within the bounds of a Joycean vision of modernity, we come to appreciate its tradition of radical upheaval in terms of the political and the spatial. When we think of the rural in Joyce we should think as much of the Irish peasantry's politics as we do of the land they farm; when we think of Dublin's streets we should think not just of the urbanites who walk them, but also the cattle. It is only through the consideration of all of these matters – the politics, the people, the places and the peregrinations – that we can come to a full understanding of Joyce beyond the Pale.

Notes

1. Patrick McCabe, 'Metemdepsychoswandayinarkloan; James Joyce and Me', *Writings on Joyce, UCD James Joyce 2012*, n.p., https://www.ucd.ie/ucdonjoyce/writings-on-joyce/articles/joyce-and-me-patrick-mccabe/index.html (accessed 12 January 2024).
2. Ibid.
3. Derek Attridge, 'Foreword', in Martha C. Carpentier (ed.), *Joycean Legacies* (New York: Palgrave Macmillan, 2015), vii.
4. Ibid., vii.
5. Frank O'Connor, 'James Joyce: A Post-Mortem', *The Bell* 5/5 (1943), 363, cited in John McCourt, *Consuming Joyce: 100 Years of 'Ulysses' in Ireland* (London: Bloomsbury Academic, 2022), 93.
6. Letter from Brian O'Nolan to Timothy O'Keeffe, in Robert Hogan and Gordon Henderson (eds), 'A Sheaf of Letters', *The Journal of Irish Literature* 3/1 (1974), 79, cited in Stephanie Boland, 'Modernism and Non-fiction: Place, Genre and the Politics of Popular Forms', PhD thesis, University of Exeter, 2017, 152.
7. Cleary, *Outrageous Fortune*, 97.
8. Ibid., 98.
9. Ibid., 98.
10. John McGahern, '*Dubliners*', in *Love of the World: Essays*, ed. Stanley van der Ziel (London: Faber and Faber, 2010), 207.
11. John Banville, 'John Banville, The Art of Fiction No. 200', interview with Belinda McKeon, *The Paris Review* 188 (2009), https://www.theparisreview.org/interviews/5907/the-art-of-fiction-no-200-john-banville, cited in Attridge, 'Foreword', xiii.
12. Banville, *The Paris Review*, n.p.
13. Breandán Ó hEithir, *Lig Sinn i gCathú* (Dublin: Sáirséal agus Dill, 1976), 205.
14. Cleary, *Outrageous Fortune*, 97–8.
15. Adele Dalsimer, *Kate O'Brien: A Critical Study* (Dublin: Gill and Macmillan, 1990), 59, cited in Aintzane Legarreta Mentxaka, '"James

Joyce is my Man"': Kate O'Brien and James Joyce', in Olga Fernández Vicente (ed.), *Joyce's Heirs: Joyce's Imprint on Recent Global Literatures* (Bilbao: Servicio de Publicaciones de la Universidad del País Vasco, 2019), 8.

16. Elizabeth Foley O'Connor, 'Kate O'Brien, James Joyce, and the "Lonely Genius"', in Martha C. Carpentier (ed.), *Joycean Legacies* (New York: Palgrave Macmillan, 2015), 11.

17. Kate O'Brien, *Pray for the Wanderer* (1938; Dublin: Arlen House, 2022), 61.

18. Kate O'Brien, *My Ireland* (London: Batsford, 1962), 148, cited in O'Connor, 'Kate O'Brien', 16.

19. O'Connor, 'Kate O'Brien', 16.

20. Mentxaka, '"James Joyce is my Man"', 17.

21. Liam Mac Con Iomaire, 'Introductory Note', in *Graveyard Clay: Cré na Cille*, trans. Liam Mac Con Iomaire and Tim Robinson (New Haven, CT: Yale University Press, 2016), viii.

22. 'Ní ghéillim orlach do mo léitheoirí ach tá lucht léite agam'; Máirtín Ó Cadhain, *Páipéir Bhána agus Páipéir Bhreaca* (Dublin: An Clóchomhar Tta, 1969), 38.

23. Cian Ó hÉigeartaigh, 'Máirtín Ó Cadhain: Politics and Literature', *The Canadian Journal of Irish Studies* 34/1 (2008), 29.

24. Ó Cadhain, *Páipéir Bhána*, 12–13.

25. Máirtín Ó Cadhain, *As an nGéibheann: Litreacha chuig Tomás Bairéad* (Dublin: Sáirséal agus Dill, 1973), 160.

26. William Brennan, 'The Irish Novel That's So Good People Were Scared to Translate It', *The New Yorker*, 17 March 2016, https://www.newyorker.com/books/page-turner/the-irish-novel-thats-so-good-people-were-scared-to-translate-it (accessed 19 January 2022).

27. David Greene, *Writing in Irish Today* (Cork: Mercier Press, 1972), 44, cited in Eoin Byrne, '"Éistear le mo ghlór!": Máirtín Ó Cadhain's *Cré na Cille* and Postcolonial Modernisms', *Irish Studies Review* 26/3 (2018), 336. There is a long tradition of comparing Ó Cadhain and Joyce in Irish language scholarship. See, for example, Radvan Markus, *Carnabhal na Marbh: 'Cré na Cille' agus Litríocht an Domhain* (Indreabhán: Leabhar Breac, 2023), 151–60; Cathal Ó Háinle, 'Ó Cadhain, an Rí Séamas II, Joyce agus Molly Bloom', in Máire Ní Annracháin (ed.), *Saothar Mháirtín Uí Chadhain, Léachtaí Cholm Cille* 37 (2007), 7–37; and Niall Ó Cuileagáin, '"A Joycean Smutmonger": Echoes of Joyce in Máirtín Ó Cadhain's Rural Modernism', *Review of Irish Studies in Europe* 7 (2024), 58–76, https://doi.org/10.32803/rise.v7i1.3249 (accessed 7 May 2024).

28. César Abin, 'James Joyce, Caricature', *transition* 21 (1932), 256.

Bibliography

1901 Census of Ireland, Limerick, District Electoral Division (DED) Grange, Grange Lower, House 15, John Clancy Household; digital image, 'Household Return (Form A)', The National Archives of Ireland, http://www.census.nationalarchives.ie/ (accessed 19 January 2022).

Æ [George Russell], *Imaginations and Reveries* (Dublin: Maunsel, 1915).

Aalen, F .H. A., 'The Irish Rural Landscape: Synthesis of Habitat and History', in F. H. A. Aalen, Kevin Whelan and Matthew Stout (eds), *Atlas of the Irish Rural Landscape* (Toronto: University of Toronto Press, 1997), 4–30.

Abin, César, 'James Joyce, Caricature', *transition* 21 (1932), 256.

Adkins, Peter, 'The Eyes of That Cow: Eating Animals and Theorizing Vegetarianism in James Joyce's *Ulysses*', *Humanities* 6/3 (2017), https://doi.org/10.3390/h6030046 (accessed 23 February 2024).

Alexander, Neal, and James Moran, 'Introduction: Regional Modernisms', in Neal Alexander and James Moran (eds), *Regional Modernisms* (Edinburgh: Edinburgh University Press, 2013), 1–21.

Allingham, William, *Laurence Bloomfield in Ireland* (1864; New York: Garland, 1979).

Anderson, Benedict, *Imagined Communities: Reflections on the Origin and Spread of Nationalism* (1983; London: Verso, 2016).

'Andrew Boorde', in *Britannica Academic*, Encyclopædia Britannica, 20 July 1998, https://www.britannica.com/biography/Andrew-Boorde (accessed 14 September 2024).

Arensberg, Conrad Maynadier, and Solon Toothaker Kimball, *Family and Community in Ireland*, 2nd edn (Cambridge, MA: Harvard University Press, 1968).

Arnold, David, 'Europe, Technology, and Colonialism in the 20th Century', *History and Technology* 21/1 (2006), 85–106.

Arnold, Matthew, *On the Study of Celtic Literature* (London: Smith, Elder, 1867).

Attridge, Derek, 'Foreword', in Martha C. Carpentier (ed.), *Joycean Legacies* (New York: Palgrave Macmillan, 2015), vii–xx.

Bakhtin, M. M., *The Dialogic Imagination: Four Essays*, ed. Michael Holquist, trans. Caryl Emerson and Michael Holquist (1981; Austin, TX: University of Texas Press, 2014).

Banville, John, 'John Banville, The Art of Fiction No. 200', interview with Belinda McKeon, *The Paris Review* 188 (2009) https://www.theparisreview.org/interviews/5907/the-art-of-fiction-no-200-john-banville (accessed 12 January 2024).

Baron, Scarlett, *'Strandentwining Cable': Joyce, Flaubert, and Intertextuality* (Oxford: Oxford University Press, 2012).

Barthes, Roland, 'The *Blue Guide*', in *Mythologies*, trans. Annette Lavers (New York: Farrar, Straus and Giroux, 1972), 74–7.

Beckett, Samuel, 'Dante . . . Bruno. Vico . . Joyce', in *Our Exagmination Round his Factification for Incamination of Work in Progress* (1929; New York: New Directions, 1972), 1–22.

'beithe-luis(-nin)', *eDil*, dil.ie/5598 (accessed 19 November 2020).

Bell, Jonathan, and Mervyn Watson, *A History of Irish Farming, 1750–1950* (Dublin: Four Courts Press, 2008).

Benjamin, Roy, 'Waking the King: Faction and Fission in *Finnegans Wake*', *James Joyce Quarterly* 46/2 (2009), 305–20.

Berman, Marshall, *All That is Solid Melts into Air: The Experience of Modernity* (1982; London: Penguin, 1988).

Bew, Paul, 'The Land League Ideal: Achievements and Contradictions', in P. J. Drudy (ed.), *Ireland: Land, Politics and People* (Cambridge: Cambridge University Press, 1982), 77–92.

Bishop, John, *Joyce's Book of the Dark: 'Finnegans Wake'* (Madison, WI: University of Wisconsin Press, 1993).

Bluemel, Kristin, and Michael McCluskey, 'Introduction: Rural Modernity in Britain', in Kristin Bluemel and Michael McCluskey (eds), *Rural Modernity in Britain: A Critical Intervention* (Edinburgh: Edinburgh University Press, 2018), 1–16.

Boes, Tobias, *Formative Fictions: Nationalism, Cosmopolitanism, and the 'Bildungsroman'* (Ithaca, NY: Cornell University Press, 2012).

Boland, Stephanie, 'The "Cornish Tokens" of *Finnegans Wake*: A Journey Through the Celtic Archipelago', *James Joyce Quarterly* 54/1 (2016), 105–18.

———— 'Modernism and Non-fiction: Place, Genre and the Politics of Popular Forms', PhD thesis, University of Exeter, 2017.

Bowker, Gordon, *James Joyce: A New Biography* (New York: Farrar, Straus and Giroux, 2011).

Boyd, Elizabeth F., 'James Joyce's Hell-Fire Sermons', *Modern Language Notes* 75/7 (1960), 561–71.

Bradbury, Malcolm, 'The Cities of Modernism', in Malcolm Bradbury and James McFarlane (eds), *Modernism: A Guide to European Literature 1890–1930* (1976; London: Penguin, 1991), 96–104.

Bradley, John, 'The Purpose of the Pale: A View from Kilkenny', in Michael Potterton and Thomas Herron (eds), *Dublin and the Pale in the Renaissance, c.1540–1660* (Dublin: Four Courts Press, 2011), 51–67.

Brannigan, John, *Archipelagic Modernism: Literature in the Irish and British Isles, 1890–1970* (Edinburgh: Edinburgh University Press, 2015).

Brazeau, Robert, '"The Sassenach wants his morning rashers": The Colonial Market and the Commodified Animal in "Telemachus"', *James Joyce Quarterly* 58/1–2 (2020), 19–35.

Brennan, William, 'The Irish Novel That's So Good People Were Scared to Translate It', *The New Yorker*, 17 March 2016, https://www.newyorker.com/books/page-turner/the-irish-novel-thats-so-good-people-were-scared-to-translate-it (accessed 19 January 2022).

Brick, Martin, 'Joyce's Overlisting Eshtree: A Genetic Approach to Sacred Trees in *Finnegans Wake*', *Genetic Joyce Studies* 12 (2012), https://www.geneticjoycestudies.org/articles/GJS12/GJS12_Brick (accessed 19 November 2020).

Browne, Stephen J., *Ireland in Fiction: A Guide to Irish Novels, Tales, Romances, and Folklore* (Dublin: Maunsel, 1916).

Browning, Robert, *The Major Works*, ed. Adam Roberts (Oxford: Oxford University Press, 2005).

Budgen, Frank, *James Joyce and the Making of 'Ulysses', and Other Writings* (Oxford: Oxford University Press, 1972).

Buell, Lawrence, *The Future of Environmental Criticism* (Oxford: Blackwell, 2005).

Byrne, Eoin, '"Éistear le mo ghlór!": Máirtín Ó Cadhain's *Cré na Cille* and Postcolonial Modernisms', *Irish Studies Review* 26/3 (2018), 335–46.

Camden, William, *Camden's Britannia* (Oxford: Edmund Gibson, 1695).

Campbell, Fergus, *Land and Revolution: Nationalist Politics in the West of Ireland 1891–1921* (Oxford: Oxford University Press, 2005).

Campbell, Joseph, and Henry Morton Robinson, *A Skeleton Key to 'Finnegans Wake': Unlocking James Joyce's Masterwork* (1944; Novato, CA: New World Library, 2005).

Capie, Forrest, and Richard Perren, 'The British Market for Meat, 1850–1914', *Agricultural History* 54/4 (1980), 502–15.

Castle, Gregory, *Modernism and the Celtic Revival* (Cambridge: Cambridge University Press, 2001).

'Cavan', *Britannica Academic*, Encyclopædia Britannica, 8 April 2013, https://www.britannica.com/place/Cavan-county-Ireland (accessed 14 September 2024).

Cavender, Anne L., 'The Ass and the Four: Oppositional Figures for the Reader in *Finnegans Wake*', *James Joyce Quarterly* 41/4 (2004), 665–87.

Chakrabarty, Dipesh, *Provincializing Europe: Postcolonial Thought and Historical Difference*, 2nd edn (2000; Princeton: Princeton University Press, 2008).

Cheah, Pheng, 'Introduction Part II: The Cosmopolitical—Today', in Pheng Cheah and Bruce Robbins (eds), *Cosmopolitics: Thinking and Feeling Beyond the Nation* (Minneapolis, MN: University of Minnesota Press, 1998), 20–41.

Cheng, Vincent J., *Joyce, Race, and Empire* (Cambridge: Cambridge University Press, 1995).

_____ '"Terrible Queer Creatures": Joyce, Cosmopolitanism, and the Inauthentic Irishman', in Michael Patrick Gillespie (ed.), *James Joyce and the Fabrication of an Irish Identity* (Amsterdam: Rodopi, 2001), 11–38.

Clare, Liam, 'The Dublin Cattle Market', *Dublin Historical Record 55/2* (2002), 166–80.

Cleary, Joe, 'Introduction: Ireland and Modernity', in Joe Cleary and Claire Connolly (eds), *The Cambridge Companion to Modern Irish Culture* (Cambridge: Cambridge University Press, 2005), 1–21.

_____ *Outrageous Fortune: Capital and Culture in Modern Ireland* (Dublin: Field Day, 2007).

Clifford, James, 'Traditional Futures', in Mark Salber Phillips and Gordon Schochet (eds), *Questions of Tradition* (Toronto: University of Toronto Press, 2004), 152–68.

Colum, Mary, *Life and the Dream* (New York: Doubleday, 1947).

Conmee, John S., *Old Times in the Barony* (1895; Dublin: Catholic Truth Society of Ireland, 1911).

Connolly, Thomas E., *The Personal Library of James Joyce: A Descriptive Bibliography*, 2nd edn (1955; Buffalo, NY: University of Buffalo, 1957).

Cosgrove, Art, 'Anglo-Ireland and the Yorkist Cause', in Art Cosgrove (ed.), *A New History of Ireland: Volume II, Medieval Ireland 1169–1534* (Oxford: Oxford University Press, 2008), 557–68.

_____ 'The Emergence of the Pale', in Art Cosgrove (ed.), *A New History of Ireland: Volume II, Medieval Ireland 1169–1534* (Oxford: Oxford University Press, 2008), 533–56.

_____ 'Ireland beyond the Pale, 1399–1460', in Art Cosgrove (ed.), *A New History of Ireland: Volume II, Medieval Ireland 1169–1534* (Oxford: Oxford University Press, 2008), 569–90.

Cullen, Brendan, 'The Pale Rampart at Clongowes Wood College', *Local History Journal* 21 (2016), 30–34, https://localhistory.ie/?mdocs-file=455 (accessed 22 February 2021).

Cullingford, Elizabeth Butler, 'Phoenician Genealogies and Oriental Geographies: Joyce, Language and Race', in Marjorie Howes and Derek Attridge (eds), *Semicolonial Joyce* (Cambridge: Cambridge University Press, 2000), 219–39.

Cunningham, Patrick, 'The Evolution of Cattle and Cattle Farming Systems: The Genetic Evidence', in Margaret Murphy and Matthew Stout (eds), *Agriculture and Settlement in Ireland* (Dublin: Four Courts Press, 2015), 1–13.

Curtis, L. Perry, *Apes and Angels: The Irishman in Victorian Caricature*, 2nd edn (Washington, DC: Smithsonian Books, 1996).

Daly, Leo, *James Joyce and the Mullingar Connection* (Dublin: Dolmen Press, 1975).

'The Danish Parallel', *Irish Homestead*, 13 August 1904, 662–3.

Davis, Thomas Osborne, *The Poems of Thomas Davis* (Dublin: James Duffy, 1846).

Davitt, Michael, *The Fall of Feudalism in Ireland or The Story of the Land League Revolution* (London and New York: Harper & Brothers, 1904).

De Paor, Louis, 'Réamhrá | Introduction', in Louis de Paor (ed.), *Leabhar na hAthghabhála: Poems of Repossession* (Hexham: Bloodaxe, 2016), 13–28.

Deane, Seamus, 'Introduction', in James Joyce, *Finnegans Wake* (1939; London: Penguin, 2000), vii–xlix.

_____ 'Joyce the Irishman', in Derek Attridge (ed.), *The Cambridge Companion to James Joyce*, 2nd edn (Cambridge: Cambridge University Press, 2004), 31–53.

_____ 'Notes', in James Joyce, *A Portrait of the Artist as a Young Man* (London: Penguin, 2000), 277–329.

Deane, Vincent, 'Joyce, Moranism, and the Opal Hush Poets', *Dublin James Joyce Journal* 5 (2012), 66–81.

_____ 'Sewing a Dream Together: "Work in Progress" 1923–4', *Dublin James Joyce Journal* 14–15 (2021–22), 102–25.

Donaghy, Caroline, and Eoin Grogan, 'Navel-gazing at Uisneach, Co. Westmeath', *Archaeology Ireland* 11/4 (1997), 24–6.

Doyle, Laura, and Laura Winkiel (eds), *Geomodernisms: Race, Modernism, Modernity* (Bloomington, IN: Indiana University Press, 2005).

Doyle, Patrick, *Civilising Rural Ireland: The Co-operative Movement, Development and the Nation-state, 1889–1939* (Manchester: Manchester University Press, 2019).

Draper, Hal, *The Adventures of the Communist Manifesto* (Alameda, CA: Center for Socialist History, 2004).

Drudy, P. J., 'Introduction', in P. J. Drudy (ed.), *Ireland: Land, Politics and People* (Cambridge: Cambridge University Press, 1982), 1–9.

Duffy, Enda, 'Drumcondra Modernism: Joyce's Suburban Aesthetic', in Marjorie Elizabeth Howes (ed.), *Irish Literature in Transition, 1880–1940*, IV (Cambridge: Cambridge University Press, 2020), 229–45.

Dukova, Anastasia, *A History of the Dublin Metropolitan Police and its Colonial Legacy* (Dublin: Palgrave Macmillan, 2016).

Eagleton, Terry, *Heathcliff and the Great Hunger: Studies in Irish Culture* (London: Verso, 1995).

Eglinton, John, *Anglo-Irish Essays* (Dublin: The Talbot Press, 1917).

Eglinton, John, W. B. Yeats, Æ and William Larminie (eds), *Literary Ideals in Ireland* (London: T. Fisher Unwin, 1899).

Eliot, T. S., '*Ulysses*, Order and Myth', in *Selected Prose of T.S. Eliot*, ed. Frank Kermode (San Diego, CA: Harcourt, 1975), 175–8.

Ellmann, Richard, *The Consciousness of Joyce* (Oxford: Oxford University Press, 1977).

_____ *James Joyce*, rev. edn (Oxford: Oxford University Press, 1982).

Everett-Heath, John, 'Pale of Settlement', in *The Concise Oxford Dictionary of World Place Names*, 5th edn (Oxford: Oxford University Press, 2019), https://www.oxfordreference.com/view/10.1093/

acref/9780191882913.001.0001/acref-9780191882913-e-10232 (accessed 19 January 2022).

Fairhall, James, 'The Bog of Allen, the Tiber River, and the Pontine Marshes: An Ecocritical Reading of "The Dead"', *James Joyce Quarterly* 51/4 (2014), 567–600.

―――― 'Eco-criticism, Joyce, and the Politics of Trees in the "Cyclops" Episode of *Ulysses*', *Irish Studies Review* 20/4 (2012), 367–87.

Fathers of the Society of Jesus, *A Page of Irish History: Story of University College, Dublin, 1883–1909* (Dublin: The Talbot Press, 1930).

Fitzgerald, Patrick, and Brian Lambkin, *Migration in Irish History, 1607–2007* (London: Palgrave Macmillan, 2008).

Fogarty, Anne, '"I Think He Died for Me": Memory and Ethics in 'The Dead'', in Oona Frawley and Katherine O'Callaghan (eds), *Memory Ireland: James Joyce and Cultural Memory*, IV (Syracuse, NY: Syracuse University Press, 2014), 46–61.

―――― 'States of Memory: Reading History in "Wandering Rocks"', in Ellen Carol Jones and Morris Beja (eds), *Twenty-First Joyce* (Gainesville, FL: University Press of Florida, 2004), 56–81.

'Foot-and-mouth disease (FMD)', *Britannica Academic*, Encyclopædia Britannica, 3 February 2012, https://www.britannica.com/science/foot-and-mouth-disease (accessed 14 September 2024).

Ford, Charles, 'Dante's Other Brush: *Ulysses* and the Irish Revolution', *James Joyce Quarterly* 29/4 (1992), 751–61.

Foster, John Wilson, *Fictions of the Irish Literary Revival: A Changeling Art* (Syracuse, NY: Syracuse University Press, 1987).

Foster, R. F., *Modern Ireland, 1600–1972* (London: Penguin, 1989).

Foucault, Michel, 'Of Other Spaces', trans. Jay Miskowiec, *Diacritics*, 16/1 (1986), 22–7.

Frawley, Oona, *Irish Pastoral: Nostalgia and Twentieth-Century Irish Literature* (Dublin: Irish Academic Press, 2005).

Freeman's Journal, 6 September 1912, p. 6, The British Newspaper Archive, https://www.britishnewspaperarchive.co.uk/viewer/BL/0000056/19120906/072/0006 (accessed 20 January 2022).

Friedman, Susan Stanford, *Planetary Modernisms: Provocations on Modernity Across Time* (New York: Columbia University Press, 2015).

Fuse, Mikio, Robbert-Jan Henkes and Geert Lernout, 'Emendations to the Transcription of *Finnegans Wake* Notebook VI.B.14', *Genetic Joyce Studies* 10 (2010), https://www.geneticjoycestudies.org/static/issues/GJS10/GJS10_B14Word_errata.pdf (accessed 19 November 2020).

Garvin, John, *James Joyce's Disunited Kingdom and the Irish Dimension* (Dublin: Gill and Macmillan, 1976).

Geheber, Philip Keel, 'Assimilating Shem into the Plural Polity: Burrus, Caseous, and Irish Free State Dairy Production', in Onno Kosters, Tim Conley and Peter de Voogd (eds), *A Long the Krommerun: Selected Papers from the Utrecht James Joyce Symposium* (Amsterdam: Brill/Rodopi, 2016), 127–39.

Gibbons, Luke, *Joyce's Ghosts: Ireland, Modernism, and Memory* (Chicago: University of Chicago Press, 2015).

———— *Transformations in Irish Culture* (Cork: Cork University Press in Association with Field Day, 1996).

Gifford, Don, and Robert J. Seidman, *Ulysses Annotated: Notes for James Joyce's Ulysses*, 2nd edn (Berkeley, CA: University of California Press, 1988).

Gladwin, Derek, 'Joyce the Travel Writer: Space, Place and the Environment in James Joyce's Nonfiction', in Robert Brazeau and Derek Gladwin (eds), *Eco-Joyce: The Environmental Imagination of James Joyce* (Cork: Cork University Press, 2014), 176–94.

Glasheen, Adaline, *Third Census of 'Finnegans Wake'* (Berkeley, CA: University of California Press, 1977).

Glotfelty, Cheryll, 'Introduction: Literary Studies in an Age of Environmental Crisis', in Cheryll Glotfelty and Harold Fromm (eds), *The Ecocriticism Reader: Landmarks in Literary Ecology* (Athens, GA: University of Georgia Press, 1996), xv–xxxvii.

Gold, Moshe, 'A Proverbial Tale of Tree or Stone: Joyce's Rewriting of Plato's Reminders', *Joyce Studies Annual* 11 (2000), 66–101.

Guinnane, Timothy, *The Vanishing Irish: Households, Migrations, and the Rural Economy in Ireland, 1850–1914* (Princeton, NJ: Princeton University Press, 1997).

Gwynn, Stephen, *The History of Ireland* (London: Macmillan, 1923).

Hannigan, Ken, '"Up In His Hat": Joyce and John Francis Byrne: The Wicklow Connections', *Dublin James Joyce Journal* 11 (2018), 47–72.

Hart, Clive, *Structure and Motif in 'Finnegans Wake'* (Evanston, IL: Northwestern University Press, 1962).

———— 'Wandering Rocks', in Clive Hart and David Hayman (eds), *James Joyce's 'Ulysses': Critical Essays* (Berkeley, CA: University of California Press, 1977), 181–216.

Hayter, Arthur D., 'Ireland Beyond the Pale', *Fortnightly Review* 41/241 (1887), 61–72.

Hegglund, Jon, *World Views: Metageographies of Modernist Fiction* (Oxford: Oxford University Press, 2012).

Heise, Ursula K., 'The Hitchhiker's Guide to Ecocriticism', *PMLA* 121/2 (2006), 503–16.

Higgins, Michael D., and John P. Gibbons, 'Shopkeeper-graziers and Land Agitation in Ireland, 1895–1900', in P. J. Drudy (ed.), *Ireland: Land, Politics and People* (Cambridge: Cambridge University Press, 1982), 93–117.

Hirsch, Edward, 'The Imaginary Irish Peasant', *PMLA* 106/5 (1991), 1116–33.

Hobsbawm, Eric, 'Introduction: Inventing Traditions', in Eric Hobsbawm and Terence Ranger (eds), *The Invention of Tradition* (Cambridge: Cambridge University Press, 1983), 1–14.

Hooper, Glenn, 'The Isles/Ireland: The Wilder Shore', in Peter Hulme and Tim Young (eds), *The Cambridge Companion to Travel Writing* (Cambridge: Cambridge University Press, 2002), 174–90.

Horgan, Mervyn, 'Anti-Urbanism as a Way of Life: Disdain for Dublin in the Nationalist Imaginary', *The Canadian Journal of Irish Studies* 30/2 (2004), 38–47.

Horkheimer, Max, and Theodor Adorno, *Dialectic of Enlightenment: Philosophical Fragments* (1944; Stanford, CA: Stanford University Press, 2002).

Howes, Marjorie, '"Goodbye Ireland I'm going to Gort": Geography, Scale, and Narrating the Nation', in Marjorie Howes and Derek Attridge (eds), *Semicolonial Joyce* (Cambridge: Cambridge University Press, 2000), 58–77.

Jameson, Fredric, *Modernism and Imperialism*, Field Day Pamphlet 14 (Derry: Field Day, 1988).

Johnson, Jeri, 'Explanatory Notes', *Dubliners* (Oxford: Oxford University Press, 2008), 194–279.

Jones, David, 'The Issue of Land Distribution: Revisiting *Graziers, Land Reform and Political Conflict in Ireland*', in Fergus Campbell and Tony Varley (eds), *Land Questions in Modern Ireland* (Manchester: Manchester University Press, 2013), 117–48.

Jones, Michael, 'The Concept of Cultural Landscape: Discourse and Narratives', in Hannes Palang and Gary Fry (eds), *Landscape Interfaces: Cultural Heritage in Changing Landscapes* (Dordrecht: Springer, 2003), 21–51.

Jordan, Thomas E., *The Census of Ireland, 1821–1911: General Reports and Extracts*, III (Lewiston, NY: Edwin Mellen Press, 1998).

Joyce, James, *Dubliners* (1914; Oxford: Oxford University Press, 2008).

——— *Finnegans Wake* (1939; London: Penguin, 2000).

——— *The James Joyce Archive*, ed. Michael Groden et al. (New York: Garland, 1977–79).

——— *Letters of James Joyce*, ed. Stuart Gilbert (London: Faber and Faber, 1957).

——— *Letters of James Joyce*, vol. 2, ed. Richard Ellmann (London: Faber and Faber, 1966).

——— *Letters of James Joyce*, vol. 3, ed. Richard Ellmann (London: Faber and Faber, 1966).

——— *Occasional, Critical, and Political Writing*, ed. Kevin Barry (London: Oxford University Press, 2000).

——— *Poems and Shorter Writings*, ed. Richard Ellmann, A. Walton Litz and John Whittier-Ferguson (London: Faber and Faber, 1991).

——— *A Portrait of the Artist as a Young Man* (1916; London: Penguin, 1966).

——— *Selected Letters of James Joyce*, ed. Richard Ellmann (London: Faber and Faber, 1975).

_____ *Stephen Hero* (1944; London: Granada, 1981).

_____ *Ulysses*, ed. Hans Walter Gabler (1922; New York: Vintage, 1986).

Joyce, P. W., *The Origin and History of Irish Names of Places*, I (Dublin: M.H. Gill & Son, 1869).

Joyce, Stanislaus, *My Brother's Keeper*, ed. Richard Ellmann (London: Faber and Faber, 1958).

Kane, Brendan, 'Languages of Legitimacy? *An Ghaeilge*, the Earl of Thomond and British Politics in the Renaissance Pale, 1600–24', in Michael Potterton and Thomas Herron (eds), *Dublin and the Pale in the Renaissance, c.1540–1660* (Dublin: Four Courts Press, 2011), 267–79.

Kenner, Hugh, 'The Making of the Modernist Canon', *Chicago Review* 34/2 (1984), 49–61.

_____ *The Mechanic Muse* (Oxford: Oxford University Press, 1987).

Kershner, Brandon, 'Joyce Beyond the Pale', in Robert Brazeau and Derek Gladwin (eds), *Eco-Joyce: The Environmental Imagination of James Joyce* (Cork: Cork University Press, 2014), 123–35.

Kiberd, Declan, *Inventing Ireland: The Literature of the Modern Nation* (London: Vintage, 1996).

Killeen, Terence, 'On the Authorship of a *Freeman* Sub-Editorial', *James Joyce Online Notes*, https://www.jjon.org/joyce-s-environs/price (accessed 19 January 2022).

Knight, Charles, *The Popular History of England: An Illustrated History of Society and Government from the Earliest Period to Our Own Times*, II (Boston, MA: Estes and Lauriat, 1874).

Kupinse, William J., 'Private Property, Public Interest: Bloom's Ecological Fantasy in "Ithaca"', *James Joyce Quarterly* 52/3–4 (2015), 593–621.

Lacivita, Alison, *The Ecology of 'Finnegans Wake'* (Gainesville, FL: University Press of Florida, 2015).

_____ 'Trouble in Paradise: Violence and the Phoenix Park in *Finnegans Wake*', *James Joyce Quarterly* 51/2 (2014), 317–31.

Lai, Yi-Peng, 'The Tree Wedding and the (Eco)Politics of Irish Forestry in "Cyclops": History, Language and the Viconian Politics of the Forest', in Robert Brazeau and Derek Gladwin (eds), *Eco-Joyce: The Environmental Imagination of James Joyce* (Cork: Cork University Press, 2014), 91–110.

Laird, Heather, '"[H]e daren't show his nose with the Molly Maguires looking for him to let daylight through him for grabbing the holding of an evicted tenant": *Ulysses*, the Cattle Economy, and the Unwritten Agrarian Code', *James Joyce Quarterly* 59/2 (2022), 211–29.

Lalor, James Fintan, 'Tenant Right Meeting in Tipperary', in L. Fogarty, *James Fintan Lalor: Patriot & Political Essayist, 1807–1849* (Dublin: The Talbot Press, 1918), 47–51.

'The Land Question', *Freeman's Journal*, 20 September 1880, p. 7, col. 4, The British Newspaper Archive, https://www.britishnewspaperarchive.co.uk/viewer/BL/0000056/18800920/033/0007?browse=true (accessed 3 January 2024).

Lane, Leeann, '"It Is in the Cottages and Farmers' Houses That the Nation Is Born": AE's "Irish Homestead" and the Cultural Revival', *Irish University Review* 33/1 (2003), 165–81.

Lanigan, Liam, *James Joyce, Urban Planning, and Irish Modernism: Dublins of the Future* (London: Palgrave Macmillan, 2014).

Leerssen, Joseph Theodoor, *Mere Irish & Fíor-ghael: Studies in the Idea of Irish Nationality, Its Development and Literary Expression Prior to the Nineteenth Century* (Amsterdam: John Benjamins, 1986).

—— 'Wildness, Wilderness, and Ireland: Medieval and Early-Modern Patterns in the Demarcation of Civility', *Journal of the History of Ideas* 56/1 (1995), 25–39.

Lefebvre, Henri, *Du rural à l'urbain* (1970; Paris: Anthropos, 2001).

—— *On the Rural: Economy, Sociology, Geography*, ed. Stuart Elden and Adam David Morton, trans. Robert Bononno (Minneapolis, MN: University of Minnesota Press, 2022).

—— *The Production of Space*, trans. Donald Nicholson-Smith (Oxford: Blackwell, 1991).

—— *La révolution urbaine* (Paris: Gallimard, 1970).

—— *The Urban Revolution*, trans. Robert Bononno (Minneapolis, MN: University of Minnesota Press, 2003).

Lehan, Richard, 'Joyce's City', in Bernard Benstock (ed.), *James Joyce: The Augmented Ninth* (Syracuse, NY: Syracuse University Press, 1988), 247–61.

Lewis, Percy Wyndham, *Time and Western Man* (London: Chatto and Windus, 1927).

Lloyd, David, *Irish Culture and Colonial Modernity 1800–2000: The Transformation of Oral Space* (Cambridge: Cambridge University Press, 2011).

—— *Irish Times: Temporalities of Modernity* (Dublin: Keough-Naughton Institute for Irish Studies, University of Notre Dame/Field Day, 2008).

Logographos, 'The Rampart of the Pale', *The Clongownian* 1 (1895), 10–12.

Lyons, F. S. L., *Ireland Since the Famine* (London: Weidenfeld and Nicolson, 1971).

Mac Cana, Proinsias, 'Early Irish Ideology and the Concept of Unity', in Richard Kearney (ed.), *The Irish Mind: Exploring Intellectual Traditions* (Dublin: Wolfhound, 1984), 56–78.

Mac Con Iomaire, Liam, 'Introductory Note', in *Graveyard Clay: Cré na Cille*, trans. Liam Mac Con Iomaire and Tim Robinson (New Haven, CT: Yale University Press, 2016), vii–xxxiii.

MacKillop, James, *A Dictionary of Celtic Mythology* (Oxford: Oxford University Press, 1998).

Mangan, James Clarence, *Selected Poems of James Clarence Mangan*, ed. Jacques Chuto, Rudolf Patrick Holzapfel, Peter van de Kamp and Ellen Shannon-Mangan (Dublin: Irish Academic Press, 2003).

Manganiello, Dominic, *Joyce's Politics* (London: Routledge and Kegan Paul, 1980).

Mao, Douglas (ed.), *The New Modernist Studies* (Cambridge: Cambridge University Press, 2021).

Mao, Douglas, and Rebecca L. Walkowitz, 'The New Modernist Studies', *PMLA* 123/3 (2008), 737–48.

Markus, Radvan, *Carnabhal na Marbh: 'Cré na Cille' agus Litríocht an Domhain* (Indreabhán: Leabhar Breac, 2023).

Marx, Karl, and Friedrich Engels, *The Communist Manifesto*, trans. Samuel Moore (1848; London: Pluto Press, 2008).

Mathew, P. J., '"A.E.I.O.U": Joyce and the *Irish Homestead*', in Anne Fogarty and Timothy Martin (eds), *Joyce on the Threshold* (Gainesville, FL: University Press of Florida, 2005), 151–68.

———— *Revival: The Abbey Theatre, Sinn Féin, the Gaelic League and the Co-operative Movement* (Cork: Cork University Press in association with Field Day, 2003).

Mattar, Sinéad Garrigan, *Primitivism, Science, and the Irish Revival* (Oxford: Oxford University Press, 2004).

Matthews, Terence, 'An Emendation to the Joycean Canon: The Last Hurrah for "Politics and Cattle Disease"', *James Joyce Quarterly* 44/3 (2007), 441–53.

McCabe, Patrick, 'Metemdepsychoswandayinarkloan; James Joyce and Me', *Writings on Joyce, UCD James Joyce 2012*, https://www.ucd.ie/ucdonjoyce/writings-on-joyce/articles/joyce-and-me-patrick-mccabe/index.html (accessed 12 January 2024).

McCall, Patrick Joseph, *Songs of Erinn* (Dublin: M.H. Gill & Son, 1899).

McCarthy, Conor, *Modernisation: Crisis and Culture in Ireland 1969–1992* (Dublin: Four Courts Press, 2000).

McCourt, John, *Consuming Joyce: 100 Years of 'Ulysses' in Ireland* (London: Bloomsbury Academic, 2022).

———— 'Queering the Revivalist's Pitch: Joycean Engagements with Primitivism', in Maria McGarrity and Claire A. Culleton (eds), *Irish Modernism and the Global Primitive* (New York: Palgrave Macmillan, 2009), 17–39.

McCrea, Barry, 'Privatising *Ulysses*: Joyce before, during and after the "Celtic Tiger"', *European Joyce Studies* 22 (2013), 81–93.

McGahern, John, *Love of the World: Essays*, ed. Stanley van der Ziel (London: Faber and Faber, 2010).

McGarrity, Maria, and Claire A. Culleton, 'Introduction', in Maria McGarrity and Claire A. Culleton (eds), *Irish Modernism and the Global Primitive* (New York: Palgrave Macmillan, 2009), 1–14.

McHugh, Roland, *Annotations to 'Finnegans Wake'*, 4th edn (Baltimore, MD: Johns Hopkins University Press, 2016).

McIntyre, Caitlin, '"We Are All Animals": James Joyce, Stephen Dedalus, and the Problem of Agriculture', *Humanities* 6/3 (2017), https://doi.org/10.3390/h6030072 (accessed 23 February 2024).

McMahon, Timothy G., 'Cultural Nativism and Irish-Ireland: *The Leader* as a Source for Joyce's *Ulysses*', *Joyce Studies Annual* 7 (1996), 67–85.

Mentxaka, Aintzane Legarreta, '"James Joyce is my Man": Kate O'Brien and James Joyce', in Olga Fernández Vicente (ed.), *Joyce's Heirs: Joyce's Imprint on Recent Global Literatures* (Bilbao: Servicio de Publicaciones de la Universidad del País Vasco, 2019), 8–23.

Meredith, Dianne, 'Hazards in the Bog: Real and Imagined', *Geographical Review* 92/3 (2002), 319–32.

Mignolo, Walter, 'The Many Faces of Cosmo-polis: Border Thinking and Critical Cosmopolitanism', *Public Culture* 12/3 (2000), 721–48.

Mink, Louis O., *A 'Finnegans Wake' Gazetteer* (Bloomington, IN: Indiana University Press, 1978).

Moran, D. P., *The Philosophy of Irish Ireland* (Dublin: James Duffy, 1905).

———— *Tom O'Kelly* (Dublin: Cahill, James Duffy, 1905).

Morrison, Steven, 'Introduction', in Steven Morrison and Andrew Gibson (eds), *Joyce's 'Wandering Rocks'* (Leiden: Brill, 2002), 1–16.

Morson, Gary Saul, and Caryl Emerson, *Mikhail Bakhtin: Creation of a Prosaics* (Stanford, CA: Stanford University Press, 1990).

Murphy, Margaret, and Matthew Stout, 'Introduction', in Margaret Murphy and Matthew Stout (eds), *Agriculture and Settlement in Ireland* (Dublin: Four Courts Press, 2015), xvi–xxx.

Nairn, Tom, *The Break-Up of Britain: Crisis and Neo-Nationalism*, 2nd edn (1977; London: Verso, 1981).

———— 'The Curse of Rurality: Limits of Modernisation Theory', in John A. Hall (ed.), *The State of the Nation: Ernest Gellner and the Theory of Nationalism* (Cambridge: Cambridge University Press, 1998), 107–34.

Nash, John, *James Joyce and the Act of Reception: Reading, Ireland, Modernism* (Cambridge: Cambridge University Press, 2006).

Neill, Crispian, 'The Afflatus of Flatus: James Joyce and the Writing of Odor', *James Joyce Quarterly* 53/3 (2016), 307–26.

Nolan, Emer, *James Joyce and Nationalism* (London: Routledge, 1995).

Norris, Margot, '*Finnegans Wake*', in Derek Attridge (ed.), *The Cambridge Companion to James Joyce*, 2nd edn (Cambridge: Cambridge University Press, 2004), 161–84.

Ó Cadhain, Máirtín, *As an nGéibheann: Litreacha chuig Tomás Bairéad* (Dublin: Sáirséal agus Dill, 1973).

———— *Páipéir Bhána agus Páipéir Bhreaca* (Dublin: An Clóchomhar Tta, 1969).

Ó Cuileagáin, Niall, '"Is he as innocent as his speech?": Rural Hiberno-English in *Stephen Hero* and *A Portrait of the Artist as a Young Man*', in Serenella Zanotti (ed.), *Joyce Studies in Italy 21: Language and Languages in Joyce's Fiction* (Rome: Anicia, 2019), 113–26.

———— '"A Joycean Smutmonger": Echoes of Joyce in Máirtín Ó Cadhain's Rural Modernism', *Review of Irish Studies in Europe* 7 (2024), 58–76, https://doi.org/10.32803/rise.v7i1.3249 (accessed 7 May 2024).

_____ '"Rus in Urbe": The Semi-Rural Liminal Zones of *Ulysses*', *Dublin James Joyce Journal* 14–15 (2021–22), 18–35.

Ó Dónaill, Niall, *Foclóir Gaeilge-Béarla* [*Irish–English Dictionary*] (Dublin: An Gúm, 1977).

Ó Háinle, Cathal, 'Ó Cadhain, an Rí Séamas II, Joyce agus Molly Bloom', in Máire Ní Annracháin (ed.), *Saothar Mháirtín Uí Chadhain, Léachtaí Cholm Cille* 37 (2007), 7–37.

O Hehir, Brendan, *A Gaelic Lexicon for 'Finnegans Wake' and Glossary for Joyce's Other Works* (Berkeley, CA: University of California Press, 1967).

Ó hÉigeartaigh, Cian, 'Máirtín Ó Cadhain: Politics and Literature', *The Canadian Journal of Irish Studies* 34/1 (2008), 28–32.

Ó hEithir, Breandán, *Lig Sinn i gCathú* (Dublin: Sáirséal agus Dill, 1976).

Ó Raghallaigh, Liam, 'Captain Boycott: Man and Myth', *History Ireland* 19/1 (2011), 28–31.

O'Brien, Joseph V., *'Dear, Dirty Dublin': A City in Distress, 1899–1916* (Berkeley, CA: University of California Press, 1982).

O'Brien, Kate, *Pray for the Wanderer* (1938; Dublin: Arlen House, 2022).

O'Brien, Paul, 'Primitive Communism and The Blasket Islands', *Irish Marxist Review* 4/12 (2015), 32–39.

O'Callaghan, Katherine, 'Joyce's "treeless hills": Deforestation and Its Cultural Resonances', in Oona Frawley and Katherine O'Callaghan (eds), *Memory Ireland: James Joyce and Cultural Memory*, IV (Syracuse, NY: Syracuse University Press, 2014), 95–111.

_____ 'The Riddle of the Brocken Spectre: Reading *Finnegans Wake* on the Top of Croagh Patrick', *James Joyce Quarterly* 56/1–2 (2018–19), 133–53.

_____ 'Solastalgic Modernism and the West in Irish Literature, 1900–1950', in Malcolm Sen (ed.), *A History of Irish Literature and the Environment* (Cambridge: Cambridge University Press, 2022), 150–72.

O'Connor, Elizabeth Foley, 'Kate O'Brien, James Joyce, and the "Lonely Genius"', in Martha C. Carpentier (ed.), *Joycean Legacies* (New York: Palgrave Macmillan, 2015), 11–32.

O'Dea, Dathalinn, 'James Joyce the Regionalist: The *Irish Homestead*, *Dubliners*, and Modernism's Regional Affect', *Modern Fiction Studies* 63/3 (2017), 475–501.

O'Kelly, Seumas, *Wet Clay* (Dublin: The Talbot Press, 1918).

O'Leary, Philip, *The Prose Literature of the Gaelic Revival, 1881–1921: Ideology and Innovation* (University Park, PA: Pennsylvania State University Press, 1994).

O'Neill, Christine, '"A Faint Mortal Odour": The Elusive World of Smell in *A Portrait of the Artist as a Young Man*', *Dublin James Joyce Journal* 5 (2012), 82–98.

O'Neill, Timothy, *Life and Tradition in Rural Ireland* (London: Dent, 1977).

O'Toole, Fintan, 'Going West: The Country versus the City in Irish Writing', *The Crane Bag* 9/2 (1985), 111–16.

Owens, Cóilín, *Before Daybreak: 'After the Race' and the Origins of Joyce's Art* (Gainesville, FL: University of Florida Press, 2013).

———— 'The Mystique of the West in Joyce's "The Dead"', *Irish University Review* 22/1 (1992), 80–91.

Pearson, Nels, *Irish Cosmopolitanism: Location and Dislocation in James Joyce, Elizabeth Bowen, and Samuel Beckett* (Gainesville, FL: University Press of Florida, 2015).

Phillips, Mark Salber, 'Introduction: What is Tradition When it is Not "Invented"? A Historiographical Introduction', in Mark Salber Phillips and Gordon Schochet (eds), *Questions of Tradition* (Toronto: University of Toronto Press, 2004), 3–29.

Pinamonti, Giovanni Pietro, *Hell opened to Christians, to caution them from entering into it, or, Considerations on the infernal pains: proposed to our meditation to avoid them: and distributed for every day in the week* (Derby: Thomas Richardson & Son, 1845).

Platt, Len, 'The Buckeen and the Dogsbody: Aspects of History and Culture in "Telemachus"', *James Joyce Quarterly* 27/1 (1989), 77–86.

———— *Joyce and the Anglo-Irish: A Study of Joyce and the Literary Revival* (Amsterdam: Rodopi, 1998).

———— *Joyce, Race and 'Finnegans Wake'* (Cambridge: Cambridge University Press, 2007).

———— 'Moving in Times of Yore: Historiographies in "Wandering Rocks"', in Steven Morrison and Andrew Gibson (eds), *Joyce's 'Wandering Rocks'* (Leiden: Brill, 2002), 141–54.

Potterton, Michael, 'Introduction: the FitzGeralds, Florence, St Fiachra and a Few Fragments', in Michael Potterton and Thomas Herron (eds), *Dublin and the Pale in the Renaissance, c.1540–1660* (Dublin: Four Courts Press, 2011), 19–47.

Pound, Ezra, '"Dubliners" and Mr. James Joyce', *The Egoist* 1/14 (1914), 267.

Power, Arthur, *Conversations with James Joyce*, ed. Clive Hart (London: Millington, 1974).

Quirke, Sinéad, 'A Gatehouse to Beyond the Boundaries of the Pale: Reflection on Rathcoffey, Co. Kildare', in Michael Potterton and Thomas Herron (eds), *Dublin and the Pale in the Renaissance, c.1540–1660* (Dublin: Four Courts Press, 2011), 104–24.

Rees, Alwyn, and Brinley Rees, *Celtic Heritage: Ancient Tradition in Ireland and Wales* (London: Thames and Hudson, 1961).

'A Report on The Milk Supply of Large Towns: Its Defects and Their Remedy. II Source and Distribution of the Milk to Towns', *British Medical Journal*, 28 March 1903, https://doi.org/10.1136/bmj.1.2204.739 (accessed 10 June 2021).

Rifkin, Jeremy, *Beyond Beef: The Rise and Fall of the Cattle Culture* (New York: Dutton, 1992).

Rindisbacher, Hans J., *The Smell of Books: A Cultural-Historical Study of Olfactory Perception in Literature* (Ann Arbor, MI: University of Michigan Press, 1993).

'River Corrib (Galway Fishery)', *Salmon Ireland*, https://salmonireland.com/rivers/western-rivers/river-corrib-galway-fishery/ (accessed 19 November 2020).

Robbins, Bruce, 'Introduction Part I: Actually Existing Cosmopolitanism', in Pheng Cheah and Bruce Robbins (eds), *Cosmopolitics: Thinking and Feeling Beyond the Nation* (Minneapolis, MN: University of Minnesota Press, 1998), 1–19.

Sauer, Carl Ortwin, 'The Morphology of Landscape', in Carl Ortwin Sauer and John Leighly (eds), *Life and Land: A Selection of the Writings of Carl Ortwin Sauer* (Berkeley, CA: University of California Press, 1967), 315–50.

Schein, Richard H., 'Cultural Traditions', in James S. Duncan, Nuala C. Johnson and Richard H. Schein (eds), *A Companion to Cultural Geography* (Oxford: Blackwell, 2004), 11–23.

Schot, Roseanne, 'Uisneach Midi a medón Érenn: A Prehistoric "Cult" Centre and "Royal Site" in Co. Westmeath', *The Journal of Irish Archaeology* 15 (2006), 39–71.

Scott, Bonnie Kime, 'John Eglinton: A Model for Joyce's Individualism', *James Joyce Quarterly* 12/4 (1975), 347–57.

――― *Joyce and Feminism* (Bloomington, IN: Indiana University Press, 1984).

Sen, Malcolm, 'Introduction: Culture, Climate, Capital, and Contagion', in Malcolm Sen (ed.), *A History of Irish Literature and the Environment* (Cambridge: Cambridge University Press, 2022), 1–32.

Sherwin-White, A. N., and Andrew William Lintott, 'peregrini', in *The Oxford Classical Dictionary* (Oxford: Oxford University Press, 2005), https://www.oxfordreference.com/view/10.1093/acref/9780198606413.001.0001/acref-9780198606413-e-4859 (accessed 20 AprIL 2020).

Shirley, Rosemary, *Rural Modernity, Everyday Life and Visual Culture* (Farnham: Ashgate, 2015).

Shovlin, Frank, *Journey Westward: Joyce, Dubliners and the Literary Revival* (Liverpool: Liverpool University Press, 2012).

Simmel, Georg, 'The Metropolis and Mental Life', in *The Sociology of Georg Simmel*, ed. and trans. Kurt H. Wolff (Glancoe, IL: Free Press, 1950), 409–24.

Slote, Sam, Marc A. Mamigonian and John Turner, *Annotations to James Joyce's 'Ulysses'* (Oxford: Oxford University Press, 2022).

Smith, Cynthia E., 'The Land-Tenure System in Ireland: A Fatal Regime', *Marquette Law Review* 76/2 (1993), 469–84.

Smith, Mark M., *Sensing the Past: Seeing, Hearing, Smelling, Tasting, and Touching in History* (Berkeley, CA: University of California Press, 2007).

Smyth, Gerry, 'Irish Literary Criticism During the Revival', in Marjorie Elizabeth Howes (ed.), *Irish Literature in Transition, 1880–1940*, IV (Cambridge: Cambridge University Press, 2020), 339–55.

_____ *Space and the Irish Cultural Imagination* (London: Palgrave Macmillan, 2001).

Spengler, Oswald, *The Decline of the West: Form and Actuality*, trans. Charles Francis Atkinson (New York: Alfred A. Knopf, 1926).

Stewart, Bruce, 'Joyce at Tara', in Theo D'haen and José Lanters (eds), *Troubled Histories, Troubled Fictions: Twentieth-Century Anglo-Irish Prose* (Amsterdam: Rodopi, 1995), 61–94.

Stout, Geraldine, and Matthew Stout, 'Early Landscapes: From Prehistory to Plantation', in F. H. A. Aalen, Kevin Whelan and Matthew Stout (eds), *Atlas of the Irish Rural Landscape* (Toronto: University of Toronto Press, 1997), 31–63.

Synge, John Millington, *The Aran Islands* (1907; Oxford: Oxford University Press, 1995).

_____ *The Complete Plays* (London: Methuen Drama, 1990).

Thacker, Andrew, *Moving Through Modernity: Space and Geography in Modernism* (Manchester: Manchester University Press, 2003).

Thrane, James R., 'Joyce's Sermon on Hell: Its Source and Its Backgrounds', *Modern Philology* 57/3 (1960), 172–98.

Tindall, William York, *A Reader's Guide to 'Finnegans Wake'* (London: Thames and Hudson, 1969).

Trevor-Roper, Hugh, 'The Invention of Tradition: The Highland Tradition of Scotland', in Eric Hobsbawm and Terence Ranger (eds), *The Invention of Tradition* (Cambridge: Cambridge University Press, 1983), 15–42.

Trotsky, Leon, 'Lessons of the Dublin Events', in *The Lace Curtain* 1, trans. Brian Pearce (Dublin: New Writers' Press, 1970), 58–59.

Turner, Michael, *After the Famine: Irish Agriculture, 1850–1915* (Cambridge: Cambridge University Press, 1996).

Tymoczko, Maria, *The Irish 'Ulysses'* (Berkeley, CA: University of California Press, 1994).

Ua Laoghaire, Peadar, *Niamh* (Dublin: Irish Book Co., 1907).

Valente, Joseph, 'James Joyce and the Cosmopolitan Sublime', in Mark A. Wollaeger, Victor Luftig and Robert Spoo (eds), *Joyce and the Subject of History* (Ann Arbor, MI: University of Michigan Press, 1996), 59–80.

Van Mierlo, Wim, 'The Greater Ireland beyond the Sea: James Joyce, Exile and Irish Imagination', in Andrew Gibson and Len Platt (eds), *Joyce, Ireland, Britain* (Gainesville, FL: University Press of Florida, 2006), 178–97.

_____ *James Joyce and Cultural Genetics: The Joycean Genome* (London: Bloomsbury Academic, 2023).

Vico, Giambattista, *New Science*, trans. David Marsh, 3rd edn (1744; London: Penguin, 1999).

Watson, Jay, *William Faulkner and the Faces of Modernity* (Oxford: Oxford University Press, 2019).

Welton, Thomas A., 'Notes on the Census of Ireland, 1911', *Journal of the Royal Statistical Society* 77/2 (1914), 205–13.

Whelan, Kevin, 'The Memories of "The Dead"', *The Yale Journal of Criticism* 15/1 (2002), 59–97.

———— 'The Modern Landscape: From Plantation to Present', in F. H. A. Aalen, Kevin Whelan and Matthew Stout (eds), *Atlas of the Irish Rural Landscape* (Toronto: University of Toronto Press, 1997), 67–103.

Williams, Raymond, *The Country and the City* (London: Chatto and Windus, 1973).

Woolf, Robert Lee, 'Introduction', in William Allingham, *Laurence Bloomfield in Ireland* (1864; New York: Garland, 1979), v–xi.

Yeats, William Butler, *The Countess Cathleen*, in David R. Clark and Rosalind E. Clark (eds), *The Collected Works of W.B. Yeats, Volume II: The Plays* (London: Palgrave, 2001), 27–63.

———— *Yeats's Poems*, ed. A. Norman Jeffares (London: Palgrave Macmillan, 1989).

Zapf, Hubert, 'Cultural Ecology of Literature – Literature as Cultural Ecology', in Hubert Zapf (ed.), *Handbook of Ecocriticism and Cultural Ecology* (Berlin: De Gruyter, 2016), 135–53.

———— 'Ecocriticism, Cultural Ecology, and Literary Studies', *Ecozon@* 1/1 (2010), 136–47.

Index

EU Authorised Representative:

Easy Access System Europe Mustamäe tee 50, 10621 Tallinn, Estonia

gpsr.requests@easproject.com

Printed and bound by CPI Group (UK) Ltd, Croydon, CR0 4YY

18/07/2025

01918970-0003